Environmental Monitoring Using Artificial Intelligence

Scrivener Publishing
100 Cummings Center, Suite 541J
Beverly, MA 01915-6106

Publishers at Scrivener
Martin Scrivener (martin@scrivenerpublishing.com)
Phillip Carmical (pcarmical@scrivenerpublishing.com)

Environmental Monitoring Using Artificial Intelligence

Edited by

A. Suresh

T. Devi

N. Deepa

and

Ali Kashif Bashir

Scrivener Publishing

WILEY

This edition first published 2025 by John Wiley & Sons, Inc., 111 River Street, Hoboken, NJ 07030, USA and Scrivener Publishing LLC, 100 Cummings Center, Suite 541J, Beverly, MA 01915, USA

For more information about Scrivener publications please visit www.scrivenerpublishing.com.

Wiley Global Headquarters
111 River Street, Hoboken, NJ 07030, USA

For details of our global editorial offices, customer services, and more information about Wiley products visit us at www.wiley.com.

Library of Congress Cataloging-in-Publication Data

ISBN 978-1-394-27036-1

Front cover images supplied by Adobe Firefly
Cover design by Russell Richardson

Set in size of 11pt and Minion Pro by Manila Typesetting Company, Makati, Philippines

Printed in the USA

10 9 8 7 6 5 4 3 2 1

Contents

Preface

In this book, readers are invited to explore a diverse array of topics centered around the theme of environmental monitoring and technological innovation. From transformative trends in AI for environmental monitoring to the utilization of advanced sensor technologies, each chapter offers a deep dive into the cutting-edge techniques and applications driving progress in this field. Through insightful discussions and case studies, insights into how these tools enable more precise and efficient tracking of environmental changes, from climate patterns to biodiversity dynamics, are revealed. Furthermore, the role of smart environmental monitoring systems, IoT advancements, and remote sensing technologies in providing real-time data on environmental conditions is explored, paving the way for smarter, more resilient communities and ecosystems.

Moreover, the integration of AI, Natural Language Processing (NLP), and sensor technologies facilitates data-driven decision-making, enhances resource efficiency, and promotes sustainability in various sectors, from agriculture to urban planning. Each chapter offers a glimpse into the future of environmental monitoring, where innovative technologies pave the way for smarter, more resilient communities and ecosystems. Join us as this exploration navigates through these chapters, uncovering the remarkable potential of AI, NLP, and sensor technologies in safeguarding our environment and shaping a more sustainable future for generations to come.

Chapter 1: Transformative Trends in AI for Environmental Monitoring: Challenges, Applications involves leveraging advanced data analytics, machine learning, and remote sensing to enhance the precision and efficiency of tracking environmental changes. These technologies enable the monitoring of climate change, pollution, and biodiversity in real time, offering predictive insights that facilitate proactive environmental management. Key applications include automated wildlife tracking, optimizing renewable energy deployment, and detecting deforestation. However, several challenges impede widespread adoption. High computational costs and the need for extensive, high-quality data are significant technical barriers. Data privacy and ethical concerns also pose challenges, as the extensive data collection required can infringe on individual privacy rights. Additionally, the deployment of AI systems in remote or underdeveloped regions can be difficult due to infrastructure limitations. Finally, despite these challenges, the integration of AI in environmental monitoring promises substantial benefits, enhancing our ability to protect natural resources and respond to environmental threats more effectively. Addressing these challenges is crucial for maximizing AI's potential in this field.

Chapter 2: Fundamentals of AI and NLP in Environmental Analysis involve using advanced algorithms and machine learning techniques to process and interpret vast amounts of environmental data. AI models can analyze patterns, predict trends, and make data-driven decisions, enabling more accurate and efficient environmental monitoring and management. Natural Language Processing (NLP), a subfield of AI, plays a crucial role in environmental analysis by processing and analyzing textual data from diverse sources such as research papers, policy documents, and social media. NLP techniques can extract relevant information, identify trends, and summarize large volumes of text, aiding in the synthesis of environmental knowledge. Together, AI and NLP facilitate the integration of multiple data sources, from satellite imagery to sensor networks and textual data, providing comprehensive insights into environmental conditions. They enable automated monitoring, early warning systems for natural disasters, and informed policy-making. Finally, the integration of these technologies enhances our capacity to understand and address complex environmental challenges.

Chapter 3: Smart Environmental Monitoring Systems: IoT and Sensor-Based Advancements provide real-time, accurate data on environmental conditions. IoT devices, interconnected through networks, collect data from various sensors measuring parameters such as air and water quality, temperature, humidity, and soil moisture. These sensors are often deployed in remote or inaccessible areas, continuously transmitting data to centralized systems for analysis. Advancements in sensor technology have led to the development of highly sensitive, low-power sensors capable of detecting minute changes in environmental conditions. These sensors, combined with IoT, enable continuous monitoring and rapid response to environmental changes, improving the ability to predict and mitigate environmental hazards. The integration of IoT and sensors in SEMS facilitates better resource management, pollution tracking, and disaster preparedness. These systems support data-driven decision-making, enhancing the ability to protect and sustain natural resources. Finally, the ongoing improvements in sensor accuracy, energy efficiency, and connectivity are driving the evolution of more sophisticated and responsive environmental monitoring solutions.

Chapter 4: Remote Monitoring Advancements: A New Approach to Biodiversity Conservation by utilizing cutting-edge technologies like drones, satellite imagery, and automated camera traps. These tools provide continuous, non-invasive monitoring of wildlife and habitats, offering detailed insights into species distribution, behavior, and population dynamics. Drones equipped with high-resolution cameras and sensors can access remote or difficult-to-reach areas, capturing real-time data on flora and fauna. Satellite imagery enables large-scale environmental monitoring, tracking changes in land use, deforestation, and habitat fragmentation over time. Automated camera traps, with AI integration, can identify and track species, reducing human intervention and minimizing disturbance to wildlife. These remote monitoring technologies enhance the accuracy and scope of biodiversity data collection, facilitating timely and informed conservation strategies. They enable early detection of threats, such as poaching or habitat degradation, and support the implementation of targeted conservation measures. Finally by providing comprehensive and precise data, remote monitoring advancements are crucial for effective biodiversity conservation in an era of rapid environmental change.

Chapter 5: Smart Water Solutions: A Case Study on Drone-Led Hydrological Investigation of Water Diversion from Lakshmiyapuram Catchment to Sivakasi Periyakulam Tank involves drones equipped with high-resolution cameras and LiDAR sensors that were deployed to assess and map the water diversion pathways and catchment characteristics. The drones collected detailed aerial imagery and topographical data, enabling precise mapping of the catchment area and water flow patterns. This data was used to identify potential inefficiencies and blockages in the diversion channels, as well as to monitor the water levels and storage capacity of the Sivakasi Periyakulam Tank. The drone-led investigation provided a comprehensive understanding of the hydrological dynamics, facilitating informed decision-making for improving water management and distribution. The use of drones significantly reduced the time and cost associated with traditional ground-based surveys, demonstrating the effectiveness of smart water solutions in enhancing the efficiency and sustainability of water resource management.

Chapter 6: Sustainable Waste Management as a Key Feature for Smart City where smart cities integrate advanced technologies to create sustainable environmental solutions, enhancing urban living while minimizing ecological footprints. Utilizing IoT, big data, and AI, smart cities monitor and manage resources efficiently, addressing challenges like pollution, waste, and energy consumption. Key solutions include smart grids that optimize energy distribution, reducing wastage and incorporating renewable sources. Intelligent transportation systems alleviate traffic congestion and lower emissions through real-time data analysis and adaptive traffic management. Waste management is revolutionized by smart bins and recycling systems that monitor fill levels and optimize collection routes. Water management benefits from sensors that detect leaks and monitor usage, ensuring efficient distribution and conservation. Air quality is continuously monitored, enabling prompt responses to pollution and health risks. Green infrastructure, such as vertical gardens and green roofs, enhances urban biodiversity and mitigates heat islands. Finally by integrating these technologies, smart cities promote sustainability, improving quality of life and fostering resilience against environmental challenges.

Chapter 7: Sensor Technologies for Environmental Data Collection where sensor technologies are essential for accurate environmental data collection, covering a wide range of parameters. Air quality sensors measure pollutants like particulate matter, carbon monoxide, and ozone, crucial for monitoring urban pollution and health impacts. Water quality sensors track pH, dissolved oxygen, and contaminants, aiding in aquatic ecosystem health and safe drinking water management. Soil moisture sensors optimize agricultural irrigation, improving crop yields and water conservation. Temperature and humidity sensors provide critical data for weather forecasting, climate studies, and environmental control systems. Remote sensing technologies, including satellite and aerial sensors like LiDAR and multispectral cameras, offer large-scale monitoring of deforestation, land use, and topographical changes. Acoustic sensors detect wildlife sounds and human activities, assisting in biodiversity conservation and poaching prevention. Integrating these sensors into IoT networks allows for real-time data collection and analysis, supporting informed decision-making and sustainable environmental management. Future advancements aim to enhance sensor durability, reduce costs, and improve data integration.

Chapter 8: Significance and Advancement of Sensor Technologies for Environmental Analysis where sensor technologies are vital for precise environmental data collection across various domains. Air quality sensors measure pollutants such as particulate matter, carbon monoxide, and ozone, essential for monitoring urban air quality and health impacts. Water quality sensors track parameters like pH, dissolved oxygen, and contaminants, aiding in the management of aquatic ecosystems and ensuring safe drinking water. Soil moisture sensors are crucial for agriculture, optimizing irrigation and improving crop yields by measuring soil water content. Temperature and humidity sensors provide key data for weather forecasting, climate research, and environmental control systems. Remote sensing technologies, including satellites and aerial sensors like LiDAR and multispectral cameras, enable large-scale monitoring of deforestation, land use, and topographical changes. Acoustic sensors detect sounds from wildlife and human activities, supporting biodiversity conservation and anti-poaching efforts. Integrating these sensors into IoT networks allows real-time data collection and analysis, facilitating informed decision-making for sustainable environmental management.

Chapter 9: Texture-Based Classification of Organic and Pesticidal Spinach Using Machine Learning to differentiate between these two categories based on textural features extracted from images. Machine learning models, such as convolutional neural networks (CNNs) or support vector machines (SVMs), are trained on datasets containing images of both organic and pesticidal spinach. The texture features extracted from these images capture subtle differences in visual patterns, such as leaf surface texture, color variations, and structural characteristics. These features serve as input to the machine learning model, which learns to classify spinach samples into organic or pesticidal categories based on the extracted texture information. By leveraging machine learning for texture-based classification, this approach offers a non-destructive and efficient method for distinguishing between organic and pesticidal spinach, aiding in quality control and ensuring consumer safety in the agricultural industry.

Chapter 10: Deep Bidirectional LSTM for Emotion Detection through Mobile Sensor Analysis employs a sophisticated neural network architecture to analyze data collected from sensors in mobile devices. Bidirectional LSTMs enable the model to capture temporal dependencies in the sensor data by processing it both forwards and backwards through time. The deep architecture incorporates multiple LSTM layers, allowing the model to learn complex patterns and representations from the sequential sensor data. By leveraging bidirectional processing and deep learning techniques, the model can effectively capture nuanced patterns indicative of different emotional states. This approach enables mobile devices to infer users' emotions in real-time based on sensor data, such as accelerometer or gyroscope readings. Applications include personalized user experiences, mental health monitoring, and emotion-aware interfaces, enhancing human-computer interaction and emotional well-being.

Chapter 11: A Comparative Analysis of AlexNet and ResNet for Pneumonia Detection involves evaluating the performance of two convolutional neural network (CNN) architectures in accurately identifying pneumonia from medical images, such as chest X-rays. AlexNet, a pioneering CNN model, consists of several convolutional and pooling layers followed by fully connected layers. ResNet, on the other hand, introduces residual connections, which help mitigate the vanishing gradient problem and enable training of deeper networks. The analysis involves training and testing both models on a dataset of chest X-ray images labeled for pneumonia presence. Metrics such as accuracy, sensitivity, specificity, and area under the receiver operating characteristic curve (AUC-ROC) are typically used to assess performance. Results from the comparative analysis provide insights into the effectiveness of each model for pneumonia detection, aiding in the selection of the most suitable architecture for medical image analysis tasks.

Chapter 12: Comparison of Borewell Rescue L-Type Different Arm with Different Materials involves evaluating the performance of rescue tools designed for retrieving individuals trapped in borewells. These tools typically feature an L-shaped arm mechanism constructed from various materials such as steel, aluminum, or composite materials. The comparison assesses factors such as strength, durability, weight, and cost-effectiveness of each arm material. Steel arms offer high strength and durability but may be heavy and prone to corrosion. Aluminum arms are lightweight but may sacrifice some strength. Composite materials offer a balance between strength, weight, and corrosion resistance but may be more expensive. The evaluation considers the effectiveness of each arm material in practical rescue scenarios, including ease of deployment and manipulation in confined spaces. Ultimately, the comparison aims to identify the most suitable arm material that maximizes performance and safety in borewell rescue operations.

Chapter 13: Optimizing Almond and Walnut Farming: A U-Net-Powered Deep Learning Approach for Energy Efficiency Prediction and Damage Assessment involves predicting energy efficiency and assessing damage using a U-Net-powered deep learning approach. The U-Net architecture is utilized to analyze aerial imagery and predict energy efficiency by identifying areas with potential damage or inefficiencies in irrigation or pest control. This deep learning model processes satellite or drone imagery to detect signs of stress or damage in orchards, such as water stress, pest infestations, or disease outbreaks. By accurately predicting energy efficiency and assessing damage, farmers can optimize resource allocation, prioritize interventions, and minimize crop losses. The U-Net -powered approach offers a precise and efficient method for monitoring orchard health, enabling timely interventions to improve energy efficiency and mitigate damage. By leveraging deep learning and remote sensing technologies, almond and walnut farmers can enhance sustainability, productivity, and resilience in their farming practices.

Chapter 14: Enhancing Sustainable Management of Waste Dump Sites with Smart Drones and Geospatial Tech: Air Quality Monitoring and Analysis involves smart drones equipped with sensors flying over dump sites, collecting real-time data on air pollutants like methane, carbon dioxide, and volatile organic compounds (VOCs). Geospatial technology integrates drone data with geographical information systems (GIS), providing spatial context for air quality measurements. This enables precise mapping of pollution hotspots and identification of areas with elevated health risks. The data collected by smart drones and analyzed using geospatial techniques facilitate proactive management strategies, such as implementing gas collection systems, optimizing waste disposal practices, and mitigating environmental impacts. By monitoring air quality in real time and analyzing spatial patterns, waste dump site managers can make informed decisions to minimize pollution and protect public health while promoting sustainable waste management practices.

Chapter 15: Voltage Veggies: A Shocking Revolution in Agriculture where Voltage Veggies represents a revolutionary approach to agriculture by harnessing the power of electricity to enhance plant growth and productivity. This innovative technique involves applying controlled electrical currents to soil or plants, stimulating nutrient uptake, improving water efficiency, and boosting overall crop yield. By optimizing plant metabolism and root development, Voltage Veggies can accelerate plant growth, shorten crop cycles, and increase resilience to environmental stressors like drought or disease. Additionally, this method may reduce the need for chemical fertilizers and pesticides, promoting sustainable farming practices. Voltage Veggies holds promise for addressing global food security challenges by maximizing agricultural productivity while minimizing resource inputs and environmental impacts. As research and development in this field advance, Voltage Veggies could revolutionize the way crops are cultivated, ushering in a new era of electrified agriculture.

Chapter 16: Emperor Penguin Optimized Loop Selection Process for Routerless NoC Design where the Emperor Penguin Optimized Loop Selection Process (EPO-LSP) is a novel algorithm inspired by the behaviors of emperor penguins for designing routerless Network-on-Chip (NoC) architectures. In this approach, the movement patterns of emperor penguins, which involve forming loops to maintain communication and conserve energy in harsh environments, are emulated to optimize the selection of loops in NoC designs. EPO-LSP algorithmically determines the most efficient paths for data transmission within an NoC without relying on traditional routers. By leveraging the natural behaviors of emperor penguins, it aims to minimize energy consumption, latency, and resource usage while maximizing throughput and fault tolerance. This innovative approach offers a promising solution for designing efficient and robust NoC architectures, particularly in resource-constrained and energy-sensitive environments. By mimicking nature's strategies, EPO-LSP demonstrates the potential for bio-inspired algorithms to address complex engineering challenges with elegance and efficiency.

Chapter 17: Case Study on Flyover Construction and the Air Quality Measurement by the Emission Level of Pollutants where in a case study on flyover construction, air quality measurements were conducted to assess the emission levels of pollutants during the construction process. Monitoring stations were strategically placed near the construction site and in surrounding areas to capture data on pollutants such as particulate matter (PM), nitrogen oxides (NOx), sulfur dioxide (SO2), and volatile organic compounds (VOCs). The study involved continuous monitoring of air quality before, during, and after construction activities. Emission sources, such as heavy machinery, vehicles, and material transportation, were identified and quantified to evaluate their impact on air quality. By analyzing the emission levels of pollutants, the study provided insights into the environmental impact of flyover construction and identified potential mitigation measures to minimize air pollution. This information is crucial for informing regulatory decisions, implementing pollution control measures, and safeguarding public health in urban areas undergoing infrastructure development.

The editors thank the contributors most profoundly for their time and effort.

Dr. A. Suresh
Dr. T. Devi
Dr. N. Deepa
Dr. Ali Kashif Bashir

1

Transformative Trends in AI for Environmental Monitoring: Challenges, Applications

Leena Sri R.[1], Divya Vetriveeran[2*], Rakoth Kandan Sambandam[2], Jenefa J.[2] and Karthikeyan Thangavel[3]

[1]Thiagarajar College of Engineering, Madurai, India
[2]CHRIST (Deemed to be) University, Kengeri, Bangalore
[3]University of Technology and Applied Sciences, Al Khuwair, Muscat, Oman

Abstract

The integration of artificial intelligence (AI) and machine learning (ML) is reshaping environmental monitoring, responding to the escalating complexities of issues like climate change and pollution. This article presents a comprehensive overview of current trends, challenges, and applications in AI-driven environmental monitoring. While technologies like remote sensing and Internet of Things (IoT) have improved data resolution, the sheer volume necessitates AI for efficient processing. The review emphasizes the role of AI in real-time monitoring, providing timely insights critical for addressing natural disasters and pollution. Exploring various environmental monitoring verticals—air and water quality, climate change modeling, biodiversity, and disaster prediction—the article highlights AI's versatility in addressing diverse concerns. Challenges such as data quality, bias, interpretability, and privacy are examined, underlining ethical considerations in biased models impacting marginalized communities. This chapter discusses common environmental modeling methodologies, ranging from empirical to geospatial modeling, elucidating their advantages and challenges.

Keywords: Artificial intelligence, environment monitoring and modeling, deep learning models, AI challenges, research directions

**Corresponding author*: divya.vetriveeran@christuniversity.in

A. Suresh, T. Devi, N. Deepa and Ali Kashif Bashir (eds.) Environmental Monitoring Using Artificial Intelligence, (1–28) © 2025 Scrivener Publishing LLC

1.1 Introduction

Environmental monitoring is a vital practice that involves systematically collecting and analyzing data to track changes in the environment. This process plays a crucial role in early pollution detection, enabling timely intervention to prevent widespread environmental damage. Additionally, it supports sustainable resource management by providing insights into the availability and quality of natural resources like water. Biodiversity conservation benefits from ecosystem monitoring, helping assess the health of various species and their habitats. Environmental monitoring also contributes to tracking climate change, aiding scientists in understanding long-term trends and making predictions. Moreover, it directly impacts public health by assessing air and water quality, identifying potential risks associated with pollution. Regulatory compliance is another key aspect, ensuring industries adhere to environmental standards. This practice generates valuable data for research, educates the public about environmental issues, and fosters a sense of responsibility towards nature, ultimately contributing to a balanced and sustainable coexistence with the planet.

i. **Need for technology in environmental monitoring**
   The realm of environmental monitoring confronts significant challenges driven by the growing complexity of environmental issues, such as climate change and pollution. Conventional monitoring methods often struggle to deliver real-time, comprehensive data in the face of these dynamic and expansive challenges. The need for more accurate and nuanced information has become paramount, demanding the integration of advanced technologies. Technologies like remote sensing and satellite imagery offer a broader, more detailed perspective, addressing the challenge of better spatial and temporal resolution. Moreover, the sheer volume of data generated requires sophisticated tools like big data analytics and artificial intelligence (AI) to automate processing, identify patterns, and predict trends.

   Real-time monitoring, facilitated by advanced sensor networks and Internet of Things (IoT) technologies, emerges as a critical solution to address environmental challenges promptly. These innovations enable continuous data collection and transmission, providing timely insights into changing conditions. This proves invaluable in responding to sudden events such as natural disasters or pollution incidents. However, the need for improved accessibility and affordability of these advanced monitoring technologies remains a crucial aspect. Making these tools more widely available ensures that communities, regardless of economic status, can actively participate in environmental stewardship, promoting a more inclusive and effective approach to environmental management.

ii. Need for AI to solve these challenges

Machine learning (ML) and artificial intelligence (AI) stand as crucial pillars in addressing the multifaceted challenges of environmental monitoring. Their capacity to handle vast datasets efficiently is pivotal, unraveling intricate patterns and correlations that elude traditional methods. This capability is instrumental in gaining profound insights into complex environmental processes, facilitating a more nuanced understanding of factors at play. Additionally, the predictive modeling prowess of ML and AI empowers environmental scientists to anticipate and prepare for future challenges, whether related to climate change impacts or the likelihood of pollution events. By leveraging historical data, these technologies contribute to a proactive approach, enhancing the efficacy of strategies for environmental management.

Furthermore, ML and AI enhance the precision of data interpretation, a critical aspect in environmental monitoring where accuracy is paramount. Their ability to distinguish relevant signals from noise ensures more reliable monitoring results. This is particularly beneficial in addressing challenges associated with the demand for better spatial and temporal resolution. Equally significant is their role in real-time monitoring, as these technologies enable automated analysis of streaming data, ensuring the swift detection of abnormalities or shifts in environmental conditions. In summary, the integration of ML and AI into environmental monitoring processes significantly advances the field, offering improved data processing, predictive capabilities, enhanced accuracy, and real-time responsiveness to environmental challenges.

1.2 Literature Verticals

There are several verticals in which the monitoring had been done. Some of them include the following:

i. **Air quality monitoring**
Machine learning algorithms analyze air quality data, predicting pollutant levels and identifying sources of pollution. This aids in developing more effective air quality management strategies.

ii. **Satellite imagery and remote sensing**
AI has been utilized to analyze satellite imagery for environmental monitoring purposes. This includes applications such as deforestation detection, land cover classification, and monitoring changes in ecosystems.

iii. **Water quality assessment**
Machine learning models have been applied to assess water quality parameters, including the detection of contaminants in rivers and lakes. These models can provide real-time insights, aiding in the management of water resources.

iv. **Climate change modeling**
AI and machine learning are used to analyze climate data, predict future climate trends, and assess the impact of climate change on ecosystems. This includes the development of models to understand complex climate dynamics.

v. **Biodiversity monitoring**
Researchers have explored the use of machine learning for biodiversity conservation. This includes species identification through image and sound analysis, as well as monitoring the health of ecosystems.

vi. **Natural disaster prediction and response**
AI algorithms are applied to analyze data related to natural disasters, such as hurricanes, earthquakes, and wildfires. These models help in predicting the occurrence of disasters and planning effective response strategies.

vii. **Noise pollution monitoring**
Machine learning has been employed to monitor and analyze noise pollution in urban areas. This involves the use of sensors and algorithms to assess noise levels and identify sources of excessive noise.

viii. **Integration of IoT devices**
The combination of AI and the Internet of Things (IoT) devices is explored for real-time monitoring. This includes the deployment of sensor networks to collect environmental data, which is then analyzed using machine learning algorithms.

1.3 Key Methodologies in Literature Review

i. **Air quality prediction**

The paper by [1] shows that non-linear machine learning models, such as Random Forest and Support Vector Regression, effectively predict air quality using meteorological and traffic data, potentially reducing the need for air pollution sensors. This study by [2] proposes an AI-based framework for air quality prediction, aiming to achieve the best precision by utilizing controlled solicitation AI calculations and vehicle traffic office datasets. The research by the authors [3] shows that an AI-based system effectively predicts air pollutants in urban environments, aiding in short-term measures to improve air quality and life quality.

The novel optimal-hybrid model by the authors [4], effectively predicts air quality index (AQI) using secondary decomposition, AI methods, and optimization algorithms, providing accurate and reliable information for environmental and public health. The study by the authors [5] shows that Deep Learning models are the most suitable for air quality classification in IoT-based networks with low-cost sensors, providing accurate results for public presentation.

ii. **Source identification of air pollutants using AI**

Based on the research by the authors [6], artificial neural network (ANN) is the most accurate machine learning algorithm for identifying indoor pollutant sources, with ANN outperforming support vector machine (SVM) and k-nearest neighbor (KNN) in detecting release masses. There had been researches wherein the monitoring has been made efficient, and one such methodology was proposed by the authors [7]. This real-time calculation platform using Flink and Automatic Identification System (AIS) data can improve the estimation of ship air pollutant emissions, supporting blue-sky defense war and improving air pollution monitoring in water transportation.

There have been several research studies using satellite imaging that helps in proper monitoring of pollution in major cities. One such research is by the authors [8]. The F-RCNN-based aircraft identification framework accurately detects airplanes in satellite images, improving air pollution source identification in smart cities with a detection rate of 92%.

iii. **Predictive modelling of pollutant levels with machine learning**

There has been research on several machine learning algorithms that are under research that helps in the ease of prediction and monitoring pollution risk. One such research by the authors [9] reports that, the KNN-DNN model, combining K-Nearest Neighbor (KNN) and Deep Neural Network (DNN), effectively improves fine-grained air quality analysis by using unlabeled samples and utilizing input variables like temperature, humidity, pollutants, and source type. There has been research on improving the time taken for the analysis, and one such research by the authors [10] has the following promising results. Our Deep Q-network-based UAV Pollution Tracking (DUPT) solution can rapidly identify unhealthy polluted areas and saves 28% of the total time compared to existing solutions. The authors [12] have researched the use of IoT for air quality classification using sensors.

iv. **Deep learning applications in air quality monitoring**

With the rise in deep learning algorithms, there have been several research studies in the field of air quality monitoring too. One such research by the authors [11] shows the following results: Deep features extracted by CNN and fed to an extreme learning machine can accurately predict air pollution levels in smartphones, with a 66.92% accuracy compared to other conventional methods. Deep Learning models are the most suitable for air quality classification in IoT-based networks with low-cost sensors, providing accurate results for public presentation. There have been several research studies on convolutional neural networks and one such research by authors [12] shows that the proposed Convolutional Neural Network–based approach efficiently detects anomalous episodes in urban ozone maps, compared to other deep learning methods. The authors [13] proposes an ensemble approach for Multi-Source Transfer Learning, which improves air quality prediction by transfer learning from multiple source to a target, overcoming data shortage issues.

v. **AI for environmental monitoring**

The paper by the authors [14] recommends a greater use of satellite imagery and data in the enforcement of environmental, social and governance goals, but it does not specifically mention AI applications in satellite imagery analysis for environmental monitoring. The paper by the authors [15] discusses the objective selection of AI applications for onboard deployment in satellite missions, including the Copernicus Hyperspectral Imaging Mission for the Environment (CHIME). It does not specifically mention AI applications in satellite imagery analysis for environmental monitoring. There have also been researches that help in building datasets for environmental monitoring. The paper [16] discusses an automatic tool for creating datasets for AI applications in the Earth Observation context, but it does not specifically mention AI applications in satellite imagery analysis for environmental monitoring.

vi. **Deforestation detection as a part of environmental monitoring using AI**

Satellite-based deforestation detection using deep learning has been explored in several research papers. Fodor and Conde introduced a deep learning–based approach using Convolutional Neural Network (CNN) and multimodal satellite imagery to estimate deforestation and detect wildfires in the Amazon forest [17] Solórzano *et al.* evaluated that utilizing multispectral and synthetic aperture radar images, the U-Net 3D spatio-temporal deep learning algorithm demonstrates significant potential in detecting deforestation within a tropical rainforest in Southeast Mexico [18]. Ankalkoti presented a deep learning–based approach for the early detection of forest wildfires from satellite images, employing data preprocessing, model training, and inference steps [19]. Kang *et al.* proposed a deep learning–based forest fire detection algorithm using high temporal resolution satellite images, achieving better performance than traditional methods [20]. Wang *et al.* used a deep learning method to detect deforestation in large-scale scenarios based on high-resolution optical remote sensing images, achieving accurate results in detecting deforestation and capturing the changing area's boundary [21].

vii. **AI and machine learning in climate change impact assessment**

AI and machine learning techniques are being increasingly used in climate change impact assessment. These methods offer the potential to accurately model and predict the future of the climate system, aiding in our understanding of climate change and its effects [22]. Machine learning algorithms, such as artificial neural networks, decision tree modeling, and regression analysis have been applied to evaluate the effects of climate change on crop production [23][24]. These techniques can integrate information from high-dimensional datasets and provide timely and accurate forecasts of crop production, which are crucial for policy assessments and global food security [25]. In addition, machine learning has been used to analyze spatio-temporal dynamics of risk factors, assess multi-hazard interactions, and analyze future scenarios under climate change [26]. These applications have shown promising results in improving climate change risk assessment and supporting decision-making processes.

1.4 Most Common Methods in Environmental Monitoring

There have been several intelligent methodologies for several environmental monitoring techniques. There have been some classic methodologies in the literature that have their own advantages of implementations beyond the limitations. Some of those methodologies in literature are listed below in Table 1.1.

1.5 AI Architectures for Environmental Monitoring

Several architectures and frameworks have been developed to enhance the effectiveness of environmental monitoring using artificial intelligence (AI). These architectures leverage various machine learning and deep learning techniques to address specific challenges in environmental monitoring. Here are some notable architectures:

LSTMs, a type of recurrent neural network (RNN), are effective for time series analysis in environmental monitoring. They excel at capturing temporal dependencies and have been applied to predict air quality, water quality, and other environmental parameters. The latest research by the authors [39] has developed an architecture for the advance prediction of coastal groundwater levels. The architecture developed by the authors are as follows in Figure 1.1.

Table 1.1 Common environmental monitoring methodologies.

Methodology	Description	Application Areas	Advantages	Challenges and limitations
Empirical Modeling [27]	Relies on observed data to develop relationships	Air quality modeling, hydrological modeling	Simple, data-driven, applicable with limited data	Limited generalization, may not capture dynamics
Analytical Modeling [28]	Involves mathematical equations to represent systems	Groundwater flow modeling, climate modeling	Provides theoretical insights, computationally efficient	Limited to simplified systems, may lack realism
Numerical Modeling [29]	Uses numerical simulations to solve complex equations	Weather forecasting, ocean circulation modeling	Captures complex interactions, spatial and temporal detail	Computationally intensive, requires high resources
Statistical Modeling [30]	Applies statistical methods to analyze relationships	Species distribution modeling, trend analysis	Can handle uncertainties, useful for pattern recognition	Assumes statistical relationships, may oversimplify
Agent-Based Modeling (ABM) [31]	Represents individual agents and their interactions	Ecological systems, land-use change modeling	Captures emergent behaviors, suitable for complex systems	Data-intensive, calibration challenges

(*Continued*)

Table 1.1 Common environmental monitoring methodologies. (*Continued*)

Methodology	Description	Application areas	Advantages	Challenges and limitations
Machine Learning (ML) [32]	Utilizes algorithms to learn patterns from data	Air quality prediction, biodiversity assessment	Adaptable to various data types, automated pattern recognition	Black-box nature, potential for bias and overfitting
Geospatial Modeling [33]	Integrates spatial data to model geographic phenomena	Land cover change modeling, urban planning	Incorporates spatial relationships, useful for spatial analysis	Relies on accurate spatial data, complexity in data integration
Hybrid Modeling [34]	Combines multiple modeling approaches for synergy	Integrated water resource management, ecosystem modeling	Leverages strengths of different models, enhances accuracy	Complexity in model integration, increased computational burden
Remote Sensing [35]	Uses satellite or aerial imagery for Earth observation	Land cover mapping, deforestation monitoring	Provides real-time data, wide coverage	Limited temporal resolution, dependency on weather conditions
System Dynamics Modeling [36]	Represents dynamic feedback loops within a system	Urban growth modeling, ecological systems	Captures system behaviors over time, useful for policy analysis	Requires detailed understanding of system dynamics

(*Continued*)

Table 1.1 Common environmental monitoring methodologies. (*Continued*)

Methodology	Description	Application areas	Advantages	Challenges and limitations
Life Cycle Assessment (LCA) [37]	Evaluates environmental impacts of products or systems	Product design, waste management	Considers entire life cycle, supports sustainable decision-making	Relies on accurate input data, limited for complex systems
IoT-based Sensor Framework [38]	Sensor-based environment sensing for precision agriculture	Agriculture, Land Modeling	Captures the prime parameters of the environment under study	Relies on the sensor performance and data capture clarity

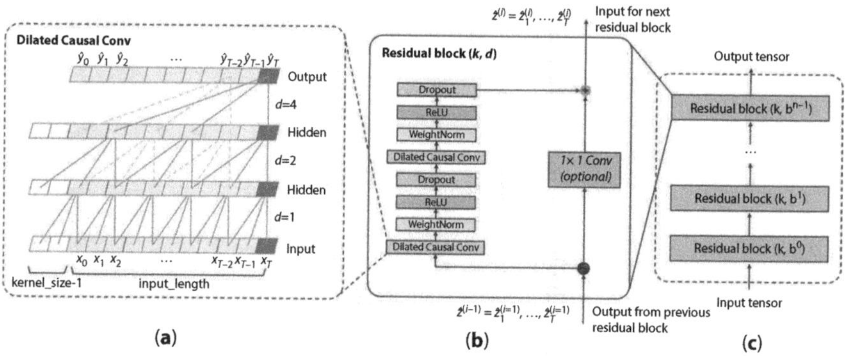

Figure 1.1 Convolution and LSTM model for environmental monitoring.

i. **Convolutional Neural Networks (CNN) for image analysis**
CNNs are widely used for analyzing satellite imagery and remote sensing data in environmental monitoring. These networks can identify patterns, detect changes in land cover, monitor deforestation, and assess the impact of urbanization on ecosystems. The authors [40] have used the CNN architecture for the vegetation monitoring in Karnataka, India, and the architecture is given in Figure 1.2.

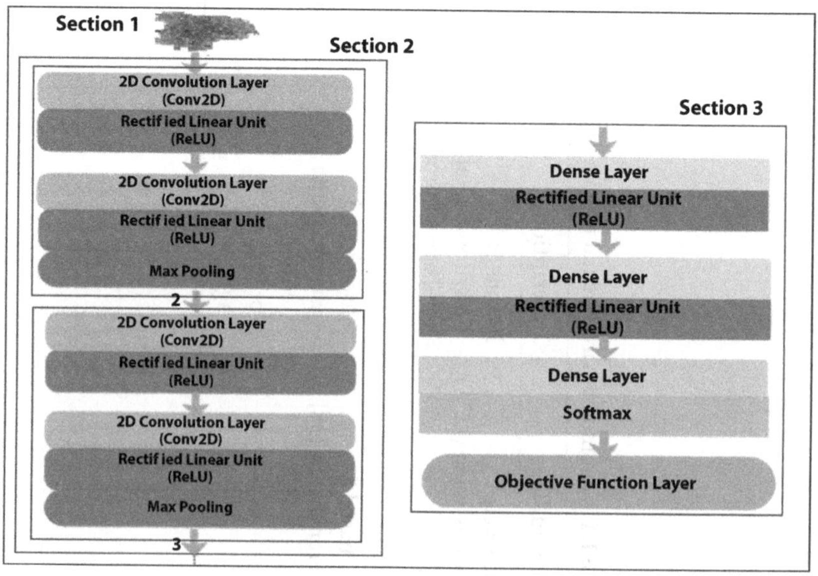

Figure 1.2 CNN model for vegetation monitoring.

ii. **Random forest and Support Vector Machines (SVM) for air quality prediction**
Ensemble methods like Random Forest and SVM have been employed for air quality prediction. These models combine the strengths of multiple algorithms, providing accurate predictions based on meteorological and traffic data. The authors [41] have implemented the machine learning model for a better preprocessing, and the proposed architecture is as given in Figure 1.3.

iii. **Hybrid models for integrated monitoring**
Hybrid models combining different machine learning approaches, such as the integration of neural networks with optimization algorithms, have shown effectiveness in predicting air quality indices. These models leverage the strengths of various techniques for improved accuracy.

iv. **U-Net 3D for deforestation detection**
U-Net 3D, a spatio-temporal deep learning algorithm, has been applied to detect deforestation in tropical rainforests. This architecture considers both spatial and temporal dimensions, enhancing the accuracy of deforestation monitoring. The authors [42] have used the residual convolutional blocks for improved learning the forest changes using satellite images with early convergence as the network deepens. The proposed architecture is as shown in Figure 1.4.

v. **Deep Q-network (DQN) for UAV pollution tracking**
DQN, a deep reinforcement learning algorithm, has been used for UAV pollution tracking. The Deep Q-network-based

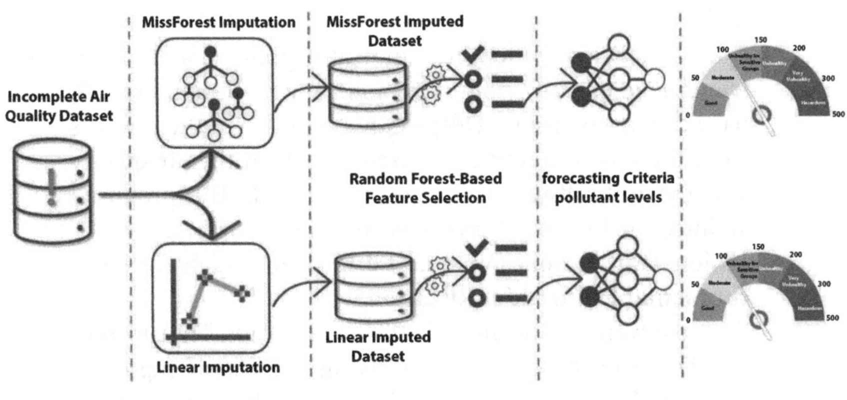

Figure 1.3 Machine learning in environment modeling and prediction.

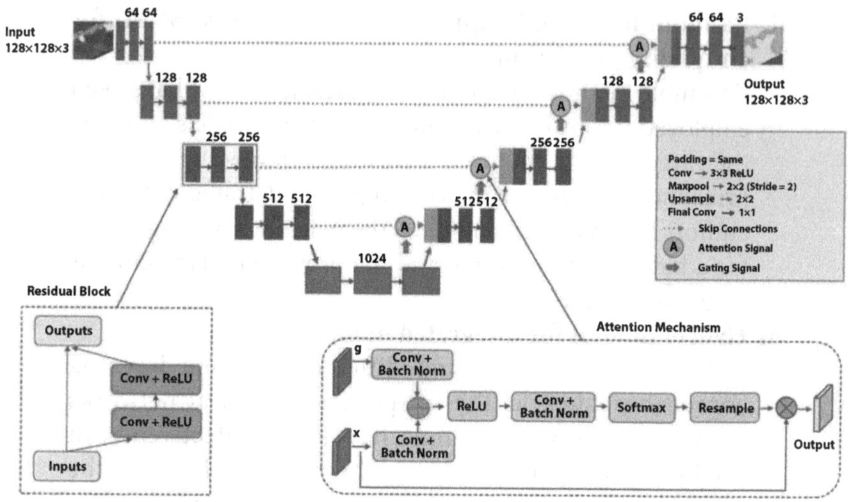

Figure 1.4 CNN model for forest change study.

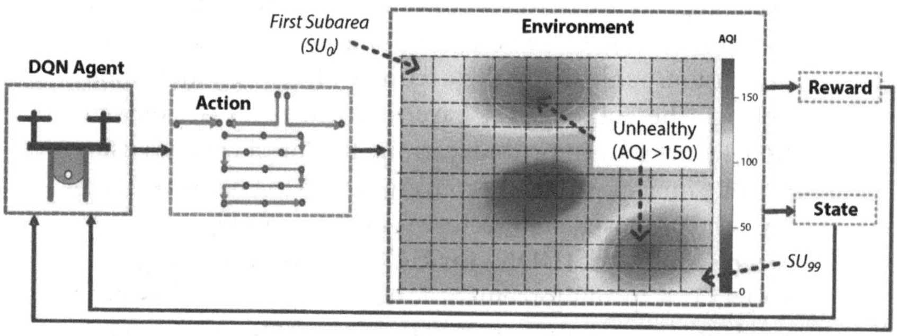

Figure 1.5 DQN Architecture for environment modelling.

solution efficiently identifies unhealthy polluted areas, contributing to effective pollution monitoring. The authors [10] have effectively used a Deep- Q network to get the rewards from the environment and based on which the air quality and the unhealthy areas were recognised. The proposed architecture by the authors is as given in Figure 1.5.

vi. **Vision Transformer (ViT) and diffusion models for environmental feature identification**

Recent advancements include the use of Vision Transformer and Diffusion models for identifying and classifying environmental features. These architectures show promise in

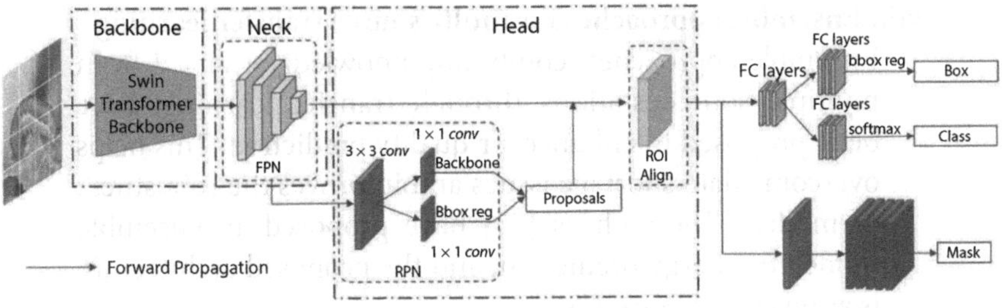

Figure 1.6 Transformer model for agricultural land monitoring.

enhancing the efficiency of environmental monitoring and preservation. One such architecture was developed by the authors [43] for agriculture monitoring as shown in Figure 1.6.

vii. **F-RCNN-based aircraft identification for air pollution source identification**

The F-RCNN-based aircraft identification framework, utilizing convolutional neural networks, accurately detects airplanes in satellite images. This has been applied to improve air pollution source identification in smart cities. One such research by the authors [44] has used an F-RCNN model for ozone depletion identification in stratosphere. The proposed architecture is given in Figure 1.7.

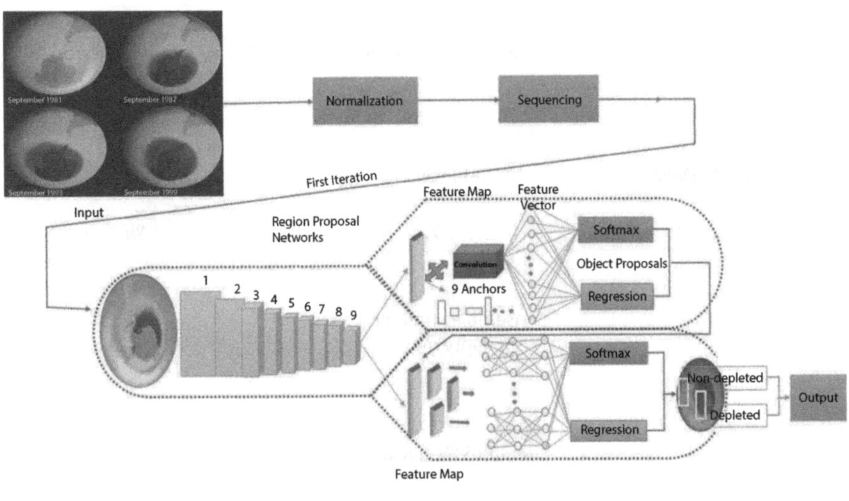

Figure 1.7 F-RCNN model for environment modeling.

viii. **Ensemble approaches for multi-source transfer learning**
Ensemble approaches, combining knowledge learned from multiple source stations through transfer learning, have been proposed to enhance air quality prediction. This helps overcome data shortage issues and improves the robustness of models. The authors [45] have proposed an ensemble model for energy prediction, and the proposed architecture is as given in Figure 1.8.

ix. **AI-SIoT for enhanced integration in environmental monitoring systems**
The deep integration of AI in environmental monitoring systems, particularly through the use of AI-SIoT (Artificial Intelligence in the Semantic Internet of Things), has been explored. This integration significantly improves the accuracy, performance, efficiency, and reliability of monitoring systems. One such architecture by the authors [46] is given in Figure 1.9.

These architectures demonstrate the diverse applications of AI in environmental monitoring, showcasing their effectiveness in handling specific challenges within different domains of environmental science. The choice of architecture often depends on the nature of the data, the specific environmental parameter being monitored, and the desired outcomes of the monitoring system.

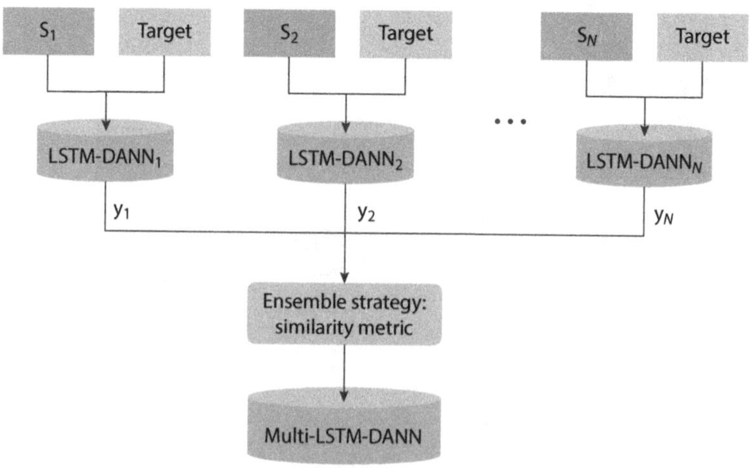

Figure 1.8 Ensemble learning for energy prediction.

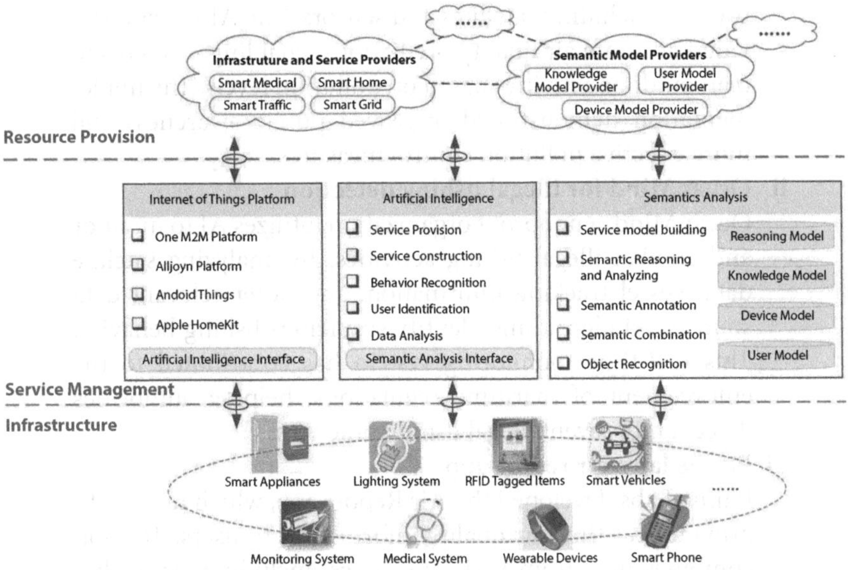

Figure 1.9 Semantic IoT architecture.

1.6 Applications of AI in Environmental Monitoring

Recent advancements in AI, such as Vision Transformer and Diffusion models, have shown promise in environmental monitoring and preservation, particularly in identifying and classifying environmental features [47]. Artificial Neural Networks have been successfully applied in environmental quality monitoring, with the implementation of MATLAB leading to improved accuracy in evaluation results [48]. AI technologies have also been used to enhance efficiency in environmental monitoring and asset management, including the observation of bird behavior and condition assessment of concrete defects [49]. The deep integration of AI in environmental monitoring systems, particularly through the use of AI-SIoT, has been shown to significantly improve accuracy, performance, efficiency, and reliability [50]. A few examples of successful applications of AI in environmental monitoring, showcasing real-world implementations and their outcomes are given as follows.

i. **IBM's green horizon project**

IBM implemented the Green Horizon Project in Beijing to address air quality challenges. The project used AI algorithms to analyze historical and real-time data from various sources, including satellites and sensors. The AI system provided accurate air quality predictions, enabling residents to plan outdoor activities based on pollution levels. The implementation demonstrated improved public awareness and more effective pollution control measures.

ii. **OceanMind for illegal fishing detection**
OceanMind, a nonprofit organization, utilizes AI to monitor and combat illegal fishing activities. By analyzing satellite data, vessel tracking information, and other relevant data sources, AI algorithms identify suspicious fishing behavior. This real-time monitoring system has contributed to the enforcement of maritime regulations, helping authorities detect and prevent illegal fishing practices.

iii. **Plume labs' air report app**
Plume Labs developed the Air Report app, which uses AI to provide real-time air quality information to users. The app combines data from various sources, including air quality monitoring stations, weather conditions, and traffic patterns. Through machine learning, it delivers personalized air quality forecasts and recommendations to users, empowering them to make informed decisions about outdoor activities.

iv. **Smart water management in Barcelona**
Barcelona implemented a smart water management system that utilizes AI to monitor water quality and consumption. Sensors and IoT devices collect data on water quality parameters and consumption patterns. AI algorithms analyze this data to detect anomalies, leaks, and contamination events, enabling authorities to respond promptly and optimize water resource management.

v. **Predictive flood modeling in Houston**
Researchers in Houston used AI for predictive flood modeling to enhance flood risk assessment. By analyzing historical weather data, river levels, and terrain information, machine learning algorithms can predict flood events with greater accuracy. This application aids in early warning systems and allows for more effective evacuation planning and flood mitigation strategies.

vi. **Wildlife conservation with TrailGuard AI**
The TrailGuard AI system, developed by Intel and RESOLVE, employs AI-powered cameras to combat wildlife poaching. The cameras use deep learning algorithms to identify and

alert authorities about potential poaching activities in real time. The system has been successfully deployed in protected areas, contributing to wildlife conservation efforts by deterring illegal activities.

vii. **CityTree's air pollution filtration**
CityTree, a mobile installation, utilizes AI to address urban air pollution. The installation combines moss cultures with IoT technology to filter and monitor air quality. The AI algorithms optimize the performance of the moss cultures based on environmental conditions. Successful deployments in urban areas have demonstrated improvements in local air quality.

viii. **Google's environmental insights explorer**
Google's Environmental Insights Explorer uses AI to estimate carbon emissions and air pollution levels in cities. By combining data from Google Maps and other sources, it provides city officials with insights into greenhouse gas emissions, helping them make informed decisions for sustainable urban planning.

ix. **Water quality monitoring in Lake George, New York**
The Jefferson Project at Lake George utilizes AI to monitor water quality in real time. Autonomous underwater vehicles equipped with sensors collect data on temperature, nutrients, and algae levels. AI algorithms analyze this data, providing insights into the lake's health and aiding in early detection of potential issues.

x. **Airthinx indoor air quality monitoring**
Airthinx, an indoor air quality monitoring solution, employs AI algorithms to analyze data from sensors measuring various air pollutants indoors. This real-time monitoring system helps businesses and institutions optimize ventilation, ensuring healthier indoor environments.

xi. **NASA's Earth Observing System Data and Information System (EOSDIS)**
NASA's EOSDIS utilizes AI to analyze vast amounts of Earth observation data collected by satellites. AI algorithms process and extract valuable information, contributing to climate research, natural disaster monitoring, and the understanding of global environmental changes.

xii. **Waze for traffic management and emissions reduction**
Waze, a navigation app, utilizes AI algorithms to optimize traffic flow and reduce congestion. By providing real-time

traffic information and suggesting alternate routes, Waze contributes to emissions reduction and more efficient transportation in urban areas.

xiii. **Solar forecasting for renewable energy integration**
AI is employed in solar forecasting to enhance the integration of renewable energy sources. By analyzing weather patterns, cloud cover, and historical data, AI models can predict solar energy production, allowing for better grid management and increased efficiency in renewable energy utilization.

xiv. **Eco-friendly farming with The Climate Corporation**
The Climate Corporation, owned by Bayer, employs AI to help farmers optimize their agricultural practices. AI algorithms analyze weather data, soil conditions, and historical crop performance to provide personalized recommendations for planting, irrigation, and fertilization, promoting sustainable and efficient farming.

xv. **Urban greening with tree-planting drones**
Drones equipped with AI technology are used for urban greening initiatives. These drones can identify suitable locations for tree planting by analyzing factors such as soil quality and available space. The automated process helps enhance urban biodiversity and mitigate the urban heat island effect.

1.7 Challenges and Limitations of Using AI in Environment Modeling

i. **Data quality and availability**
Challenge: The effectiveness of AI models relies heavily on the quality and availability of data. Incomplete, biased, or inaccurate datasets can lead to flawed predictions and decisions.
Limitation: In some regions or for specific parameters, obtaining reliable and comprehensive datasets may be challenging, hindering the development and accuracy of AI models.

ii. **Bias in data and algorithms**
Challenge: If historical data used for training AI models contain biases, the algorithms may perpetuate and even

exacerbate existing biases, leading to unfair or discriminatory outcomes.

Ethical consideration: Biased AI models can result in environmental injustice, disproportionately affecting marginalized communities. It is crucial to address bias in both data collection and algorithmic decision-making.

iii. **Interpretable models**

Challenge: Many AI models, especially complex ones like deep neural networks, are considered "black boxes" because their decision-making processes are not easily interpretable. Understanding how and why a model makes a specific prediction can be challenging.

Ethical consideration: Lack of interpretability raises ethical concerns, especially in cases where decisions impact human lives or the environment. Transparent models are essential for accountability and trust.

iv. **Privacy concerns**

Challenge: Environmental monitoring often involves collecting data from various sources, including IoT devices and sensors. Protecting individuals' privacy while collecting and utilizing this data is a significant challenge.

Data privacy issues: As AI systems process personal or sensitive information, there is a risk of privacy breaches. Striking a balance between data utility and privacy is essential.

v. **Limited generalization**

Challenge: AI models trained on specific datasets may struggle to generalize well to different geographical locations, climates, or ecosystems. This limitation can affect the adaptability of models across diverse environmental contexts.

Limitation: Models developed for one region or ecosystem may not perform as effectively when applied elsewhere, requiring retraining or adaptation.

vi. **Computational resources and energy consumption**

Challenge: Training sophisticated AI models demands substantial computational resources and energy. The environmental impact of such resource-intensive processes can counteract the positive intentions of AI applications in environmental monitoring.

Ethical consideration: Considering the environmental cost of AI development is crucial for ensuring that the overall impact is environmentally sustainable.

vii. Human-AI collaboration

Challenge: Over-reliance on AI systems without sufficient human oversight can lead to errors or misinterpretations. The need for human expertise and decision-making remains critical.

Ethical consideration: Decisions that have significant environmental and societal consequences should involve human judgment and ethical considerations beyond what AI algorithms can provide.

viii. Security risks

Challenge: AI systems are susceptible to adversarial attacks, where malicious actors manipulate input data to deceive the model. This poses security risks in critical environmental monitoring applications.

Limitation: Ensuring the robustness of AI models against attacks is an ongoing challenge that requires continuous research and development.

1.8 Future Directions

The future directions of AI in environmental monitoring hold tremendous potential for advancing sustainability, resilience, and our understanding of complex ecosystems. Here are some key areas where AI is expected to make significant contributions:

i. **Enhanced prediction and adaptation**

AI will play a crucial role in improving the accuracy of environmental predictions. Advanced machine learning models will be employed to enhance climate models, predict extreme weather events, and provide more accurate assessments of environmental changes. This will enable better preparedness and adaptive strategies in the face of climate change.

ii. **Precision conservation and restoration**

AI technologies, including machine learning and computer vision, will be increasingly used for precision conservation and ecosystem restoration. This involves targeted interventions based on detailed monitoring and analysis, such as precision planting, invasive species management, and habitat restoration.

iii. **Autonomous environmental monitoring systems**
The development of autonomous monitoring systems, equipped with AI capabilities, will become more prevalent. These systems, including drones and underwater robots, will autonomously collect and analyze environmental data, providing real-time insights into ecosystems, air and water quality, and biodiversity.

iv. **Cross-domain integration**
Future AI applications will focus on integrating data from various environmental domains. Cross-domain integration will enable a more holistic understanding of complex interactions between different components of the environment, facilitating better-informed decision-making and policies.

v. **Explainable AI for decision support**
The need for transparency and accountability in decision-making processes will drive the development of explainable AI models. Understanding how AI arrives at specific conclusions will be crucial for gaining trust in environmental decision support systems, especially in areas like land use planning and natural resource management.

vi. **Citizen science and crowdsourcing**
AI will be integrated into citizen science initiatives and crowdsourcing platforms to leverage large-scale data collection. Machine learning algorithms will aid in analyzing diverse datasets contributed by the public, enhancing our understanding of local environmental conditions and promoting community engagement in environmental monitoring.

vii. **Resilience planning and risk assessment**
AI will assist in developing comprehensive resilience plans for urban and natural environments. By analyzing historical data, predicting future scenarios, and identifying vulnerabilities, AI models can contribute to effective risk assessment and the development of strategies to enhance resilience in the face of environmental challenges.

viii. **Quantifying ecosystem services**
AI will be applied to quantify and assess the value of ecosystem services. Machine learning models can help in understanding the contributions of ecosystems to human well-being, facilitating more informed decision-making around sustainable resource management and conservation.

ix. **Ethical and fair AI practices**
The future of AI in environmental monitoring will also involve a focus on ethical and fair AI practices. Ensuring unbiased data, addressing algorithmic biases, and incorporating diverse perspectives in the development and deployment of AI systems will be critical for responsible environmental management.

x. **Integration with emerging technologies**
AI will continue to integrate with emerging technologies such as blockchain, edge computing, and 5G networks. This integration will enhance the efficiency of data collection, processing, and sharing, enabling more robust and responsive environmental monitoring systems. As AI technologies continue to evolve, interdisciplinary collaboration and a strong emphasis on ethical considerations will be essential for harnessing the full potential of AI in environmental monitoring, contributing to a more sustainable and resilient future.

1.9 Conclusion

In conclusion, environmental monitoring stands as a critical practice, essential for understanding and managing the complexities of our ever-changing ecosystems. The integration of advanced technologies, particularly artificial intelligence (AI), has emerged as a transformative force in addressing the challenges posed by climate change, pollution, and resource management. The need for real-time, comprehensive data has driven the adoption of technologies like remote sensing, big data analytics, and the Internet of Things (IoT). AI, with its capacity to handle vast datasets and predict trends, plays a pivotal role in providing nuanced insights into environmental processes. It enhances precision, accuracy, and adaptability in monitoring air and water quality, predicting climate changes, and assessing biodiversity. The literature review highlights diverse verticals, from air quality prediction to deforestation detection, where AI is making significant contributions. In this dynamic landscape, the continual evolution of AI, coupled with interdisciplinary collaboration and a commitment to ethical principles, offers a path towards a more sustainable and resilient coexistence with our planet. Environmental monitoring, powered by AI, stands poised at the forefront of shaping a future where technology harmonizes with nature for the benefit of both.

Acknowledgements

The authors are grateful for the facilities provided by the Thiagarajar College of Engineering, Madurai, CHRIST (Deemed to be University), Bengaluru, and University of Technology and Applied Sciences, Muscat, for the facilities offered to carry out this work.

References

1. Gryech, I., Ghogho, M., Elhammouti, H., Sbihi, N., Kobbane, A., Machine learning for air quality prediction using meteorological and traffic related features. *J. Ambient Intell. Smart Environ.*, 12, 379–391, 2020, https://doi.org/10.3233/AIS-200572.
2. Nitheesh, M., Gokulakrishnan, R., Devadas, P., Air Prediction by Given Attribute Based on Supervised with Classification Machine Learning Approach, pp. 413–420, 2021, https://doi.org/10.1007/978-981-15-8752-8_42.
3. Petry, L., Meiers, T., Reuschenberg, D., Borujeni, S., Arndt, J., Odenthal, L., Erbertseder, T., Taubenböck, H., Müller, I., Kalusche, E., Weber, B., Käflein, J., Mayer, C., Meinel, G., Gengenbach, C., Herold, H., Design and Results of an AI-Based Forecasting of Air Pollutants for Smart Cities. *ISPRS Annals of the Photogrammetry, Remote Sensing and Spatial Information Sciences*, 2021, https://doi.org/10.5194/isprs-annals-viii-4-w1-2021-89-2021.
4. Wu, Q. and Lin, H., A novel optimal-hybrid model for daily air quality index prediction considering air pollutant factors. *Sci. Total Environ.*, 683, 808–821, 2019, https://doi.org/10.1016/j.scitotenv.2019.05.288.
5. Bogdanović, N., Koprivica, M., Markovic, G., Machine Learning for Air Quality Classification in IoT-based Network with Low-cost Sensors. *2021 15th International Conference on Advanced Technologies, Systems and Services in Telecommunications (TELSIKS)*, pp. 303–306, 2021, https://doi.org/10.1109/TELSIKS52058.2021.9606379.
6. Huang, Y., Gao, Z., Zhang, H., Comparison of common machine learning algorithms trained with multi-zone models for identifying the location and strength of indoor pollutant sources. *Indoor Built Environ.*, 30, 1142–1158, 2020, https://doi.org/10.1177/1420326X20931576.
7. Zhang, J., Tang, P., Lv, T., A real-time calculation platform of ship air pollutant emission based on Flink. *2022 5th International Conference on Advanced Electronic Materials, Computers and Software Engineering (AEMCSE)*, pp. 785–788, 2022, https://doi.org/10.1109/aemcse55572.2022.00157.
8. Niture, N. and Abdellatif, I., AI Based Airplane Air Pollution Identification Architecture Using Satellite Imagery. *2020 IEEE Cloud Summit*, pp. 150–155, 2020, https://doi.org/10.1109/IEEECloudSummit48914.2020.00029.

9. Zhao, Y., Wang, L., Zhang, N., Huang, X., Yang, L., Yang, W., Co-Training Semi-Supervised Learning for Fine-Grained Air Quality Analysis. *Atmosphere*, 2023, https://doi.org/10.3390/atmos14010143.
10. Mohammed, A., Sultan, S., Cho, S., Pyun, J., Powering UAV with Deep Q-Network for Air Quality Tracking. *Sensors (Basel, Switzerland)*, 22, 2022, https://doi.org/10.3390/s22166118.
11. Rahimi, S. and Sajedi, H., Monitoring air pollution by deep features and extreme learning machine. *J. Exp. Theor. Artif. Intell.*, 31, 517–531, 2019, https://doi.org/10.1080/0952813X.2019.1572658.
12. Cárdenas-Montes, M., Detection of anomalous episodes in urban Ozone maps. *Expert Syst.*, 38, 2020, https://doi.org/10.1111/exsy.12636.
13. Dhole, A., Ambekar, I., Gunjan, G., Sonawani, S., An Ensemble Approach to Multi-Source Transfer Learning for Air Quality Prediction. *2021 International Conference on Computing, Communication, and Intelligent Systems (ICCCIS)*, pp. 70–77, 2021, https://doi.org/10.1109/ICCCIS51004.2021.9397138.
14. Yang, Z. and Broby, D., Sustainable Finance: AI Applications in Satellite Imagery and Data, 2020.
15. Wijata, A.M., Bobichon, Y., Vitulli, R., Celesti, M., Camareo, R., Gascon, F., Longépé, N., Nieke, J., Gumiela, M., Nalepa, J., Taking Artificial Intelligence into Space through Objective Selection of Hyperspectral Earth Observation Applications: To Bring the "Brain" Close to the "Eyes" of Satellite Missions. *IEEE Geosci. Remote Sens. Mag.*, 2023, doi: 10.1109/MGRS.2023.3269979.
16. Sebastianelli, A., Del Rosso, M.P., Ullo, S.L., Automatic Dataset Builder for Machine Learning Applications to Satellite Imagery, arXiv: Image and Video Processing, 2020.
17. Fodor, G. and Conde, M.V., Rapid Deforestation and Burned Area Detection using Deep Multimodal Learning on Satellite Imagery, arXiv preprint arXiv:2307.04916, 2023.
18. Solórzano, J.V., Mas, J.F., Gallardo-Cruz, J.A., Gao, Y., de Oca, A.F.M., Deforestation detection using a spatio-temporal deep learning approach with synthetic aperture radar and multispectral images. *ISPRS J. Photogramm. Remote Sens.*, 199, 87–101, 2023.
19. Toan, N.T., Cong, P.T., Hung, N.Q.V., Jo, J., A deep learning approach for early wildfire detection from hyperspectral satellite images, in: *2019 7th International Conference on Robot Intelligence Technology and Applications (RiTA)*, 2019, November, IEEE, pp. 38–45.
20. Kang, Y., Jang, E., Im, J., Kwon, C., A deep learning model using geostationary satellite data for forest fire detection with reduced detection latency. *GISci. Remote Sens.*, 59, 1, 2019–2035, 2022.
21. Wang, Z., Liu, D., Liao, X., Pu, W., Wang, Z., Zhang, Q., SiamHRnet-OCR: A Novel Deforestation Detection Model with High-Resolution Imagery and Deep Learning. *Remote Sens.*, 15, 2, 463, 2023.
22. Sodha, K., Pati, P., Rajput, D., Solanki, H., Review of the Study Climate Change Impact Assessment on the Gujarat Coastline: The Role of Artificial

Intelligence, Statistical, Mathematical and Geographic Information Systems (GIS). *Int. Assoc. Biol. Comput. Dig.*, 2, 1, 241–244, 2023.

23. Singh, S., Babu, K.S., Singh, S., Machine learning approach for climate change impact assessment in agricultural production, in: *Visualization techniques for climate change with machine learning and artificial intelligence*, pp. 317–335, Elsevier, 2023.
24. Mauro Ferrario, D., Furlan, E., Torresan, S., Maraschini, M., Critto, A., Harnessing Machine Learning and Deep Learning applications for climate change risk assessment: a survey, in: *EGU General Assembly Conference Abstracts*, 2022, May, pp. EGU22-6568.
25. Anshul, and Singh, R., Crop Yield Prediction and Climate Change Impact Assessment Using Machine Learning Technology in Agriculture, in: *Information and Communication Technology for Competitive Strategies (ICTCS 2022) Intelligent Strategies for ICT*, pp. 349–362, Springer Nature Singapore, Singapore, 2023.
26. Zennaro, F., Furlan, E., Simeoni, C., Torresan, S., Aslan, S., Critto, A., Marcomini, A., Exploring machine learning potential for climate change risk assessment. *Earth Sci. Rev.*, 220, 103752, 2021.
27. Beven, K. and Freer, J., Equifinality, data assimilation, and uncertainty estimation in mechanistic modelling of complex environmental systems using the GLUE methodology. *J. Hydrol.*, 249, 1-4, 11–29, 2001.
28. Bear, J., *Dynamics of fluids in porous media*, Courier Corporation, 2013.
29. Anderson, M.P. and Woessner, W.W., *Applied groundwater modeling: Simulation of flow and advective transport*, Academic Press, 1992.
30. Hastie, T., Tibshirani, R., Friedman, J., *The elements of statistical learning: Data mining, inference, and prediction*, Springer, 2009.
31. Railsback, S.F. and Grimm, V., *Agent-based and individual-based modeling: A practical introduction*, Princeton University Press, 2012.
32. Hastie, T., Tibshirani, R., Friedman, J., *The elements of statistical learning: Data mining, inference, and prediction*, Springer, 2001.
33. Longley, P.A., Goodchild, M.F., Maguire, D.J., Rhind, D.W., *Geographic information systems and science*, John Wiley & Sons, 2015.
34. Jakeman, A.J., Letcher, R.A., Norton, J.P., Ten iterative steps in development and evaluation of environmental models. *Environ. Modell. Software*, 21, 5, 602–614, 2006.
35. Jensen, J.R., *Remote sensing of the environment: An Earth resource perspective*, Pearson, 2007.
36. Forrester, J.W., *Industrial dynamics*, MIT Press, 1961.
37. ISO 14040:2006, Environmental management - Life cycle assessment - Principles and framework. International Organization for Standardization.
38. Sathiyapriya, K., Thaiyalnayaki, S., Sambandam, R.K., Anuranjani, K., Vetriveeran, D., Smart Precision Irrigation Techniques Using Wireless Underground Sensors in Wireless Sensors. *2022 8th International Conference*

on Advanced Computing and Communication Systems (ICACCS), Coimbatore, India, pp. 2072–2077, 2022, doi: 10.1109/ICACCS54159.2022.9785190.

39. Zhang, X., Dong, F., Chen, G., Dai, Z., Advance prediction of coastal groundwater levels with temporal convolutional and long short-term memory networks. *Hydrol. Earth Syst. Sci.*, 27, 1, 83–96, 2023.
40. Mahendra, H.N., Mallikarjunaswamy, S., Subramoniam, S.R., An assessment of vegetation cover of Mysuru City, Karnataka State, India, using deep convolutional neural networks. *Environ. Monit. Assess.*, 195, 4, 526, 2023.
41. Alkabbani, H., Ramadan, A., Zhu, Q., Elkamel, A., An Improved Air Quality Index Machine Learning-Based Forecasting with Multivariate Data Imputation Approach. *Atmosphere*, 13, 7, 1144, 2022, https://doi.org/10.3390/atmos13071144.
42. Kalinaki, K., Malik, O.A., Lai, D.T.C., FCD-AttResU-Net: An improved forest change detection in Sentinel-2 satellite images using attention residual U-Net. *Int. J. Appl. Earth Obs. Geoinf.*, 122, 103453, 2023.
43. Wu, T., Shi, L., Zhang, L., Wen, X., Lu, J., Li, Z., RS Transformer: A Two-Stage Region Proposal Using Swin Transformer for Few-Shot Pest Detection in Automated Agricultural Monitoring Systems. *Appl. Sci.*, 13, 22, 12206, 2023, https://doi.org/10.3390/app132212206.
44. Aslam, B., Alrowaili, Z.A., Khaliq, B., Manzoor, J., Raqeeb, S., Ahmad, F., Ozone depletion identification in stratosphere through faster region-based convolutional neural network. *Comput. Mater. Continua*, 68, 2159–2178, 2021.
45. Fang, X., Gong, G., Li, G., Chun, L., Peng, P., Li, W., A general multi-source ensemble transfer learning framework integrate of LSTM-DANN and similarity metric for building energy prediction. *Energy Build.*, 252, 111435, 2021, doi: 10.1016/j.enbuild.2021.111435.
46. Guo, K., Lu, Y., Gao, H., Cao, R., Artificial Intelligence-Based Semantic Internet of Things in a User-Centric Smart City. *Sensors*, 18, 5, 1341, 2018, https://doi.org/10.3390/s18051341.
47. Di Ciaccio, F., Russo, P., Troisi, S., Does: A deep learning-based approach to estimate roll and pitch at sea. *IEEE Access*, 10, 29307–29321, 2022.
48. Zhao, K., He, T., Wu, S., Wang, S., Dai, B., Yang, Q., Lei, Y., Application Research of Artificial Neural Network in Environmental Quality Monitoring. *Int. J. Pattern Recognit. Artif. Intell.*, 33, 12, 1959039, 2019.
49. Settemsdal, S., Machine learning and artificial intelligence as a complement to condition monitoring in a predictive maintenance setting, in: *SPE Oil and Gas India Conference and Exhibition*, 2019, April, SPE, p. D012S025R001.
50. Zhang, X., Shu, K., Rajkumar, S., Sivakumar, V., Research on deep integration of application of artificial intelligence in environmental monitoring system and real economy. *Environ. Impact Assess. Rev.*, 86, 106499, 2021.

2

Fundamentals of AI and NLP in Environmental Analysis

Sreedevi Chikkudu and Suresh Annamalai*

Department of Networking and Communications, School of Computing, College of Engineering and Technology, SRM Institute of Science and Technology, SRM Nagar, Kattankulathur, Chennai, Tamil Nadu, India

Abstract

Recent advancements in Artificial Intelligence (AI), Natural Language Processing (NLP), and Artificial Intelligence of Things (AIoT) have created transformative opportunities to enhance and optimize the environmental performance of smart cities. This study employs a unified evidence synthesis framework that integrates aggregative, configurative, and narrative synthesis methods, providing a comprehensive analysis of the impacts of AI, NLP, and AIoT on environmental sustainability in urban areas. The study delves into critical research questions concerning the core principles of emerging smarter eco-cities, including their design, infrastructure, and governance models. It also explores the key drivers behind the realization of these eco-cities, such as technological advancements, policy initiatives, and societal demands for sustainable living environments. Furthermore, the study investigates the primary AI, NLP, and AIoT solutions that contribute to environmental sustainability practices in smart cities. This includes technologies like predictive analytics for energy efficiency, smart waste management systems, and AI-powered urban planning tools that optimize resource allocation and reduce environmental impact. The findings of this study enrich our understanding of how AI, NLP, and IoT technologies can positively impact sustainable urban development. However, they also highlight the challenges associated with their implementation, such as data privacy concerns, technological dependencies, and the need for interdisciplinary collaboration among stakeholders. Overall, these insights empower policymakers, urban planners, and technology developers to advance the integration of eco-urbanism and AI-driven urbanism. By making more informed decisions and designing policies that prioritize environmental

**Corresponding author*: prisu6esh@yahoo.com; suresha2@srmist.edu.in

A. Suresh, T. Devi, N. Deepa and Ali Kashif Bashir (eds.) Environmental Monitoring Using Artificial Intelligence, (29–44) © 2025 Scrivener Publishing LLC

well-being, stakeholders can create smarter and more sustainable cities for the future.

Keywords: Artificial intelligence of things, natural language processing, predictive analytics, artificial intelligence, smart waste management systems, AI-driven, comprehensive analysis

2.1 Introduction

The rapid and merging evolution of artificial intelligence (AI) and the Internet of Things (IoT) has led to groundbreaking progress across various industries, particularly in climate change, environmental sustainability, and urban development. This unprecedented collaboration has given rise to smarter eco-cities, underscoring the indispensable role of Artificial Intelligence of Things (AIoT) integration and garnering widespread attention and anticipation. Within this dynamic landscape, AIoT emerges as a promising force, poised to offer innovative solutions to the escalating environmental challenges confronting smart eco-cities and, by extension, smart cities. At the forefront of this technological revolution, AIoT has vast potential to explore novel pathways for reducing energy consumption, enhancing resource efficiency, optimizing waste management processes, refining transportation systems, safeguarding biodiversity, and ultimately mitigating the overall environmental impact.

As AIoT advances, its applications in a variety of areas provide not just solutions to existing environmental issues, but also the ability to anticipate future ones. These pioneering breakthroughs usher in a new era, altering the urban development landscape to reflect the unstoppable march of urbanization and the growing complications of environmental degradation. The ultimate goal is to transform cities into hubs of knowledge, environmental consciousness and sustainability. Smart eco-cities are evolving into places where technology effortlessly blends with environmental care, promoting a healthy coexistence of urbanization and ecological preservation. As the industry grows, stakeholders must collaborate to ensure that AIoT technologies are utilized properly, taking into consideration ethical concerns, data security, and long-term environmental consequences. The convergence of AI and the IoT within smart eco-cities represents a promising frontier. This integration holds the potential not only to enhance urban life but also to make substantial contributions to global initiatives aimed at forging a more sustainable and resilient future.

AI is not only reshaping technological landscapes but is also fundamentally transforming the fabric of urban settings. Its role as a critical driving force in developing smart cities and smart eco-cities highlights its disruptive and revolutionary potential, placing it at the forefront of these advancements. This influential position has instigated fundamental changes in intricate interactions, influencing subsystems' behaviors and reactions to their surroundings. The ongoing impact of AI has led to significant alterations in urban processes and practices, indicating a clear trend towards greater proper alignment with data-driven scientific urbanism. This paradigm shift emphasizes increased reliance on data analytics, machine learning, and AI to optimize resource utilization, decision-making processes, and overall urban functionality.

This paradigm shift is characterized by an increased emphasis on data analytics, machine learning, and AI to enhance resource utilization, decision-making processes, and overall urban functionality. As AI permeates urban environments, its influence on urban processes and activities accelerates, buoyed by the exponential expansion of computing power. This growth is especially crucial in addressing the vast influx of data from diverse sources facilitated by the Internet of Things (IoT).

The combination of AI, NLP and IoT has emerged as a powerful accelerator for environmentally sustainable urban development. IoT's inherent strength is its capacity to generate enormous amounts of data through networked devices and sensors scattered throughout cities. AI then applies complicated models and algorithms to thoroughly examine and comprehend this data. This relationship encourages informed decision-making, real-time monitoring, and predictive analytics, all of which contribute to ecologically friendly urban solutions. Furthermore, the integration of AI, NLP and IoT is not limited to data analysis. it affects many elements of urban life. From optimizing energy use and garbage management to enhancing transportation systems and conserving natural resources, AI and IoT are enabling a complete approach to sustainable urban development.

As technology advances, there is an increasing emphasis on constructing resilient and adaptive urban ecosystems that can successfully respond to environmental concerns while still fostering a high quality of life for people. Finally, the interconnected areas of AI and IoT are altering not just the technological environment, but also the very fabric of urban life. The joint power of AI and IoT offers immense potential for ecologically sustainable urban development, and as these technologies advance, they promise to usher in an era in which cities become not just smarter, but also more resilient, responsive, and environmentally conscientious.

The centralized infrastructure of the Internet of Things (IoT) is grappling with significant challenges, primarily attributed to the overwhelming volume of data generated and processed. To navigate this expansive data landscape effectively, it becomes imperative to deploy robust AI and NLP prototypes and algorithms. These AI and NLP technologies play a crucial role in managing data storage, flow, and processing within IoT networks, extracting valuable insights from the vast data pool.

Among these considerations, the concept of AIoT emerges due to several distinguishing features that set it apart from other IoT techniques. AIoT takes advantage of correlations between AI/NLP and IoT technologies, introducing new layers of intelligent and efficient processing of data, analysis, and decision-making abilities. One significant advantage of AIoT is its ability to facilitate real-time data discernment, statistical analysis, and adaptive responses. This is accomplished by seamlessly integrating AI/NLP and DL/ML capabilities into IoT machines and systems, resulting in improved overall system performance.

One key differentiator for AIoT is its ability to effectively address the challenges posed by the vast and varied information generated within the extensive network of interrelated devices that characterises the IoT landscape. Moreover, AIoT not only addresses the challenge of efficiently delivering substantial data through a dispersed sensor network design but also excels in the analysis and contextualization of intricate and diverse data sources. This proficiency enables the deployment of more sophisticated applications across various sectors.

In essence, the introduction of AIoT unfolds a plethora of opportunities for optimization, innovation, and automation across diverse industries, ranging from climate change and environmental sustainability to the development of intelligent eco-cities. Beyond its role in data management, AIoT proves indispensable for the functioning of smart cities, contributing to the enhancement of eco-cities. Its remarkable potential extends to effectively addressing complex environmental concerns by offering solutions that surpass traditional IoT capabilities.

The integration of Natural Language Processing (NLP) with AIoT introduces a heightened level of complexity. NLP empowers robots to comprehend and respond to human language, fostering more intuitive interactions and enhancing user experiences within smart city environments. Additionally, the application of natural language processing enables the rapid analysis of textual data, facilitating tasks such as sentiment analysis to evaluate public opinions on environmental activities and policies. In summary, the convergence of AI, IoT, and NLP within the framework of AIoT not only revolutionizes data management but also propels innovation, sustainability, and automation across various sectors. As this technology progresses, its adaptive and intelligent capabilities hold the potential to tackle intricate challenges, make substantial contributions to environmental conservation efforts, and contribute to the development of a more resilient and interconnected future.

2.2 AI and NLP Techniques

AI/NLP, a field known for emulating human intelligent behavior using devices or computers with cognitive capabilities, plays a crucial role in this chapter. In this context, AI encompasses any device or system capable of observing its environment and taking actions to achieve specific goals. AI robots, particularly noteworthy in their capabilities, acquire knowledge about their surroundings, enhance performance through experiential learning, and tackle complex problems akin to human processes.

AI systems demand diverse skills, including the analysis and learning from external data, employing the synergy of natural computing (NC) and Machine Learning (ML). NC, a multifaceted approach, not only simulates human cognitive functions using techniques like fuzzy logic (FL), computer vision (CV), and NLP but also addresses the intricate aspects of human intellect and emotion. Its applications extend to decision assistance, strategic planning, sequential activities, self-improvement, and self-learning. Moreover, NC involves imitating natural phenomena and utilizing raw materials as computer mediums, contributing to the advancement of machine learning algorithms.

Evolutionary Computing (EC), drawing inspiration from biological processes such as evolution and ecology, finds frequent application in continuous optimization, especially within complex settings involving numerous variables. ML, often rooted in FL, intricately models human thought and cognition using degrees of truth ranging from 0 to 1. FL, a key component, is utilized in fuzzy c-means clustering, a method that categorizes data points into clusters based on probability score attribution, further showcasing the depth of AI/NLP's impact and capabilities. CV uses ML to extract information from visual input, detect patterns, and make informed decisions. ML interacts with or is a tool for several AI models, including NLP, FL, and CV. This integration of many methodologies within the AI framework demonstrates the adaptability and interconnectedness of AI systems in emulating and improving human-like cognitive processes. Optimization, particularly in complicated settings involving many variables. Machine Learning, which may be based on FL, models human thought and cognition using degrees of truth ranging from 0 to 1. FL is used in fuzzy c-means clustering, which divides data points into clusters depending on possibility score attribution. CV uses ML to extract data from detect patterns and visual input and make educated decisions. ML interacts with or is a tool for several AI/NLP models, including NLP, CV, and FL. This integration of many methodologies inside the AI framework demonstrates the adaptability and interconnection of AI systems in imitating and improving human-like cognitive processes.

NLP is critical to computers' ability to comprehend, analyze, modify, and synthesize human language. In the context of smart cities, NLP is critical for promoting effective communication between people and intelligent technology. It promotes intelligent interactions and decision-making across a variety of sectors, including smart planning, governance, transportation, and municipal services. The use of NLP in smart cities improves service delivery and communication channels, and generates useful insights from public feedback. A wide range of AI and NLP methodologies have acquired substantial popularity, notably in AI/NLP and AIoT applications focusing on environmental sustainability, climate change, and intelligent cities. Prominent methodologies comprise:

2.2.1 Artificial Neural Network (ANN)

Inspired by the human brain, ANNs excel in pattern recognition, making them valuable for tasks like data categorization and regression.

2.2.2 Support Vector Machine (SVM)

A model for classification and regression analysis that employs supervised learning, detecting patterns and relationships within data with exceptional proficiency.

2.2.3 Linear Regression (LR)

A fundamental statistical tool for modeling the connection between dependent and independent variables, commonly used in predictive analytics.

2.2.4 Random Forests (RF) and Decision Trees (DT)

Serve in classification, regression, and decision-making, offering visual representations of potential results.

2.2.5 Adaptive Neuro-Fuzzy Inference System (ANFIS)

Integrating neural networks and fuzzy logic, ANFIS manages uncertainties and makes decisions by leveraging linguistic and numerical data.

2.2.6 Batch-Normalization (BN)

Enhances the training process of deep neural networks through the normalization of intermediate feature values, mitigating concerns like gradient issues.

2.2.7 Convolutional Neural Networks (CNNs)

Indispensable for environmental monitoring, particularly in the analysis of visual data due to their efficacy in image processing and recognition.

2.2.8 Deep Neural Networks (DNNs)

Composed of numerous layers, DNNs demonstrate proficiency in acquiring hierarchical data representations, empowering them to make intricate decisions.

2.2.9 Genetic Algorithm (GA)

Based on natural selection, genetic algorithms are optimization approaches used to solve complicated issues.

Supervised learning techniques in ML include LR, RF, DT, ANN, Generalized Linear Models (GLM), SVM, and Bayesian Networks (BN) for regression, classification, or a combination. Deep Learning (DL) is a biologically inspired version of ML employing algorithms like DNNs, CNNs, and Recurrent Neural Networks, simulating human cognition for quicker and more efficient decision-making. DL relies on neural networks with input, hidden, and output layers to gain data representation and create relationships across the various levels of abstraction, extracting useful insights from complex datasets.

2.3 AI Models and NLP System with Data Science Cycle

Effectively managing and deciphering the growing volume of continually changing and interconnected data generated by the IoT necessitates strong computing and analytical skills. The proliferation of dynamic and interconnected data from IoT has given rise to AIoT, a technological structure aimed at optimizing IoT operations, refining data management and analytics structures, improving human-machine interactions, and elevating processes for making decisions. AIoT combines IoT devices and sensors with AI models and methodologies to enable sophisticated analysis, real-time insights, intelligent decision-making, sophisticated analysis, and autonomous behavior. AIoT operates by manipulating and interacting in a dynamic environment, using ML and DL to improve control precision. These technologies also play important roles in facilitating bidirectional interactions, thereby contributing to the seamless integration of AI/IoT.

The convergence of big data, AI, and IoT results in more creative and effective applications across multiple industries, fostering discovery and enabling disruptive solutions. As IoT generates large amounts of big data, AI becomes increasingly important for analyzing, comprehending, and making optimal decisions within various urban systems. IoT is the foundation for data-driven AI analytics, allowing complex processes to be carried out efficiently while extracting valuable knowledge from utilized intelligence. AIoT integrates intelligence and decision-making capabilities into IoT applications and systems. The AI-NLP/AIoT system is built around five pillars: detection, perception, learning, visualization, and action. This conceptual framework is adaptable to a variety of applications, allowing for the customization of requirements, unique qualities, and objectives.

For example, Zhang and Tao investigate AIoT advancements in perception, learning, reasoning, and behavior within intelligent transportation, grids, and buildings. This entails imbuing smart devices with human-like cognitive and behavioral abilities, which are critical for system efficiency. This demand has resulted in the development of AIoT, a technical framework aimed at improving the efficiency of IoT operations, interactions between humans and machines, data management and analytics models, and processes for making choices. AIoT combines IoT devices and sensors with AI models and methodologies, allowing for advanced analysis, real-time insights, intelligent decision-making, and autonomous behavior. It operates by manipulating and interacting with a dynamic environment, with ML and DL playing critical roles in improving control precision and supporting multimodal communications.

The convergence of big data with AI and IoT is instrumental in creating more innovative and efficient applications across diverse sectors, fostering innovation, and enabling disruptive solutions. As IoT generates substantial amounts of big data, AI becomes pivotal for analyzing, comprehending, and making optimal decisions within various urban systems. IoT is the cornerstone for data-driven AI analytics, allowing complex processes to be executed effectively while extracting valuable knowledge from applied intelligence. The resurgence of AI is fueled by the abundance and potency of big data, supported by increased computing storage capacity and real-time data processing speeds.

AIoT provides the integration of intelligence and capacity for decision-making into IoT systems and applications. The AI/NLP/AIoT system is built upon five pillars: detection, perception, learning, visualisation, and action. This conceptual framework, shown in Figure 2.1, is adaptable to a variety of applications, tailoring itself to specific characteristics, requirements, and goals.

An AI-NLP/AIoT-powered infrastructure stands out for its ability to interpret unstructured data and generate meaningful insights to guide choices and actions. This necessitates the complex interaction of multiple computing skills and processes. Machine perception is a critical feature in which the system uses input data from multiple sensors to infer environmental characteristics such as identifying objects, action recognition, image categorizing, and interpretation of language. Machine observation seeks to convert sensory data into useful information, enabling the system to detect and comprehend its surroundings in the real world. The collection and interpretation of sensory information are critical components of the learning process. The most common learning technique is machine learning, which enables the system to learn through experience rather than explicit programming. This includes collecting and processing training data, developing ML models, delivering data, and allowing the system to learn to recognize patterns or predict outcomes. The end result is a

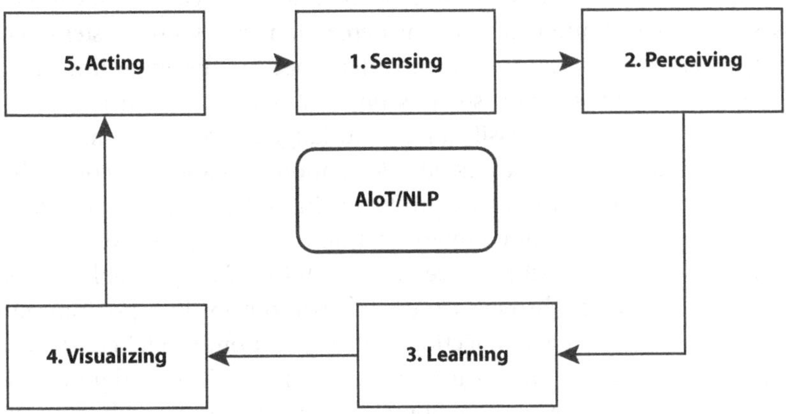

Figure 2.1 Perspective on the data science cycle.

machine learning model that can perform predictive, descriptive, prognostic, and prescriptive tasks, as well as recommend actions. Within machine learning, there are three subcategories:

2.3.1 Supervised Learning

Trained on labeled datasets to recognize items or entities.

2.3.2 Semi-Unsupervised Learning/Unsupervised Learning

Discovers similarities in unlabeled data, like patterns or trends.

2.3.3 Reinforcement Learning

Trained through failure and trial to make the best judgements, relevant in scenarios such as self-driving cars or automating regular tasks.

Few-shot learning, transduction learning, multitasking learning, federated learning, and transfer learning are additional classifications within the realm of machine learning. The utilization of extensive datasets to augment learning and adaptability underscores the significance of DL. DL has garnered substantial attention in AIoT applications due to its ability to enhance system intelligence, particularly in dynamic and complex environments, utilizing unsupervised and reinforcement learning paradigms. ML is fundamentally concerned with optimizing system performance by leveraging data. DL is increasingly favored for managing complex and dynamic scenarios in IoT applications. An AI/AIoT-powered system can analyze unprocessed data to derive actionable insights, enabling well-informed decision-making. This involves a series of interdependent computational capabilities and processes. A crucial component, machine perception, enables the system to utilize input data from various sensors to infer aspects of the environment. This encompasses responsibilities such as pose estimation, action recognition, object detection, image classification, and language recognition. Machine perception transforms unprocessed information into a logical comprehension of the physical environment, producing insightful conclusions. Sensory data acquisition and accurate interpretation are vital aspects of the learning process. ML, the most advanced approach to learning, enables systems to acquire knowledge through experience without explicit programming. The process includes data collection and preparation, model construction and training, and ML system learning and prediction. The final product is a machine learning model capable of making predictions, providing descriptions, making prognostications, and recommending actions. Supervised learning (trained with labeled datasets), unsupervised/semi-unsupervised learning, and reinforcement learning are three subcategories of machine learning. Various algorithms, including few-shot learning, federated learning, transfer learning, and transduction learning, contribute to the system's multifaceted capabilities.

To enhance the system's capacity for generating dependable decisions and learning from interpreted data and computations, training ML models often requires the use of enormous datasets. In this context, DL plays a crucial role by enhancing the system's capacity to learn and adapt to various scenarios, especially in unsupervised and reinforcement learning techniques. DL has proven critical in augmenting the intelligence of IoT applications, enabling them to efficiently navigate dynamic and intricate environments. In essence, ML involves the continuous improvement of performance and intelligence in applications powered by AI and the Internet of Things.

2.4 Environmental Analysis Using AIoT and NLP

Addressing ecological challenges requires a holistic approach. The incorporation of scholarly research in renewable energy and energy conservation underscores the need for a diverse array of strategies, including technological advancements, policy development, and behavioral changes. These components play a crucial role in achieving sustainable energy practices across various contexts. Review studies focusing on water resources conservation explore topics such as the impact of climate change on water resources, effective water management practices, and conservation strategies. Emphasizing the critical nature of sustainable practices and integrated water resource management, these assessments aim to mitigate water scarcity and safeguard water resources for the foreseeable future. In the realm of waste management, literature evaluations shed light on the transformative effects of AI on waste management processes. The implementation of predictive maintenance, optimized collection routes, and refined waste classification positions AI and Decision Support Systems (DSS) as powerful tools for fostering sustainable waste management practices, reducing environmental impact, and enhancing resource efficiency. Research on biodiversity and ecosystem services adds significantly to our understanding of biodiversity conservation and the critical role of ecosystem services in maintaining human well-being. These evaluations highlight the importance of incorporating services provided by ecosystems into processes for making decisions, habitat restoration, and conservation efforts, as well as advocating for practices that promote sustainable development.

Scholarly research into sustainable transportation addresses a variety of issues, including electric vehicles, intelligent transportation systems and multimodal transportation alternatives. These studies show that sustainable transportation alternatives have the possibility to reduce carbon dioxide emissions, improve air quality, and facilitate urban movement. In climate change adaptation and mitigation, a thorough examination of existing research improves our understanding of the challenges and potential advantages. These evaluations evaluate policy frameworks, mitigation strategies, and adaptation strategies for reducing greenhouse gas emissions and increasing climate change resilience. These comprehensive assessment studies significantly improve our understanding of environmentally sustainable development and global warming. They emphasize the importance of using comprehensive methodologies, encouraging interdisciplinary collaboration, and taking technical and policy considerations into account in order to effectively confront and overcome the complexities effectively.

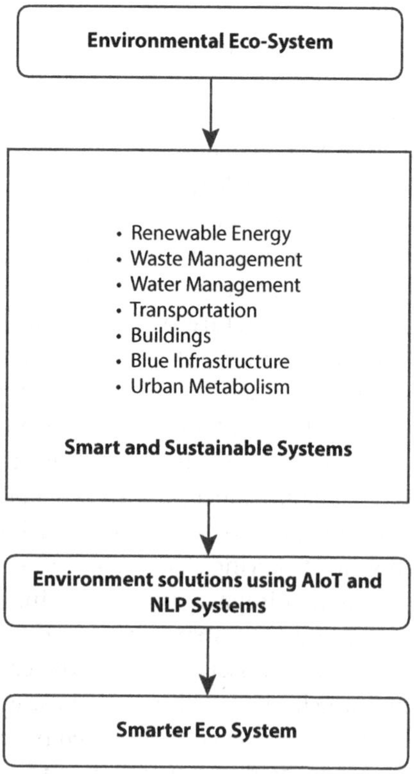

Figure 2.2 An overview of environmental analysis using AIoT and NLP.

The Figure 2.2 illustrates how AIoT and NLP can be used to analyze and improve various aspects of the environment, leading to a smarter and more sustainable eco-system. The essence of eco-cities lies in the creation of urban environmental systems that minimize resource input and waste output. A concise definition of eco-cities is "an urban environmental system in which input (of resources) and output (of waste) are minimized." The prevalence of eco-cities today reflects a diverse range of approaches and solutions tailored to address environmental challenges in various urban contexts. The conceptualization, implementation, and development of eco-cities are notably diverse, resulting in a spectrum of ideas, aspirations, and concepts rather than a singular, definitive definition.

At their core, eco-cities are urban areas meticulously planned and constructed to prioritize ecological balance and sustainability. Their overarching objectives include fostering a harmonious relationship between humanity and nature and minimizing ecological footprints. Key priorities encompass energy efficiency, the adoption of renewable energy sources, reduction of pollution, incorporation of green spaces, promotion of sustainable transportation, and conservation of resources. The fundamental goal is to create a habitat that supports the well-being of residents, promotes ecological harmony with the surrounding environment, and advances both social integration and economic growth.

The main objective of eco-cities is to create urban environments that are environmentally conscious, low-carbon, and resilient, thereby actively steering towards a more sustainable future. Creating smart eco-cities is a complex task impacted heavily by policy instruments, technological advancements, and environmental considerations. These cities use technological advancement to optimize urban systems for sustainable and implement innovative, eco-friendly solutions in response to environmental issues. However, policy instruments play an important role in establishing and directing the trajectory of smart cities. Policy structure, incentives, and regulations foster the adoption of innovative technologies and environmentally friendly practices. They ensure the seamless integration of intelligent solutions into urban settings, in line with the vision of technologically progressive and environmentally conscious urban environments. Successful policy implementation is critical to fully leveraging technological advancements and addressing environmental challenges, ultimately contributing to the realization of smart cities. The smart cities and governance are inextricably linked and mutually reinforcing, with governance serving as the foundation for policy development and implementation. Urban policy, which includes actions, plans, laws, rules, and regulations, is critical in mobilizing and aligning stakeholders to manage intelligent cities. Deploying data-driven solutions and advancing environmental sustainability require specific policies, so policy instruments are essential in strategizing, executing, and overseeing innovative eco-city initiatives.

Key policy instruments facilitating smart eco-cities include the following:

1. Government regulations: Implement regulations specifying sustainability requirements and standards for smart eco-city outcomes, encompassing targets for waste management, energy efficiency, and renewable energy integration.
2. Financial incentives: Local authorities and governments can provide financial incentives, such as grants, tax, and subsidies, to encourage integrating sustainable practices and intelligent technologies within smart eco-city initiatives.
3. Public-private partnerships: Collaboration between governments, technology firms, research institutions, energy companies, and industry players to develop and implement long-term solutions leveraging knowledge, resources, and financing.
4. Open data initiatives: Enabling access and analysis of information for policymakers, businesses, and researchers to develop intelligent solutions. Facilitating data exchange from diverse sources, such as IoT devices and sensors, promotes collaboration and fosters evidence-based decision-making processes. This involves encouraging the seamless sharing of information to support the creation of well-informed decisions.
5. Certification programs and standards: Establishing technical prerequisites, cybersecurity protocols and data privacy principles to ensure the reliability, interoperability, and security of intelligent resolutions in smart eco-cities.

By providing direction, incentives, and regulations that promote technological creation and sustainable development and improve the well-being of inhabitants, these policy instruments collectively create a conducive atmosphere for realizing smart cities. The influence of policies on defining sustainable development for cities explains the variations in approaches and priorities across nations.

Bibliography

ADEME, General principles for the environmental labelling of consumer products, methodological standard for the environmental assessment of digital services. Technical report, ADEME, 2021.

Anthony, L.F.W., Kanding, B., Selvan, R., Carbontracker: Tracking and Predicting the Carbon Footprint of Training Deep Learning Models, arXiv:2007.03051, 2020.

Baldé, C.P., Forti, V., Gray, V., Kuehr, R., Stegmann, P., The global e-waste monitor 2017: Quantities, flows and resources, United Nations University, International Telecommunication Union, and International Solid Waste Association, 2017.

Berkhout, P.H., Muskens, J.C., Velthuijsen, J.W., Defining the rebound effect. *Energy Policy*, 28, 6, 425–432, 2000.

Berthoud, F., Bzeznik, B., Gibelin, N., Laurens, M., Bonamy, C., Morel, M., Schwindenhammer, X., Estimation de l'empreinte carboned'une heure.coeur de calcul. Research report, UGA - Université Grenoble Alpes; CNRS; INP Grenoble; INRIA, 2020.

Bol, D., Pirson, T., Dekimpe, R., Moore's law and ICT innovation in the anthropocene, in: *Proceedings of the IEEE Design and Test in Europe Conference*, Grenoble, France, pp. 1–5, 2021.

Bracquené, E., De Bock, Y., Duflou, J., Sustainability impact assessment of an intelligent control system for residential heating. *Procedia CIRP*, 90, 232–237, 2020, CIRP Life Cycle Engineering (LCE) Conference.

Cardon, D., Cointet, J.-P., Mazières, A., Libbrecht, E., Neurons spike back. *Reseaux*, 211, 5, 173–220, 2018.

Coroamă, V.C. and Pargman, D., Skill rebound: On an unintended effect of digitalization, in: *Proceedings of the 7th International Conference on ICT for Sustainability, ICT4S2020*, Association for Computing Machinery, New York, NY, USA, pp. 213–219, 2020.

Henderson, P., Hu, J., Romoff, J., Brunskill, E., Jurafsky, D., Pineau, J., Towards the Systematic Reporting of the Energy and Carbon Footprints of Machine Learning, 2020.

Hilty, L.M. and Hercheui, M.D., ICT and sustainable development, in: *What kind of information society? Governance, virtuality, surveillance, sustainability, resilience*, pp. 227–235, Springer, 2010.

Horner, N.C., Shehabi, A., Azevedo, I.L., Known unknowns: indirect energy effects of information and communication technology. *Environ. Res. Lett.*, 11, 10, 103001, 2016.

ITU-T, Methodology for environmental life cycle assessments of information and communication technology goods, networks and services. Technical report, ITU-T, 2014.

Lacoste, A., Luccioni, A., Schmidt, V., Dandres, T., Quantifying the Carbon Emissions of Machine Learning, arXiv:1910.09700, 2019.

Lannelongue, L., Grealey, J., Inouye, M., Green Algorithms: Quantifying the carbon emissions of computation, 2020.

Li, D., Chen, X., Becchi, M., Zong, Z., Evaluating the Energy Efficiency of Deep Convolutional Neural Networks on CPUs and GPUs, in: *IEEE International Conferences on Big Data and Cloud Computing (BDCloud), Social Computing and Networking (SocialCom), Sustainable Computing and Communications (SustainCom) (BDCloud-SocialCom-SustainCom)*, 2016.

Ligozat, A.-L. and Luccioni, A., A Practical Guide to Quantifying Carbon Emissions for Machine Learning Researchers and Practitioners. Technical report, LISN and MILA, 2021.

Patterson, D., Gonzalez, J., Le, Q., Liang, C., Munguia, L.-M., Rothchild, D., So, D., Texier, M., Dean, J., Carbon emissions and large neural network training, arXiv:2104.10350, 2021.

3

Smart Environmental Monitoring Systems: IoT and Sensor-Based Advancements

D. Roja Ramani[1]*, B. Ben Sujitha[2] and Shrikant Tangade[3]

[1]Computer Science and Engineering, New Horizon College of Engineering, Bengaluru, India
[2]Department of Computer Science and Engineering, Noorul Islam Centre for Higher Education, Kumaracoil, Thuckalay, India
[3]Department of Mathematics, University of Padova, Padova, Italy

Abstract

In today's environmentally conscious era, with challenges ranging from air quality and water pollution to radiation issues, the importance of thorough monitoring has become more pronounced than ever. Recent breakthroughs in technology, particularly the rapid evolution of the Internet of Things (IoT) and innovative sensor technologies, have ushered in an era of sophisticated and intelligent environmental monitoring (IEM). This manuscript offers a comprehensive review of groundbreaking contributions and research undertakings within the realm of IEM. The domains covered span the spectrum, from the meticulous tracking of air and water quality to the discerning evaluation of radiation pollution and agricultural systems. These investigations are classified according to their precise objectives, with each scrutinized in terms of the sensor technologies deployed, deep learning methodologies applied, and classification techniques employed. The culmination of this meticulous analysis yields recommendations and insights that underscore the profound influence of IEM research on the evolution of environmental monitoring practices. The authors critically assess how the synergy of deep learning, sensor innovations, and IoT connectivity is reshaping environmental monitoring into an astute and efficient system. This paper advocates for the formulation of robust deep learning methodologies, the refinement of denoising strategies, and the establishment of stringent standards for wireless sensor networks (WSNs). It is within this framework that the future of IEM is envisioned, promising to elevate precision and reliability in environmental monitoring endeavors.

**Corresponding author*: rosevsroja@gmail.com

A. Suresh, T. Devi, N. Deepa and Ali Kashif Bashir (eds.) Environmental Monitoring Using Artificial Intelligence, (45–60) © 2025 Scrivener Publishing LLC

Keywords: Intelligent environmental monitoring, sensor devices, industrial automation, smart farming, air quality

3.1 Introduction

The synergy between Internet of Things (IoT) and cloud computing propels forward-thinking solutions by capturing data from IoT systems and processing it efficiently with cloud resources. This study is centered on an immediate environmental monitoring system, emphasizing temperature and humidity parameters. Through the incorporation of sensors like DHT11 and leveraging cloud services like ThingSpeak, the system guarantees seamless data storage, analysis, and visualization. Security is maintained through the Advanced Encryption Standard (AES) algorithm. The results are conveniently accessed and presented via a mobile application interfacing with the ThingSpeak cloud platform [1]. Global sustainability hinges on factors like the economy and education, but environmental health is paramount. Monitoring the environment is crucial for ensuring clean, hazard-free surroundings, vital for citizens' well-being. Environmental monitoring (EM) tackles issues like pollution and disasters, with recent advances like AI and IoT shaping it into smart environment monitoring (SEM) systems. These systems, utilizing wireless networks and sensors, play a key role in managing pollution and adverse effects, contributing to the design of smart cities. Standards and protocols are essential for effective implementation, prompting studies on developing them for IoT-based SEM systems [2]. Global agriculture grows with the population, demanding enhanced production. Climate change and population growth concern crop management. Real-time systems, such as Arduino with sensors like DHT11, enable reliable environmental monitoring. Ethernet shields provide internet connectivity, while IoT and cloud computing streamline data management. ThingSpeak and IFTTT are used for analysis and automation, monitoring temperature and humidity and triggering alerts in this research. The paper covers related work, proposed systems, results, and conclusions with future ideas.

The world's sustainable development relies on factors like the economy and education, but the environment is crucial for human well-being [4]. Monitoring is vital to ensure citizens' health, addressing pollution challenges through environmental monitoring (EM) [2]. Recent technological advancements, especially in AI and machine learning, have transformed EM into a smart system. Smart cities, using wireless networks for pollution monitoring, are replacing traditional urban planning methods [6].

Figure 3.1 illustrates the SEM system monitoring water contamination via IoT and sensors, connected to the cloud. Additionally, the SEM system addresses diverse environmental issues through the utilization of wireless sensor networks (WSNs) and IoT devices.

The landscape of operational health and environmental systems has been significantly reshaped by the incorporation of the Internet of Things (IoT), utilizing sensors and devices to convert data streams into intelligent location-based services [1–4]. Within the framework of IoT, the Wireless Sensor Network (WSN) assumes a pivotal role, finding applications across various fields [5, 6]. Numerous cities are either currently in the process of deploying or planning to deploy WSNs to establish expansive wireless coverage on a city-wide scale [7]. In the sphere of environmental and health monitoring applications, the design of WSNs holds immense significance, as it can be a critical factor determining life and death outcomes. The primary goal is to ensure that these networks consistently and universally deliver environmental and health services, irrespective of location or time. The deployment of such WSNs presents challenges, particularly considering the high cost of sensors. It is therefore essential to strategically position a minimal number of sensors to achieve maximum coverage of a region. Adding to the complexity is the constraint imposed by sensor batteries, which hampers the continuous provision of health and environmental services. This limitation is particularly notable in challenging environmental terrains such as mountains, forests, and groundwater, as well as in sensitive areas within hospitals where frequent battery replacement is impractical. To address these challenges, deploying WSNs in a manner that minimizes energy consumption

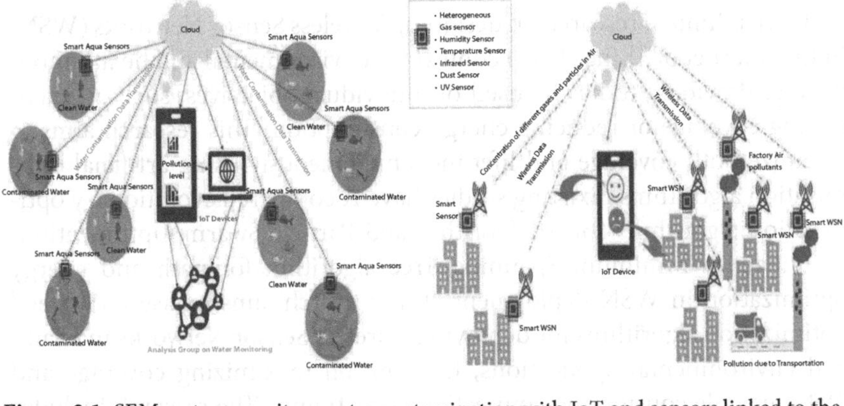

Figure 3.1 SEM system monitors water contamination with IoT and sensors linked to the cloud, while also addressing environmental issues using WSNs and IoT device [2].

by sensors becomes imperative. Consequently, achieving optimal coverage and effectively managing energy consumption emerge as two critical considerations in the deployment of WSNs for environmental and health applications.

Crafting a reliable network necessitates meticulous attention to its topology, encompassing the arrangement of elements within an IoT network. This entails decisions about sensor numbers, their locations, communication protocols, packet size, and radio range [1, 8]. Topology, a fundamental aspect of IoT network architecture, governs the network to seamlessly deliver environmental and health services across diverse environments [1]. In this context, the strategic positioning of sensors plays a crucial role in shaping an appropriate network topology, exerting a significant influence on its reliability, security, and safety [8–12]. Addressing the challenge of determining optimal sensor locations within the network, framed as a deployment issue in WSN-based environmental and health systems, can be effectively tackled through the application of Geospatial Information Systems (GIS). This approach proves invaluable for efficient environmental and health planning [13–15]. WSN deployment poses a multi-objective optimization dilemma, aiming to identify the most suitable sensor node locations in the network to ensure the seamless provision of environmental and health services, while managing conflicting objectives such as lifetime and coverage [16, 17]. Drawing on insights from [18], the utilization of Multi-Criteria Decision Making (MCDM) and Evolutionary Multi-Objective Optimization (EMO) algorithms is crucial for addressing these intricate multi-objective optimization problems. This research specifically focuses on EMO algorithms, widely recognized for their effectiveness in handling multi-objective optimization challenges across diverse fields.

There is limited research on designing Wireless Sensor Networks (WSN) in the Internet of Things (IoT) context for environmental and health monitoring. Previous studies focused on individual objectives, such as maximizing coverage or reducing energy consumption. This research aims to optimize both coverage and lifetime simultaneously using artificial optimization algorithms. Existing studies haven't compared evolutionary optimization algorithms (Bees Algorithm and Particle Swarm Optimization) or utilized a Minimum Spanning Tree algorithm for path and energy optimization in WSN deployment. This research aims to use GIS-based optimization algorithms for deploying Wireless Sensor Networks in health and environmental applications, focusing on maximizing coverage and lifetime while considering connectivity constraints. The research includes a review of prior studies, the application of the Minimum Spanning Tree algorithm to minimize energy consumption, and a comparison between the Bees Algorithm and Particle Swarm Optimization for GIS-based WSN deployment based on convergence rate, constancy repeatability, and modeling complexity.

3.2 Essential Elements and Factors for Environmental Monitoring with IoT

3.2.1 Sensor Devices

Sensors are fundamental components employed in environmental monitoring, serving the purpose of measuring various critical parameters [7]. These parameters encompass temperature, humidity, air quality, water quality, soil moisture, and light levels. The versatility of these sensors allows for deployment in diverse settings, including field environments, on structures, and even on vehicles and drones. In the context of environmental monitoring, temperature sensors gauge the thermal conditions of the surroundings, humidity sensors measure moisture levels in the air, and air quality sensors assess the composition of the atmosphere for pollutants. Water quality sensors, on the other hand, are designed to evaluate the condition of water sources, ensuring they meet specified standards. Soil moisture sensors provide insights into the moisture content of the soil, which is crucial for agricultural and ecological studies. Additionally, light level sensors contribute to understanding the intensity of natural or artificial light in a given location. The deployment flexibility of these sensors is noteworthy. They can be strategically placed in the field to capture real-world conditions, affixed to structures for continuous monitoring, or mounted on vehicles and drones for mobile data collection. This detailed and varied sensor data is essential for comprehensive environmental analysis and decision-making in fields ranging from agriculture and ecology to urban planning and air quality management.

3.2.2 Data Acquisition

In the process of continuous data collection, sensors operate by routinely acquiring information at predefined intervals. These sensors serve as data capture devices, collecting details on parameters such as temperature, humidity, air quality, and more, depending on their specific functionalities. The collected data is then relayed to a central node or a cloud-based platform for further processing and analysis.

Wireless communication protocols, including Wi-Fi, cellular networks, LoRa WAN, and Zigbee, play a crucial role in transmitting the gathered information to the designated central location. This wireless transmission ensures real-time or near-real-time delivery of data, contributing to timely insights and decision-making.

The central node or cloud-based platform serves as a hub for data processing and analysis. Here, advanced algorithms and analytics tools can be employed to derive meaningful insights from the collected data. This may involve identifying patterns, trends, anomalies, or correlations within the dataset.

The utilization of wireless communication protocols is pivotal in facilitating seamless and efficient data transmission, allowing for the integration of sensors in various environments, including remote locations and mobile platforms. The comprehensive process of data collection, transmission, and analysis is fundamental in applications such as environmental monitoring, IoT systems, and other fields where real-time information is crucial for informed decision-making.

3.2.3 Data Mastery and Storage Brilliance

Sensor data undergoes processing and is subsequently stored on either cloud platforms or local servers. The utilization of cloud platforms is particularly favored for IoT environmental monitoring due to their scalability and the ease of accessing data from any geographical location. The cloud infrastructure not only ensures efficient storage but also facilitates seamless integration with diverse IoT devices, enhancing the overall effectiveness of environmental monitoring systems. The scalability aspect allows for the accommodation of varying data volumes, making it a versatile and robust solution for handling the dynamic and evolving nature of environmental data.

3.2.4 Data Analysis

Sophisticated analytics and machine learning algorithms play a pivotal role in delving into the intricacies of the gathered data. Through this process, profound insights are extracted, enabling the creation of predictive models to anticipate environmental shifts or identify anomalies. This advanced analysis goes beyond surface-level observations, providing a deeper understanding of patterns and trends in the monitored environment. Such comprehensive insights empower decision-makers with valuable information for proactive and informed environmental management.

3.2.5 Visualizing Insights

Disseminating information to users is achieved through dynamic web-based dashboards, user-friendly mobile applications, or other intuitive interfaces. These platforms serve as portals for users to engage with and interpret the data effectively. Visualization tools, characterized by their sophistication, enable researchers, government agencies, and the broader public to gain a comprehensive understanding of environmental conditions and trends.

Web-based dashboards, designed for real-time updates, provide an interactive and visually appealing experience. Mobile applications extend accessibility, ensuring users can stay informed on environmental data regardless of their location. The use of alternative interfaces caters to diverse preferences and needs, enhancing the inclusivity of data dissemination.

These visualization tools go beyond mere representation, facilitating an immersive experience that fosters deeper comprehension. Researchers can explore intricate patterns, government agencies can make informed decisions, and the public can stay informed and engaged. Overall, the multi-faceted approach to data presentation enriches the accessibility and utility of valuable insights derived from environmental data.

3.2.6 Alert Mechanism

Environmental monitoring systems excel in providing captivating alerts and notifications, activated by predetermined conditions or the discernment of irregularities. This feature facilitates rapid responses to critical scenarios, such as heightened pollution or occurrences of extreme weather events. The system's agility ensures timely interventions, promoting heightened awareness and effective environmental stewardship.

3.2.7 Synergizing Connectivity

IoT-based environmental monitoring systems have the capacity to seamlessly integrate with various systems and diverse data sources. These may include weather forecasts, GIS (Geographical Information System), and historical data. This integration aims to offer a holistic perspective on environmental conditions, presenting a comprehensive and interconnected view.

3.2.8 Energy Efficiency

A paramount consideration in the realm of IoT environmental monitoring is the strategic design for energy efficiency, particularly crucial for prolonged and remote deployments. The goal is to ensure that sensors and devices within the Internet of Things ecosystem are adept at optimizing power consumption. Certain IoT sensors and devices are purposefully engineered to operate seamlessly over extended periods, relying on energy-conserving mechanisms. This may involve leveraging battery power, allowing these devices to function autonomously without frequent replacements or recharging. Furthermore, the implementation of innovative designs enables some devices to draw power from renewable energy sources, such as solar panels. In essence, energy optimization in IoT environmental monitoring not only enhances the sustainability of operations but also contributes to the feasibility of deploying sensors in remote locations. This thoughtful approach to power management aligns with the broader goals of achieving efficiency and resilience in environmental monitoring system.

3.2.9 Securing Environmental Data

Guaranteeing the protection of data transmitted and stored in IoT environmental monitoring systems is paramount, considering the consequential nature of sensitive environmental information. To fortify the resilience of these systems against potential threats, it is essential to institute robust security measures. This encompasses the implementation of encryption, stringent access control protocols, and regular security audits. By adopting this comprehensive approach, the confidentiality and integrity of environmental data are upheld, thereby mitigating risks and instilling confidence in the reliability of IoT-based monitoring systems.

3.2.10 Adhering to Regulatory Standards

The seamless integration of IoT environmental monitoring systems into diverse applications and locations necessitates a meticulous approach to regulatory adherence. Depending on the specific context, these systems must align with a myriad of regulations and standards to ensure ethical and legal compliance. Crucially, compliance with environmental regulations is essential, as it ensures that the monitoring processes are conducted responsibly, with due consideration for the impact on ecosystems. Simultaneously, adherence to data privacy regulations is imperative to safeguard sensitive information collected by these systems. This comprehensive regulatory alignment involves continuous monitoring and adjustment to stay abreast of evolving legal frameworks. By meticulously following these standards, IoT environmental monitoring systems not only ensure their own legitimacy but also contribute to ethical and responsible environmental practices.

3.3 Diverse Avenues and Methodologies in IoT Environmental Applications

3.3.1 Agricultural Surveillance

Leveraging a spectrum of methodologies, such as AI (Artificial Intelligence), ML (Machine Learning), and DL (Deep Learning), is essential for the comprehensive monitoring of soil moisture, temperature, and humidity in precision agriculture. AI contributes by analyzing complex patterns in data, providing predictive insights for informed decision-making. ML algorithms enhance the system's ability to adapt and improve predictions over time, optimizing resource allocation. DL, with its deep neural networks, excels in extracting intricate relationships within datasets, further refining the precision of agricultural monitoring. Integrating these advanced technologies ensures a holistic approach to precision agriculture, where real-time data analytics and intelligent decision support systems lead to efficient crop management, reduced resource wastage, and overall enhanced productivity. Figure 3.2 illustrates digital technology in smart farming for efficient and sustainable agriculture.

3.3.2 Air Quality Surveillance

The incorporation of AI enhances the system's capability to analyze intricate patterns in real-time air quality data, enabling predictive modeling and early identification of emerging pollution trends. ML algorithms actively adapt to changing conditions, refining predictions in real-time and optimizing response strategies based on dynamic environmental factors. DL, with its deep neural networks, excels in real-time recognition of complex relationships within diverse datasets, contributing to the precision and immediacy of air quality assessments. This comprehensive and real-time approach to air quality monitoring ensures that interventions can be swiftly implemented, contributing to the creation of healthier urban environments and the protection of public well-being. Figure 3.3 illustrates IoT-enabled air quality and traffic monitoring utilizing regression analysis [8].

Figure 3.2 Smart farming employs digital tech for efficient and sustainable agriculture [7].

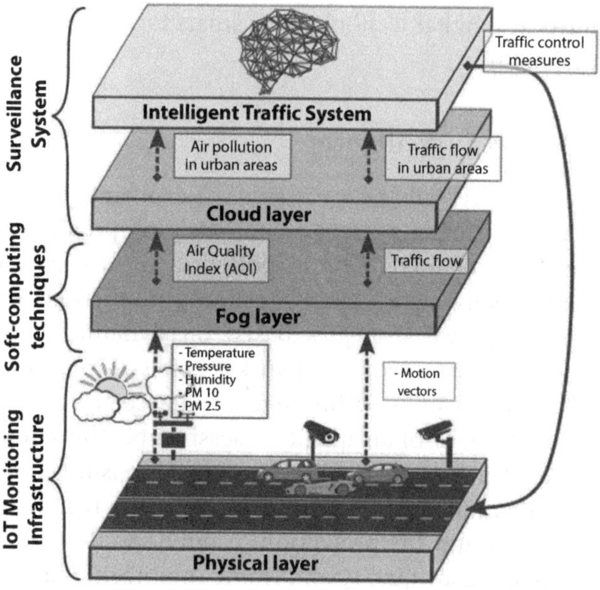

Figure 3.3 IoT facilitates air quality and traffic monitoring through regression analysis [8].

3.3.3 Aquatic Quality Surveillance

Surveillance involves harnessing cutting-edge computational technology to assess and mitigate pollution in lakes, rivers, and oceans. Incorporating recent computational technology, such as AI (Artificial Intelligence), ML (Machine Learning), and IoT (Internet of Things), revolutionizes water quality monitoring. Advanced sensors equipped with IoT capabilities are deployed in aquatic environments, continuously collecting real-time data on parameters like chemical composition, microbial content, and physical characteristics. The integration of AI and ML algorithms facilitates the analysis of this data, identifying intricate patterns and anomalies. The use of recent computational technology enables swift and data-driven decision-making. It enhances the efficiency of pollution control measures, contributing to the preservation of aquatic ecosystems. This approach ensures that environmental authorities and researchers have access to up-to-date and detailed information, ultimately promoting the sustainable management of water resources. Figure 3.4 depicts an intelligent system that integrates real-time monitoring and advanced data management for efficient water and wastewater treatment [9].

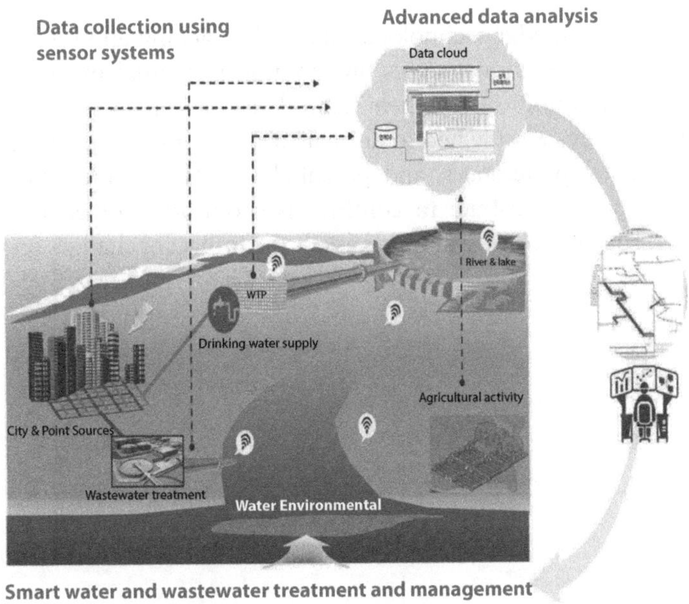

Figure 3.4 Smart system integrating real-time monitoring and advanced data management for water and wastewater treatment [9].

3.3.4 Urban Intelligence

Urban intelligence employs contemporary methodologies to sustainably govern traffic, waste, and energy consumption in smart cities. In the context of smart cities, current methodologies involve the integration of IoT (Internet of Things), AI (Artificial Intelligence), and data analytics to optimize the management of urban infrastructure. For traffic, smart sensors and AI algorithms monitor and predict congestion, enabling dynamic traffic control systems to alleviate bottlenecks. Regarding waste management, IoT-enabled sensors in waste bins transmit real-time data, optimizing collection routes and schedules. Additionally, AI algorithms aid in identifying patterns to enhance recycling practices and reduce environmental impact. In energy consumption, smart grids equipped with IoT devices facilitate real-time monitoring and control. AI algorithms analyze usage patterns, enabling predictive maintenance and optimizing energy distribution. This contemporary approach to urban governance ensures efficiency, sustainability, and improved quality of life in smart cities. Figure 3.5 is a visualization showcasing urban intelligence and the core components essential for smart city infrastructure [10].

3.3.5 Preserving Wildlife

Employing cutting-edge technologies like GPS tracking and satellite imagery, wildlife conservation focuses on monitoring animal movements and environmental conditions in their natural habitats. Real-time data from GPS tracking devices attached to animals provides insights into migration patterns, habitat preferences, and potential threats. Satellite imagery and sensor networks contribute to continuous monitoring of environmental parameters, helping conservationists assess the impact of changes on wildlife

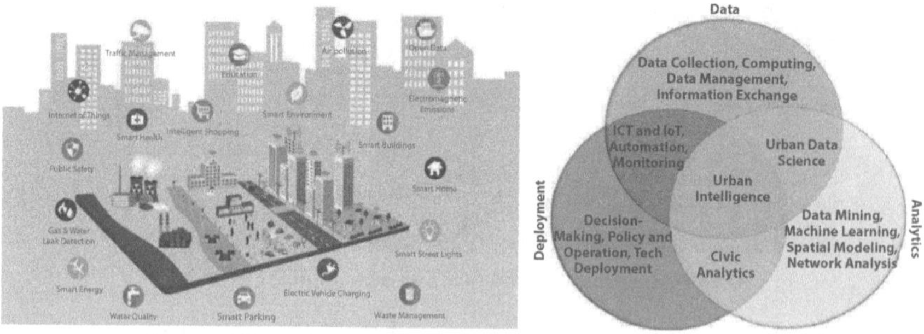

Figure 3.5 Urban intelligence and fundamental elements of smart city [10].

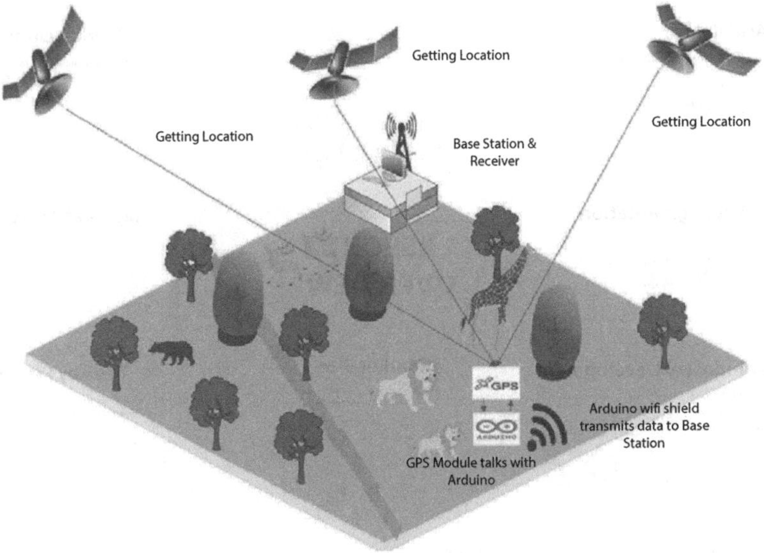

Figure 3.6 Arduino-based wildlife animal protection system with tracking and alarm [11].

populations. This integrated approach aids in implementing targeted strategies for biodiversity preservation. Figure 3.6 describes a wildlife animal protection system utilizing Arduino for tracking and alarming purposes [11].

3.3.6 Sustainable Industrial Practices

Employing advanced monitoring systems to oversee emissions, energy usage, and resource allocation ensures both environmental sustainability and compliance within industrial operations. The implementation of cutting-edge technologies, including sensors, IoT devices, and data analytics, enables real-time tracking of emissions during production. Continuous monitoring of energy consumption optimizes efficiency and identifies opportunities for enhancement. In tandem, resource utilization, including raw material consumption and waste generation, is closely observed. The integration of data analytics facilitates informed decision-making, fostering sustainable practices and compliance with stringent environmental regulations. This holistic and technology-driven approach not only prioritizes environmental responsibility but also enhances operational efficiency within industrial processes. Figure 3.7, a comprehensive illustration of industrial automation, showcases the integration of advanced technologies for enhanced industrial processes and control [12].

Figure 3.7 Industrial automation [12].

3.4 Conclusion

In summary, IoT-based environmental monitoring systems, equipped with an intricate array of sensors, data analytics, and real-time capabilities, play a pivotal role in preserving our environment. Covering applications ranging from precision agriculture to wildlife conservation and industrial processes, these systems offer a comprehensive approach to comprehending and tackling environmental issues. The incorporation of visualization tools, prompt alerts, and adherence to regulations ensures a rapid and well-informed response to critical situations, contributing to pollution control and sustainable resource management. As technology progresses, the potential of these systems to nurture resilient and environmentally conscious communities becomes increasingly evident, marking significant strides toward a more sustainable and protected planet.

References

1. Shetty, S., An Intelligent and Secure Real-Time Environment Monitoring System for Healthcare Using IoT and Cloud Computing with the Mobile Application Support, in: *Image Based Computing for Food and Health Analytics: Requirements, Challenges, Solutions and Practices*, R. Tiwari, D. Koundal, S. Upadhyay (Eds.), Springer, Cham, 2023, https://doi.org/10.1007/978-3-031-22959-6_5.

2. Ullo, S.L. and Sinha, G.R., Advances in Smart Environment Monitoring Systems Using IoT and Sensors. *Sensors*, 20, 3113, 2020, https://doi.org/10.3390/s20113113.
3. Lutfi, Z.F., Ahmed, D.S., Hussien, N.M., Mohialden, Y.M., Mohammed, I.S., Mous, N.J., Design and Implementation of an Internet of Things-based Environmental Monitoring System. *Int. J. Intell. Syst. Appl. Eng.*, 2023, ISSN:2147-6799.
4. Antonopoulos, C., Kerasiotis, F., Koulamas, C., Papadopoulos, G., Koubias, S., Experimental evaluation of the waspmote platform power consumption targeting ambient sensing, in: *2015 4th Mediterranean Conference on Embedded Computing (MECO)*, pp. 124–128, 2015, https://doi.org/10.1109/MECO.2015.7181882.
5. Jamil, M.S., Jamil, M.A., Mazhar, A., Ikram, A., Ahmed, A., Munawar, U., Smart Environment Monitoring System by Employing Wireless Sensor Networks on Vehicles for Pollution Free Smart Cities. *Procedia Eng.*, 107, 480–484, 2015, [CrossRef].
6. https://www.lingayasvidyapeeth.edu.in/iot-based-environmental-monitoring-system
7. https://faperta.umsu.ac.id/2023/04/13/pengertian-pentingnya-dan-cara-kerja-smart-farming
8. Martín-Baos, J.A., Rodriguez-Benitez, L., García-Ródenas, R., Liu, J., IoT based monitoring of air quality and traffic using regression analysis. *Appl. Soft Comput.*, 115, 108282, 2022, ISSN 1568-4946, https://doi.org/10.1016/j.asoc.2021.108282.
9. Park, J., Kim, K.T., Lee, W.H., Recent Advances in Information and Communications Technology (ICT) and Sensor Technology for Monitoring Water Quality. *Water*, 12, 510, 2020, https://doi.org/10.3390/w12020510.
10. https://www.axis.com/blog/secure-insights-de/was-ist-eine-smart-city
11. Gor, M., *et al.*, GATA: GPS-Arduino based tracking and alarm system for protection of wildlife animals. *2017 International Conference on Computer, Information and Telecommunication Systems (CITS)*, pp. 166–170, 2017.
12. https://www.linkedin.com/pulse/industrial-automation-software-market
13. Clarke, K.C., McLafferty, S.L., Tempalski, B.J., On epidemiology and Geographic Information Systems: a review and discussion of future directions. *Emerg. Infect. Dis.*, 2, 2, 85, 1996.
14. Tzeng, G.H. and Huang, J.J., *Multiple attribute decision making: Methods and applications*. CRC Press, 2011.
15. Deb, K., Pratap, A., Agarwal, S., Meyarivan, T., A fast and elitist multi-objective genetic algorithm: NSGA-II. *IEEE Trans. Evol. Comput.*, 6, 2, 182–197, 2002.
16. Georgiadis, C.K. and Perlepes, L.P., GIS for environmental management: analysis and visualization of spatial data. *J. Environ. Prot. Ecol. (JEPE)*, 12, 3A, 1313–1320, 2011.

17. Goyal, M. and Saxena, M., Node deployment and coverage optimization for wireless sensor networks: A survey. *Int. J. Comput. Appl.*, 2, 8, 5–10, 2008.
18. El Attar, H. and Omari, A., Efficient multi-objective optimization algorithms for WSN coverage and connectivity issues. *Sensors*, 17, 7, 1608, 2017.

4

Remote Monitoring Advancements: A New Approach to Biodiversity Conservation

D. Roja Ramani[1]*, K. Kalaiarasan[2] and Shrikant Tangade[3]

[1]*Computer Science and Engineering, New Horizon College of Engineering, Bengaluru, India*
[2]*Information Technology, M Kumarasamy College of Engineering, Karur, India*
[3]*Department of Mathematics, University of Padova, Padova, Italy*

Abstract

This research delves into the dynamic landscape of biodiversity conservation, shedding light on the profound impact of remote monitoring advancements. The preservation of Earth's rich and diverse ecosystems has become an increasingly critical endeavor, and modern technology has ushered in a new era of conservation. Remote monitoring methods have revolutionized the way we approach biodiversity conservation. By leveraging cutting-edge technologies, such as satellite imagery, drones, and sensor networks, we gain a real-time and comprehensive view of ecosystems and their inhabitants. This not only aids in safeguarding endangered species but also in understanding the intricate interplay of ecosystems at large. Our study explores the diverse array of remote monitoring techniques used in biodiversity conservation, emphasizing their potential to significantly enhance our conservation efforts. From tracking migratory patterns of wildlife to monitoring the health of fragile habitats, these advancements provide invaluable data that guide informed decision-making. Furthermore, we delve into the ethical and environmental considerations that come hand in hand with these technologies. Striking a balance between innovation and the welfare of the natural world is of utmost importance in the pursuit of sustainable conservation practices. In conclusion, this research underscores the transformative role of remote monitoring in biodiversity conservation. By harnessing these technologies, we are better equipped to protect our planet's biodiversity and pave the way for a more sustainable and harmonious coexistence between humans and the natural world.

**Corresponding author*: rosevsroja@gmail.com

A. Suresh, T. Devi, N. Deepa and Ali Kashif Bashir (eds.) Environmental Monitoring Using Artificial Intelligence, (61–70) © 2025 Scrivener Publishing LLC

Keywords: Biodiversity indicators, ecosystem services, artificial intelligence, machine learning, deep learning, AI Drones

4.1 Introduction

A considerable cohort of researchers and an expanding community of applied conservationists are employing artificial intelligence (AI) for the automated monitoring of species. Algorithms, utilizing data from optical, acoustic, or thermal sensors deployed in the field or mounted on drones, aircraft, or satellites, demonstrate the ability to identify species and, in certain cases, estimate population abundance. The use of AI in these applications provides notable advantages, such as significantly improved efficiency, repeatability, and accuracy in data processing compared to the manual analysis methods of the past [1]. AI plays a pivotal role in the processing of acoustic and thermal data. Platforms like Wildlife Insights and WildMe utilize machine and deep learning algorithms to automate species identification. The Microsoft AI for Earth MegaDetector is essential for detecting animals in camera trap images. AI applications extend beyond terrestrial species to coral reef monitoring, and user-friendly apps such as PictureThis and iNaturalist enable instantaneous plant species identification. Biodiversity monitoring benefits from acoustic data analysis, as demonstrated by Rainforest Connection Arbimon, and the utilization of thermal imagery, as observed in the drone-based identification of koalas and deer. Despite improvements in accessibility to biodiversity knowledge, challenges persist in raising awareness, reducing data transfer costs, and ensuring inclusive technology access. Addressing biases in training data remains critical for models to generalize effectively across diverse geographic and taxonomic domains.

The concept of "climate change effect" denotes a prolonged alteration in the fundamental framework of the natural world. The increasing human population poses a substantial hazard to biodiversity, putting the well-being of our planet at risk. The decline in biodiversity reduces the population of wild animals, initiating a cascading effect that can disrupt ecosystems and result in their breakdown. Preserving Earth's biodiversity is crucial for the sustenance of all ecosystems. However, existing monitoring systems fall short in their global reach to effectively tackle this challenge comprehensively. Traditional methods, coupled with the labor-intensive efforts of researchers, prove inadequate for the effective conservation of biodiversity. To overcome these limitations, essential contemporary technologies like artificial intelligence (AI) and machine learning (ML) have come to the forefront. Their streamlined operation plays a crucial role in contemporary conservation initiatives, offering vital support for the preservation of Earth's biodiversity.

4.2 Indicators of Primary Biodiversity

Predicting vital derived metrics essential for analyzing, reporting, and managing biodiversity across diverse geographical and temporal dimensions is gaining prominence. This extends beyond direct species recognition and observation, focusing on Essential Biodiversity Variables. The continuous accumulation of new data, including more detailed classifications of terrestrial and aquatic ecosystems, enhances our understanding of the intricate interplay between abiotic and biotic variables, along with the factors influencing community composition. Figure 4.1 offers a comprehensive illustration of the organizational structure for Essential Biodiversity Indicators. Proficiency in interpreting species behaviors, extracting rich data, and discerning traits from both acoustic and occurrence data is demonstrated. At the population level, seamless integration with satellite data enables global predictions and automated species abundance estimation. In conservation,

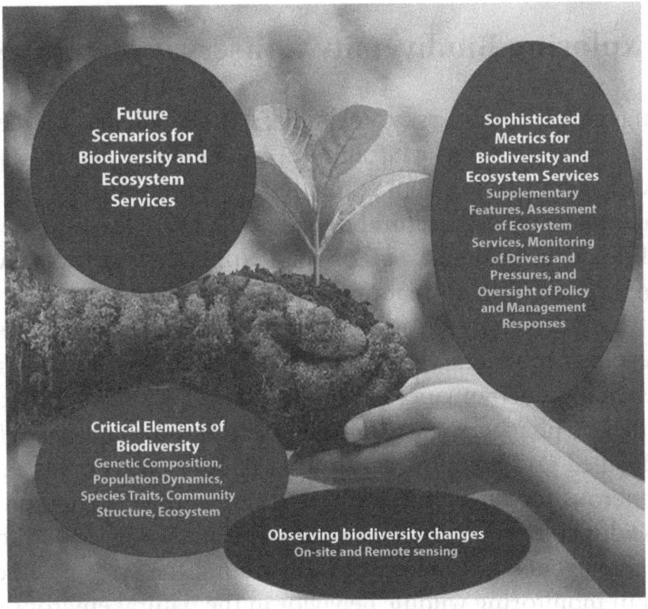

Figure 4.1 Organization of essential biodiversity indicators.

meticulous analysis of crowd-sourced images is employed to monitor wildlife activities. Zooming in on the community level, invaluable contributions are made to derive metrics of species diversity through molecular ecology, predicting genetic diversity with precision. This contribution extends to ecosystem-level metrics, providing insightful assessments of functioning and integrity. Furthermore, there is significant streamlining of workflows related to biodiversity data, enhancing efficiency and accuracy.

The scope extends beyond traditional monitoring, excelling in modeling intricate environmental variables. In the domain of imagery analysis, adept classification of land cover, estimation of carbon stocks, and enhanced capabilities for fire monitoring are observed. Despite commendable advancements, challenges persist in scaling these systems for broader accessibility, especially for less technologically advanced user groups, presenting an ongoing area for improvement and innovation. Safeguarding biodiversity for future generations is essential, and modern techniques like artificial intelligence (AI) and machine learning (ML) emulate human efforts in conservation. The dynamic advancements in AI and ML prove invaluable for addressing challenges such as illegal wildlife trade and monitoring environmental health. The integration of these technologies revolutionizes wildlife conservation efforts, providing efficient solutions to combat threats to global fauna and flora [2].

4.3 Exploring Biodiversity Conservation Strategies

Preserving global biodiversity encounters the challenge of identifying, recognizing, and tracking wild animals. AI emerges as a key player in safeguarding rare species from extinction, providing surveillance against threats like poaching and natural disasters. Machine learning revolutionizes wildlife conservation by predicting extinction risks and evaluating global impacts on both animals and humans. Motion-sensor cameras, or "camera traps," driven by AI, automate animal identification, transforming wildlife ecology practices. In the Anthropocene era, where human activity drives change, AI-enhanced cameras boost forest safety by detecting threats such as poachers, ensuring the protection of animals. Figure 4.2 gives a detailed and complex description of how AI cameras detect and track numerous footsteps in the forest. The lengthy explanation demonstrates the difficult process of recognizing and analyzing these tracks using artificial intelligence technology, demonstrating the system's efficacy and precision in monitoring wildlife behavior in the natural environment.

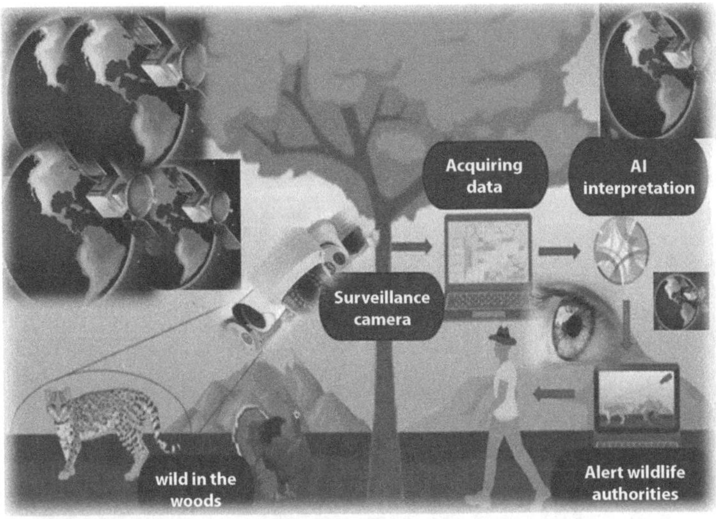

Figure 4.2 AI cameras detected tracks in the forest.

4.4 AI Enhancing Animal Observation Images

By automating species counts, detection, recognition, and identification, artificial intelligence (AI) plays an important role in biodiversity monitoring. Image bounding box annotation for visibility, semantic segmentation for object detection, and species identification are all part of this. AI can also help identify and deter poaching by using security cameras with night vision and object recognition. By monitoring online sales and trade operations, the Internet Monitoring System aids in the tracking of potentially invasive species. Robotics driven by artificial intelligence and drone surveillance aid in livestock management, animal monitoring, and waste identification. Acoustic sensors are used to detect bat species passively and to alert authorities to abnormalities. Satellite imaging with high resolution aids in animal surveying, detection, and monitoring. The transformative impact of AI technology is evident across these biodiversity conservation efforts. Figure 4.3 depicts an example of animal counting utilizing AI drones.

4.5 AI and ML for Preserving Flora

Human civilizations have caused ecological imbalances and biodiversity loss, emphasizing the crucial requirement for plant life survival. Plants

Figure 4.3 Counting animals with AI drones.

meet important human needs such as food, medicine, and shelter, as well as providing a critical habitat for a diverse spectrum of species. Trees and forests serve an important role in decreasing greenhouse gas emissions and producing oxygen, both of which are essential for the existence of a healthy ecosystem. Unfortunately, more than 20% of plant species are threatened, highlighting the critical importance of conservation actions. AI is proving to be a good solution for solving these issues and safeguarding plant species. AI employs a variety of strategies, including Artificial Neural Network methods. These algorithms investigate regional patterns, morphologies, ecosystem traits, and climate changes to estimate the conservation status of 150,000 plant species. This method aids in the identification of endangered plants and provides critical data for conservation efforts.

AI also plays a crucial role in tracking changes in plant genotypes and phenotypes. Leveraging the synergy of AI and scientific breakthroughs allows for the identification of optimal genome combinations, enhancing plants' adaptability to dynamic environments and aiding in the creation of climate-resilient varieties that contribute to biodiversity preservation. Figure 4.4 provides a detailed illustration of the varied functions of artificial intelligence in the conservation of forests and plants.

In pest management, AI-driven artificial neural networks predict the geographic distribution of polyphagous plant pests, providing insights for proactive measures. Addressing taxonomic challenges, autonomous

Figure 4.4 AI's diverse roles in conserving forests and plants.

systems powered by AI efficiently collect extensive data, facilitating the identification of new plant species and enriching global botanical knowledge. Beyond plant-focused applications, AI plays a pivotal role in addressing broader environmental challenges, from predicting and managing wildfires using neural networks and machine learning to forecasting invasive species' distribution patterns with support vector machines. In agriculture, a spectrum of machine learning techniques, including Decision Trees, Regression Analysis, Bayesian belief networks, and soft computing methods, supports pest management, temperature forecasting, and overall agricultural practices. Semantic Data Masters, employing ML techniques, integrate remote sensing data to model species' dispersal capacities and identify priority conservation areas. The collective impact of these AI applications signifies a transformative force in advancing our understanding of plant life, preserving biodiversity, and ensuring a sustainable future.

4.6 Deep Learning Tracks Terrestrial Mammals via Satellites

Cutting-edge technologies in satellite remote sensing and machine learning present unprecedented opportunities for swiftly and precisely monitoring global biodiversity. These innovations hold the potential to uncover fresh ecological insights on spatial scales crucial for effective population and ecosystem management. In this study, we introduce a robust and adaptable deep learning pipeline designed to automatically identify and tally large herds of migratory ungulates, such as wildebeest and zebra, in the Serengeti-Mara ecosystem. Utilizing fine-resolution (38-50 cm) satellite imagery, the results demonstrate precise detection of nearly 500,000 individuals across extensive areas and diverse habitats, achieving an outstanding overall F1-score of 84.75% (Precision: 87.85%, Recall: 81.86%) [3]. This research underscores the capacity of satellite remote sensing and machine learning techniques to autonomously and accurately quantify extensive terrestrial mammal populations in highly varied landscapes. Additionally, we explore the potential of satellite-derived species detections to advance fundamental insights into animal behavior and ecology. Figure 4.5 illustrates how deep learning enables the satellite-based monitoring of varied terrestrial mammal populations.

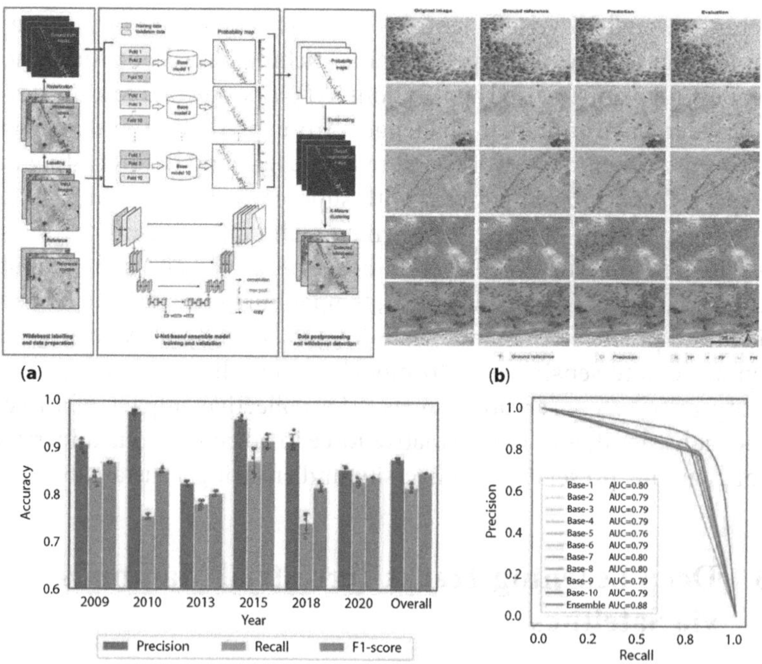

Figure 4.5 Satellite-based monitoring of diverse terrestrial mammal populations is made possible through deep learning [3].

4.7 Conclusion

Wildlife preservation is attainable through adeptly training AI models, incorporating deep learning with relevant machine learning datasets for animal identification. The effective deployment of machine learning algorithms, along with deep learning capabilities, serves as a shield for various plant species, providing protection against pests and diseases and fostering environmental robustness. The potential of artificial intelligence, especially with the integration of deep learning, to prevent the extinction of endangered plants underscores its pivotal role in sustaining ecological vitality. Looking ahead, future enhancements in AI technologies offer the promise of even more advanced and efficient conservation strategies. As we harness the power of AI, including deep learning, for conservation, there is an opportunity for continued innovation and refinement. However, it is crucial to approach these advancements responsibly, ensuring that the application of AI in conservation is guided by ethical considerations and a commitment to maximizing benefits while minimizing potential adverse impacts on both human and ecological systems.

References

1. Weinstein, A computer vision for animal ecology. *J. Anim. Ecol.*, 2017, https://doi.org/10.1111/1365-2656.12780.
2. Kumar, V., Kumar, N., Kumar, S., Kumar, A.V., Implication of Computer-Based Strategies in Biodiversity Conservation: A Review. *IOSR J. Pharm. Biol. Sci. (IOSR-JPBS)*, 18, 1 Ser. I, 19–27, Jan.-Feb. 2023, e-ISSN:2278-3008, p-ISSN:2319-7676.
3. Wu, Z., Zhang, C., Gu, X., *et al.*, Deep learning enables satellite-based monitoring of large populations of terrestrial mammals across heterogeneous landscape. *Nat. Commun.*, 14, 3072, 2023, https://doi.org/10.1038/s41467-023-38901-y.

5

Smart Water Solutions: A Case Study on Drone-Led Hydrological Investigation of Water Diversion from Lakshmiyapuram Catchment to Sivakasi Periyakulam Tank

I. Baskar[1], A. Haamidh[1], S. Suriya[1]* and K. Parameswari[2]

[1]*Department of Civil Engineering, Mepco Schlenk Engineering College, Sivakasi, Tamil Nadu, India*

[2]*Department of Civil Engineering, University of Technology and Applied Sciences Muscat, Oman*

Abstract

Drones have become more vital in the field of surveying and mapping. Drones, the so-called Unmanned Aerial Vehicles (UAVs) fitted with necessary sensors, have revolutionized the field of mapping, offering unparalleled advantages in terms of efficiency, cost-effectiveness, and data precision. This chapter presents a comprehensive exploration of Smart Water Solutions through a case study utilizing drone technology to dissect water movement from Lakshmiyapuram catchment to Sivakasi Periyakulam Tank. The study utilizes a variety of post-processing techniques in addition to real-time data collection to generate outputs such as Orthomosaic Maps, Digital Surface Models, and 3D models. The investigation encompasses a comprehensive assessment on hydrological dynamics on orthomosaic visualization. The integration of the post-processed drone-driven images and hydrological analysis offers a holistic understanding of the water dynamics in the specified region of study. The chapter also demonstrates how these Smart Water Solutions provide actionable insights for optimizing water resource management and attempts to promote sustainable practices in similar geographical contexts. The results play a crucial role for policy makers involved in environmental monitoring and planning by providing guidance for decision formulation towards

**Corresponding author*: suriya.svu@gmail.com

A. Suresh, T. Devi, N. Deepa and Ali Kashif Bashir (eds.) Environmental Monitoring Using Artificial Intelligence, (71–102) © 2025 Scrivener Publishing LLC

adoption of sustainable practices and development of efficient strategies for water conservation and distribution.

Keywords: Drone, UAVs, sensors, environmental monitoring, sustainable practices

5.1 Introduction

Understanding the complex dynamics for water diversion within a watershed is essential for efficient resource management and environmental conservation. Conventional research techniques for hydrological investigation are found to be time-consuming and resource-intensive. In recent years, aircraft and satellites have been the main sources of remotely sensed water resource data. Nevertheless, these platforms are mostly applicable at the highest spatial scales [1]. The inability to acquire data on demand, which is frequently required to capture the highly transient processes operating at fine spatial scales required for the planning and management of water resources (such as freshwater abstraction), and the assessment of water quality, is made impossible by the lack of finer resolution data and the temporal rigidity of these platforms [2]. In recent years, drone technology has become a transformative tool in hydrological monitoring, which provides efficiency in data collection, good spatial coverage and cost-effectiveness. There has been a growing emphasis on the use of drones for hydrological research. It offers a unique opportunity for a better understanding of water drainage processes holistically. The water ways from catchment to tank becomes a crucial component in water resource management as it impacts on ecological stability, population expansion, and agricultural production [3]. It is a challenging task to provide timely and thorough data on vast and geographically diverse locations. Drones have sensors on board that can record high-resolution photos and topographic data and offers a dynamic solution to bridge this gap. The potential of drone-based technology in hydrological investigations has been brought to light by recent studies. Drone-based Large-Scale Particle Image Velocimetry (LSPIV) measurements are more precise and sensitive to tracer transit [4].

The drones can be used for hydrological investigation, including digital forensic analysis of Remotely Piloted Aircraft System (RPAS), impact of climate change on hydrological conditions, disaster damage investigation, flood management, drought assessment, traffic information collection, crop water requirement, irrigation management, habitat assessment and probabilistic hydrological modeling [5–8]. Drones have diverse applications in hydrological investigation and it has the potential to provide valuable data for various hydrological studies [9]. Drones can support asset management, conduct flow and water quality monitoring, traffic volume investigation collect high spatial resolution data for improved model parameterization [10]. Low-altitude drone survey, ground photos, and high-resolution satellite data can be used to identify vegetation along the canal and assess the hydraulic changes [11].

Drones can be effectively utilized to conduct hydrogeological assessment of a distant stream reach, yielding important data on the exchange of surface and groundwater [12]. In an artificial lake scenario, unmanned aerial vehicles can be employed to characterize, monitor, appraise, and model soil and water resources in a cost-effective and on-demand manner [13]. Hydrological study using Unmanned Aerial Vehicles (UAVs) outfitted with diverse sensors and imaging technologies coupled with machine learning technologies can be adopted to achieve accuracy [14–16]. Ridolfi *et al.* [17] developed a system for measuring water levels using drones and cameras, with encouraging results. Together, these studies show how useful drone-led research may be for improving our knowledge of hydrological systems. The use of artificial intelligence and UAV photogrammetry can be used to manage natural disaster [18, 19]. Their study used AI approaches for hazard identification and detection in addition to a compact, user-friendly UAV-based investigative process for areas affected by natural disasters. Drone mapping accuracy and productivity for use in catastrophe investigations was also assessed. They also highlighted the possibility of photogrammetry based drone mapping technology as an alternative to labor-intensive disaster site surveying.

High-resolution studies of headwater network dynamics and surface connectivity at various spatiotemporal scales can be obtained using drone-based Thermal InfraRed (TIR) technology. It could close the knowledge gap between model simulations and field observations, improving the knowledge of hydrological processes. It also has potential for assessing dynamics of surface saturation and the headwater network, which are important for understanding streamflow response at the catchment outlet [20]. Salamh *et al.* [21] highlighted the need for digital forensic investigation processes to assist in supporting the presentation of forensically sound evidence in legal proceedings, especially when it comes to instances involving Remotely Piloted Aerial Systems (RPAS) like drones. The authors propose a technical forensic process for the analysis of RPAS forensic artifacts, which can reduce the complexity of the identification and investigation of drones. This process focuses on developing a technical drone investigation process that can be applied to various types of drones. Sapac *et al.*

[22] focused on the investigation of low- and high-flow characteristics of karst catchments under climate change. The study used a lumped conceptual hydrological model to investigate the impact of climate change on the hydrological conditions of the Ljubljanica River catchment. The results indicate that a decrease in summer precipitation could lead to lower low-flow values for the investigated areas, increasing the vulnerability of karst areas. On the other hand, mean flow and high-flows could increase in the future, indicating the need for additional focus on water resource management in karst areas. Multiple point predictions can be done using a single hydrological model with various parameter extracted from the simulation. Beyond the scientific aspects, the case study addresses the broader implications of water diversion on local communities and ecosystems. The present study aims to capture high-resolution imagery and topographic data for a comprehensive mapping of the study area, focusing on water diversion. The study attempts to answer the following research questions:

- How does the use of drone technology enhance the efficiency of data collection for hydrological analysis for proper water diversion?
- What impact does the incorporation of remote sensing technologies with drone data have on the overall reliability and completeness of hydrological data pertaining to water diversion?
- To what extent does the use of drones coupled with a Geographic Information System (GIS) aid in sustainable water resource management by providing insightful information about water diversion impacts?
- How might the insights gained from a drone-led hydrological study contribute in decision-making processes related to water resource management?

Based on the above research questions, the objectives of the study were framed as follows:

- Investigate the role of drone technology in capturing high-resolution imagery and topographic data for a comprehensive mapping of the study area
- Examine the integration of drone-derived data with Geographic Information System (GIS) tools to generate hydrological models

- Perform hydrological analysis to comprehend and evaluate the movement and distribution of water in the study area
- Develop best practices for mitigation, aiming to guide future watershed management strategies and contribute to sustainable water resource utilization.

The study area chosen for investigation is Lakshmiyapuram catchment to Sivakasi Periyakulam Tank, Tamil Nadu, India. This area is affected by extensive soil mining posing an environmental hazard disrupting natural percolation and flow of water. Hence, the study area is surveyed using a drone for its real-time data acquisition followed by extensive post-processing and subsequent hydrological analysis. Drone technology and optical sensing together will provide a novel observational tool to perform the study by enabling precise and non-invasive surface flow observations. It is anticipated that the use of drones to assess surface flow would advance knowledge of surface water processes and the overall hydrological response of natural systems.

5.2 Software Used

5.2.1 GPS Essentials Application

GPS Essentials is a mobile application designed for Global Positioning System (GPS) navigation and location-related functions. The primary role of this application is to assist users in real-time navigation using GPS technology. This tool was employed to determine the live coordinates (Latitude, Longitude & Elevation) precisely for the boundary points. These coordinates are crucial for outlining the boundaries and serve as reference points for the drone to collect the necessary data. Moreover, GPS Essentials distinguishes itself with its exceptional mapping capabilities, enabling users to efficiently track routes and designate waypoints. The application boasts a digital compass that supports both magnetic and true north, thereby enhancing the accuracy of orientation. The essential information required for navigation is provided to the user by offering real-time altitude and speed data. The app is user friendly and it is very simple to export data such as coordinates, tracks and waypoints. The app allows easy and smooth integration with other tools or platforms. The app can support multiple coordinate systems and it provides provision for meteorological data. The app ensures the determination of a precise boundary and thus helps the user, providing better navigation and data collection efficiency. This is an essential tool for users who rely on GPS technology for their jobs.

5.2.2 Google Earth Pro

Google Earth Pro is a popular application that offers advanced mapping and geographical exploration capabilities. It provides users with an immersive experience by leveraging satellite imagery and aerial views. Google Earth Pro is utilized to visualize and analyze geographical data. It aids in identifying key features and landmarks, contributing to a comprehensive understanding of the terrain. This application proves invaluable in the planning and decision-making processes related to the study. Furthermore, Google Earth Pro enables users to make their own maps and 3D figures effortlessly. This allows users to adjust their view of things based on what they require totally. The smart gear inside the tool makes it simple to measure lengths, sizes and heights. They are beneficial for plenty of distinctive jobs such as planning urban areas, inspecting the environment and constructing matters. The app includes one more additional parameter time for images, letting customers view old satellite statistics and examine changes over time. Google Earth Pro is a notable preference of researchers as it's easy to use and has effective features. It enables them to view the arena up close on a shifting map. Google Maps is interconnected to other Google services. This easy platform shifting makes it easy to get more information from there, making it a total and much-needed tool in the world of maps and places.

5.2.3 Drone Deploy

Drone Deploy is a widely used application for drone mapping and aerial data analysis. This powerful tool allows users to plan, fly, and analyze drone missions for various purposes. Drone Deploy is instrumental in capturing aerial imagery and generating detailed maps. By leveraging this application, critical data points can be collected and analyzed, enhancing the ability to make informed decisions based on aerial perspectives. Drone Deploy gives a simple-to-use system that makes planning missions easier. It lets people set up flight routes and take photos with accuracy. The app works with lots of jobs, like farming and building. It helps by giving good and current pictures to see what's happening there. It can also make 3D models and height maps, giving a full picture of the area studied. When drone flights gather information, users can quickly look at it all with real-time processing. The online system lets many people work together easily. They can see and study the gathered data from anywhere without any problem over the internet. Thus, Drone Deploy has become a vital tool for people who need quick and definite drone maps and people who survey and collect data from the sky and analyze data.

5.2.4 QGIS

QGIS, or Quantum GIS, is a versatile, open-source Geographic Information System (GIS) software. It serves as a powerful tool for mapping, spatial analysis, and data visualization. QGIS can be employed to handle and analyze geospatial data. This software allows creating maps, performing spatial analyses, and making informed decisions based on a comprehensive understanding of geographic information.

In addition, QGIS has a wide range of feature set which can easily adapt to various geospatial data formats. Users can easily customize their GIS experience to meet the specific needs of their projects through different plugins and extensions available in the software. QGIS software is community-driven and open-source which allows for continuous upgrades and enhancements. Hence, users can always rely on the software to stay up to date with emerging technology and trends. QGIS's user-friendly design is ensured by its seamless operation on Mac, Windows, and Linux operating systems. QGIS is a reliable and essential tool for experts due to its user-friendly interface and robust functionalities for creation of visually striking thematic maps, analysis of complex spatial data, and interpreting and managing of huge geodatabases.

5.2.5 Pix 4D Mapper

Pix4D Mapper is widely used software designed for photogrammetry and 3D mapping applications. It is particularly valuable for converting drone-captured images into accurate and detailed maps, models, and geospatial data. Pix4D Mapper plays a crucial role in processing aerial imagery acquired by drones. By leveraging its advanced algorithms, precise 3D maps and models can be generated by providing valuable insights and aiding decision-making processes. This application significantly contributes to the ability to analyze and interpret geospatial data effectively. The more highlighting feature is that the Pix4D Mapper excels in its ability to seamlessly integrate with various sensors and platforms, ensuring compatibility with diverse drone systems. Its user-friendly interface and intuitive workflow empower professionals in fields such as surveying, agriculture, and urban planning to harness the power of geospatial data without requiring extensive technical expertise. The software's commitment to accuracy and detail makes it an indispensable tool for projects demanding precision, ranging from topographic mapping to infrastructure assessment. Whether it's creating detailed terrain models or conducting volumetric measurements, Pix4D Mapper continues to be at the forefront of transforming aerial imagery into actionable insights, making it an essential asset in the toolkit of professionals engaged in spatial data analysis and decision support.

5.3 Methodology

5.3.1 Drone Preprocessing

Drone preprocessing is a crucial phase in the workflow of drone data analysis, which involves several steps to enhance the quality and accuracy of raw data collected by drones. The detailed breakdown of the key processes involved in drone preprocessing is given below.

5.3.1.1 Collection of GPS Coordinates

GPS points are gathered for creating a map; the procedure involves collecting boundary coordinates systematically to form a closed polygon. The steps are outlined to gather GPS points. To set up the GPS coordinates for mapping, GPS Essentials app on the smartphone is installed and the application is launched. The home screen is navigated to access the settings tab. In the settings, "Position datum" to World Geodetic System 1984 is configured and the units are set to meters. Then in the home screen, waypoints are selected, and the plus icon at the bottom right corner is tapped. GPS coordinates are noted by standing at the location, observing the screen, and taking note of certain parameters, such as ensuring many satellites and a precision within 5 m. The device position is adjusted as needed by moving around until the parameters fall within the desired range. Once the parameters are satisfactory, name and symbol are assigned to the coordinate, and the "create" icon is clicked. The process is repeated at each location until a closed boundary of the area is established. The above steps ensure an accurate GPS point collection for mapping the collected data. Figure 5.1 illustrates the boundary points marked using GPS.

5.3.1.2 Generation of .kmlfile

After gathering all the coordinates, the three dots icon located at the upper-right corner of the screen is tapped. The export option is chosen from the

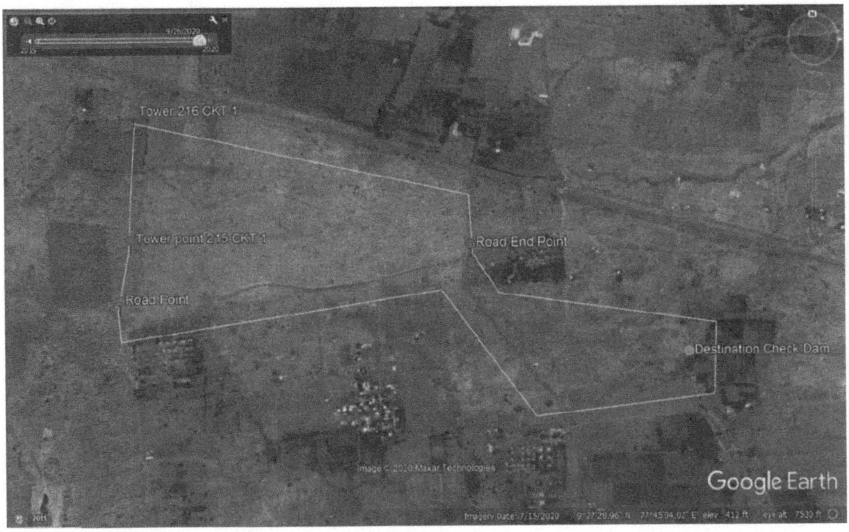

Figure 5.1 Boundary marking of points using GPS.

dropdown menu. The KML (Google Earth) format is chosen, and data should be sent to the Gmail account via email.

5.3.1.3 Generation of the Ground Map

Upon receiving the email, download the attached .kmlfile. Ensure that Google Earth Pro is installed on your system, and launch the application. Open the previously downloaded .kmlfile within Google Earth Pro; the software will prompt you to visually mark the collected coordinates on the virtual globe. Define the area boundaries accurately by utilizing the "add polygon" option located in the top menu. Connect all the gathered coordinates to form a closed polygon, thereby creating a well-defined area on the map. After successfully adding the polygon, the map will reflect the intended spatial representation. To preserve your work, save the file in .kmlformat. This comprehensive process ensures the successful translation of collected GPS coordinates into a tangible and accurate visual representation using Google Earth Pro.

5.3.1.4 Creating Flight Plan

The flight plan is generated by signing up for Drone Deploy and accessing the home screen. The flight plan is created by initiating a new project

Figure 5.2 Drone flight planning over the study area.

within the application by selecting the "New Project" tab option. The specific location details for the targeted area are entered. Once the location is set, the "Create Project Here" option is clicked to assign a name to the project for easy identification. Following this step, a side menu will emerge, which presents various options. Within this menu, the "File" option is located and clicked. This action prompts the upload of a .kmlfile, previously created using Google Earth to define specific geographical parameters. Upon successful file upload, a map will be dynamically generated on the right side of the screen, featuring either vertical or horizontal path lines as shown in Figure 5.2. In the subsequent phase, users have the option to set flight parameters such as flight altitude and access more advanced settings, including but not limited to overlap (ensuring a minimum of 75%), flight speed, and other parameters based on specific project requirements. It is important to note that adjusting these parameters will inherently influence factors such as flight time, the number of batteries required, and the total number of images captured. After configuring all the settings, software simulation must proceed to verify the proper functionality and execution of the work.

5.3.1.5 *Collection of Data*

An environmentally conscious and efficient workflow for drone operations is established by the following steps: the first step involves downloading and installing both the DJI GO4 and Drone Deploy applications in the mobile device, which serves as the interface with the drone's radio transmitter.

Once installed, it is essential to fine-tune the default settings in DJI GO4 by navigating to the device settings, accessing the Apps section, selecting DJI GO4, and clearing any default settings. This ensures a smooth transition between applications. After preparing the mobile device, power on the drone and a connection with the radio transmitter is initiated. The DJI GO4 app is launched to assess crucial parameters. The firmware version must be checked to ensure that it is up to date for optimal performance. The GPS status is verified to guarantee a stable and accurate connection. The general flying condition of the drone is evaluated by ensuring that all systems are functioning correctly.

Once satisfied with the drone condition, DJI GO4 app is closed and the Drone Deploy application is opened. The Drone Deploy account must be logged in within the app in order to access mission planning and data collection features. The Drone Deploy app is designed to seamlessly detect the connected drone, simplifying the setup process. The app establishes a GPS lock, ensuring precise positioning of the drone during flight. With the drone connected and the GPS locked, the mission can be initiated within the Drone Deploy app. The mission parameters such as altitude, waypoints, and flight path are defined to tailor the drone movements to the specific requirements of the data collection task. The autonomous nature of the Drone Deploy app allows the drone to follow a predefined flight path, collecting data as programmed. In the event of issues with drone detection, Drone Deploy app must be exited, the drone should be restarted and an attempt made to reconnect. The troubleshooting process ensures a reliable connection between the app and drone. Throughout the mission, the entire progress should be monitored through the Drone Deploy app to ensure that data collection is proceeding according to plan.

Upon completion of the aerial survey, the captured images are meticulously transferred and stored on a computer for subsequent post-processing. The drone captured approximately 611 images of the study area. These images are subjected to post-processing using specific tools. The objective of this post-processing is to elevate the quality and precision of the collected data, enabling the generation of diverse and insightful outputs. The post-processing tools employed in this phase played a crucial role in refining the raw imagery and extracting valuable information essential for the project objectives. The quantity and caliber of images obtained during the drone mission are paramount, influencing the accuracy and reliability of the final outputs. The post-processing stage is pivotal, serving as a transformative bridge from raw data to actionable insights and meaningful visualizations. In essence, the detailed post-processing of the drone-captured images (Figure 5.3) constitutes a critical facet of the

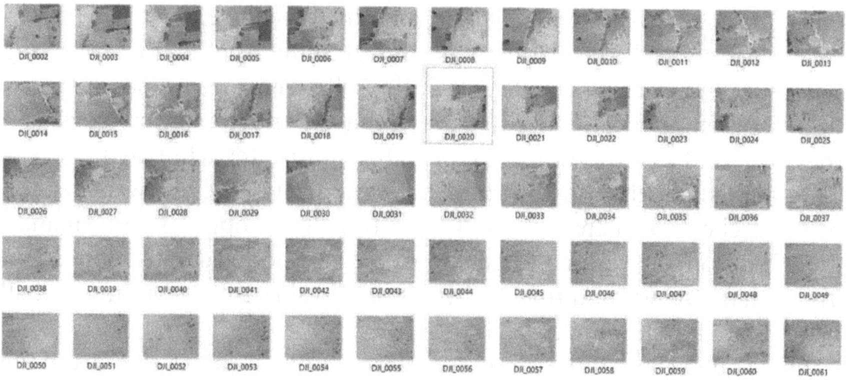

Figure 5.3 Drone-captured images.

workflow, ensuring that the collected data is not only effectively harnessed but also contributes significantly to the success and outcomes of the overarching project. This methodical approach underscores the importance of precision in image processing for the realization of project goals and objectives.

5.3.2 Drone Data Preprocessing

3D modeling is crucial in various geospatial applications, and using drone data enhances the accuracy and detail of these models. This step explores the steps involved in 3D modeling using Bentley Context Capture.

5.3.2.1 Reviewing the Data

Before initiating the modeling process, it is essential to review the drone data. This involves assessing data types (imagery, point clouds), ensuring data quality, and identifying potential challenges or anomalies. In case, if the images lack clarity, blurry shall be removed before uploading.

5.3.2.2 Uploading the Data

On completion of reviewing the data, the same drone data is uploaded into Bentley Context Capture by following a step-by-step guide. The file organization and data compatibility must be considered and the software interface for efficient data upload must be understood clearly. On confirming, all the photos containing the input images must be added. Once the images are uploaded, they will appear as a group along with the list of images. They can be reviewed before being rendered for final modeling.

5.3.2.3 *Addition of Ground Control Points (GCPs)*

Ground Control Points (GCPs) are another parameter vital to achieve global accuracy. The model accuracy can be improved by adding GCPs for georeferencing. GCPs are collected and integrated into the project, and their impact on spatial accuracy is observed. Once the GCPs are added, each point is marked in at least three uploaded images as input. Once all GCPs are marked precisely in images, .kml file format is chosen to save the file and the saved file is exported. As soon as it is done, Google Earth will automatically open and the ground control points will be marked showing the targeted location. To continue with the modeling process, .XML file must be generated and aero triangulation must be performed.

5.3.2.4 *Aero Triangulation*

Aero triangulation is a photogrammetric process that determines the spatial relationship between multiple overlapping images taken from different perspectives. It establishes the precise positions of the ground points by triangulating the intersections of corresponding rays projected from different photos. The generated .xml file generated is submitted for aero triangulation and the completed 3D view can be seen as an output.

5.3.2.5 *Reconstruction Settings*

In this step, the unnecessary data is clipped to reduce the processing time and system capabilities. The object can be tightly fit inside the bounding box to remove its surroundings.

5.3.2.6 *Production*

The final step is production, which gives the 3D model of the object. Various models can be generated based on the user requirements. After the production is complete, the generated 3D model can be seen in the 3D view tab. The 3D reference model serves as a prerequisite for the generation of various other post-processing outputs such as orthophoto/Digital Surface Model (DSM).

5.3.3 Drone Data: Post-Processing-Outputs

5.3.3.1 Orthomosaic Map

An orthomosaic map is a high-resolution, georeferenced aerial image created by stitching together multiple individual images captured during a drone survey. It corrects distortions caused by terrain and camera angles, providing a seamless, accurate representation of the surveyed area. An orthophotograph can be used to measure true distances because it is an accurate representation of the Earth's surface, having been adjusted for topographic relief, lens distortion, and camera tilt. The orthomosaic map of the study area is depicted in Figure 5.4. As a step toward validation, the distance between any two points is measured in the orthomosaic map. As shown in Figure 5.4, the distance between the Tower point (A) and the Dam destination (B) is found to be 1.751 km. Similarly, surface area is calculated using an orthomosaic map. An orthomosaic map for surface area measurements in the upstream and downstream of the study area is illustrated in Figure 5.5a and b. The area between the tower points and road point and dam point region are selected and the values of 98.26 acres and 42.03 acres are found, respectively. The complete area of the site surveyed using a drone is found to be 167.68 acres as indicated in Figure 5.6.

5.3.3.2 Digital Surface Model (DSM)

A digital surface model represents the elevation of the Earth surface and all objects on it, including vegetation, buildings, and terrain features. It is generated from drone data and provides a comprehensive view of the landscape. It is useful in terrain analysis, flood modeling, and infrastructure planning. It distinguishes surface features and aids in understanding the

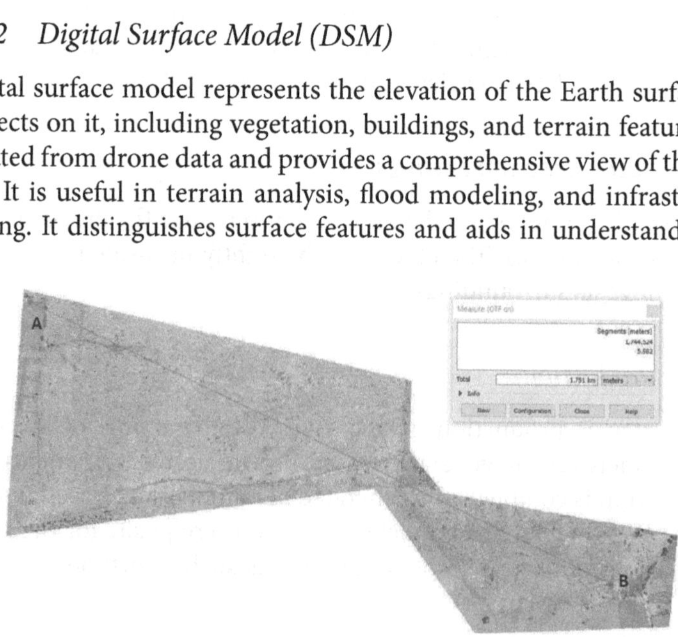

Figure 5.4 Orthomosaic map.

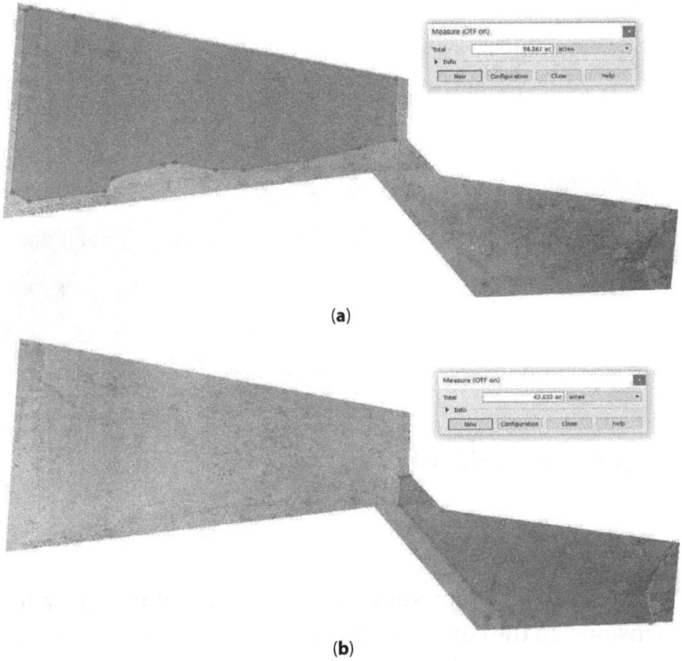

Figure 5.5 (a) Orthomosaic map for surface area measurements in the upstream of the study area. (b) Orthomosaic map for surface area measurements in the downstream of the study area.

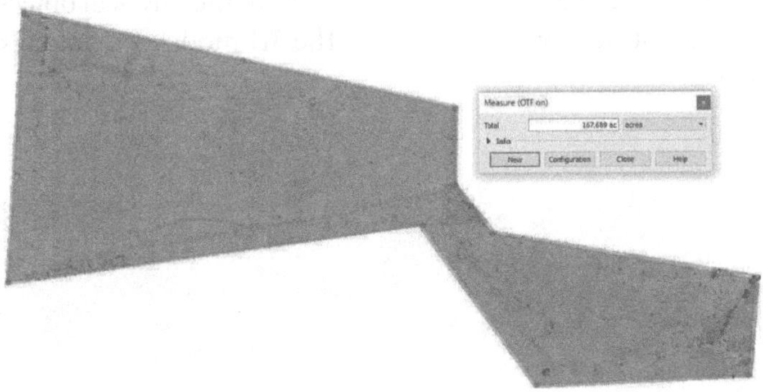

Figure 5.6 Orthomosaic map for whole area measurements.

topography of the study area. The digital surface model generated clearly shows the lowest elevation surface which is marked in blue and the highest elevation surface of the site, which is marked in red. The elevation values of the site vary from 138.8 m to 153.1 m as shown in the scale with colour and value variations (Figure 5.7).

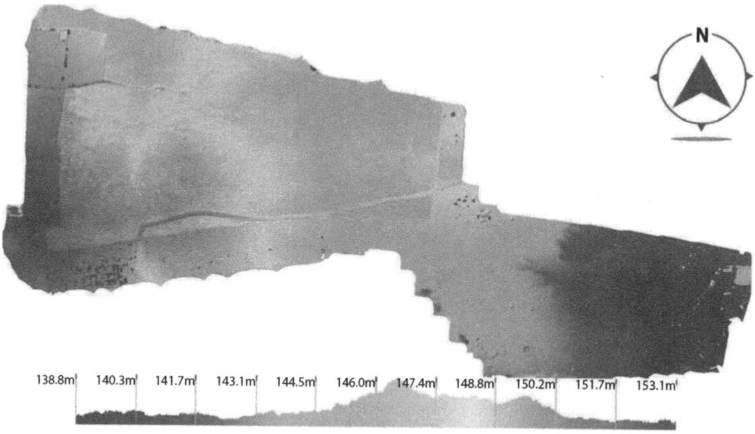

Figure 5.7 Digital surface model of the study area.

5.3.3.3 3D Model

A 3D model is a digital representation of a physical object or terrain in three dimensions. In the context of drone data, 3D models are often created using photogrammetric techniques, allowing for a realistic visualization of the surveyed area. One of the important outputs of the drone survey is 3D model generation of the study area. A 3D model provides 3D visualization of the plot from which one can measure the actual distance between two points, surface area and volume measurement of the physical objects along with feature identification and marking. The 3D model generated is shown in Figure 5.8.

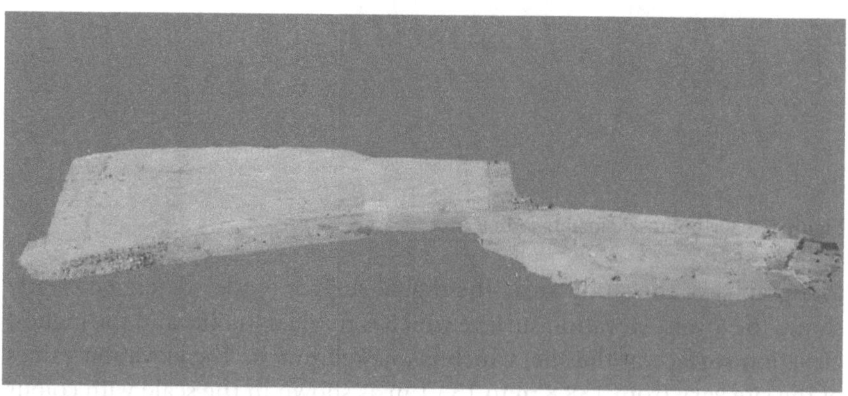

Figure 5.8 Generated 3D model of the study area.

With the help of the generated 3D model, volume calculations can be performed, integrating elevation differences across the site. The cut volume signifies the volume of the earthwork to be excavated, whereas the fill volume represents the volume of earthwork required to achieve the desired elevation. Methodologies such as grid-based, triangulation, or voxel-based approaches are generally performed based on software and site complexity. The accuracy of estimates depends on factors such as data resolution, model precision, and calculation methodology. Visualizing cut and fill volumes within the 3D model aids in comprehension and effective project planning and hence this process plays a vital role in engineering projects, providing crucial insights for optimal resource allocation and cost estimation. Any surface selected within the 3D model will give an estimate of the cut and fill volume of the study area as shown in Figure 5.9. As indicated, a particular surface area of 37,251 sq m is selected in the site, which gave the cut and fill volumes of 14100.518 cubic m and 15116.671 cubic m, respectively. Similarly, coordinate measurements are also carried out on the 3D model and are validated as shown in Figure 5.10. Every point or pixel in the 3D model represents the latitude/longitude/elevation values (position) of that point of the site. As shown in Figure 5.10, the selected point of the study area shows the position coordinate values of 9.4643915N (latitude), 77.7345327E (longitude), 150.295 m (elevation from mean sea level).

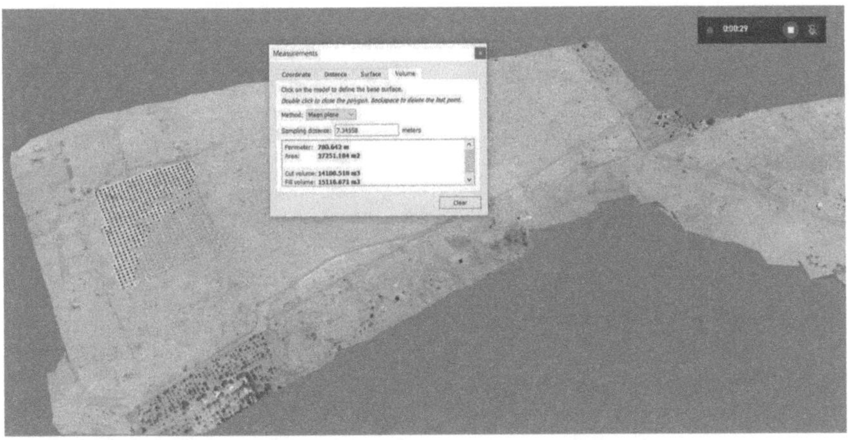

Figure 5.9 Estimate of cut and fill volume.

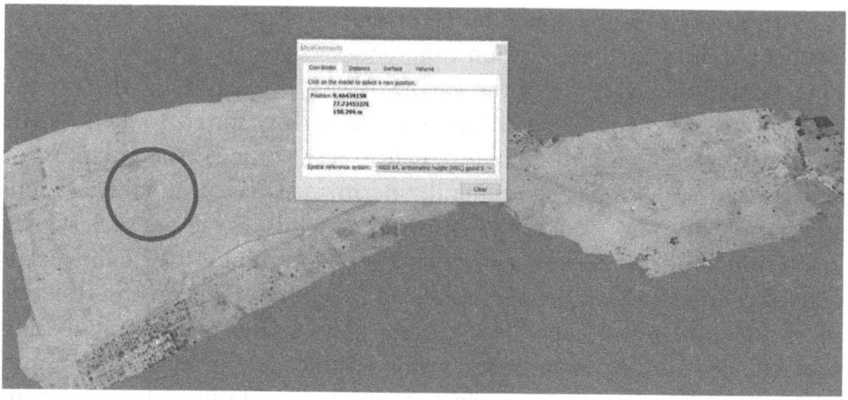

Figure 5.10 Coordinate measurement on the generated 3D model.

5.3.3.4 *Contour Map*

A contour map displays lines connecting points of equal elevation on the Earth's surface. These lines, known as contour lines, help in visualizing the shape of the terrain and changes in elevation. The contour interval is the difference between the levels of consecutive contour lines on a map. The contour interval is kept constant in the given map. The contour interval is drawn at 1 m intervals for the study area (as shown in Figure 5.11). Contours are also overlaid on the orthomosaic map for better understanding of the elevations in the site with respect to the actual visualization of the site (Figure 5.12).

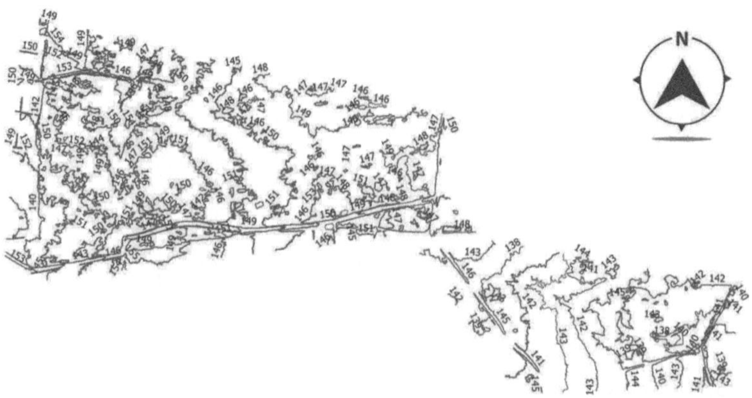

Figure 5.11 Contour map of the study area.

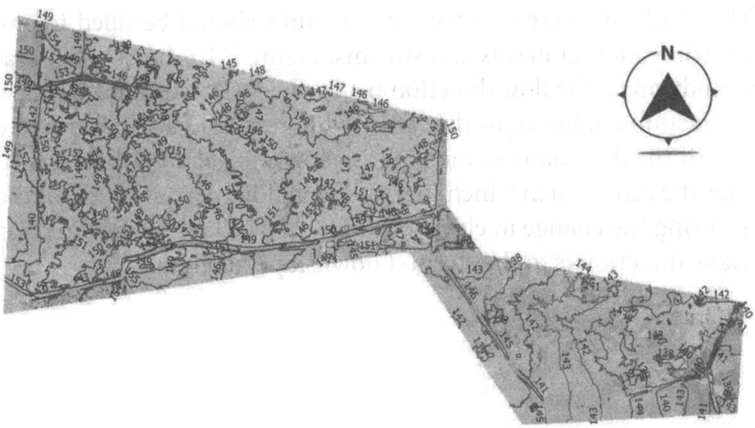

Figure 5.12 Contours overlayed on orthomosaic map.

These generated outputs are often interconnected. For instance, an orthomosaic map serves as a base for overlaying other information, whereas a DSM is used to generate a 3D model. Contour maps can be derived from DSMs, thereby enhancing their utility in terrain analysis. However, accurate geo-referencing, proper ground control point placement and precise photogrammetric techniques contribute to the reliability and quality of these outputs.

5.3.4 Hydrological Analysis

Hydrological analysis is conducted using QGIS software on the outputs obtained from the post-processing of drone data. The outputs such as fill and flow direction, stream line and stream order, water outlet and the water catchment area, fill volume estimation, terrain elevation range, streamline overlayed on ortho mosaic, outlet trace and expected excavation volume are generated.

5.3.4.1 Fill and Flow Direction

Fill represents flow accumulation, indicating areas of water accumulation or potential flooding. Flow direction identifies the direction of water flow in the landscape. These outputs are crucial for identifying the drainage patterns of the site, areas prone to water accumulation, and overall watershed characteristics. Fill is the first step in the hydrological analysis where the software identifies the entire sink that is present in the raster digital Surface

Model and fills it to create a flat terrain. Sinks should be filled to ensure proper delineation of basins and streams. Figure 5.13 shows the fill raster of the study area. The flow direction inside the QGIS software is prepared using direction coding algorithm where different colors are distributed to identify all the directions of the flow as shown in Figure 5.14. Each color indicates the direction in which the water will flow. An output raster is created showing the change in elevation from each cell along the direction of flow (flow direction is to the steepest downslope neighbor).

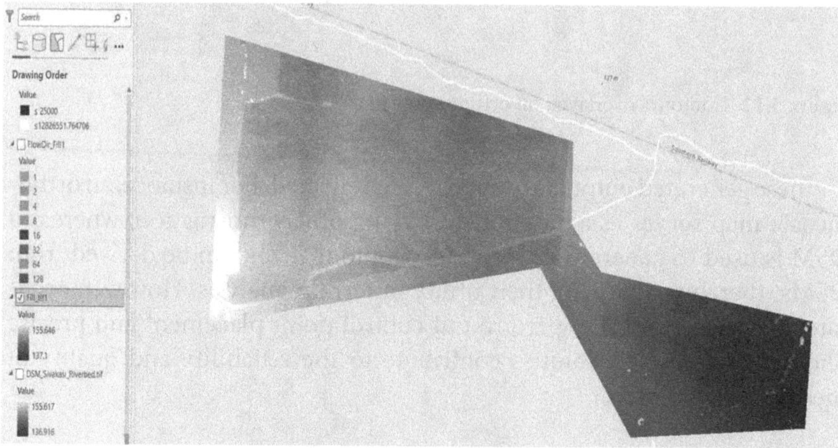

Figure 5.13 Fill raster of the study area.

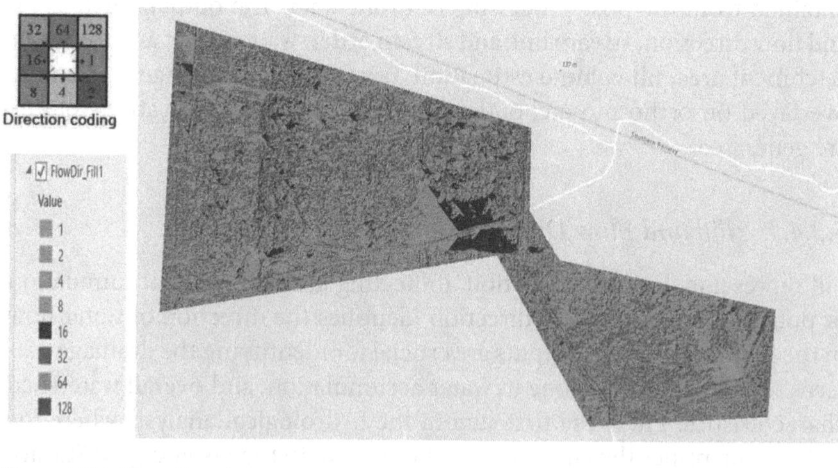

Figure 5.14 Flow direction.

5.3.4.2 *Streamline and Stream Order*

In hydrology, a streamline is a graphical representation of the flow direction of water across a landscape, revealing the natural pathways that water would take from higher to lower elevations. The streamlines are generated through the analysis of terrain data and streamlines visually depict the flow patterns, aiding in the identification of drainage pathways and concentrated flow areas. They play a crucial role in watershed delineation, flood modeling, and hydrological analysis, providing valuable insights for land-use planning and environmental management. Stream order is a hierarchical classification system that categorizes streams within a watershed on the basis of their position in the drainage network. For instance, first-order streams are the smallest, unbranched streams, and when two first-order streams converge, they form a second-order stream. Visualization of stream order on maps helps to characterize the structure of the drainage network, with higher-order streams representing larger watercourses. Understanding stream order is fundamental for watershed management, enabling assessments of contributions from different streams, and predicting the impacts of land-use changes on stream ecosystems. Together, streamlines and stream order contribute to a comprehensive understanding of surface water dynamics in a given landscape. The streamlines marked clearly will show the direction in which the rain water flow takes place along the surface elevations as shown in Figure 5.15. Stream order defines the number of streams interconnected; the higher the order number the higher the number of streams connected to it. For the study area shown, four stream orders are created by the software in which the highest stream order four (blue colour) connects all other streams together. There

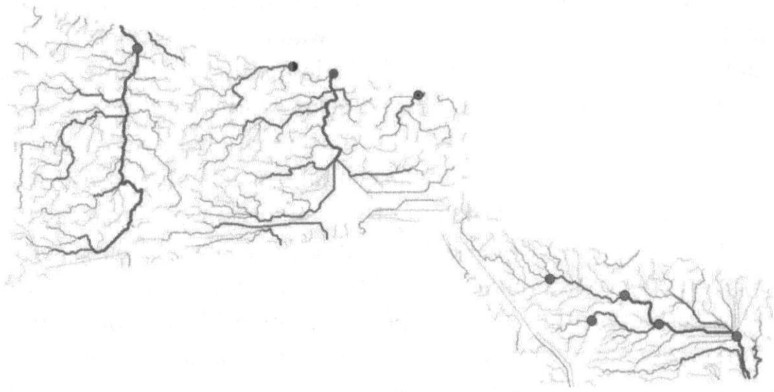

Figure 5.15 Streamlines for the study area.

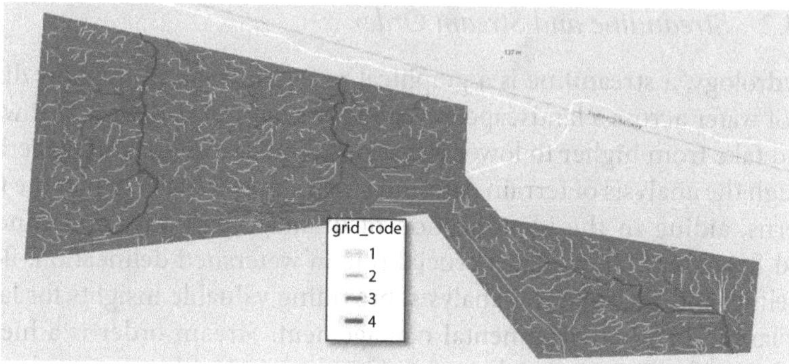

Figure 5.16 Stream order for the study area.

are three highest order streams (blue colour) in the study area as shown in Figure 5.16.

5.3.4.3 *Water Outlet and Water Catchment Areas*

In hydrology, a water outlet refers to a specific location where water is discharged from a particular area, usually at the lowest elevation point or through a designated drainage pathway. Determining water outlets is crucial for understanding the natural flow patterns within a landscape, identifying potential discharge points, and assessing the overall drainage network. In GIS and hydrological modeling, the precise location of water outlets is often delineated through the analysis of terrain data, such as Digital Elevation Models (DEMs). This information is essential for various applications, including watershed management, flood risk assessment, and infrastructure planning, as it aids in pinpointing areas where water exits a particular terrain. Similarly, the water catchment area often represents the geographical area that contributes runoff water to a specific water outlet. GIS tools, based on hydrological analysis define these catchment areas by considering the topography and flow patterns. Understanding water catchment areas is vital for managing water resources, predicting the volume and timing of runoff, and assessing the potential impacts of land-use changes on the overall hydrological system. The delineation of water catchment areas is integral to effective water resource planning and environmental management, providing valuable insights into the interconnected nature of surface water flow within a landscape. In Figure 5.17, each outlet marked with different symbols and along with their geographic locations in terms of latitude and longitude can be identified clearly. Similarly, in Figure 5.18, the area of the water catchment is represented in different colors.

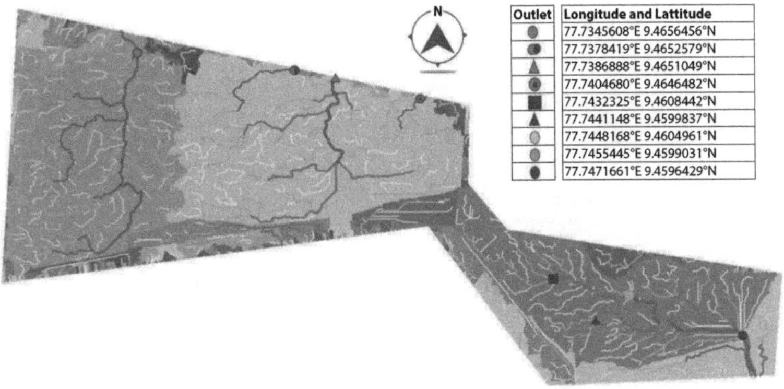

Figure 5.17 Water outlet along with its geographic location.

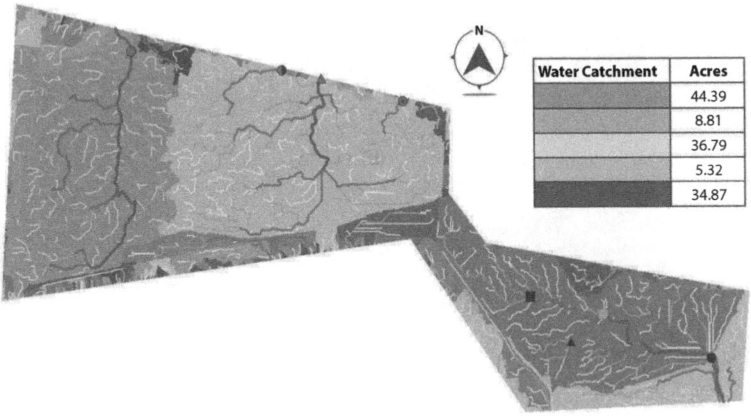

Figure 5.18 Water catchment area.

5.3.4.4 *Fill Volume Estimation*

Fill volume estimation is a critical aspect of hydrological and engineering analysis that involves calculating the volume of material, such as soil or sediment, required to achieve a desired topography or surface configuration. This process is particularly relevant in construction and earthwork projects, where understanding the quantity of material to be excavated (cut) or added (fill) is essential for project planning and resource allocation. Estimation is often conducted using GIS software and digital terrain models, such as those derived from drone data. By comparing the existing terrain with the desired final surface, the cut and fill volumes can be determined. Accurate fill volume estimation is crucial for optimizing earthwork

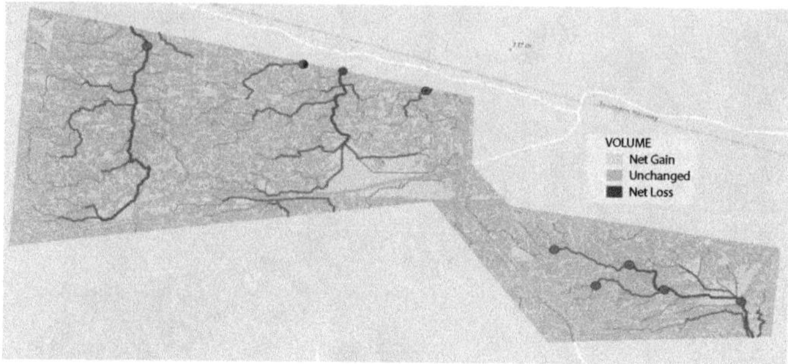

(a)

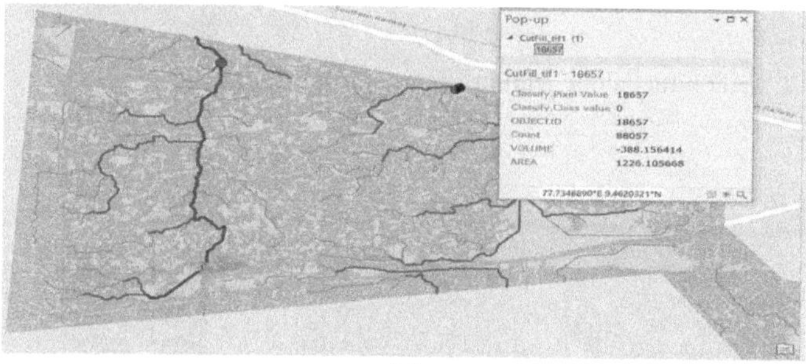

(b)

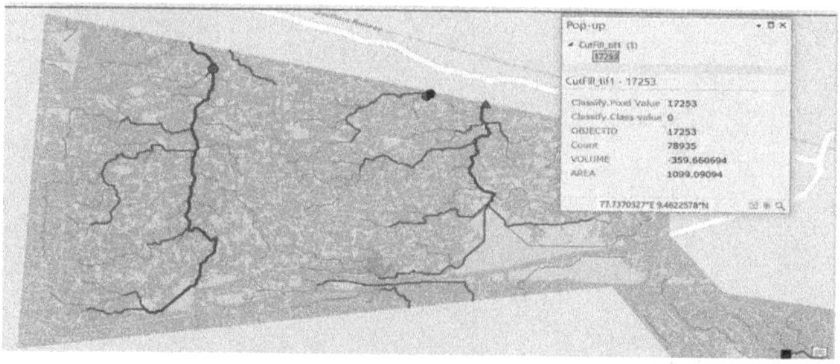

(c)

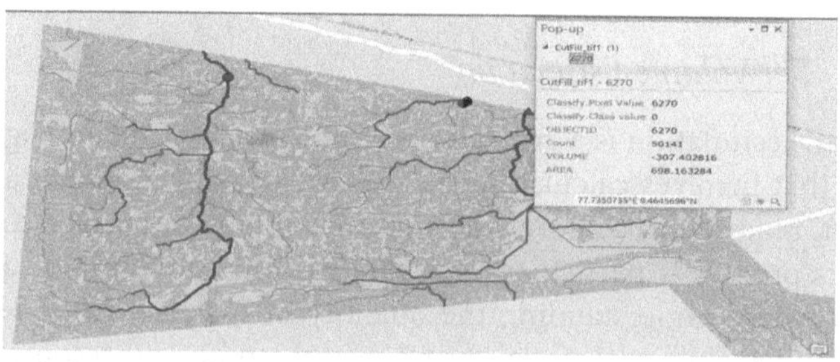

(d)

Figure 5.19 (a-d) Fill volume estimation of the study area.

operations, minimizing costs, and ensuring the efficient management of soil movements during site development. This information is fundamental for engineers, planners, and construction professionals to effectively plan and execute projects while considering the environmental and economic implications of earthwork activities. For the study area, fill volume estimation is performed. The net gain (yellow) is the region where soil must be filled. The total volume of soil that must be filled in all the sinks in the site is approximately 32,471 cubic meters (Figure 5.19 a to d).

5.3.4.5 *Terrain Elevation Range*

Terrain elevation range is a fundamental metric in geospatial analysis that characterizes the vertical variability of the landscape by defining the difference between the highest and lowest elevation points within a given area. This range is determined using digital elevation models (DEMs) or other topographic datasets representing elevation values across the terrain. A wide elevation range indicates significant relief, whereas a narrow range indicates a flat terrain. Understanding the terrain elevation range is crucial for various applications, including hydrological modeling, land-use planning, and environmental assessments. In hydrology, for instance, it helps to identify areas of potential flooding or drainage issues by highlighting variations in the topography of the landscape. The terrain elevation range provides valuable insights for decision-makers and planners, allowing them to comprehend the overall topographical characteristics of a region, assess its suitability for specific purposes, and make informed choices in fields such as infrastructure development and natural resource management. Figure 5.20 shows a visualization of the surface elevation in a particular range. Different colours indicate different terrain elevations of the surface and are important for understanding the site elevations. For example, the purple colour region is a higher elevation region than the orange colour region and similarly the orange colour region is a higher elevation region than the red one.

5.3.4.6 *Stream Order Overlayed on Orthomosaic*

Stream order overlayed on an orthomosaic combines two essential geospatial datasets to provide a comprehensive understanding of landscape hydrological features. Stream order, a classification system for streams based on their hierarchical position within a watershed, is overlaid onto an orthomosaic—a detailed, georeferenced aerial image or map capturing the surface features of the area. This overlay allows for a visual representation

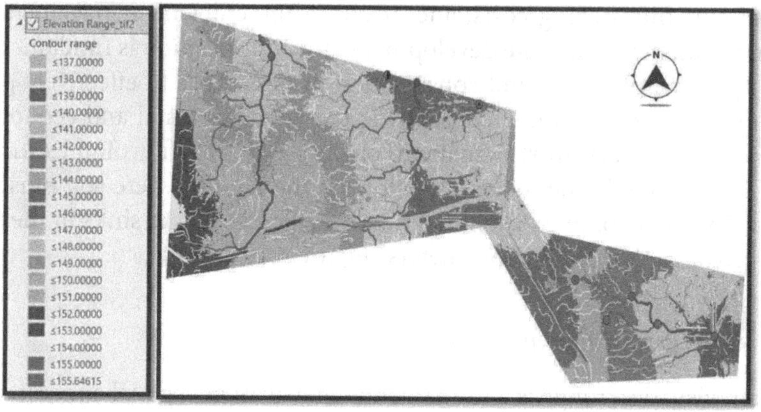

Figure 5.20 Visualization of surface elevation.

of the stream order within the context of the landscape, offering valuable insights into the relationship between the stream network and the surrounding terrain. The orthomosaic provides a high-resolution visual backdrop, while the stream order classification enhances the interpretation of hydrological patterns. This integrated approach aids in watershed delineation, identification of stream hierarchies, and assessment of the spatial distribution of different stream orders across the landscape. Figure 5.20 shows the stream order overlayed on an orthomosaic for a better visualization and understanding of the streams with respect to the site.

5.3.4.7 *Expected Earthwork Estimation*

An integrated water flow path is established by interconnecting all identified outlets to form continuous route guiding water to the designated endpoint approximately 1.822 km away. Figure 5.21 serves as a crucial reference, aiding in pinpointing outlet locations concerning "A," the lower leg Tower point, and "F," the road end point, with North assumed as the zero-degree reference. By connecting these outlets systematically, a comprehensive water flow network is constructed, facilitating a detailed understanding of the landscape's drainage patterns. This interconnected path plays a pivotal role in watershed management, providing insights into potential water accumulation points and aiding planners and environmental scientists in making informed decisions related to water resource sustainability and infrastructure.

The study area is delineated into five watersheds using DEM data. A rainfall of 100 mm, 300 mm, and 500 mm is assumed to pour in the study

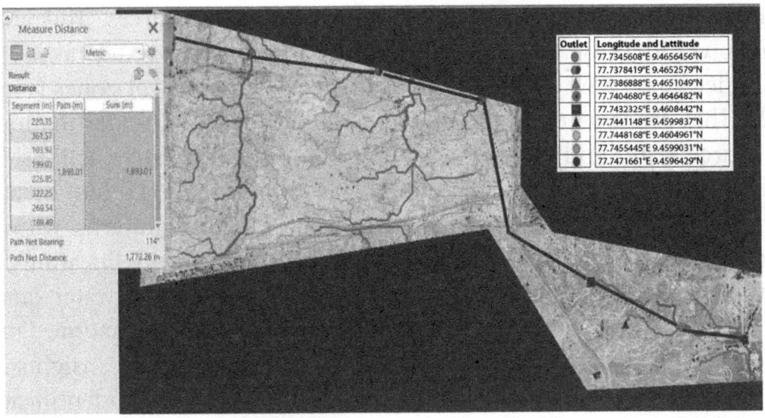

Figure 5.21 Major outlet – geographic locations.

area and the amount of water that could be collected is determined by multiplying the watershed area by the corresponding rainfall data. This method allows for a quick determination of the volume of water that could be collected as indicated in Table 5.1 from the landscape, providing valuable insights into the potential water resources available for use.

5.3.4.8 Outlet Trace

Outlet trace refers to the process of systematically tracing the flow path from a specific location, often a water outlet or discharge point, and

Table 5.1 Estimate of volume of water against rainfall.

Catchment	Area of the catchment		Water level for various rainfall (cubic m)		
	Acres	Sq m	10 cm	30 cm	50 cm
1	44.39	179640	17964	53892	89820
2	8.81	35653	3565	10696	17826
3	36.79	148884	14888	44665	74442
4	5.32	21529	2153	6459	10765
5	34.87	141114	52682	158046	263410
Total	130.18	526820	52682	158046	263410

back through the drainage network to its upstream sources. This analysis involves identifying and mapping the pathways that water takes from the outlet upstream to the contributing areas or catchment zones (Figure 5.22). This process enables users to track and identify the destination of the source water and paves the way for planning alternative actions. The outlet trace is conducted using digital elevation models (DEMs) or other topographic datasets to understand the natural flow patterns within a watershed (Figure 5.23). This information is valuable for delineating contributing areas, assessing the upstream factors influencing water quality and quantity, and identifying potential sources of contamination. Outlet trace is a vital step in watershed management which provides insights into the interconnected nature of water flow and facilitates the identification of critical points for environmental monitoring, land-use planning, and infrastructure design. As a validation step the outlet water flow from the

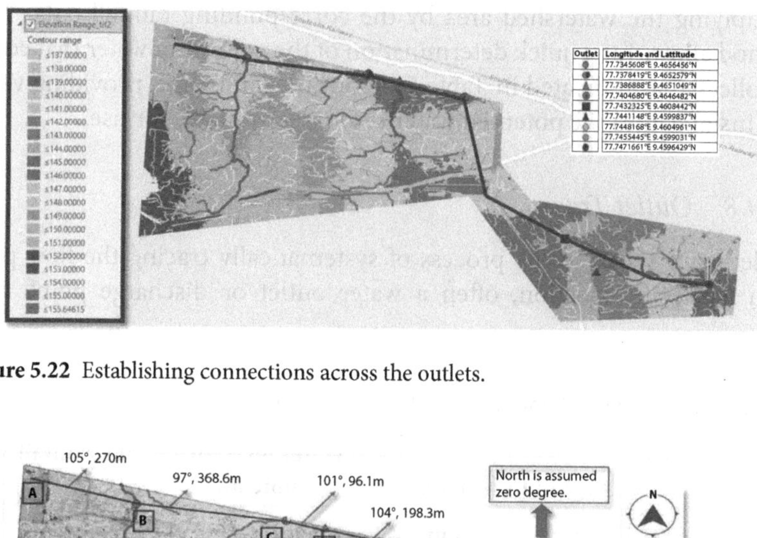

Figure 5.22 Establishing connections across the outlets.

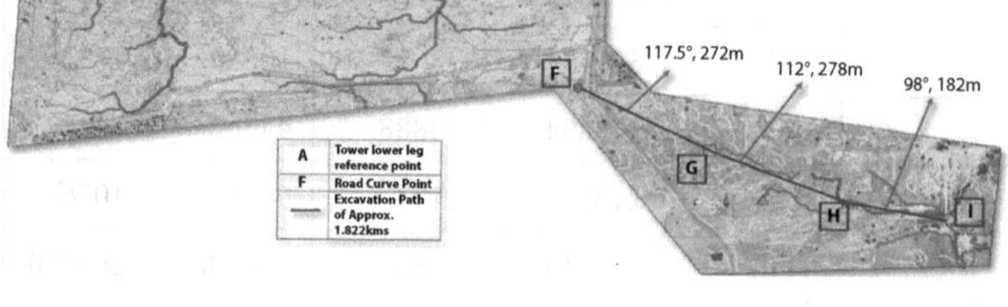

Figure 5.23 Directions of the outlets.

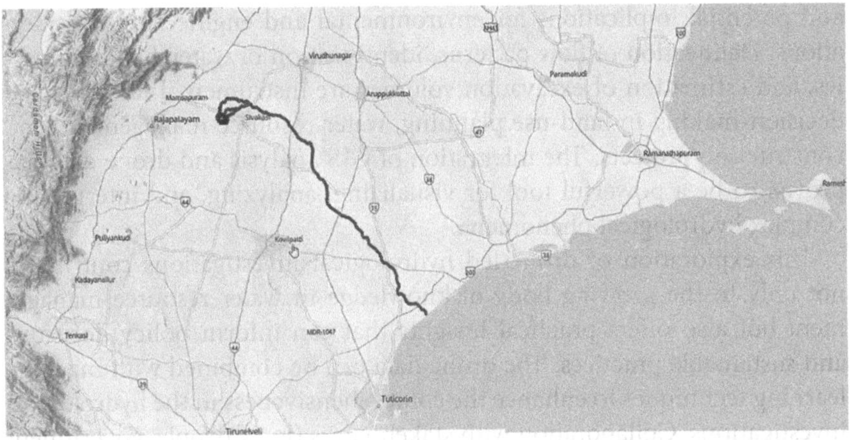

Figure 5.24 Water outlet trace in the study area.

study area has been traced and the water flow connects with Vaippar River before ending the flow into the sea as shown in Figure 5.24.

5.4 Conclusion and Recommendation

The drone-led hydrological investigation conducted in the case study has yielded valuable information about water diversion in the study area. Drone technology is found to be an effective and efficient means of gathering high-resolution spatial data by allowing for analyzing the hydrological dynamics of the study area. Precise mapping and monitoring capabilities of drones have made it easier to identify possible problem locations and necessitates taking preventative action to minimize water stagnation or related problems. The accelerated precise data collection by drones helps in saving time and human resources. The above study has emphasized the significance of using cutting-edge technologies, including drones, in hydrological studies, providing a scalable and economical approach for monitoring large and complex watersheds.

Hydrological analysis conducted using QGIS software on post-processed drone data has provided valuable insights into the intricate dynamics of the landscape water systems. The outputs, including fill and flow direction, streamline and stream order, water outlet, water catchment area, fill volume estimation, terrain elevation range, stream line overlayed on orthomosaic, outlet trace, and expected excavation volume, collectively contribute to a holistic understanding of the hydrological characteristics and potential implications for environmental and engineering considerations. Delineation of flow patterns, identification of watershed boundaries, and estimation of excavation volumes are instrumental for informed decision-making in land-use planning, water resource management, and construction projects. The integration of GIS analysis and drone data has proven to be a powerful tool for visualizing, analyzing, and interpreting complex hydrological phenomena.

This exploration of drone-led hydrological investigations contributes not only to the growing body of knowledge in water resource management but also offers practical insights that can inform policy decisions and sustainable practices. The drone data can be combined with machine learning techniques to enhance the comprehensiveness in the hydrological investigations. Collaboration with stakeholders (local people, government officials and non-governmental organizations) can be adopted to improve data collection and validation. This will promote community involvement in sustainable water management practices. Zoning regulations, conservation measures and awareness programs can be initiated to reduce the anthropogenic activities on the waterways. Further research can explore the impact of climate change on the hydrological processes of the watershed, constituting a potential future scope for this study.

In conclusion, this chapter underscores the importance of leveraging advanced geospatial technologies to unravel the complexities of water systems, fostering sustainable practices and effective planning for future developments. By leveraging the capabilities of drone technology, we anticipate uncovering new perspectives on water diversion within a watershed, ultimately contributing to the responsible and efficient utilization of this vital resource.

Acknowledgement

We express our deep sense of gratitude to Mr. Arun Jeya Prakash, director and CEO of Aviocian Technologies Private Limited, New Delhi, for providing expertise and assistance with drone technology.

References

1. Xue, J. and Su, B., Significant remote sensing vegetation indices: A review of developments and applications. *J. Sens.*, 2017, DOI: 10.1155/2017/1353691.

2. Chabot, D., Trends in drone research and applications as the Journal of Unmanned Vehicle Systems turns five. *J. Unmanned Veh. Syst.*, 2018, DOI: 10.1139/juvs-2018-0005.
3. Mcdonald, W., Drones in urban stormwater management: a review and future perspectives. *Urban Water J.*, 2019, DOI: 10.1080/1573062X.2019.1687745.
4. Tauro, F., Petroselli, A., Arcangeletti, E., Assessment of drone-based surface flow observations. *Hydrol. Processes*, 2015, DOI: 10.1002/hyp.10698.
5. McCabe, M., Rodell, M., Alsdorf, D., Miralles, D., Uijlenhoet, R., Wagner, W., Lucieer, A., Houborg, R., Verhoest, N., Franz, T., Shi, J., Gao, H., Wood, E., The Future of Earth Observation in Hydrology. *Hydrol. Earth Syst. Sci.*, 2017, DOI: 10.5194/hess-21-3879-2017.
6. Cancela, J.J., González, X.P., Vilanova, M., Mirás-Avalos, J.M., Water Management Using Drones and Satellites in Agriculture. *Water*, 2019, DOI: 10.3390/w11050874.
7. Bouabdelli, S., Meddi, M., Zeroual, A., Alkama, R., Hydrological drought risk recurrence under climate change in the karst area of Northwestern Algeria. *J. Water Clim. Change*, 2020, DOI: 10.2166/wcc.2020.207.
8. Dyer, J.L., Moorhead, R.J., Hathcock, L., Identification and Analysis of Microscale Hydrologic Flood Impacts Using Unmanned Aerial Systems. *Remote Sens.*, 2020, DOI: 10.3390/rs12101549.
9. Papacharalampous, G., Koutsoyiannis, D., Montanari, A., Quantification of predictive uncertainty in hydrological modelling by harnessing the wisdom of the crowd: Methodology development and investigation using toy models, 2019, DOI: 10.13140/RG.2.2.32868.22401.
10. Moon-Yeob, L., Je-Jin, P., Tae-Hee, J., Tae-Jun, H., Establishment of Traffic Information Image Collection System Using Drones. *KSCE J. Civ. Environ. Eng. Res.*, 401–408, 2020.
11. Kulkarni, A. and Nagarajan, R., Drone survey facilitated weeds assessment and impact on hydraulic efficiency of canals. *ISH J. Hydraul. Eng.*, 2018, DOI: 10.1080/09715010.2018.1520653.
12. Briggs, M.A., Wang, C., Day-Lewis, F.D., Williams, K.H., Dong, W., Lane, J.W., Return flows from beaver ponds enhance floodplain-to-river metals exchange in alluvial mountain catchments. *Sci. Total Environ.*, 2019, DOI: 10.1016/j.scitotenv.2019.05.336.
13. Sibanda, *et al.*, Application of Drone Technologies in Surface Water Resources Monitoring and Assessment: A Systematic Review of Progress, Challenges, and Opportunities in the Global South. *Drones*, 2022, DOI: 10.3390/drones6050131.
14. Acharya, B., Bhandari, M., Bandini, F., Pizarro, A., Perks, M., Joshi, D.R., Wang, S., Dogwiler, T., Ray, R., Kharel, G., Sharma, S., Unmanned Aerial Vehicles in Hydrology and Water Management: Applications, Challenges, and Perspectives. *Water Resour. Res.*, 2021, DOI: 10.1029/2021WR029925.

15. Koutalakis, P., Tzoraki, O., Zaimes, G., UAVs for Hydrologic Scopes: Application of a Low-Cost UAV to Estimate Surface Water Velocity by Using Three Different Image-Based Methods. *Drones*, 2019, DOI: 10.3390/drones3010014.
16. Baig, Z., Khan, M., Mohammad, N., Brahim, G., Drone Forensics and Machine Learning: Sustaining the Investigation Process. *Sustainability*, 2022, DOI: 10.3390/su14084861.
17. Ridolfi, E. and Manciola, P., Water Level Measurements from Drones: A Pilot Case Study at a Dam Site. *Water (Switzerland)*, 2018, DOI: 10.3390/w10030297.
18. Kim, S., Kim, T., Sim, J., Applicability assessment of UAV mapping for disaster damage investigation in Korea. *ISPRS - International Archives of the Photogrammetry, Remote Sensing and Spatial Information Sciences*, 2019, DOI: 10.5194/isprs-archives-XLII-3-W8-209-2019.
19. Kim, S.S., Shin, D.Y., Lim, E.T., Jung, Y.H., Cho, S.B., Disaster Damage Investigation using Artificial Intelligence and Drone Mapping. *International Archives of the Photogrammetry, Remote Sensing and Spatial Information Sciences*, 2022.
20. Dugdale, S., Klaus, J., Hannah, D., Looking to the Skies: Realising the Combined Potential of Drones and Thermal Infrared Imagery to Advance Hydrological Process Understanding in Headwaters. *Water Resour. Res.*, 2022, DOI: 10.1029/2021WR031168.
21. Salamh, F., Karabiyik, U., Rogers, M., RPAS Forensic Validation Analysis Towards a Technical Investigation Process: A Case Study of Yuneec Typhoon H. *Sensors*, 2019, DOI: 10.3390/s19153246.
22. Sapac, K., Medved, A., Rusjan, S., Bezak, N., Investigation of Low- and High-Flow Characteristics of Karst Catchments under Climate Change. *Water*, 2019, DOI: 10.3390/w11050925.

6

Sustainable Waste Management as a Key Feature for Smart City: A Case Study of Vadodara, Gujarat, India

Sahil Menghani[1], Hardik Giri Gosai[1], Parashuram Kallem[1,2], Payal Desai[3] and Uma Hapani[1]*

[1]*Department of Environmental Studies, Faculty of Science, The Maharaja Sayajirao University of Baroda, Vadodara, Gujarat, India*
[2]*Department of Environmental and Public Health, College of Health Sciences, Abu Dhabi University, Abu Dhabi, United Arab Emirates*
[3]*Foundation for Ecological Security, Anand, Gujarat, India*

Abstract

In the present day, the development of smart cities is crucial for India's progress towards achieving high-quality growth. This development is essential for promoting urban innovation and establishing India as a leader in innovation. On the other hand, there are still problems with Municipal Solid Waste Management (MSWM) in India as a result of the country's rapidly expanding population, densely populated cities, varied cultural backgrounds, and shifting lifestyles. This study examines the solid waste reduction system in the Sama neighbourhood of Vadodara and involved surveying 150 homes to determine their awareness, attitudes, and desire to participate in the program. A comparative study was conducted on sustainable waste management and the existing generalized waste management to assess their efficiency. The survey showed varying levels of source knowledge among respondents, and they were unsatisfied with the current waste management scenario in their locality. The generalized waste management process ends with dumping at a landfill site, while sustainable waste management provides value-added products and incentives for waste management. This study serves as a baseline source for local managing bodies to understand residents' perceptions of waste management and fill in the gaps for long-term sustainability in making smart cities.

**Corresponding author*: umahapani18@gmail.com

A. Suresh, T. Devi, N. Deepa and Ali Kashif Bashir (eds.) Environmental Monitoring Using Artificial Intelligence, (103–132)

Keywords: Circular economy, incentives, smart cities, questionnaire, waste management

6.1 Introduction

Over the last twenty years, cities have undergone significant transformation due to technological and economic advancements, resulting in a substantial increase in urbanization. The growing population necessitates better infrastructure and services, which demand continuous monitoring. However, there are a lot of issues that cities have to deal with, such as social isolation, poverty, inadequate infrastructure, and pollution. As a result, raising people's standard of living in cities becomes crucial. Technological developments have made it easier to evaluate how well a city is performing in terms of service delivery, creating sustainable urban environments, and improving the standard of living. Urban life has become more active for both locals and tourists thanks to technology, and cities are getting better at recognizing the needs of their citizens and offering pertinent services and solutions [1].

These technological developments are frequently employed as sensors in urban infrastructure, which includes traffic control systems, wastewater management strategies, and other systems that enable system monitoring and improved performance—better known as "smart cities." Is it a smart city, though? If cities exclusively use technology, are they still intelligent? Smart cities are an emerging 21st-century global phenomenon; they are promoted as an answer to the problems that urbanisation is currently facing [2]. The idea of a smart city has been more prevalent in recent times, and its roots may be traced back to the initial integration of information technology in urban settings. Many studies have looked at the definitions and traits of smart cities in the scientific literature, identifying and categorizing different elements and components [3]. Figure 6.1 depicts the components of smart cities [4]. In recent years, the idea of the smart city has gained attention in both governmental and scholarly discourse. However, there is no universal standard for smart cities, even though smart urbanism is being discussed in an increasing amount of research and being implemented worldwide. The fact that there isn't a single, accepted definition for such a widely accepted idea is very useful; perhaps it's time to give up trying to find a solution and focus on defining smart cities in a way that makes sense for the situation at hand [5].

According to Ramprasad [3], using networked infrastructure to support social, cultural, and urban advancement while boosting political

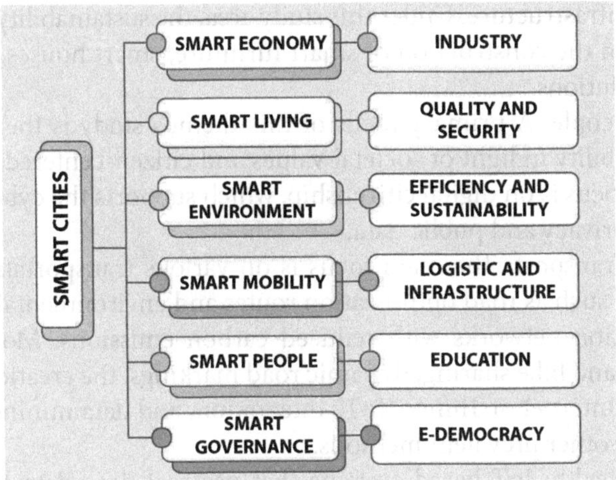

Figure 6.1 Components of smart cities.

and economic efficiency is one of the traits that characterize a smart city. Furthermore, there is a focus on social and environmental sustainability as a crucial strategic component, business-driven urban development, and careful study of the impact of social and relational capital on urban growth. In an attempt to improve the quality of life and performance of cities, the concept of smart cities emerged from modern technological advancements; however, the rate of technology advancements and their integration into urban lifestyles has outpaced the emergence of new ideas and definitions [1].

In an effort against climate change, smart cities are essential, and emerging intelligent technologies are believed to have a significant impact on reducing greenhouse gas emissions and improving urban energy efficiency. These technologies need to be resource-efficient, affordable, lean, integrated, and intelligent. In addition to the environmental sustainability goals, they should also have an impact on the population's well-being and financial sustainability [6].

According to Mundada and Mukkamala [7], the following are some areas in which smart cities' sustainable development objectives can be found.

Smart Environment: The main field of study for this theme is the Information and Communications Technology (ICT) sustainability component of mitigating climate change. Another important component is thought to be the waste management decision support system. Additionally common are tools for simulating investigations of renewable energy resources.

Smart Infrastructure: Under this study area, the sustainability element is prevalent in the construction of smart furniture, smart houses, and smart lighting solutions.

Smart People: A primary focus of this theme's study is the evaluation of sustainability in light of societal values and citizen-centered objectives. Here, the focus is on digital citizenship, which supports the cyber-physical theory of privacy and public data.

Smart Transport: The main focus is on various transportation-related challenges, such as road optimization routes and environmentally friendly transportation networks with reduced carbon emissions. Model shuttle routes, car and bike sharing, dynamic road markings, the creation of smart bikes with Internet of Things (IoT) integration, and data mining for parking lots are other prevalent methods.

Smart Health: IoT-based systems that use real-time data to measure knee angles and the use of artificial intelligence (AI) to provide precise diagnosis and efficient treatment are two of the main research topics.

Smart Education: A novel technique for creating virtual public libraries is offered, and smart learning is given an innovative spin with the use of satellite data.

Smart Government: In this industry, sustainability is concentrated on creating digital and effective public administrations. Using smart governance and urban data together creates fully realised ideal cities.

Smart Technology: It focuses on utilizing a wide range of technologies and methods for sustainable development goals with the adoption of techniques like fuzzy neural networks, ubiquitous computing, cloud data integration with IoT devices, data mining, mobile applications, augmented reality, and the innovation of smart decision support systems.

Large-scale, high-budget initiatives called smart city projects are meant to bring about changes in the environment and society [8]. Sustainable Development Goals (SDGs) and thoughtful urban planning form the foundation of sustainability. The SDGs are derived from the United Nations 2030 Agenda, which offers an action plan focused on three axes: people, the planet, and prosperity. These are a list of priorities that deal with the most significant problems that mankind is now experiencing. The concept of sustainability is widespread in all facets of life and requires our attention due to the irresponsible use of natural resources and environmental damage. More precisely, the notion of sustainable development in the context of a smart city is a multifaceted term that encompasses elements that are strongly tied to the quality of life on the social, political, and economic fronts. It comprises meeting the current demands of residents in a smart city while avoiding endangering the needs of future generations, within achievable limits that include environmental sensitivity and the pursuit of enhancing quality of life via technology advancement. Reducing consumption, recycling different resources, changing production and consumption patterns, using different forms of renewable energy, and implementing intelligent transportation systems are the most common ways that sustainability in smart cities is defined [9].

6.1.1 Essential Features of Indian Smart Cities

The global urban population is expanding quickly, particularly in emerging nations like India, which is causing a constant expansion in both the number and size of urban centres in terms of both demographics and geography [10]. India is one of several emerging nations where the transition from rural to urban areas is happening quickly. This change is indicated by the fact that the population of urban regions is expanding faster than that of rural ones. India's urban population increased, rising from around 27.8% (286 million) in 2001 to 31.2% (377 million) in 2011. By 2030, it is expected to reach 40%, and by 2050, it will surpass 50%. The growing population is causing cities to face challenges in maintaining their infrastructure and offering services. One approach that is being used to successfully and efficiently address these issues is the creation of smart cities [10]. The unplanned and unpredictable nature of India's urbanisation is a major contributing factor to nearly every issue. Three broad categories can be used to group the main issues arising from the country's urbanisation, some of which may overlap in different ways. First, infrastructure, which refers to the institutional, social, and physical infrastructure. Second, governance and management, which includes essentially how urban infrastructure and services are provided. Third, sustainability refers to using the right technology to achieve sustainability for the economy, society, and environment. Collectively, these roles support the social and economic frameworks that are necessary for metropolitan regions to flourish and for the welfare of their residents [11].

In an attempt to establish the framework for 100 smart cities in five years, the Indian Ministry of Urban Development (MoUD) initiated the Smart Cities Mission (SCM) (FY 2015-16 to FY 2019-20) [12, 13]. However, the SCM does not specify the exact characteristics that must exist in a smart city. Through the facilitation of local area development, which consists of three components, the SCM seeks to improve people's quality of life and foster economic progress by area-based development, which attempts to raise living conditions throughout the city by renovating and repurposing existing spaces, even impoverished neighborhoods. New parts of the city will be developed through green-field initiatives in order to accommodate the expanding urban population. The goal of pan-city development is to implement certain intelligent fixes to the infrastructure that exists in the city today [14].

According to the Ministry of Housing and Urban Affairs (MoHUA) [12, 13], cities will need to draft their Smart City Proposal (SCP), which must include a strategy for resource mobilization, a vision, and the expected results for upgrading infrastructure and implementing smart applications. While a specific paradigm is not mandated, it is anticipated that the SCPs would encompass several infrastructure services and intelligent solutions. The requirements for an SCP include a number of important components: a dependable electricity supply, with a minimum of 10% coming from solar power; sufficient water supply, including stormwater collection and wastewater reuse; comprehensive sanitation practices, including solid waste management and rainwater collection; adoption of smart metering systems; development of a strong IT infrastructure and digitization; encouragement of pedestrian-friendly environments; intelligent traffic management solutions; pedestrian-only zones and smart parking facilities; creatively utilizing open spaces; and improving aesthetics by replacing overhead electric [12, 13].

Cities will need to add more smart applications to this list in order to boost their SCP. Apart from the essential elements mentioned earlier, a minimum of 80% of the buildings in both redeveloped and greenfield smart city models must to be ecologically sustainable and energy-efficient. Moreover, at least 15% of the housing available in greenfield sites should be affordable. It is crucial to emphasize that the planned smart city and the SCPs need to be appropriately prepared, especially considering the rivalry among towns to be included in the Smart Cities Mission. Strategic planning concepts will be used by smart cities to produce SCPs, which will include pan-city efforts and area-based development plans. Since the goals and resources of all government agencies, parastatals, private organizations, and individuals are integrated into the SCP preparation process, the SCP is collaborative. It is acknowledged that States and Urban Local Bodies (ULBs) would need expert support to prepare the SCPs, as the process is rather difficult. There are two options for getting technical support: working with hand-holding organizations and consulting businesses [12, 13].

In addition to the smart city designations given to some other projects, such as Dholera in Ahmedabad, Gujarat, other green field developments, such as Lavasa in Pune, Maharashtra, Gift City in Gandhinagar, Gujarat, and Kochi Smart City in Kerala, have also been conceptualized and built in India under the auspices of sustainable and smart cities. However, they are insufficient in both quantity and size to keep up with the nation's rate of urbanisation and demand; as such, brownfield development is desperately needed [15]. The Indian government's vision for smart cities is made up of components rather than a clear description. Every smart city ought to have a special edge over the competition in terms of job creation and business activity. A well-defined policy agenda that can be put into practice to build and fortify institutional, social, physical, and financial infrastructure is necessary to get the competitive edge. Given that smart cities are still relatively new in India, stakeholders and policymakers must comprehend how Indian smart cities might fit into the larger global smart city ecosystem. To begin with, assessing Indian cities requires a deep understanding of technology and the current status of smart city development [16].

6.1.2 Waste Management in Smart Cities

Our planet is predicted to produce over 27 billion metric tons of trash by 2050. Asia will produce one-third of this trash, with China and India contributing the most because of their fast expansion [17]. It is estimated that every individual residing in urban India by 2025 would produce around 0.7 kilogram of solid trash. This quantity is four to six times greater than what was produced in 1999. The issues of trash management have grown along with the population, necessitating the use of decentralized waste management techniques. This can be accomplished through programs like self-help groups or NGOs that are specifically focused on solid waste management. It has been noted that India's metropolitan regions generate over 170,000 tons of rubbish every day as a result of changing lifestyles and population increase. This equates to about 62 million tons annually, with a 5% yearly growth predicted [17].

Pressure to provide a sustainable approach to waste management and incorporate methods that would yield the most realistically feasible ecologically friendly alternative is mounting on waste management planners and regulators [18]. Growing urban populations and recent industrial and economic advancements are seen to be the main reasons behind rising garbage production and the ensuing contamination of the environment [19]. As waste generators within the waste management system, consumers provide a challenge to the implementation of waste reduction, waste separation, and effective waste handling rules if the social component is disregarded [20].

A few key components are needed for the complicated system of waste management to be sustainable. The three elements of sustainability—the environment, society, and economy—should be taken into consideration when evaluating the effects of our choices and actions in a holistic manner. Specifically, sustainable waste management uses a systems approach to look into the connections between these problems and aims to balance the sustainability aspects in order to make well-informed judgments [19]. Sustainability in waste management has received a lot of attention recently, as governments and businesses all over the world have pledged to reduce their environmental impact. The idea of a circular economy—where trash is seen as an asset rather than an issue—has gained popularity as a way to build a more sustainable future. Designing products and processes to reduce waste generation, promoting reuse and recycling, and recovering valuable resources from waste are all part of it [21]. Reduce, reuse, and recycle waste materials are greatly aided by the informal sector in low-income and middle-income nations like India. Approximately 34 million individuals worldwide are employed in the recycling industry. The informal sector is defined as low-tech, labour-intensive, small-scale, generally unregistered, uncontrolled manufacturing or supply of goods and services. It is pitiful to learn that between one million and two million individuals, or 1% to 2% of the city's entire population, are employed in the uncontrolled informal sector, where poor women and children may also be seen working in recycling operations [22].

Solid waste management (SWM), is seen as essential to urban environmental planning. Urban trash volumes are rising due to a number of factors such as rising living standards, changing demographics, increased consumerism, and population growth. According to World Bank projections, the quantity of municipal solid waste (MSW) generated from metropolitan areas is expected to double by the end of 2025, from 1.3 million tons in 2012. Annually, India generates 62 million tonnes of waste, including 15 lakh tonnes of e-waste, 0.17 million tonnes of biological waste, 7.90 million tonnes of hazardous waste, and 5.60 million tonnes of plastic waste. The Central Pollution Control Board (CPCB) estimates that by 2030, the country's garbage production will reach 165 million tonnes per year. The average daily amount of rubbish created by each individual in Indian municipalities ranged from 0.2 to 0.7 kilograms [23].

The development of infrastructure and systems planning will be significantly influenced by growing waste patterns. The improper handling and disposal of waste has a significant negative influence on the ecological footprint. In underdeveloped countries, waste is either burnt or dumped outdoors since land is readily available and the economy is viable. As per the 2014 UN Climate Summit [24], the third-largest source of emissions of anthropogenic methane is MSW landfills. Soil, surface water, and groundwater are contaminated by metals and other dangerous compounds discovered in landfill leachate. The development of integrated waste management systems is encouraged by the Municipal Solid Waste Management Rules of 2016, which place a strong emphasis on source-specific collection, home composting/bio-methanation, material and energy recovery, and wet and dry segregation. It is recommended that local authorities develop a strong strategy and infrastructure for solid waste management (SWM) in order to replace outdated and unsustainable practices [23, 24].

Programs for recycling that offer incentives are certain to expand into other markets. The recycling processes in place now, while functional, are inefficient. Household garbage recycling is still thought to be a labor-intensive task. Recyclers in unstable marketplaces struggle to discover viable ways to gather recyclable materials, while people around the world battle to recycle their garbage. This non-equivalent demand-supply connection results in an uneven situation in garbage collection and recycling because of the system's ineffective recycling services [25]. Under a traditional incentive-based recycling system, recyclable garbage from households may be collected in three ways: Residents sell their recyclable waste to door-to-door recycling collectors; residents exchange monetary rewards for delivering their recyclables to the designated pickup sites; or residents can receive incentives in return for recycling their materials in the proper smart recycling containers [26]. Similar systems like these have been in place in other cities in the current market. Nevertheless, these systems only incorporate simple data records and statistics as well as crude channels of communication between locals, recycling businesses, and government agencies. The goal of the smart system is to improve the affordability, sustainability, and cleanliness of metropolitan areas through incentive-based recycling services [25].

According to Esmaeilian [26], the vital subject of how smart cities may be utilized to handle waste management in particular and environmental challenges in general has to be covered in academic study. Thus, sustainable waste management has become essential to achieving sustainable development goals and moving toward a more sustainable society [27]. For smart cities management of waste is crucial. Therefore, the present chapter aims to evaluate the public apathy toward waste management and comparison of existing generalised waste management systems with smart sustainable waste management practices in Sama area, Vadodara City, Gujarat, India.

6.1.3 Indian Status of Solid Waste Management

The Central Pollution Control Board's (CPCB) 2020-21 annual report states [28], India produces 160038.9 tons of solid garbage per day (TPD), which is a massive quantity of rubbish. 152749.5 TPD are gathered out of this, demonstrating an amazing 95.4% efficiency rate. In contrast, 29427.2 TPD (18.4%) end up in landfills, while only 79956.3 TPD (50%) receive the appropriate processing. Remarkably, a sizeable portion of 50655.4 TPD (31.7%) is still missing (Table 6.1). The study also highlights the concerning finding that Delhi produces the most solid garbage per person, followed by Lakshadweep and Mizoram. On the other hand, Lakshadweep generates the least amount of solid waste among all the states in India. The report further highlights the trend in waste generation per capita, which shows a marginal decrease over the past six years (Figure 6.2). Additionally, the percentage of treated solid waste has increased significantly, rising from 19.96% in 2015-16 to 49.96% in 2020-21 (see Figure 6.3). Simultaneously, there has been a favorable trend in the percentage of solid waste intended for landfilling, which has dropped from 54% in 2015-16 to 18.4% in 2020-21 (see Figure 6.4). The analysis emphasizes a significant gap in solid waste management despite these gains, with a drop from 40.99% in 2015-16 to 31.70% in 2020-21. Figure 6.5 illustrates this tendency and emphasizes how urgently the problem needs to be resolved. There are now 1924 landfill sites known to exist; 305 of them are finished, 126 are being built, 341 are in use, 17 are exhausted, and 11 are covered. When it comes to locations, Maharashtra (382), Madhya Pradesh (341), and Karnataka (221) are in the lead. Maharashtra has the most waste sites—137—followed by Karnataka (52) and Uttar Pradesh (86). Twelve states and union territories (Gujarat, Assam, Bihar, Chhattisgarh, Haryana, Karnataka, Maharashtra, Manipur, Odisha, Punjab, Tamil Nadu, and Chandigarh) have not given city-specific information [28].

6.2 Material and Methodology

6.2.1 Study Area

Gujarat is a western Indian state that contains the city of Vadodara, the elegant metropolis of Gujarat State, which is situated between latitudes 22°18′N and longitude 73°16′E (Figure 6.6). It spans around 148.95 km^2 and is elevated to a height of 129 m (423 ft). The city experiences a moderately tropical climate. The city's temperature ranges from 8 - 46 °C. There

Table 6.1 India's state-wise solid waste generation and its management (TPD).

State	Solid waste generated	Collected	Treated	Landfilled
Andhra Pradesh	6898	6829	1133	205
Arunachal Pradesh	236.51	202.11	Nil	27.5
Assam	1199	1091	41.4	0
Bihar	4281.27	4013.55	NP	No
Chhattisgarh	1650	1650	1650	0
Goa	226.87	218.87	197.47	22.05
Gujarat	10373.79	10332	6946	3385.82
Haryana	5352.12	5291.41	3123.9	2167.51
Himachal Pradesh	346	332	221	111
Jammu & Kashmir	1463.23	1437.28	547.5	376
Jharkhand	2226.39	1851.65	758.26	1086.33
Karnataka	11085	10198	6817	1250
Kerala	3543	964.76	2550	NP
Madhya Pradesh	8022.5	7235.5	6472	763.5
Maharashtra	22632.71	22584.4	15056.1	1355.36 (Unscientifically disposed = 6221.5)
Manipur	282.3	190.3	108.6	81.7
Meghalaya	107.01	93.02	9.64	83.4
Mizoram	345.47	275.92	269.71	0
Nagaland	330.49	285.49	122	7.5

(Continued)

Table 6.1 India's state-wise solid waste generation and its management (TPD). (*Continued*)

State	Solid waste generated	Collected	Treated	Landfilled
Odisha	2132.95	2097.14	1038.31	1034.33
Punjab	4338.37	4278.86	1894.04	2384.82
Rajasthan	6897.16	6720.476	1210.46	5082.16
Sikkim	71.9	71.9	20.35	51.55
Tamil Nadu	13422	12844	9430.35	2301.04
Telangana	9965	9965	7530	991
Tripura	333.9	317.69	214.06	12.9
Uttarakhand	1458.46	1378.99	779.85	-
Uttar Pradesh	14710	14292	5520	0
West Bengal	13709	13356	667.6	202.23
Andaman & Nicobar Islands	89	82	75	7
Chandigarh	513	513	69	444
DDDNH	267	267	237	14.5
Delhi	10990	10990	5193.57	5533
Lakshadweep	35	17.13	17.13	Nil
Puducherry	504.5	482	36	446
Total	**160038.9**	**152749.5**	**79956.3**	**29427.2**

Here - NP: Not provided, DDDNH: Dadra and Nagar Haveli and Daman and Diu

is 900 mm of rain on average every year. The literacy rate in Vadodara is 78.92%. The population is 41.7 lakh [29]. Males constitute around 52% of the population, which is a greater percentage than females. Vadodara is a multilingual city where people speak Gujarati, Hindi, Urdu, Marathi, and English. This city is home to a diverse range of ethnic groups, such as Bengalis, South Indians, and North Indians. According to Vadodara Municipal Corporation (VMC), the quantity of municipal solid waste

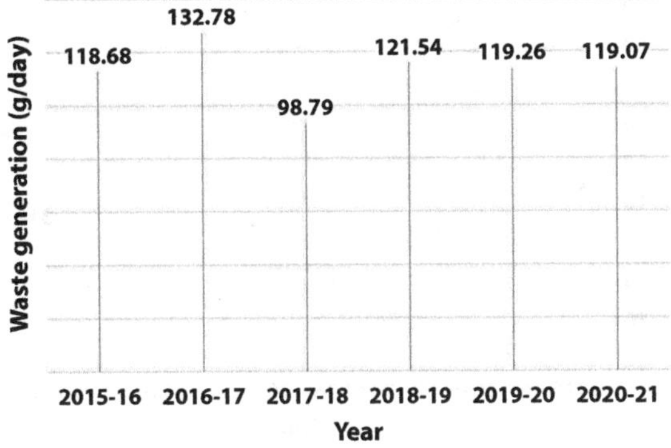

Figure 6.2 India yearly solid waste generation.

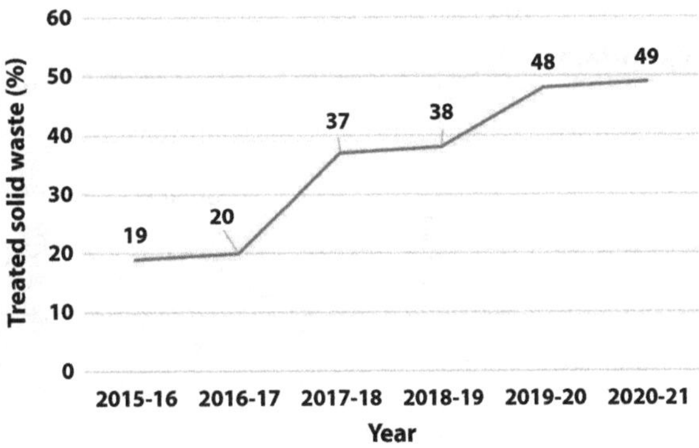

Figure 6.3 Situation of treated solid waste handling in India (%).

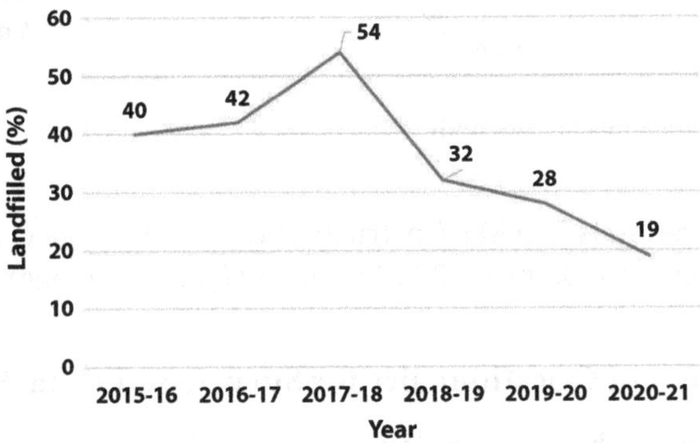

Figure 6.4 Management of solid waste landfills in India (%).

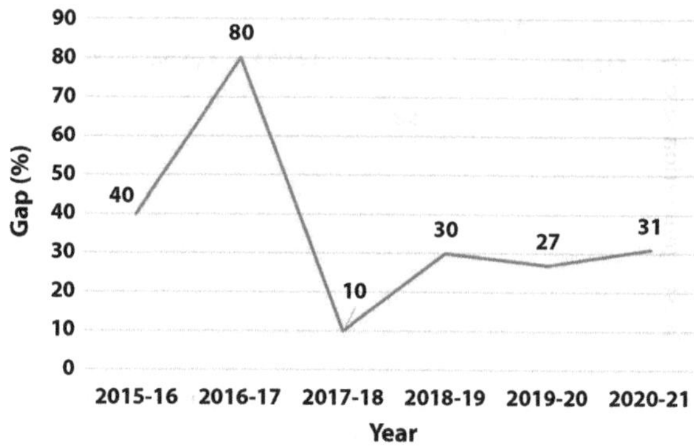

Figure 6.5 India's solid waste management gap (%).

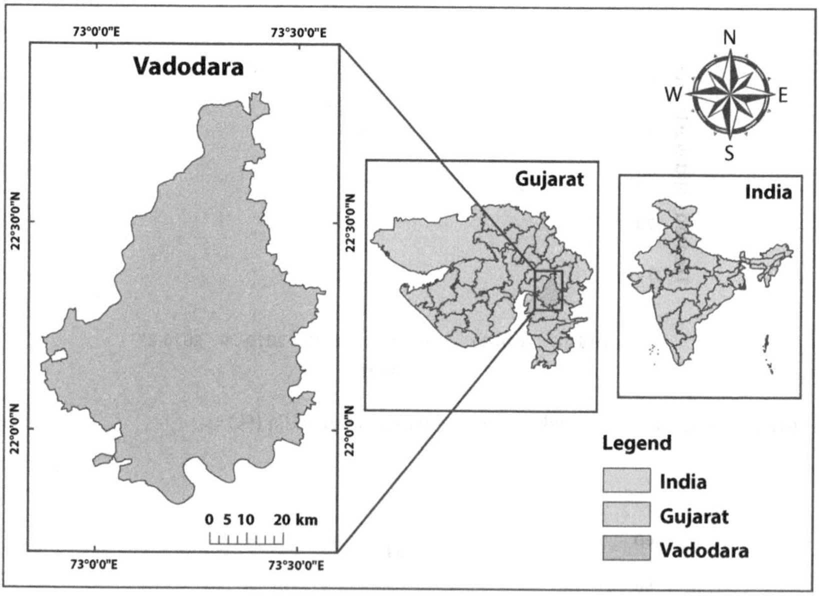

Figure 6.6 Location map of case study.

(MSW) generation is 750 MT (metric tonnes) per day. The collection and transportation of the same is 730 MT per day (yearly average) [30].

6.2.2 Design of Questionnaire for Survey, and Data Analysis

The major data gathering technique for the study was questionnaire surveys; secondary data sources included books, websites, journals, and other

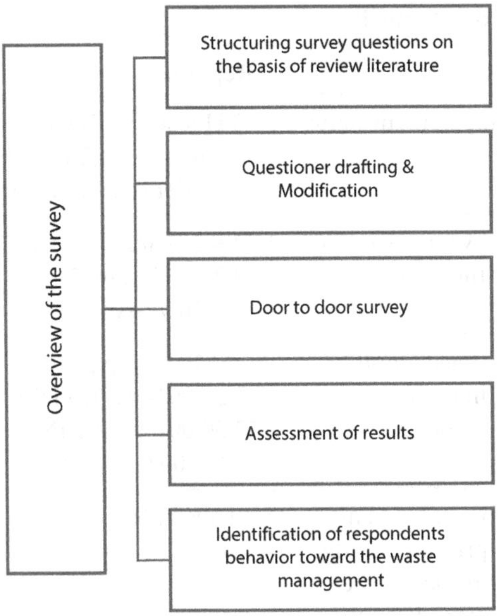

Figure 6.7 Outline of survey.

pertinent published materials (Figure 6.7). The purpose of the study was to find out how much information and willingness families in the Sama region of Vadodara, Gujarat, have about trash management and associated topics. The primary goal of the study was to gather quantitative data using two parts of questionnaires: information on the respondents' socio-demographics, as well as their level of knowledge and desire to manage trash (Table 6.2). Since Gujarati is the native language in Gujarat, India, the survey questions were structured in both Gujarati and English to make it easier and more efficient for respondents to understand. The data collection process involved visiting door-to-door at homes and conducting formal, direct first-hand interviews to gather accurate information. The respondents were assisted in filling out the questionnaires to avoid errors or misinterpretations. As a preliminary case study, the research randomly selected a total of 150 residents' homes from the Sama area, Vadodara.

6.2.3 Comparison Study of Waste Management Scenario in Vadodara

Located in the Sama area of Vadodara, the Kachre Se Azadi (KSA) foundation is an organization that provides a platform for promoting eco-friendly lifestyles and helping the environment by reducing, reusing, and recycling

Table 6.2 Survey questionnaire.

Categories	Content	Repones
Socia-demographic profile	Employment status	☐ Housewife ☐ Government employee ☐ Farmer ☐ Own business ☐ Student ☐ Private employee
	How long lived in the city?	☐ ≤ 2 years ☐ 5 years ☐ 10 - 20 years ☐ 21 - 30 years ☐ 31 - 40 years ☐ ≥ 50 years
	Average monthly household income?	☐ ≤ 10,000 INR ☐ 10,001-19,999 INR ☐ 20,001- 49,999 INR ☐ 50,001-99,999 INR ☐ ≥ 1,00,000 INR
Awareness and willingness	Do you have any prior knowledge in solid waste management?	☐ Yes ☐ No
	If yes, what is the source?	☐ Family ☐ Television ☐ Radio ☐ Public meetings ☐ Posters ☐ Academics ☐ Awareness campaign
	Type of solid waste comes out from your household?	☐ Paper ☐ Plastic ☐ Food waste ☐ Sanitary waste ☐ Tins/Cans ☐ Fibre Bags, ☐ Glass
	Do you have a public (common) dustbin for your flat/society?	☐ Yes ☐ No ☐ Unaware
	What would you say about your apartment complexes or your community's public trash can?	☐ Very good ☐ Good ☐ Bad ☐ Very bad

(Continued)

Table 6.2 Survey questionnaire. (*Continued*)

Categories	Content	Repones
	Do you believe that the way garbage is disposed of in your community is an issue?	☐ Yes ☐ No
	How would you rank the quality of solid waste management in your community?	☐ Very good ☐ Good ☐ Bad ☐ Very bad
	Do you find the generalized waste management system's waste management procedure satisfactory?	☐ Yes ☐ No
	Do you think that each and every person has an obligation to support sustainable development?	☐ Yes ☐ No
	Would you be willing to divide things into different bags for collection purposes if a recycling program was set up?	☐ Yes ☐ No

waste (Figure 6.8). During a survey period, we had the opportunity to collaborate with the KSA foundation to understand their approach to waste management, which is centred around eco-friendliness. By comparing the KSA waste collection process with the general waste collection process, one can get a better idea of the differences between them. The KSA

Figure 6.8 KSA foundation office, Sama, Vadodara.

concept has provided many people with employment opportunities and has resulted in numerous positive outcomes. It was established on August 15th, 2016, and has become a leading player in the category of eco-friendly product manufacturers in Vadodara. This esteemed business provides local people and visitors from various areas of Vadodara with a one-stop store. This business has amassed a sizable and steadily expanding clientele by operating under the philosophy that customer pleasure is just as vital as their goods and services.

6.3 Result and Discussion

6.3.1 Socio-Demographic Profile of Respondents

Solid waste management practices in developing economies face many challenges, including inadequate infrastructure and financial support, which results in poor waste management services; rising urbanization and population only serve to increase the amount of waste produced and the need for collection services in urban areas [31, 32]. The provided information outlines the socio-demographic profile of the respondents who participated in a survey (Figure 6.9). The survey team approached

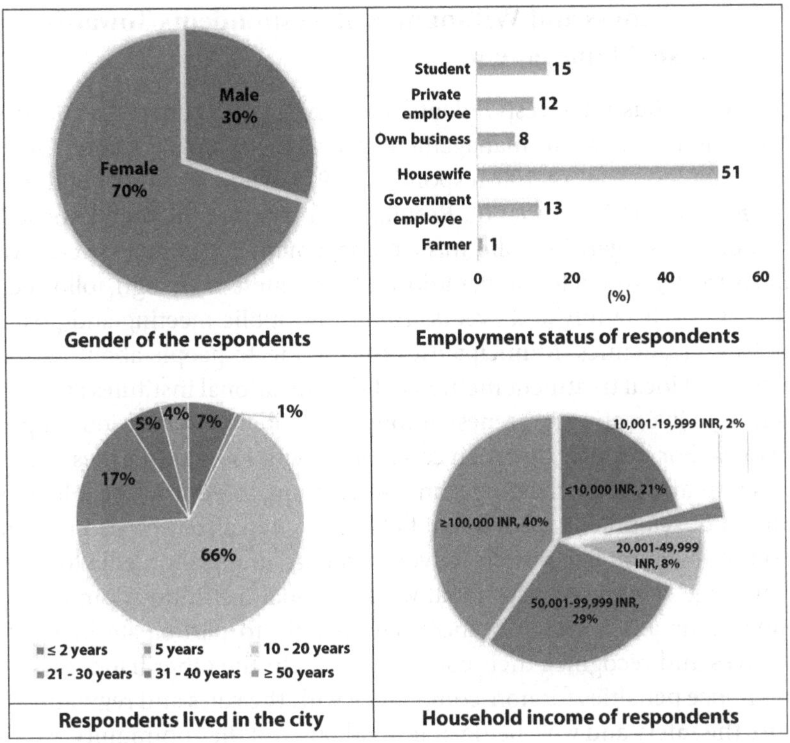

Figure 6.9 Socio-demographic profile of respondents.

150 homes randomly, out of which 100 individuals responded while 50 did not. Among the respondents, 70% were female and 30% were male. A majority of the respondents (51%) were housewives, followed by students (15%), government employees (13%), private employees (12%), business owners (8%), and farmers (1%). It was observed that around 66% of the respondents had been living in the city for 10-20 years, 17% for 21-30 years, 7% for ≤2 years, 5% for 31-40 years, 4% for ≥50 years, and 1% for 5 years. In terms of household income, 40% of the respondents had a yearly income of ≥1,00,000 INR, followed by 50,001-99,999 INR for 29%, ≤10,000 INR for 21%, 20,000-49,999 INR for 8%, and 10,000-19,999 INR for 2%. Furthermore, it was observed that waste composition significantly influenced waste management practices. Compared to lower-income groups, higher-income groups were found to utilize more packaged goods, which led to larger quantities of paper, glass, metals, plastics, and textiles [17, 33]. Regarding the low-income respondents in this study, it was observed that a variety of waste was found from their household.

6.3.2 Awareness and Willingness of Respondents Towards Waste Management

Figure 6.10 illustrates respondents' awareness and knowledge of waste management and waste management practices in their locality. On the knowledge level, out of 100 respondents, 92% were aware of solid waste management and 7% were not. Results demonstrated the high knowledge of respondents regarding solid waste management. Respondent were aware majorly (51%) from television, radio, and awareness campaign, followed by 22% from their family and events; 16% from public meeting and posters; 11% from academics. Municipalities must educate people about national policies and local treatment methods [34]. Educational institutes can play a crucial role in creating awareness among individuals about various important issues. For instance, they can collaborate with local authorities to organize seminars, group meetings, and workshops to educate people about the latest developments in different fields. They can also use various modes of communication like posters, advertisements, and print media to spread the message effectively. Additionally, educational institutions can leverage competitions and awards to encourage people to participate in various initiatives and recognize their contributions. On the other hand, they can also impose penalties for non-compliance with the rules and regulations to ensure the safety and well-being of individuals and the community at large. By working together, educational institutes and local authorities can create a safe and healthy environment for everyone to thrive in [35–37]. The waste from respondents' households was 76% paper, plastic, food waste and sanitary waste and 24% tins/cans, fibre bags and broken glass materials. It was found that household waste contains paper, glass, plastics, glass, bottles, tin, metals, ceramics and rubber [38, 39].

According to this survey, 43% of respondents had a common trashcan in their neighbourhood and 57% of respondents did not have one. When asked about their satisfaction with the garbage collection dustbin and service, for common dustbin condition, 79% had a negative response that includes 57% very bad to 22% bad condition. The remaining respondents were satisfied with dustbin conditions, including 12% very good to 9% good. It is possible that the low satisfaction level of the respondents is due to the inefficient use and management of the container system, as well as its low public acceptance. Poor public services, such as inadequate cleaning and disinfection of containers, can also contribute to this issue, leading to aesthetic and health problems. To successfully implement these systems, it is essential to provide proper municipal services, promote public awareness, and modify public attitudes and behaviour [40]. Out of 100,

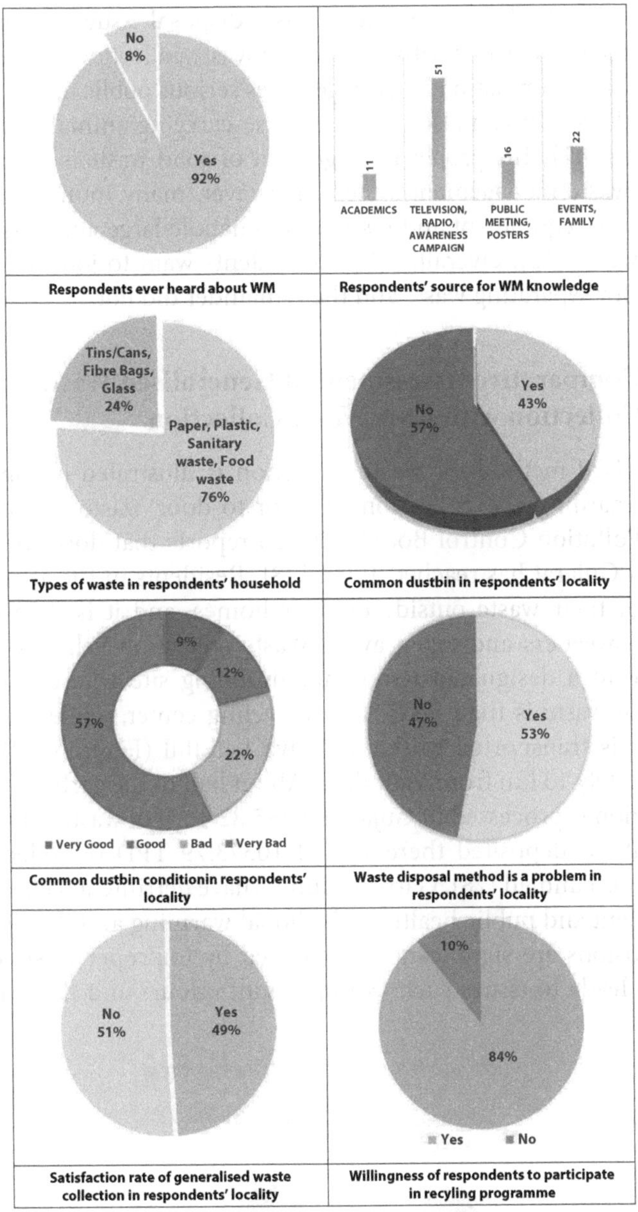

Figure 6.10 Awareness level and willingness of the respondents.

53% respondents think they had a waste disposal issue in their locality and 51% are not satisfied with generalised waste collection process in their locality. The accumulation of garbage poses serious public health and environmental risks. It can also attract disease-carrying animals like rodents and insects [41]. The proper management of solid waste is crucial to any effective waste management system. However, many municipalities lack the necessary equipment and resources to handle large amounts of disorganized waste [22]. Overall, 84% respondents want to join the recycling program for separating waste and the remainder did not.

6.3.3 Comparative Assessment of Generalised Waste Collection with KSA Waste Collection

A generalised method for waste collection is illustrated in Figure 6.11. Firstly, regarding the collection of door-to-door waste collection, the Central Pollution Control Board (CPCB) reports that door-to-door collection in Gujarat has reached 100% [28]. Residents in the area typically dispose of their waste outside of their homes, and it is then collected by street sweepers and taken away. Waste collection vehicles transport the waste to a designated temporary dumping site where it is sorted. Recyclable waste is then taken to a recycling center, while the remaining waste is transported to the Jambuva Landfill (Figure 6.12), located approximately 13 km from Vadodara. About half of the garbage produced in the region is processed in Gujarat; 3,385.82 TPD of waste is transferred to landfills or deposited there, out of 10373.79 TPD of collected solid waste that is handled [28]. Garbage dumps have detrimental effects on the environment and public health [42]. Global warming and the risk of fires and explosions are significantly influenced by improper waste disposal. This also leads to issues such as unpleasant odours and the leaching of

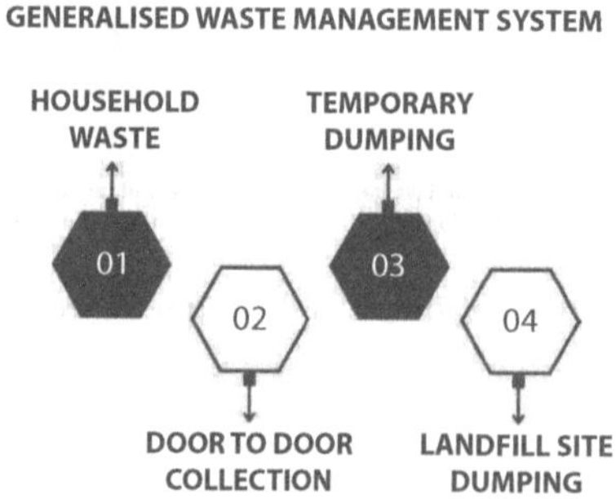

Figure 6.11 Outline of generalised waste management system.

Figure 6.12 Jambuva Landfill, Vadodara, Gujarat, India.

harmful chemicals into water reservoirs. These problems are particularly pronounced in India during the summer season when temperatures can reach an average of 45°C. The uncontrolled burning of waste at dump-sites without adequate measures produces fine particles that contribute to the formation of smog, causing respiratory diseases to become more prevalent [43]. Furthermore, summertime heat can accelerate the pace at which bacteria break down biodegradable organic matter and release a strong smell [44, 45]. Leachates, for instance, were not handled in 47% of landfills in China [46]. Lack of proper waste management has a negative impact on public health, as evidenced by an increase in infections of the nose, throat, bacteria, inflammation, breathing problems, anemia, asthma, decreased immunity, allergies, and other illnesses [43, 47]. Waste is carelessly dumped on roads, lawns, and bodies of water as a result of inadequate and insufficient SWM. Such customs were noted, for instance, in India [42, 48], South Africa [41, 49, 50], Pakistan [51], and Brazil [52], etc. Numerous studies reveal that drinking water supplies and other domestic uses are contaminated by leachate from landfill sites, posing serious health dangers to the general public [51, 53–56].

In KSA foundation waste management process (Figure 6.13), firstly they collect door-to-door dry waste that can be recycled, i.e., plastics, plastic bags, plastic bottles, cardboards, polythene bags, food packets, and other segregated dry wastes from the households. Secondly, on the basis of dry waste weight, incentive was given (Figure 6.14 a & b). The KSA foundation

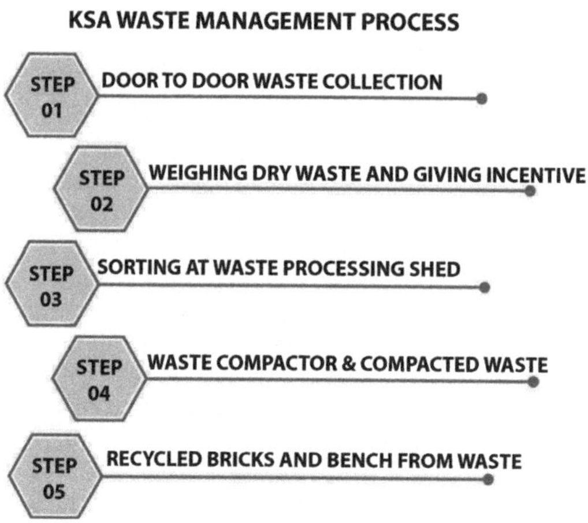

Figure 6.13 Outline of KSA waste management system.

Figure 6.14 (a) Weighing of dry waste (b) Soap given as an incentive.

provided incentives such as soaps to the individuals based on the quantities of dry wastes they provided. On the basis of dry waste, the incentive was given, i.e., 1kg soap for 1kg of dry waste (Figure 6.14b). Plans for source separation and recycling are significantly influenced by a trash tax that community members pay [57]. In this way, there are financial incentives for residents to recycle more, which reduces garbage production. The collected segregated dry wastes were transferred at KSA's waste processing shed, located in Dumad, Vadodara. After sorting of dry waste, the waste compressed with the help of waste compactor. At the end, tiles, bricks,

Figure 6.15 (a) Bio-degradable garbage waste, (b) Bench, (c) Brick, (d) Pen, (e) Notebook, (f) Compost.

benches, bamboo brush, pen pouch, pen stand, notebook were made (Figure 6.15). The end products which are made from dry wastes are used by Gujarat Air Force and Railways. For wet waste, they focus on composting with the help of their own patented instrument, i.e., Rocket composter. Converting waste into usable byproduct is good practice for waste reduction. ,Many researches have been conducted for converting waste into value-added products from a variety of waste such as plastic waste [58], citrus waste [59], agricultural biowaste [60], food waste [61], packaging waste [62], paper and pulp industry waste [63], etc.

6.4 Limitation of Study

There many aspects of smart cities but the present study only focused on the waste management aspect. The study was restricted to the Sama area; a broader study covering more city areas is recommended; this will reveal the thinking, attitude, awareness and involvement of the residents towards waste management. Future studies with a greater number of area coverage and study respondents are recommended.

6.5 Conclusion and Future Prospects

The government of India has proposed the Smart City India project with the aim of planning and implementing a future urbanized India. The project includes transforming many small or growing cities into smart cities. In a waste management case study, the respondents' knowledge and inclination were assessed, along with the distinctions between the KSA Foundation's sustainable waste management and the current, generalized waste management system. Although there are government policies for sustainable waste management, their implementation is a major concern. KSA Foundation is working on sustainable waste management, but they focus only on dry and wet waste management to create value-added products. The existing generalised waste management method needs to be urgently changed to scientifically design a waste management plan that meets national norms. The monitoring of civic duties, the strong enforcement of environmental laws, and the provision of sustainable trash collection, storage, and disposal are the obligations of local governments. It is imperative to address the health risks associated with inadequate solid waste management, which are manifested in numerous instances of rubbish littering within the research region. Waste restrictions should be enforced with penalties to deter unsustainable behavior. Additionally, local governments need to make sure that garbage collection services are provided in a sufficient geographic area, which includes underprivileged and minority areas [64, 65]. To achieve sustainable development and a circular economy, local governments must create stronger solid waste management policies that prioritize trash reduction, reuse, and recycling. The local governing body can involve KSA Foundation for the sustainable management of dry and wet waste, which will decrease some burden of recycling. The fact that residents are ignorant of waste management issues and treat garbage carelessly presents a problem for communities is one of the main causes for worry. It is the moral obligation of the people to accept and abide by the policies that the government enacts, regardless of their differences.

References

1. Keshavarzi, G., Yildirim, Y., Arefi, M., Does scale matter? An overview of the "smart cities" literature. *Sustainable Cities Soc.*, 74, 103151, 2021.
2. Bisello, A., *et al.*, *Smart and Sustainable Planning for Cities and Regions: Results of SSPCR 2019—Open Access Contributions*. Green Energy and Technology, Springer Cham, 2021.

3. Ramaprasad, A., Sánchez-Ortiz, A., Syn, T., A Unified Definition of a Smart City, Springer International Publishing, Cham, 2017.
4. Lombardi, P., *et al.*, Modelling the smart city performance. *Innovation: Eur. J. Social Sci. Res.*, 25, 2, 137–149, 2012.
5. Prasad, D. and Alizadeh, T., What Makes Indian Cities Smart? A Policy Analysis of Smart Cities Mission. *Telemat. Inform.*, 55, 101466, 2020.
6. Ahvenniemi, H., *et al.*, What are the differences between sustainable and smart cities? *Cities*, 60, 234–245, 2017.
7. Mundada, M. and Mukkamala, R.R., Smart cities for sustainability - an analytical perspective, in: *2020 Fourth World Conference on Smart Trends in Systems, Security and Sustainability (WorldS4)*, IEEE, 2020.
8. Yigitcanlar, T. and Kamruzzaman, M., Does smart city policy lead to sustainability of cities? *Land Use Policy*, 73, 49–58, 2018.
9. Burlacu, M., Boboc, R.G., Butilă, E.V., Smart Cities and Transportation: Reviewing the Scientific Character of the Theories. *Sustainability*, 14, 2022, DOI: 10.3390/su14138109.
10. Güneralp, B., *et al.*, Trends in urban land expansion, density, and land transitions from 1970 to 2010: a global synthesis. *Environ. Res. Lett.*, 15, 4, 044015, 2020.
11. Cattaneo, A., *et al.*, Economic and social development along the urban–rural continuum: New opportunities to inform policy. *World Dev.*, 157, 105941, 2022.
12. MHUA-GOI, Smart cities, 5 January 2024, [cited 2024 7 January].
13. MoUD-GOI, Smart Cities Mission Statement & Guidelines, India, 2015.
14. Gupta, K. and Hall, R.P., The Indian perspective of smart cities, in: *2017 smart city symposium prague (SCSP)*, IEEE, 2017.
15. Jawaid, M.F. and Khan, S.A., Evaluating the need for smart cities in India. *Int. J. Adv. Res. Sci. Eng. (IJARSE)*, 4, 1, 991–996, 2015.
16. Kavta, K. and Yadav, P.K., Indian Smart Cities and Their Financing: A First Look, Springer Singapore, Singapore, 2017.
17. Somani, P., Navaneethan, R.D., Thangaiyan, S., Integrated solid waste management in urban India: A mini review. *J. Phys. Conf. Ser.*, 1913, 1, 012084, 2021.
18. Salmenperä, H., *et al.*, Critical factors for enhancing the circular economy in waste management. *J. Cleaner Prod.*, 280, 124339, 2021.
19. Torkayesh, A.E., *et al.*, Integrating life cycle assessment and multi criteria decision making for sustainable waste management: Key issues and recommendations for future studies. *Renewable Sustainable Energy Rev.*, 168, 112819, 2022.
20. Azimi, A.N., Dente, S.M.R., Hashimoto, S., Social Life-Cycle Assessment of Household Waste Management System in Kabul City. *Sustainability*, 12, 2020, DOI: 10.3390/su12083217.
21. Hossain, R., *et al.*, Full circle: Challenges and prospects for plastic waste management in Australia to achieve circular economy. *J. Cleaner Prod.*, 368, 133127, 2022.

22. Kumar, A. and Agrawal, A., Recent trends in solid waste management status, challenges, and potential for the future Indian cities – A review. *Curr. Res. Environ. Sustainability*, 2, 100011, 2020.
23. Cheela, V.R.S., *et al.*, Pathways to sustainable waste management in Indian Smart Cities. *J. Urban Manage.*, 10, 4, 419–429, 2021.
24. IISD, A Summary Report of the UN Climate Summit 2014, 2014.
25. Zhou, J., *et al.*, Designing a smart incentive-based recycling system for household recyclable waste. *Waste Manage. (Oxford)*, 123, 142–153, 2021.
26. Laurieri, N., *et al.*, A Door-to-Door Waste Collection System Case Study: A Survey on its Sustainability and Effectiveness. *Sustainability*, 12, 14, 5520, 2020.
27. Seadon, J.K., Sustainable waste management systems. *J. Cleaner Prod.*, 18, 16, 1639–1651, 2010.
28. CPCB, Annual Report 2020-21 on Implementation of Solid Waste Management Rules, 2016. 2020-21, Central Pollution Control Board, New Delhi, pp. 288–446.
29. GOG, Vadodara at a Glance, Government of Gujarat, 28 December 2023, [cited 2024 7 January]; Available from: https://vadodara.nic.in/demography/#.
30. VMC, The usual approach to the carry out Solid Waste Management in the Vadodara City, [cited 2024 7 January]; Available from: https://vmc.gov.in/Department_SWM_Approach.aspx.
31. Jagaba, A.H., *et al.*, Sequencing batch reactor technology for landfill leachate treatment: A state-of-the-art review. *J. Environ. Manage.*, 282, 111946, 2021.
32. Sha'Ato, R., *et al.*, Survey of solid waste generation and composition in a rapidly growing urban area in Central Nigeria. *Waste Manage. (Oxford)*, 27, 3, 352–358, 2007.
33. Sridevi, V., *et al.*, A review on integrated solid waste management. *Int. J. Eng. Sci. Adv. Technol.*, 2, 1491–1499, 2012.
34. Sfez, S., De Meester, S., Dewulf, J., Solid waste management sector - Overview of assessment tools and methods. Externality of energy system View project Critical Raw Materials for the EU View project SEE PROFILE, May 2016, Doi 10.
35. McAllister, J., Factors influencing solid-waste management in the developing world, 2015.
36. Fernando, R.L.S., Solid waste management of local governments in the Western Province of Sri Lanka: An implementation analysis. *Waste Manage. (Oxford)*, 84, 194–203, 2019.
37. Aparcana, S., Approaches to formalization of the informal waste sector into municipal solid waste management systems in low- and middle-income countries: Review of barriers and success factors. *Waste Manage. (Oxford)*, 61, 593–607, 2017.
38. Lawal, I.M., *et al.*, Proximate analysis of waste-to-energy potential of municipal solid waste for sustainable renewable energy generation. *Ain Shams Eng. J.*, 15, 1, 102357, 2024.

39. Meena, M.D., *et al.*, Municipal solid waste: Opportunities, challenges and management policies in India: A review. *Waste Manage. Bull.*, 1, 1, 4–18, 2023.
40. Babaei, A.A., *et al.*, Household recycling knowledge, attitudes and practices towards solid waste management. *Resour. Conserv. Recycl.*, 102, 94–100, 2015.
41. Addo, I., Adei, D., Acheampong, E., Solid waste management and its health implications on the dwellers of Kumasi Metropolis, Ghana. *Curr. Res. J. Social Sci.*, 7, 3, 81–93, 2015.
42. Singh, D. and Kumar, S., Challenges of Municipal Solid Waste Management in Jalandhar, Punjab (India): A Case Study, in: *Proceedings of the 7th International Conference on Civil Engineering*, Springer Nature Singapore, Singapore, 2024.
43. Patel, J., Mujumdar, S., Srivastava, V.K., Municipal solid waste management in India – Current status, management practices, models, impacts, limitations, and challenges in future. *Adv. Environ. Res.*, 12, 2, 95–111, 2023.
44. Sankoh, F.P., Yan, X., Tran, Q., Environmental and health impact of solid waste disposal in developing cities: a case study of granville brook dumpsite, Freetown, Sierra Leone. *J. Environ. Prot.*, 2013.
45. Almulhim, A.I. and Abubakar, I.R., Understanding Public Environmental Awareness and Attitudes toward Circular Economy Transition in Saudi Arabia. *Sustainability*, 13, 18, 10157, 2021.
46. Zhuang, Y., *et al.*, Source separation of household waste: A case study in China. *Waste Manage. (Oxford)*, 28, 10, 2022–2030, 2008.
47. Abubakar, I.R., *et al.*, Environmental Sustainability Impacts of Solid Waste Management Practices in the Global South. *Int. J. Environ. Res. Public Health*, 19, 19, 2022.
48. Ramachandra, T.V., *et al.*, Municipal solid waste: Generation, composition and GHG emissions in Bangalore, India. *Renewable Sustainable Energy Rev.*, 82, 1122–1136, 2018.
49. Dlamini, S., Simatele, M.D., Serge Kubanza, N., Municipal solid waste management in South Africa: from waste to energy recovery through waste-to-energy technologies in Johannesburg. *Local Environ.*, 24, 3, 249–257, 2019.
50. Owojori, O., *et al.*, Characterisation, Recovery and Recycling Potential of Solid Waste in a University of a Developing Economy. *Sustainability*, 12, 12, 5111, 2020.
51. Akmal, T. and Jamil, F., Health impact of Solid Waste Management Practices on Household: The Case of Metropolitans of Islamabad-Rawalpindi, Pakistan. *Heliyon*, 7, 2021.
52. de Morais Lima, P. and Paulo, P.L., Solid-waste management in the rural area of Brazil: a case study in Quilombola communities. *J. Mater. Cycles Waste Manage.*, 20, 3, 1583–1593, 2018.
53. Hong, R.J., *et al.*, Life cycle assessment of BMT-based integrated municipal solid waste management: Case study in Pudong, China. *Resour. Conserv. Recycl.*, 49, 2, 129–146, 2006.

54. Dangi, M.B., Urynowicz, M.A., Belbase, S., Characterization, generation, and management of household solid waste in Tulsipur, Nepal. *Habitat Int.*, 40, 65–72, 2013.
55. Suthar, S. and Sajwan, A., Rapid impact assessment matrix (RIAM) analysis as decision tool to select new site for municipal solid waste disposal: A case study of Dehradun city, India. *Sustainable Cities Soc.*, 13, 12–19, 2014.
56. Gavilanes-Terán, I., *et al.*, Opportunities and Challenges of Organic Waste Management from the Agroindustrial Sector in South America: Chimborazo Province Case Study. *Commun. Soil Sci. Plant Anal.*, 46, sup1, 137–156, 2015.
57. Slavik, J. and Pavel, J., Do the variable charges really increase the effectiveness and economy of waste management? A case study of the Czech Republic. *Resour. Conserv. Recycl.*, 70, 68–77, 2013.
58. Kant, G., *et al.*, Chapter 7 - Waste plastic to fuel: properties, combustion characteristics and emission profile, in: *Renewable Diesel*, D. Kumar, B. Singh, S.K. Gupta (Eds.), pp. 167–189, Elsevier, 2024.
59. Sharma, K., *et al.*, Converting citrus wastes into value-added products: Economic and environmently friendly approaches. *Nutrition*, 34, 29–46, 2017.
60. Ren, L., *et al.*, Oriented conversion of agricultural bio-waste to value-added products - A schematic review towards key nutrient circulation. *Bioresour. Technol.*, 346, 126578, 2022.
61. Ng, H.S., *et al.*, Recent advances on the sustainable approaches for conversion and reutilization of food wastes to valuable bioproducts. *Bioresour. Technol.*, 302, 122889, 2020.
62. Radhakrishnan, S., Environmental Implications of Reuse and Recycling of Packaging, in: *Environmental Footprints of Packaging*, S.S. Muthu (Ed.), pp. 165–192, Springer Singapore, Singapore, 2016.
63. Salimbeni, A., *et al.*, Application of an integrated pyrolysis and chemical leaching process for pulper waste conversion into coal, hydrogen and chemical flocculating agent. *Waste Manage. (Oxford)*, 174, 549–557, 2024.
64. Olukanni, D.O., Pius-Imue, F.B., Joseph, S.O., Public perception of solid waste management practices in Nigeria: Ogun State experience. *Recycling*, 5, 2, 8, 2020.
65. Senekane, M.F., Makhene, A., Oelofse, S., A critical analysis of indigenous systems and practices of solid waste management in rural communities: The case of Maseru in Lesotho. *Int. J. Environ. Res. Public Health*, 19, 18, 11654, 2022.

7

Sensor Technologies for Environmental Data Collection

Adimulam Raghuvira Pratap and Suresh Annamalai*

Department of Networking and Communications, School of Computing, College of Engineering and Technology, SRM Institute of Science and Technology, SRM Nagar, Kattankulathur, Chennai, Tamil Nadu, India

Abstract

This paper explores the advancements and applications of sensor technologies in the domain of environmental data collection. With increasing concerns about climate change, pollution, and resource management, there is a growing demand for accurate and real-time environmental monitoring systems. Sensor technologies play a pivotal role in addressing this need by providing a cost-effective and efficient means of gathering data across various environmental parameters such as air quality, water quality, soil conditions, and biodiversity. This paper provides an overview of different types of sensors commonly used in environmental monitoring, including optical, chemical, biological, and physical sensors. Furthermore, it discusses the integration of sensor networks and data analytics techniques to enhance the capabilities of environmental monitoring systems. The challenges and opportunities associated with sensor technologies for environmental data collection are also addressed, including issues related to sensor calibration, data accuracy, power consumption, and data privacy. Finally, the paper concludes with a discussion on future trends and potential research directions in this rapidly evolving field.

Keywords: Environmental monitoring, sensor technologies, digital sensors, internet of things, machine learning

**Corresponding author*: prisu6esh@yahoo.com; suresha2@srmist.edu.in

A. Suresh, T. Devi, N. Deepa and Ali Kashif Bashir (eds.) Environmental Monitoring Using Artificial Intelligence, (133–166) © 2025 Scrivener Publishing LLC

7.1 Introduction

The socioeconomic and economic factors of our day are driving rapid and ongoing change. More people use the planet's limited natural resources on a daily basis. Our effect on the earth is growing as a result of urbanisation, energy consumption, garbage generation, and other factors, and it is not without repercussions. The world around us is becoming more polluted, which harms our physical and mental well-being. The activities of humans exert a massive influence on ourselves and our world, ranging from smog clouds in cities to contamination with unsafe waters for consumption to merely not having enough serenity to sleep peacefully. Significant changes in how we both reside as well as operate. Humans have also become far more passive throughout the past century. As the global population ages, improved lifespan puts additional strain on our healthcare systems. States have been compelled to curtail programmes like home healthcare aid to lessen rising expenses. The existing paradigm just will not be scalable in the future. We must also shift our basic method of the medical field, moving from a reactionary to a wellness-oriented approach. Here, the objective is to preserve individuals' health for as long as can be done while minimising the system's costs. It is critical to provide individuals with concrete information concerning their health and the things that influence it, whether favourably or adversely. Technologies that allow quick utilisation of data on exercise, food, and the environment, as well as cognitive data analysis and display, are crucial to promoting long-term behavioural change. The world is full of difficulties that require answers to handle critical global issues. Sensor technology can provide us with tools to handle many of the important global concerns of the twenty-first century.

7.2 Sensor Technologies

The detectors are employed in numerous current industrial processes, encompassing food fabrication and daily surveillance of operations like transportation, atmosphere, medicinal therapies, etc. They have been present for over a century, but contemporary ones with embedded ICT (information and communication technology) capabilities, known as smart sensors for short, have only been around for a little over three decades. Significant advancements have been achieved in computing, storage, energy efficiency, form factors, communication, and settings for designing software. These developments have coincided with a significant increase in perceiving capabilities. Since their introduction, biosensors have been used in a variety of goods for consumers, such as fertility, cholesterol, for example, gestation, and allergy testing. The rapid development and commercialization of inexpensive microelectronic mechanical systems sensors—like 3D accelerometers—has led to their integration into a wide range of components, including mobile phones and cars. Economical electronic sensors have accelerated the development of novel ambient sensing platforms, including ones used to monitor residential quality of the atmosphere. Widespread sensing was made possible by the abundance of low-cost sensors. Sensors and sensor networks may now be worn or incorporated into our living environments, including our clothing, with little impact on our everyday lives. The information via these monitoring devices enables new pre-emptive medical approaches by detecting possible difficulties early, such as heart disease risk, fatty liver, anaemia and so on. The sensors are becoming more utilised to track everyday behaviours, which include fitness, and provide rapid access to individual progress via mobile devices. Digital sensors now provide regular individuals with insights on the state of their water and air, as well as additional ecological issues like noise pollution. Publishing and socialising all of this information online contributes to the growing notions of citizen-led sensing. As individuals submit knowledge globally, public maps of factors such as air pollution over broad geographical regions may be created and shared.

7.3 Background of Sensing

Figure 7.1 shows the development of sensor technologies over time, highlighting key advancements and their impact on various fields. A detector is a tool that takes an intangible amount and transforms it into a signal that a tool or observation can interpret.

Critics regard the invention of the very first thermostats in 1883 to be the genesis of current technology for sensors. Sensors can take multiple forms and operate on various underlying concepts. Early sensors were fundamental devices that measured amounts of interest and produced a mechanical, electric, or optical output signal. Over the span of a decade, sensors' capabilities have greatly expanded with advancements in computers, ubiquitous communications, Web access, mobile gadgets that are smart, and integration into the cloud.

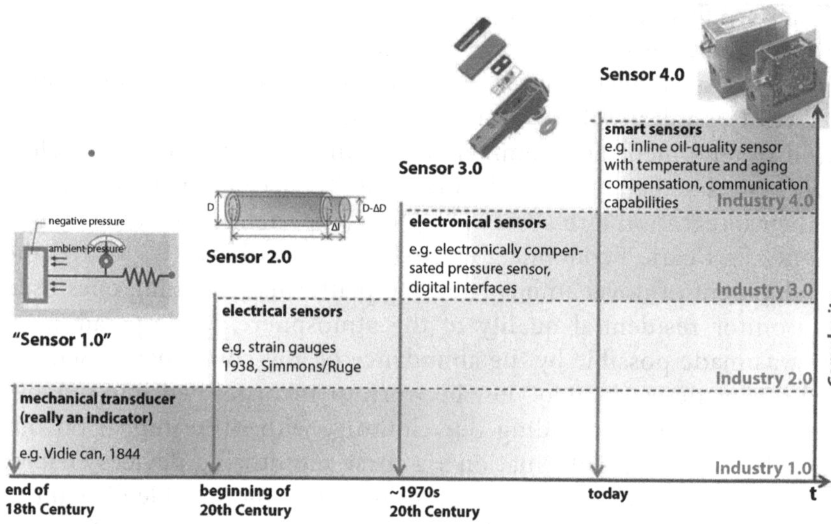

Figure 7.1 Evolutionary history of sensor technologies.

7.4 Types of Sensors

Figure 7.2 gives a block diagram of the sensing process as well as sensors' numerous different chemical, physical, and biochemical quantities, such as protein molecules, organisms, chemicals, gases, intensity of light, movement location, and noise. An apparatus that translates sensor information

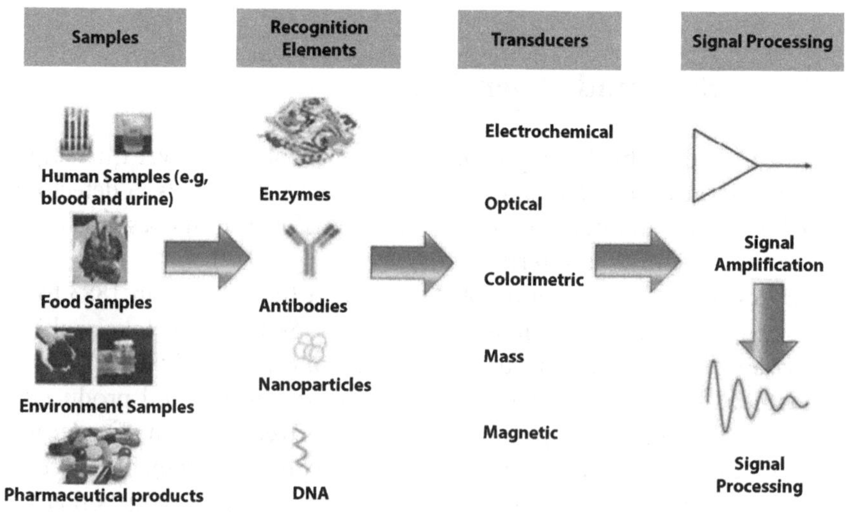

Figure 7.2 The sensing process.

into an electrical signal is called a transducer, which indicates the amount relevant to the viewer or the environment outside of it.

Table 7.1 lists various types of sensors. We can classify sensors into three types:

1. Passive and Active: Passive sensors can't detect the input on their own. Nevertheless, active sensors may detect input data autonomously.
2. Analog and Digital: Analogue sensors have a consistent response or output that is determined by one or more of its input factors. However, a digital sensor provides a binary response.
3. Scalar and vector: The scaler sensor assesses the input variables based only on their magnitudes. However, with a vector, the magnitude of the movement and aspect of the given input parameter dictates the sensor's response.

Electromechanical Sensors

Mechanical detectors operate by detecting alterations in a device or material due to an external stimulus, which leads to physical distortion of the component. Examples of such stimuli include motion, velocity, acceleration, and displacement, all of which result in measurable deformations of matter. The sensor's optoelectronic function promptly converts this input into an electrical output. Other options for output signals include thermal, optical, and magnetic.

The benefits of electrochemical sensors include the following.

- They have a high specificity for a particular gas or vapour in the parts-per-million range.
- They generate a linear output, consume little power, and provide superb resolution.
- They offer remarkable precision and repeatability.
- They are not harmed or compromised by other gases.

However, there are certain downsides connected with electrochemical sensors, including:

- They have a restricted temperature range.
- They have a short shelf life.
- They may exhibit cross-sensitivity to other gases.
- The sensor's lifetime reduces with increasing exposure to the target gas.

Table 7.1 Sensor types.

Sensor type	**Sensor**	**Type**
Mechanical sensor and electromechanical sensors	Sensor guage	Metallic Thin film Thick film Font Bulk Resistance
	Pressure	Piezoelectric Strain Gauge Potentiometric Inductive Capacitive
	Accelerometer	Piezoelectric Piezoresistive Capacitive MEMS Quantum Tunnelling Hall effect
	Gyroscope	Vibrating structure Dynamically tunned MEMS London moment
	Potentiometer	String Linear taper Linear slider Logarithmic Membrane
	Displacement	Resistive Capacitive Inductive
	Force	Hydraulic load cell Pneumatic load cell Magneto-elastic Piezoelectric Plastic deformation

(Continued)

Table 7.1 Sensor types. (*Continued*)

Sensor type	**Sensor**	**Type**
	Ultrasonic	Piezoelectric Magneto strictive
	Flow	Gas Fluid controller
Semiconductor sensor	Gas sensors	Optical gas sensor Calorimetric gas sensor Acoustic-based gas sensor Electrochemical gas sensor Metal oxide-based gas sensor Capacitance gas-based sensor
	Temperature sensors	Temperature sensor Thermistors RTD
	Magnetic sensors	Hall effect Fluxgate Capacitive proximity Magneto resistive Switch Angle
Optical sensors	Photo detectors	Photoresistor Photodiode Phototransistor Diode array Position sensitive diode CCD camera CMOS camera
	Infrared	IR LED IR photodiode Passive infrared sensor Transmissive infrared sensor IR proximity sensor IR temperature sensor IR spectroscopy sensor IR imaging sensor

(*Continued*)

Table 7.1 Sensor types. (*Continued*)

Sensor type	Sensor	Type
	Fiber optic	Humidity Temperature Pressure Strain
	Interferometers	Fabry-Perot
Electrochemical sensors	Potentiometric	Ion-Selective electrode (ISE) Coated-wire electrode Field-effect transistors (FET)
	Coulometric	Potent static coulometry Coulometric titration
	Aerometric	Clark-type Gas diffusion electrode Solid polymer electrode
	Conductometric sensor	Electrode Ultra
Biosensors	Electrochemical	Conductometric Impedimetric Coulometric Potentiometric
	Optical	Piezometric Thermometric Calorimetric

Semiconductor Sensors

The key features of these sensors include reliability, energy efficiency, long lifespan, and compact size. They find applications in various fields such as gas monitoring, pollution monitoring, breath analysis, domestic gas detection, temperature measurement, magnetism (e.g., magnetometers for six degrees of freedom applications), and optical sensing. Transistor sensors utilize solid-state memory, which allows for faster data access compared to other storage methods. Data can be written to or retrieved from solid-state memory in just a few nanoseconds, while traditional storage devices like hard disks take milliseconds to access data. Semiconductor devices are also more cost-effective. However, it's important to note that semiconductor devices are highly sensitive to temperature changes.

Optical sensors

Figure 7.3 illustrates the process of optical sensors, including light generation, detection, and signal processing. Optical sensors detect light waves, or photons, in the visible, infrared, and ultraviolet (UV) areas. They work by measuring variations in the intensity of light, whether emitted or absorbed, in proportion to a certain parameter of interest. They may also monitor changes in the phase of light beams induced by interactions or interference effects. Another common tactic is to identify when a light source is present or absent. This concept is commonly applied to sensors for automated doors and gates in order to guarantee clear paths. They are commonly employed in industrial applications to detect the presence or absence of things and to monitor liquid and material levels in tanks as well as production lines. Stepper motors and optical sensors are employed in applications where movement detection and encoded are necessary.

The potential for both online and real-time applications, low detection limits, quick reaction times, a comparatively high signal-to-noise proportion, and high responsiveness, and affordability are some of the advantages of optical sensors. However, one of the main limitations of these sensors is the lack of adequate or generic chemical probes. It is also possible to enhance the threshold of detection, which is approximated to be around 10-11 and 10-13 mol per litre of concentration in some circumstances. Utilizing sensor arrays instead of a single sensor would be the most effective approach to enhance selectivity. Additionally, future advancements in light-detecting systems primarily focus on improving the stability and reversibility of the sensitive layers.

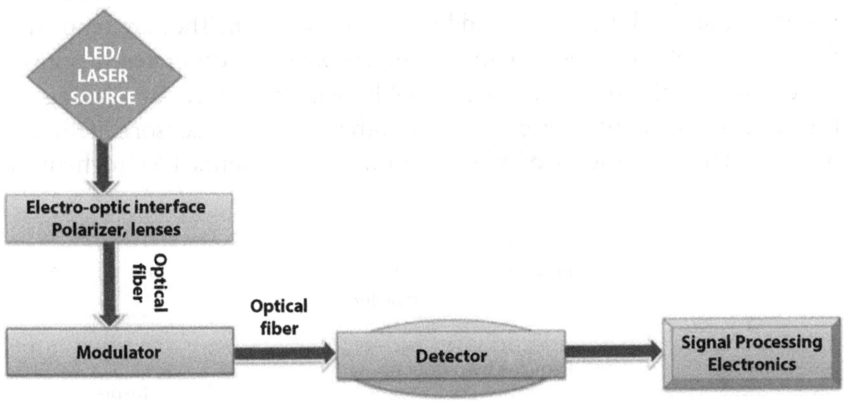

Figure 7.3 Process of optical sensors.

Electrochemical Sensors

An electrochemical detection device has three primary parts: a detection or active electrode, an analogue reference electrode, and the opposite electrode. Usually, a liquid or solid electrolyte is in interface with the aforementioned electrodes. Electrochemical sensors are used at low temperatures (<140° C) to detect pH, conductivity, ions that are dissolved, and gas dispersion. Solid electrolyte sensors, on the other hand, are used to monitor temperatures beyond 500° Celsius, such as exhaust fumes and molten metals. The basic premise of electrochemical detectors is to monitor the electrical conductivity of the material being analysed. They can be classed according to the specific measuring method utilised.

Electrochemical detectors have multiple benefits, notably minimal power consumption, a high level of sensitivity, superior reliability, and resistant to outdoor toxic effects. However, environmental factors, notably temperature, have a significant impact on their sensitivity, selectivity, and stability. Environmental circumstances have a considerable impact functional lifetime; in humid and hot conditions, for instance, a sensor's functional life is drastically shortened. Gas sensors may have cross-responsiveness to other gases. The lifespan of the sensor may potentially be shortened by oversaturating it with the target species. They can be categorized based on the particular measurement technique that is applied.

Figure 7.4 illustrates the process of electrochemical sensors, where a redox reaction occurs between the analyte and electrode, generating a measurable electrical signal. Electrochemical detection devices can detect a specific gas or vapour in parts per million. The amount of selectivity is determined by the type of detector, the specific kind of gases targeted, and the level of gas that the sensor is meant to detect. These sensors produce a linear output, use little power, and have high resolution. They are renowned for their exceptional repeatability and precision. Once calibrated to a given concentration, the sensor will dependably deliver an accurate reading for the target gas without interference from other gases. The sensor's lifetime is unaffected by the presence of other environmental vapours. Electrochemical

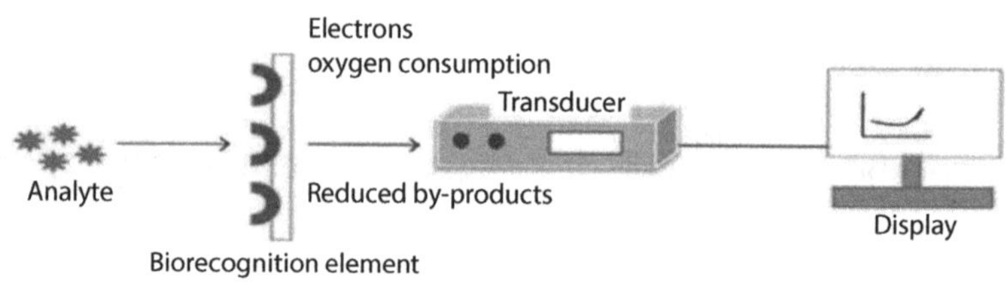

Figure 7.4 The process of electrochemical sensors.

sensors are often more cheap than other gas detection devices. Compared to infrared and PID technology, electrochemical detection devices are quite inexpensive. However, there are several drawbacks to using electrochemical sensors for detection. These include a small or restricted temperature range, a short shelf life, and cross-sensitivity to other gases. Furthermore, it is worth noting that the sensor's lifetime reduces as exposure to the target gas rises.

Biosensors

Biosensors are instruments that utilize biochemical pathways to identify a specific substance of interest in various types of samples, including chemicals, the environment, and biological materials. These sensors contain a bios component, such as an enzyme, antibody, nucleic acid, or hormone, that is immobilized within a self-contained device. The biosensor's biological component is fixed in a way that preserves its ability to function.

To produce immobilisation, many approaches are used, such as membrane trapping using physical bonding, noncovalent or covalent binding, and electroactive substances. Immobilisation technique guarantees that the biological material is in touch with the transducer. When a substance called analyte interacts with the immobilised biological substance, a transducer produces a quantifiable output, which can be a shift in color, mass, or flow. It is also possible to employ indirect approaches, in which a product is formed through a biochemical reaction between the analyte and the sensor material. This reaction produces quantifiable quantities like heat, gas, electrons, and hydrogen ions, which may be measured.

Figure 7.5 depicts the process of biosensors, which involve a biorecognition element interacting with a target analyte, resulting in a measurable

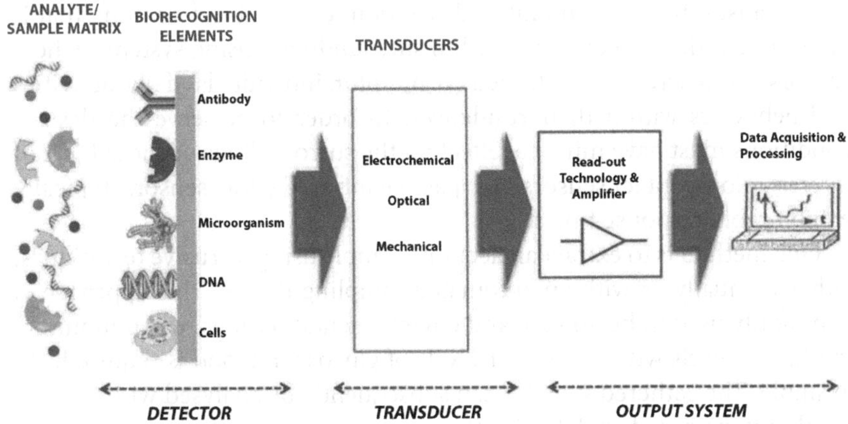

Figure 7.5 The process of biosensors.

signal. Different sensor types offer varied degrees of precision, sensitivity, specific and adaptability to a variety of environmental circumstances. Cost is also an issue to consider. Generally, more costly sensors include sophisticated features that improve their performance. There are three ways to use transducers to determine quantities of interest:

- In order for this approach to yield results, physical contact is essential. This technique can detect various substances such as liquids, gases, and even the human body. The implementation of these sensors has an impact on the condition of the sample to a certain degree.
- When detecting touch with the body, it is critical to consider comfort and biocompatibility. For example, prolonged contact with sensors might cause skin discomfort. Furthermore, sensor fouling can be an issue, making it critical to identify solutions to reduce these impacts, particularly for sensors that must remain in place for lengthy periods of time. There may also be constraints to the size and design of touch sensors. Applications for fitness and medical frequently make use of proximity sensing, notably to measure physiological variables such as electrocardiography (ECG), electromyography (EMG), and electroencephalography (EEG). Contact sensors' reaction time is determined by the speed with which the necessary quantity is conveyed to the measurement spot.

Noncontact sensing removes the requirement for physical interaction with the quantity being measured. The benefit of using this technique is that it causes the least amount of disruption to the subject or thing that is being assessed. It's frequently used in surrounding sensing systems, where sensors are discreetly positioned to monitor individuals' daily activities and behaviors within their residences. In order to preserve the desired conditions must have minimal effect on the surroundings or the subject of interest. Non-contact sensors, like passive infrared (PIR) sensors, typically exhibit rapid response times.

One method is to extract an accurate sample using intrusive techniques, either manually or with an automated sampling device. This approach is commonly used in healthcare and environmental settings, when monitoring E. coli levels within water or levels of glucose in blood is required, for example. The gathered samples can subsequently be analysed with sensors or laboratory-based analytical instruments.

The primary components of a sensor

The sensor element responds to physical stimuli, which can be of a mechanical, electrical, chemical, or biological nature. The transducer converts the gathered data into a measurable electrical signal. Signal conditioning components, such as amplifiers and filters, enhance the electrical signals. Interface electronics transform analog signals into digital signals that can be interpreted by a processor.

7.5 Applications of Sensors

Sensing technology is continually changing to meet technological breakthroughs and commercial objectives. It is critical to plan for these shifts and consider how sensing technology might be used to create more imaginative solutions.

A solid understanding of sensor technology is essential for individuals working in industrial and technical fields. Sensors play a pivotal role in creating innovative solutions and driving value. Each type of sensor has its own unique benefits and limitations. When choosing which sensor technology to utilize, it is important to consider the specific use case or application. This decision-making process may involve weighing various factors that may sometimes contradict each other. It is crucial to carefully evaluate the type of detector, hardware possibilities, container design, and usage interface in accordance with the project's particular needs.

1. Environmental Monitoring: Innovative detectors monitor environmental factors, such as soil quality, ambient temperature, and moisture. They use real-time weather data and projections to create the optimal watering plan for the yard. In the field of healthcare, these sensors are critical to digitising the sector, increasing clinic efficiency, and improving patient outcomes. Furthermore, sensors help to monitor the state of smart warehouses, allowing for faster check-ins and check-outs while simplifying day-to-day operations. Sensors are also becoming more prevalent in industrial mining to help firms optimise their operations.
2. Air: Air monitoring devices can be supplied with a variety of sensors. These types of sensors can detect a variety of atmospheric parameters, including solitary gas species, particulate matter, hydrocarbons, and metals. The specific sensors used are determined by the regulations governing air quality monitoring. Regulatory monitoring frequently requires the employment of

costly analytical tools, such as spectroscopic analysis. For example, UV fluorescence may be used to monitor sulphur dioxide, whereas O3 absorption of UV light at 254nm is used to monitor ozone. Because of the expensive cost of these devices, only a few sophisticated monitoring stations are installed in each geographic region. This leads to a low in-density deployment, which reduces the resolution of the acquired data. Air quality, particularly in densely populated metropolitan areas, may be impacted by a variety of variables such as individual emission sources, traffic patterns, and building types. The research community is becoming more interested in adopting high-density sensor deployments to collect precise information regarding air quality, particularly now that low-cost sensors are widely available. Air quality and environmental monitoring use a variety of sensing innovations, notably, optic and fibre optic sensors, and electrochemical sensors.

3. Health Care and Medical: Sensors enable the monitoring of individuals to prevent accidents resulting from falls, excessive work, heavy machinery, and various other factors. By combining sensors with advanced cognitive abilities and external resources like the environment and weather, there is the potential to completely transform our current lifestyle and work practices. Wearable technology utilizes the Internet of Things to gather, integrate, and analyze sensory information. In such systems, a sensor identifies, measures, and provides information on a specific element in the physical world.
4. Water: Sensors are used to monitor the amount of water vapour and other gases in the atmosphere. In both commercial and residential settings, moisture meters are frequently utilized in HVAC systems. Numerous industries employ such sensors., including clinics and weather stations that are used for environment observation and forecasting. Pressure sensors, on the other hand, detect changes in the pressure of gas and fluids. When pressure fluctuations occur, these sensors detect the changes and send the data to linked systems. Everyday circumstances, such as leak testing caused by degradation, rely on pressure sensors. Pressure sensors are very important in water systems since they detect pressure fluctuations or dips accurately.
5. Sound: As urbanization continues to expand and people live closer together, the problem of smog and congestion grows increasingly prevalent. The impact of noise on one's quality

of life can range from mere annoyance to significant physiological or psychological consequences. Noise pollution refers to unwanted sounds that disrupt our daily lives and activities. It can manifest as both temporary disturbances and constant nuisances. Common sources of noise pollution include vehicles, trains, airplanes, industrial activities, noisy neighbors, and recreational activities. Efforts to monitor and control noise pollution are becoming more stringent. In order to make this information easily accessible to the public, the European Directive now requires member states to periodically release accurate maps of noise levels in urban areas.

6. Soil: Various portable equipment is widely used to assess the properties and state of the soil. The field-portable FP-XRF apparatus is a frequently used instrument for contamination with metals detection. This approach has the benefit of requiring just little sample preparation, such as acid digestion. However, it is confined to analysing bulk concentrations and is best effective when an element is present in large quantities in the sample. Temperature and moisture metres, as well as penetrometers for measuring soil strength, are other popular soil analysis equipment. While these instruments often produce reliable data, they can only measure one moment in time.
7. Monitoring Recreational Activity: With growing awareness about personal health, there is an increasing demand for ready-to-use sensors that were previously limited to professional use. Consumers are now utilizing these sensors to monitor their advancement in health campaigns focused on preventing obesity and improving fitness levels. Body-worn heart rate and blood pressure monitors, integrated activity trackers, and pulse oximeters are gaining popularity for evolving field. These are combined with traditional active devices like pedometers, which are connected to software programs that provide activity analysis and encourage goal-oriented behavior.
8. Personal Safety Like Home Security: Sensors play a crucial role in safeguarding homes, as they are designed to provide timely notifications and trigger fire alarm systems. They greatly improve the chances of escaping any potential accidents. A variety of sensors are used, including location, duration, noise, and material sensors. This not only aids manufacturers in improving their processes but also promotes the well-being of employees.

9. Activity and Location Detection: In retail settings, sensors are frequently utilized to identify motion. By analyzing a customer's location, a store is able to text specific offers or incentives to their cell phone. To verify parking availability, proximity sensors are used in parking garages as well as larger venues like arenas, stores, and ports. Moisture detection sensors can be used to forecast threats to a property, such as the possibility of a pipe freezing or a burst sewage line. These sensors are also capable of detecting leaks within the house and assisting with prompt repairs.
10. Gas detection and surveillance: Ensuring the safety of individuals is of utmost importance when it comes to detecting hazardous gases. Gas sensors play a crucial role in monitoring and accurately measuring higher-than-normal levels of gas, providing a safe environment for those working with and in close proximity to such harmful gases. The field of indoor air quality also relies on gas sensor technology to effectively assess the presence and quantity of gases.

7.6 Challenges of Sensors

a. Challenges in measuring resistance

- Resistance of the leads: The wires that connect to the resistive sensor element possess their own resistance. This resistance can potentially introduce errors to the measurement, and its temperature dependence is significant enough to be of concern.
- Output impedance: The measuring network is characterized by a certain resistance, which essentially sets a minimum value for a connected resistance across the output terminals without altering the output voltage.

b. Challenges in measuring of capacitance

Stray capacitance happens when any wire in a real-world setting has a low capacitance in comparison to the ground. While working with a sensor whose output resembles a capacitor, it is critical to use caution while connecting the sensor to the remainder of the circuit. These stray capacitances cause additional capacitance in the measurement circuit, which can lead to inaccuracies.

7.7 Environmental Sensors

7.7.1 Standards and Regulations

As our awareness of our well-being and the planet's well-being grows, we develop a stronger interest in evaluating their interconnectedness. We may assess the quality of the drinking water we consume, the atmosphere that we inhale, the weather, and the noise levels around us by keeping an eye on the surroundings. Both commonly available equipment for hobbyists and highly calibrated professional devices can be used to take these types of measurements. These gadgets offer data that has the potential to greatly affect our lives. For this reason, it is essential that the devices that alert us to tainted water or abnormally elevated carbon monoxide levels do so in a precise, reliable, and timely manner.

To quantify the parameters to be measured, the measuring procedure, and data reporting, norms and standards have been developed. It is essential to comprehend these requirements and assess the sensors' capacity to meet them while developing applications. For instance, if a cheap carbon dioxide sensor can't accurately detect atmospheric levels of carbon dioxide within the range specified by indoor air quality recommendations, it can't be used in an office environment. Cheap sensors frequently fall short of the requirements. However, research is underway to see if numerous less accurate sensors may compensate for one another, producing important information similar to that of a single controlled sensor.

Environmental Noise

The phrase "environmental noise pollution" pertains to an excess of undesired or bothersome noise outdoors that has a negative impact on the well-being of individuals and wilds. Annoying sound leads to irritation, aggression, heightened stress levels, sleep disturbances, and in extreme instances, auditory impairment. The primary culprits of outdoor environmental noise are typically traffic, construction, industrial activities, and certain recreational pursuits. Indoor noise pollution can also occur, although its causes vary. Indoor noise pollution regulations may vary based on the indoor space's function. Sound restrictions are designed to regulate the amount, duration, and the noise's origin. The permitted degree of noise may also change depending on the moment of time and the disturbance's location: acceptable noise levels are much lower at night or in quieter places than during the day or in noisy locations. Sound level metres are used to measure noise levels. Table 7.2 provides the maximum allowable concentrations (threshold limit values) for different air pollutants. These devices

Table 7.2 Threshold limit values for several air pollutants.

Hazardous air pollutant	Threshold limit value (ppm)	
	8-hour weighted average	15-minute short-term exposure limit
Benzene	0.5	2.5
Xylenes	100	150
Trichlorethylene	50	100

detect sound-induced pressure changes, amplify and filter the signal, and offer decibel reading.

Before every set of readings, these instruments need to be calibrated in the field using a calibrator. The volume meter and its calibrator need to be compliant with ISO standards and undergo an annual calibration in a laboratory. Table 7.3 outlines the World Health Organization's guidelines for community noise exposure. The two main standards for detecting noise in the air are ISO 9613 and ISO 1996-2. These two specifications describe how to quantify noise from various sources. The two most widely used metrics for noise are the rated level of noise (LAr,T), which adds a penalty for more annoying tonal and impulsive noise, and the equivalent

Table 7.3 WHO noise community noise guidance.

Environment	Critical health effect	Sound level dB(A)	Time (hours)
Outdoor living areas	Annoyance	50 to 55	16
Inside bedrooms	Sleep disturbance	30	8
School classrooms	Disturbance of communication	35	During class
Industrial, commercial and traffic areas	Hearing impairment	70	24
Ceremonies and entertainment	Hearing impairment	100	4
Music through earphones	Hearing impairment	85	1

continuous sound level (ECSL), which outlines altering disturbances from all sources in terms of a single noise level over the sample period.

Ambient Air Quality

Proximity to particulate debris, liquid droplets, or gases in the atmosphere can be harmful to human health. Air pollution includes a wide variety of contaminants, both man-made and natural, such as those emitted from engine emissions and radon gas. Both mobile (vehicles, trucks, and airplanes) and stationary (manufacturing plants, refineries, and power plants) sources can produce these contaminants. There are a number of regulations in place to deal with these sources, including the European Paints Convention and the Industrial Emissions Directive, as well as limitations on emissions from maritime shipping.

Drinking water

The Public Water System Regulations, known as the National Primary Drinking Water Regulations, are a set of enforceable requirements. Table 7.4 lists the maximum allowable levels of disinfection byproducts in drinking water as set by the U.S. Environmental Protection Agency (EPA). These regulations were created expressly to protect the general public's health by minimizing the number of pollutants in drinking water. Table 7.5 lists the maximum allowable levels of disinfectants in drinking water as set by the U.S. Environmental Protection Agency (EPA). Although public water systems are the main target of these laws at the point of use, they are frequently used by regulatory authorities to monitor the quality of groundwater at the source.

Table 7.4 EPA national primary drinking water standards for byproducts disinfections.

Contaminant	Maximum contaminant level goal (mg/L)	Maximum contaminant level (mg/L)
chlorite	.8	1.0
Haloacetic Acids (Haas)	n/a	0.060
Total Trihalomethanes (TTHMs)	n/a	0.08

Table 7.5 EPA national primary drinking water standards for disinfections.

Contaminant	Maximum contaminant level goal (mg/L)	Maximum contaminant level (mg/L)
Chloramines (CI_2)	MRDLG=4	MRDLG=4.0
Chlorine (CI_2)	MRDLG=4	MRDLG=4.0
Chlorine Dioxide (CIO_2)	MRDLG=0.8	MRDLG=0.8

7.7.2 Drivers of Environmental Sensing

Multiple causes, notably technology breakthroughs, changes in culture, and financial issues are driving up interest in and usage of environmental sensors. As sensor costs fall and accuracy increases, they become more practicable for on-site monitoring. Furthermore, their adjustable nature enables creative procedures and sample methods that may be difficult and costly using standard methodologies.

Pricing

For on-site surveillance or instantaneous evaluation in laboratories, current environmental monitoring systems rely on expensive analytical devices. Mass spectrometers (MS) and gasoline chromatography (GC) are both highly sensitive and exact techniques, but they come at a price: hundreds to many thousands of euros. On the other hand, detectors built using visual, electrochemical in nature, and semiconductor-based methods are starting to be available for tens or even lower hundreds of dollars. These devices may be combined to construct discrete, self-contained platforms that serve as the foundation for distributed sensor networks that are wireless. With proper calibration procedures, these sensing devices offer inexpensive proxy to centralised significant changes for specific applications.

Smartphones

The growth of cell phones provides a low-cost solution for climate sensing as well as information gathering. In certain circumstances, cell phones act as the sensor platform. For instance, programs that monitor ambient noise can take advantage of the built-in microphone included in every smartphone. The embedded GPS feature enables data geotagging, which is critical for mobile crowdsourcing applications. Sharing data via email, SMS, or the internet is extremely helpful to regional environmental monitoring organizations. Smartphones provide a single appearance for all data-related tasks, and as more wirelessly connected ecological sensors are accessible, their use in corporate and citizen-oriented apps will only increase.

Public Sensing

People want to monitor their environment more and more as sensor systems advance and become more accessible. Taking an active role in the collection and processing of ecological information can result in shifts in perceptions, attitudes, behaviours, and overall involvement. Concerns about atmosphere, water, and food toxic, which are regularly raised in the media, as well as the obvious impacts of pollution, such as haze in cities, contribute to this increased concern. People may be particularly concerned about being exposed to environmental toxins while participating in outdoor sports such as running or jogging, especially in cities.

Online Communities

Environmental surveillance often employs on-site sampling, commonly referred to as grab sampling. Before being returned to the testing facility for examination, the specimens are collected in labeled containers or gas bags and stored in a controlled atmosphere. But this approach is time-consuming, expensive, and might not accurately depict the amount of interest, especially in dynamic contexts. with fluctuating contaminants. The delayed detection of issues could have potential implications for public health. To ensure consistent and reproducible samples, it might be necessary to integrate sensing with mechanized harvesting systems.

7.7.3 Network and Communications Technologies in Conjunction with Environmental Sensing

Numerous sensors for the environment are wirelessly capable of communicating via wireless internet, 3G/4G, or low-power devices Zigbee. When Zigbee-driven nodes are used in a mesh network topology with multihop regulations, a wider global area of coverage can be achieved than with a traditional star topology. Outside, Wi-Fi has a range of about 100 to 200 meters (300 to 600 feet), whereas 3G and 4G have far greater ranges.

For environmental applications, the capacity to place sensors over large geographic areas is essential. But in figuring out how densely to deploy, the economic factor must be taken into account in order to achieve effective communication. To achieve dependable connectivity, a compromise needs to be made when creating a network that has redundant communication fields between a large number of devices with low power consumption and just a handful of high-power devices. Since IPv6 offers end-to-end IP communication, its adoption on sensor nodes is growing.

In order to realize the Global Internet of Things notion, the procedure to connect wireless sensor network devices to the internet is made simpler. It is simpler for ecologically conscientious people to create internet-based and portable apps that can enlighten and enlighten the general public when the data is easily available online. Furthermore, system designers and users can benefit from the wide array of tools available for establishing, configuring, and maintaining these networks by utilizing IPv6-based protocols.

7.7.4 Environmental Sensors

In listing and explaining any sensor technology that could be used to gather environmental data, the technologies are arranged in accordance with the analyte, which comprises biologic infectious agents, aromatic organic chemicals, radioactive substances, and residual metals.

7.7.4.1 Metal Trace Detectors

Nanoelectrode Array

Metals that dissolved can be detected and quantified through the utilization of nanoelectrode arrays. When an electrical potential is applied, the electrodes collect signals by monitoring current and voltage. By employing techniques such as chemical vapor deposition or electron beam lithography, it is possible to deposit approximately one million separate electrodes on a square inch of substrate. The combination of the sensing electrodes and reference electrode eliminates the need for buffers, enabling the detection of contaminants in ultra-pure water. Compared to conventional electrodes, the small size and high density of these electrodes result in a signal-to-noise ratio that can be up to 103 times better. The target analytes encompass hazardous industrial compounds and metals like lead, a metal chromium in mercury, methyl-t-butyl ether, trichloroethylene, and so forth. Achieving this requires the use of multiple electrodes, coatings, and electrochemical procedures.

Laser-Induced Breakdown Spectroscopy (LIBS)

Figure 7.6 illustrates a stand-off LIBS probe head that utilizes fiber optics for laser ablation and spectroscopic data collection. By using the elemental elements that exist at the focus point, LIBS uses a laser to swiftly heat a small area that can be solid or liquid. High-precision spectroscopy tools can then be used to track the plasma's radiative relaxation. For the quick examination of toxic metals and other inorganic contaminants in soil, water, and mixed waste locations, LIBS is a useful technique. Nearly all elements can be detected by it, albeit some metals exhibit noticeably stronger emission

Figure 7.6 Stand-off LIBS probe head, Laser ablation energy and spectroscopic collection occurs through fibre optics.

than others. The specific metal, as well as the spectroscopic and detector gear used, all affect the detection limits, which are typically in the low parts per billion (ppb) regions. Among the contaminants are lead (Pb), cadmium (Cd), mercury (Hg), copper (Cu), arsenic (As), beryllium (Be), selenium (Se), and mercury (Hg). Zinc (Zn), Silver (Ag), Chromium (Cr), Iron (Fe), and Manganese (Mn) are the primary focus of LIBS investigations.

7.7.4.2 Radioisotope Sensors

With the radiation field-effect transistor, these concepts for assessing gamma radiation dose have existed for many years. The theory behind it is that high mobility electrons are permanently promoted into low mobility holes by ionizing radiation. The FET's threshold voltage shifts irreversibly as a result. Sensitivities vary from 0.01 to 5 mV per rad and are somewhat dependent on the process of creating structure. Figure 7.7 depicts a single 4-inch wafer capable of accommodating over 5000 RadFET elements, each

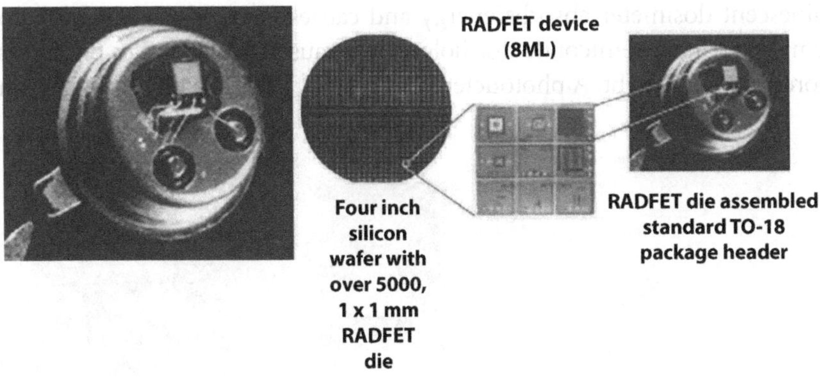

Figure 7.7 The 1 mm2 RadFET element fits on a standard TO-18 package header: Over 5000 RadFETs can be microfabricated on a single 4-inch wafer.

measuring 1 mm2 and mounted on a standard TO-18 package header. RadFET arrays can be used to fabricate filters with different threshold energies to create an energy spectrometer.

7.7.4.3 Cadmium Zinc Telluride (CZT) Detectors

Figure 7.8 showcases a handheld gamma radiation spectrometer equipped with a 1 cm2 CZT array mounted on a dip package and integrated onto a circuit board. Conveyor zone thermocouples are semiconductors detectors for radiation that sense high-energies radiation by generating current flow in response to a gate voltage. For image or spectroscopy to these may be produced in arrays. The performance and calibration of these sensors deteriorate with repeated exposure, notwithstanding their promise as sensitive sensors. Since damage may increase with radiation energy levels, it is difficult to monitor long-term performance.

7.7.4.4 Minimal-Power Pin Diode Beta Spectrometer

Commercially available pin light-emitting from Hamamatsu, Japan, were used at Zia to create a hand-held low-energy beta spectroscopy for the purpose of diagnosing tritium contaminants. The current pulses that are produced in the diode when beta particles strike it are measured by the system. Every signal is transformed by electronic circuits into a voltage pulse whose amplitude varies with the particle's energy.

7.7.4.5 Thermoluminescent Dosimeter (TLD)

Being subjected to radiation, a certain kind of crystal called a thermoluminescent dosimeter absorbs energy and causes electrons to migrate into semi-permanent semiconductor holes. Heat causes the crystal to release its stored energy as light. A photodetector is used by a TLD reader to transform

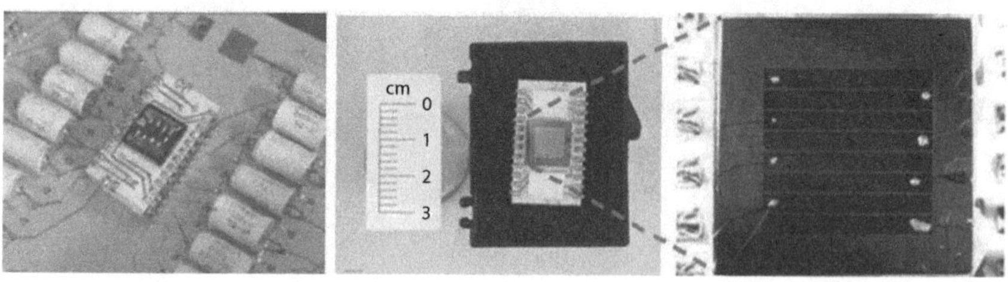

Figure 7.8 The 1 cm2 CZT array sits on a dip package on a circuit board for a handheld gamma radiation spectrometer.

this signal into a radiation dose measurement. Lithium fluoride and calcium fluoride-manganese are two frequently utilized crystals. Sandia has created TLDs with Teflon-embedded crystals to improve sensitivity. While bigger crystals are used to evaluate total exposure, thinner crystals are useful for detecting low-energy radiation. Different kinds of crystals and filters can also be used to distinguish between various energy levels.

7.7.4.6 *Identification Gamma Detector for Isotopes*

Together with the Military Risk Management Agency, Innovative Research Associates, and DOE/NNSA facilities, a radioactive detection γ detector was created. This was intended to serve as a gateway tool to locate and identify nuclear weapons and radioactive dispersal devices that were brought in an unorthodox manner.

7.7.4.7 *Neutrino Projector for Detection of Nuclear Material*

High purity germanium sensors, which require nitrogen in the form of liquid, and scintillating particles, such as sodium iodide coated with thallium (which has a limited energy resolution), are often used for gamma radiation sensors. Among the initial detectors for radiation on the market, geiger counters were also the first to measure radiation quantitatively. They are bulkier than some of the above-discussed sensors, but they cover a large radiation range and have extremely basic electronics.

7.7.4.8 *Non-Sandia Radiation Detectors*

Purified germanium detection devices, which need scintillating granules such as iodide of sodium and nitrogen in liquid form, which is doped with thallium (which has a limited energy resolution), are often used gamma radiation detectors. Among the first radiation detectors on the market, geiger counters were also the first to measure radiation quantitatively. They are bulkier than some of the above-discussed sensors, but they have a large radiation range and fairly simple electronics.

7.7.4.9 *Sensors for Organic Pollutants*

Chemically Relevant Detector Using Optical Evanescent Fiber
When electromagnetic radiation experiences total internal reflection, the energy that travels across a dielectric interface is referred to as an evanescent wave. Within a specific penetration depth, this wave can interact with matter.

Certain chemicals from a mixture can be concentrated into the area where the evanescent wave interacts by using specialized coatings as the cladding for fiber-optic cables. Low parts per million (ppm) levels of organic component detection in aqueous solutions have been achieved by the use of polymer optical wave guides. Sol-gel coatings can be used for pH monitoring. Near infrared (NIR) spectroscopy is used in sensing applications to carry out quantitative measurements. Long-distance sensing is possible because of this wavelength range's remarkable light transmission characteristics.

Reflection of Grating Light Electrolytic Spectra

Using spectroscopic analysis, Reflection of grating Light Electrolytic spectra is a technique for detecting and evaluation. It entails putting a sample of liquid that has to be evaluated upon contact with a transmission prism grating. The grating is then exposed to an incident light beam. Certain diffracted orders change from being traveling waves to evanescent waves at particular angles of incidence. The intricate index of optics of the sample and the grating's period dictate the wavelength at which this transition occurs. The intensity of a scattered order is also influenced by the sample's complicated index of diffraction. The mathematical formulae' real part represents the speed of light in the material, while the imaginary part represents light reception.

Biochemical Flow Probe Sensor in Miniature

The gauge at issue used for monitoring molecules of organic matter diffusing through a partially permeable membrane by putting it into an opening. These materials react with an agent of chemical nature to generate products that are visibly different. A fiber optic cable is used to transport light in two directions so that a spectrometer may be used to view the bands of radiation from a flash bulb. This probe can be used to find metals that are dissolved and volatile organic chemicals, particularly chlorine halo carbons in either water or air.

SAW Chemical Sensor Arrays

Figure 7.9 presents an application-specific integrated circuit featuring four vertically aligned SAW sensor elements, one of which remains uncoated for comparative frequency shift analysis with other polymer or solgel coated lines. The usual method for using acoustic sensor is to measure a drop in its primary resonance frequency, which is connected to trace mass loading on the active surface. Large-area coatings, polymer compounds, and sol-gels are frequently used to improve mass absorbing and adsorb and to offer some chemical class discrimination. Flexural plate wave, crystal quartz microbalances and surface acoustic waves sensors are among the acoustic sensors

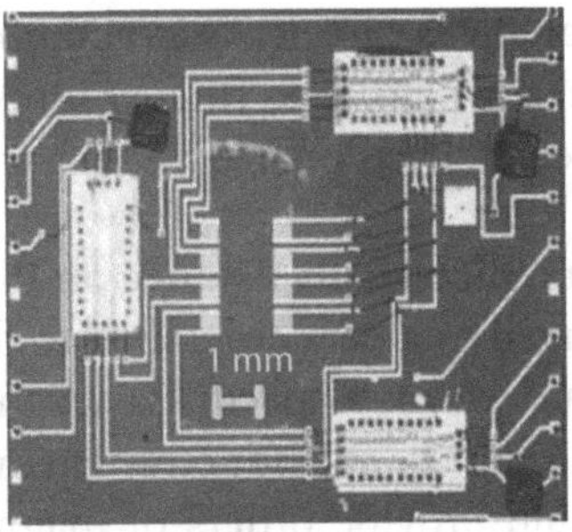

Figure 7.9 Four SAW sensor elements aligned vertically on an application specific integrated circuit. One delay line is left uncoated to compare frequency shifts of other polymer or solgel coated lines.

employed at Sandia. Coatings with different chemical characteristics have been used to accomplish chemical speciation and vapour quantification on a 6-SAW array. The materials' reactions to 14 distinct analytes—which included alcohol, ketone, organophosphonate, alkane, hydrocarbon, chlorinated hydrocarbon, and water—were assessed in a single test.

7.7.4.10 MicroChemLab (Gas Phase)

The phase of gas in order to comply with national security regulations, MicroChemLab is a small-scale gas chromatography (GC) system that was first intended for the detection of chemical warfare weapons. GC offers a wide range of applications because of its versatility. Additionally, the MicroChemLab can be tailored to meet specific needs, including the quantification of organic chemicals in explosives, natural gas, and derivatized biological fatty acids. The major components are typically a microfabricated hotplate preconcentrator (PC), a micromachined silicone chromatography gas column (μGC), and an exterior acoustical wave sensor array. Polymers, absorbent sol-gels, or large surface area adsorbent solid phase are used by the PC. The low heat capacity membrane is rapidly heated to temperatures which may reach several hundred degrees in order to release the collected analyte.

Gold Nanoparticle Chemiresistors

Despite a few exceptions, gold nanoparticle chemiresistors make use of the same basic ohmic sensing concepts as conventional chemiresistors. These sensors use gold nanoparticles electrically coupled by conductive polymer linkages rather than conventional conductive linkages. Since the conductor system is encapsulated in a nonconductive polymeric polymer, polymer swelling has no effect on resistive measurements. The polarizable polymer linkages and analytes directly interact, producing a signal that is more stable, repeatable, and sensitive. Thicker films can therefore be used, making it possible to detect levels of analyte that are lower.

Tethered Lipid Bilayers' Electric Resistance on Planar Electrodes
Lipid bilayers are arranged in a very thin layer to form this sensor. When VOCs attach or infiltrate within a specific layer, the material's ion mobility is altered. Compared to current inductive chemiresistors covered with polyelectrolyte, this could provide orders of magnitude more sensitivity. Antibodies that bind the analyte molecules are examples of molecules that recognize features that cause a significant increase in sensitivity.

MicroHound
The MicroHound is a comprehensive analytical system consisting of a tiny Ion Mobility Spectrometry and a chemical preconcentration system. Although detecting pyrotechnics is its main function, it may additionally be modified to identify semi-volatile organic chemicals in the atmosphere. Large amounts of air are drawn into the preliminary concentration process via a web of mesh that collects explosives alone. After the screen is heated, the absorbed chemicals are quickly released as a pulse and sent into the IMS's intake. The chemicals inside the IMS are ionized at a drift tube's time-gated entry. After that, the ions are electronically driven toward a detecting electrode by an inert gas that is flowing counter-flowing. The ions split from one another as they move through the drift tube.

Hyperspectral Imaging
Various filters are used to capture numerous (miniature or gigantic) infrared pictures of the same spot. Each pixel's color spectrum is thus obtained. Empirical species identification can be achieved by processing these multimodal images. This is a stand-off technique that could be used to monitor surface soil from a satellite or unmanned aerial vehicle. The biological and biomedical fields have also employed these techniques.

Chemiresistor Array
Figure 7.10 showcases Sandia's development of chemiresistor arrays featuring four conductive polymer films, strategically placed as black spots on platinum wire traces integrated onto a silicon wafer substrate. A chemiresistor sensor, known as a conductive polymer sheet, is created by placing it on a microfabricated circuit. The chemically sensitive insulating polymer is mixed with conductive carbon particles and dissolved in a solvent. The resulting ink is then applied to solid substrates (chips) with thin-film

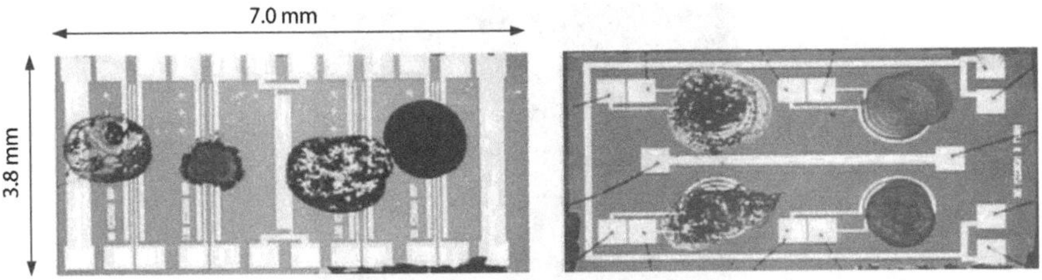

Figure 7.10 Chemiresistor arrays developed at Sandia with four conductive polymer films (black spots) deposited onto platinum wire traces on a silicon wafer substate.

platinum traces that do not intersect. When exposed to chemical vapours, the polymers absorb the chemicals, making them enlarge. The physical appearance of the sensitive granules in the polymer film is altered by these swellings, which alters the resistance that exists across the platinum-trace electrode. The electrical resistance can be monitored and recorded with an ohm meter or data logger. If the chemical vapours are removed, the swelling can be reversed, although some hysteresis may occur.

7.7.4.11 Biological Sensors

Fatty Acid Methyl Esters (FAME) Analyzer

The approach employed entails looking at entire living cells using micro hotplates. On the hotplate, a liquid sample and a chemically methylating agent are placed. Cells begin to lysis amid the hotplate's thermally stepping, which can reach 500°C in just a couple of milliseconds. This causes protein molecules to become semi-volatile FAMEs. In order to make identification and quantification easier, this procedure also acts as the injection mechanism into a μGC. Using cutting-edge instruments, by comparing the ratios of various FAMEs, bacteria can be distinguished at the gram-type, a genus as well as species levels. Sandia's goal is to reduce laboratory-scale equipment costing half a million dollars to a portable, battery-operated device.

7.7.4.12 iDEP (Insulator-Based Dielectrophoresis)

With this technique, a microfabricated set of insulated posts is subjected to an electrical field. Particles are preferentially concentrated using a polypropylene apparatus based on their size and polarization. Figure 7.11 demonstrates how electric field gradients generated by microfabricated posts can separate live and dead E. coli cells based on their electrical properties, concentrating them in specific zones. It may isolate protein in order to analyze

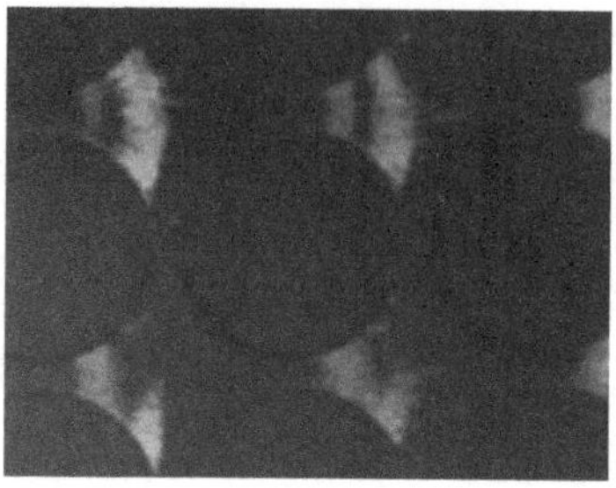

Figure 7.11 Electric field gradients created between microfabricated posts separate fluorescently tagged live and dead E.coli while dielectrophoretically concentrating them in zones.

them in the liquid MicroChemLab or other systems that employ fingerprints to identify diseases.

Bio-SAW Sensor

The usual method for using acoustic sensors is to measure a drop in the resonance frequency that is connected with mass loading. Applying certain antibody coatings to the acoustic device's active surface allows for biological detection (Figure 7.12). It just takes a few minutes to identify anthrax spores, and other antibody coatings can be used to identify other deadly threats. Using a variety of detectors with distinct coatings would boost versatility.

μProLab

The purpose of this LDRD Grand Demand apparatus is to use MIMS (molecular integrated microsystems) for the preconcentration as well as evaluation of proteins and peptides. The benefits of system downsizing will be enhanced by this architecture, resulting in greater efficiency. Simultaneously, the goal is manufacturing simplicity. Using programmable

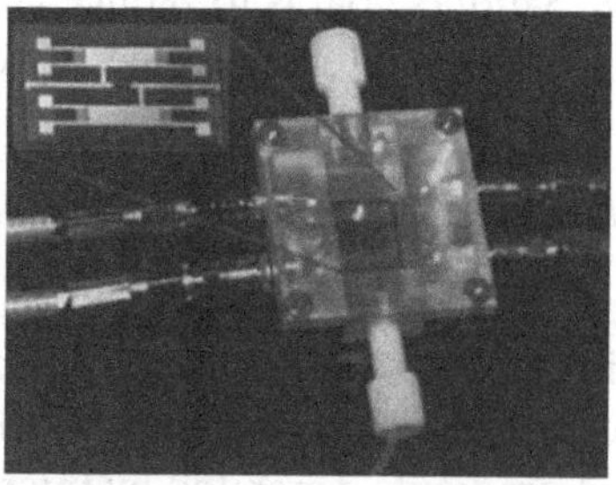

Figure 7.12 A miniaturized biosensor is shown consisting of a shear horizontal surface acoustic wave sensor coated with a molecular recognition layer. Highly specific coatings are used for biological warfare agent detection and medical diagnostics.

switchable polymers and electrokinetic trapping, it is possible to preconcentrate protein and peptide signatures 1,000 times. Other achievements to date include cast-in-place fluidic forms and coatings.

MicroChemLab (Liquid)
Figure 7.12 shows a miniaturized SH-SAW biosensor with a specific coating for detecting biological warfare agents and aiding medical diagnostics. The gas-phase MicroChemLab that was previously discussed has a liquid counterpart. This small, low-power gadget is portable and easy to use. Its main job is to quickly identify a large variety of materials both bio and inorganic in about fifteen minutes. Three different analytical techniques are used by the detector, which uses capillary electrophoresis technology. First, viruses and bacteria are identified using DNA analysis. Additionally, organisms such as viruses, bacteria, and poisons are detected using antigen-antibody Finally, poisons are identified using protein signatures. Only microfabricated channels on a single circuit board are used for fluid handling; low power electrokinetic forces are needed but high voltage is required.

7.8 Summary and Recommendations

The regulations, guidelines, and specifications related to the surveillance of environmental pollutants in water from storms, water for human consumption, pretreatment process, and the atmosphere have been delineated in this study. To act as metrics for assessing sensor technologies, the given relative terms are used to describe saturation restrictions, test rate, sampling procedure, and reporting stages.

The shortcomings of traditional sensors have made it clear that novel sensor technologies are required for surveillance of the environment. Microelectronics, wireless communications, and data analytics are just a few of the areas where technology is advancing quickly and creating new opportunities for sensor development. Innovative sensor systems that can solve new environmental concerns and get over the limitations of conventional sensors are in high demand.

These cutting-edge sensors are made to measure aspects of the environment with greater empathy, accuracy, and precision. They provide current information, computerized analysis, and predictive capabilities by utilizing cutting-edge technologies including nanotechnology, Internet of Things (IoT), computational intelligence (also known as AI), and machine learning or ML algorithms. Furthermore, these sensors are frequently more affordable than more conventional ones.

Bibliography

Marek, J. and Gómez, U.-M., MEMS (Micro-Electro-Mechanical Systems) for Automotive and Consumer, in: *Chips 2020: A Guide to the Future of Nanoelectronics*, B. Höfflinger, (Ed.), pp. 293–314, Springer-Verlag, Heidelberg, 2012.

Lee, I.-M., *et al.*, Effect of physical inactivity on major non-communicable diseases worldwide: an analysis of burden of disease and life expectancy. *Lancet*, 380, 9838, 219–229, 2013.

Shortreed, S.M., Peeters, A., Forbes, A.B., Estimating the effect of long-term physical activity on cardiovascular disease and mortality: evidence from the Framingham Heart Study. *Heart*, 99, 9, 649–654, 2013.

Park, A., Lack of Exercise as Deadly as Smoking, Study Finds, Last Update: July 18, 2012.

Babor, T.F., Alcohol consumption trends and patterns of drinking, in: *Alcohol: No Ordinary Commodity: Research and Public Policy*, T. Babor, (Ed.), pp. 23–42, Oxford Press, Oxford, UK, 2010.

American Lung Association, Smoking, 2013, http://www.lung.org/stop-smoking/about-smoking/health-effects/smoking.html.

Jha, P., Avoidable global cancer deaths and total deaths from smoking. *Nat. Rev. Cancer*, 9, 655–664, 2009.

Al-Maskari, F., Lifestyle Disease: An Economic Burden on the Health Services, UN Chronicle - Achieving Global Health, vol. XLVII (2), 2010.

United Nations, Global status report on noncommunicable disease, 2010, http://www.who.int/nmh/publications/ncd_report_full_en.pdf.

Fogel, R.W., Longer Lives and Lower Health Costs in 2040: Business Class, Last Update: July 21, 2011.

Fraden, J., *Handbook of Modern Sensors*, 4th ed., Springer, New York, 2010.

Jones, D.P., *Biomedical Sensors*, 1st ed., Momentum Press, New York, 2010.

Chen, K.Y., Janz, K.F., Zhu, W., Brychta, R.J., Redefining the roles of sensors in objective physical activity monitoring. *Med. Sci. Sports Exercise*, 44, 13–12, 2012.

Sutherland, J.W., An Introduction to Sensors and Transducers, Last Update: 2004, http://www.mfg.mtu.edu/cyberman/machtool/machtool/sensors/intro.html.

American National Standards Institute (ANSI), ISA S37.1–1975 (R1982), ed., 1975. National Research Council (NRC), Committee on New Sensor Technologies: Materials Applications Commission on Engineering Technical Systems, *Expanding the Vision of Sensor Materials*, National Academies Press, 1995.

AALIANCE, *Ambient Assisted Living Roadmap*, vol. 6, G. Van Den Broek, F. Cavallo, C. Wehrman (Eds.), IOS Press, 2010, http://ebooks.iospress.nl/volume/aaliance-ambient-assisted-living-roadmap.

Khanna, V.K., *Nanosensors: Physical, Chemical, and Biological*, CRC Press, Boca Raton, 2012.

Wang, P. and Liu, Q., *Biomedical Sensors and Measurement*, Springer-Verlag, Berlin Heidelberg, 2011.

Fink, J.K., Mechanical Sensors, in: *Polymeric Sensors and Actuators*, pp. 131–138, Wiley-Scrivener, Hoboken, Massachusetts, 2012.

Patranabis, D., *Sensors and Transducers*, 2nd ed., PHI Learning Pvt Ltd, New Delhi, 2004.

Kyowa, What's a Strain Guage, 2013, http://www.kyowa-ei.co.jp/eng/.

Kasukawa, Y., *et al.*, Relationships between falls, spinal curvature, spinal mobility and back extensor strength in elderly people. *J. Bone Miner. Metab.*, 28, 1, 82–87, 2010.

Bohannon, R.W., Literature reporting normative data for muscle strength measured by hand-held dynamometry: A systematic review. *Isokinet. Exercise Sci.*, 19, 3, 143–147, 2011.

Bretveld, R., Brouwers, M., Ebisch, I., Roeleveld, N., Influence of pesticides on male fertility. *Scand. J. Work Environ. Health*, 33, 1, 13–28, 2007.

Balabanic, D., Rupnik, M., Klemencic, A.K., Negative impact of endocrine-disrupting compounds on human reproductive health. *Reprod. Fertil. Dev.*, 23, 3, 403–416, 2011.

IHME, *The Global Burden of Disease: Generating Evidence, Guiding Policy*, Institute for Health Metrics and Evaluation, Seattle, Washington, 2013.

Quantified Self Labs, Quantified Self: self knowledge through number, 2022, http://quantifiedself.com/.

Linear-Technology, Wireless Sensor Network Challenges and Solutions, 2012, http://cds.linear.com/docs/en/white paper/wp001fa.pdf.

Ghosh, A. and Das, S.K., Coverage and connectivity issues in wireless sensor networks: A survey. *Pervasive Mob. Comput.*, 4, 3, 303–334, 2008.

Mainwaring, K. and Srivastava, L., The Internet of Things - Setting the Standards, in: *The Internet of Things: Connecting Objects*, H. Chaouchi, (Ed.), pp. 208–210, Wiley, Hoboken, New Jersey, 2010.

Conway, M., What Is Cyberterrorism and How Real Is the Threat?, in: *Law, Policy, and Technology*, P.C. Reich, and E. Gelbstein (Eds.), pp. 279–307, IGI Global, Hershey PA, 2012.

Zervous, B., Q&A on energy harvesting, wireless sensors, wireless sensor networks, Last Update: April 4 2013.

http://www.energyharvestingjournal.com/articles/q-amp-a-on-energy-harvesting-wireless-sensors- wireless-sensor-networks-00005316.asp

Boisvert, S., 3D printing enclosures for micro wireless sensors and circuits inexpensive and practical solution for company, Last Update: 2013, http://www.3dprinter.net/3d-printing-enclosures-for-micro-wireless-sensors-and-circuits.

Crisostomo, C., Monitor Air Pollution with Smartphone Accessed Portable Sensors, The Environmental Blog. Last Update: January 20, 2013, http://www.theenvironmentalblog.org/2013/01/monitor-air-pollutionsmartphone-accessed-portable-sensors/.

Sensorcon, Make Sensordrone Do Even More, Last Update: 2013, http://www.sensorcon.com/sensordrone extensions/.

Choi, S., Kim, N., Cha, H., Ha, R., Micro Sensor Node for Air Pollutant Monitoring: Hardware and Software Issues. *Sensors*, 9, 7970–7987, 2009.

Romain, A.C. and Nicolas, J., Long term stability of metal oxide-based gas sensors for e-nose environmental applications: An overview. *Sens. Actuators, B*, 146, 2, 502–506, 2010.

Grossi, M., *et al.*, A Portable Sensor with Disposable Electrodes for Water Bacterial Quality Assessment. *Sens. J. IEEE*, 13, 5, 1775–1782, 2013.

8

Significance and Advancement of Sensor Technologies for Environmental Analysis

S. Thanga Revathi[1], Mary Subaja Christo[1], A. Sathya[2] and Suresh Annamalai[1]*

[1]Department of Networking and Communications, School of Computing, College of Engineering and Technology, SRM Institute of Science and Technology, SRM Nagar, Kattankulathur, Chennai, Tamil Nadu, India

[2]Department of Artificial Intelligence and Data Analytics, Sri Ramachandra Faculty of Engineering and Technology, Chennai, Tamil Nadu, India

Abstract

Although there are many different kinds and a vast range of applications for sensors, at their core, sensors are apparatuses that identify a measuring object's feature quantity and translate it into a readable signal that is shown on an instrument. In short, sensing technology is any technology that detects amounts of physical, chemical, or biological properties and transforms them into readable signals using sensors. Sensors are readily available for almost every industrial application. Sensors provide unparalleled asset protection and can help enhance processes for demanding, mission-critical industrial applications. When a workflow calls for it, these sensors provide real-time monitoring that includes detection and reporting. Sensors send the data they monitor and collect for control and analysis, and when they detect an anomaly in a certain property, they indicate it by sending out an electrical signal. In this manner, sensors guarantee that procedures adhere to best practices while improving process effectiveness and product quality. The paper highlights how sensor node technology is able to track and record environmental data. It also provides an explanation of the different parts of the sensor technology. It is possible to further analyse and mine the massive amount of data that the sensor nodes have acquired.

***Keywords*:** Sensor technology, industrial applications, asset protection, real time monitoring, anomaly detection, process optimization, environmental monitoring

**Corresponding author*: prisu6esh@yahoo.com; suresha2@srmist.edu.in

A. Suresh, T. Devi, N. Deepa and Ali Kashif Bashir (eds.) Environmental Monitoring Using Artificial Intelligence, (167–180) © 2025 Scrivener Publishing LLC

8.1 Introduction

People are using the internet more frequently due to the growth of social media and mobile internet, which has resulted in the spread of a lot of information. Information that is considered to be hot issues or happenings on the network is that which has garnered a lot of attention and conversation in a short amount of time. Information about network hotspots must be disseminated quickly in order to monitor events, guide public opinion, and provide disaster alerts. The speed at which information is generated during the dissemination of trending content online is quite high, making it challenging to manually gather and handle.

This article gathers and processes network hotspot data using sensor technology. Network hotspot data can be captured and processed by sensors, which are capable of perceiving changes and states in the surrounding environment in a variety of ways. There have been advancements in sensor technology for information distribution, preprocessing, and acquisition in network hotspots. The primary application outcomes are listed below. Network hotspot traffic, including real-time traffic data, traffic peaks, and other information, can be observed with sensor technology. Due to changes in the economy, society, and population, we are living in a time of constant and rapid change. The planet's limited natural resources are being consumed by an increasing number of people every day. Urbanization, energy use, trash generation, and other factors are all contributing to our growing global footprint, which is not without repercussions. Our environment is becoming more polluted, which has an impact on our health and happiness. Human activity has a significant impact on both humans and the environment, from smog clouds in cities to drinking water contamination to the simple inability to have enough peace of mind to sleep peacefully at night. Our lives have become significantly more sedentary over the past century due to drastic changes in lifestyle. Growing public health problems as a result include cancer, overweight, liver disease, arteriosclerosis, and other disorders. The world's healthcare systems are under increasing strain due to rising life expectancy as the population gets older. Governments are under pressure to minimize spiraling expenses by slashing services like home healthcare support. For all intents and purposes, the current model is not future-proof.

Modern industrial applications for sensors are vast and include food processing as well as routine monitoring of things like transportation, quality of air, medical treatments, etc. Although sensors have been a part of human life for over a century, smart sensors, or contemporary sensors with advancements in technology, have only been available over the last thirty years. Significant advancements have been made in terms of computational power, energy efficiency, storage, networking choices, and environments for software development which have coincided with a notable advancement in sensing capacities. The swift advancement and industrialization of inexpensive microelectromechanical systems (MEMS) sensors, such as three-dimensional accelerometers, have resulted in their incorporation into an extensive array of gadgets, spanning automobiles to mobile phones. Accessible semiconductor sensors have sparked the development of new ambient sensing applications, like indoor air quality monitoring. Pervasive sensing emerged as a result of the wide variety of affordable sensors. With little impact on our day-to-day activities, wearable sensors are integrated into our living spaces, or even included into our clothes.

By early identification of possible problems, such as chronic heart disease, liver failures (increased levels of bilirubin in urine), anaemia and so on, data captured from these sensors is expected for promoting foresighted healthcare standards. Sensors are being utilized more and more to track everyday activities, including working out, and provide instantaneous performance data via smartphones. There is a major shift occurring in the relationship between our ambient environment and our well-being. With the use of sensor technology, the general public may now access information on environmental problems including noise pollution and the quality of the air and water. It is not appropriate, however, to think of sensors as the answer to every issue we face. Rather, they ought to be viewed as really helpful instruments. As always, the appropriate tool for the job must be used, and just like any other complicated equipment, sensors and sensor systems have advantages and disadvantages. It is essential to carefully match the sensor's operational features to the desired use case. For the duration of the necessary application, the data must have the necessary precision and stability. However, high sensitive and high precision sensors were typically more expensive; as such, their cost is carefully assessed compared to the quality for the application. They occasionally do not, however, have compelling use cases based on actual requirements that have a definite positive societal or economic impact. Unless these technologies solve a real-world problem in a novel way and outperform current solutions in terms of performance, they are not really valuable. There must also be actual, devoted data users.

8.2 Sensing and Sensor Fundamentals

The industry is always trying to develop products more efficiently and quickly. Manufacturers can achieve these objectives while upholding greater standards of quality and dependability by automating processes. A sensor is characterized as follows: A recording, functionally connected, usually electrical or optical device that reacts to an interesting physical input. In general, a sensor is an apparatus that transforms a measured value to signals that can be interpreted with the help of human or machine. In the context of measuring systems, sensor or transducer can be used. A sensor is not the same as a transducer. A sensor converts received signal to electrical waves; it gathers data from the outside environment. All that a transducer does is change the form of energy.

8.2.1 Sensing Modalities

Figure 8.1 sensor and transducer likely depicts the components and interactions involved in converting a physical quantity into a measurable electrical signal. This could include the sensor itself, which detects the physical input, and the transducer, which transforms that input into an electrical output. Numerous things such as proteins, some chemicals, a few bacteria, various gases, intensity of light, the change in position, sound, etc., which is of different forms like physical, biological and chemical variables, is measured or detected using sensors. A transducer transforms sensor readings into a signal that an observer or the outside world can use to describe the quantity of interest. Common sensing approaches are used for intended application domains considered in the following section.

Multiple types of sensors are available that can be used to measure any given quantity. Higher-priced sensors are usually equipped with more advanced features that provide superior performance qualities. Three methods exist for using sensors to measure quantities of interest, as described below.

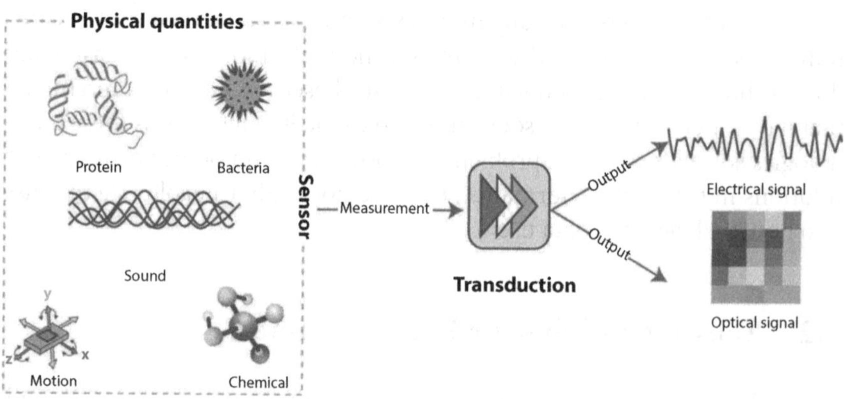

Figure 8.1 Sensor and transducer.

Contact: In order to apply this strategy, the quantity of interest must be physically touched. This method of sensing is applicable to a wide range of classes, including liquids, gases, and things like the human body. Clearly, the status of the sample or subject is disturbed to some extent when such sensors are deployed.

Noncontact: Direct contact with the quantity of interest is not necessary for this type of sensing. A benefit of this method is that it causes the least amount of disturbance to the patient or trial. This model is most commonly utilized in applications sensing environments, which track people's daily activities and behaviours in their own homes. These applications are built using sensors which are usually concealed from the user's view. These sensors use passive infrared (PIR).

Sample removal: In this method, a representative sample is intrusively collected by a person or by using automation sampling method. It is a popular practice in environmental and healthcare applications, such as monitoring blood glucose levels or E. coli levels in water. Sensors or analytical equipment housed in a lab may be used to examine such samples.

8.2.2 Sensor Types

The fundamental idea behind mechanical sensors is the measurement of changes that occur in a material or device when an input results in the material or device's mechanical deformation (Fink, 2012). Inputs that produce measurable mechanical deformation include change in direction, speed, and position. The sensor is referred to as electromechanical when it immediately transforms this input into an electrical output. This transformation of resistance brought on by strain on one constituent or group of components serves as the basis for measurement. Motion sensing can be done in four different ways: tilt (static), shock (instantaneous), vibration (periodic), and rotation. Accelerometers can measure all of these parameters, with the exception of rotation. The visible light, infrared Radiations (IR), and ultraviolet Radiations (UVR) spectral ranges of light are among the waves or photons of light that optical sensors may detect. Depending on whether a quantity of interest is absorbing or emitting light, they measure the change in light intensity. It is also possible to measure the phase shifts brought about by interference or interaction effects in light beams. Monitoring the presence or lack of a light source is another popular method. In automatic doors and gates, sensors that operate on this concept are frequently employed to make sure that the opening path is clear of obstructions. The basis of photodetector sensors is the notion of photoconductivity, which states that a target material's conductivity changes depending on whether light is present or absent. A particular region of spectrum, or range of light wavelengths, from UVR to IR, is what sensors are sensitive to. There are two types of infrared sensors: active and passive. When the sensor is in its active state, it uses an IR as a source of light, like Light Emitting Diode, to produce a beam of light that is detected by another detector (phototransistors, photodiodes, or photoelectric cells). It is possible to coat optical fibers with compounds that react to variations in humidity, temperature, or strain.

Interferometer, a tool which measures the changes in beam of light as it propagates, such as changes in wavelength or path length. Typically, the sensor makes use of two single fibers plus a light source, like a laser LED. After splitting, the light is connected into each of the two fibers. By comparing the measured quantity with a reference optical signal, one can determine whether the quantity being measured is modulating the optical signal's phase. Semiconductor sensors are frequently employed to identify dangerous gases such as carbon monoxide (CO), alcohol, hydrogen, and oxygen (O2). Home CO detectors are popular sensors used for monitoring the gas semiconductor. Biosensors recognize an analyte of concentration in different properties like changes in chemical, environmental (such as soil, air, water), and biological samples (includes saliva, blood samples and urine samples) by use of biochemical processes. In the apparatus it includes the enzyme, few antibody, or any nucleic acid, or hormone which is immobilized for using in sensors.

8.2.3 Sensor Characteristics

Since sensors normally need an electrical input to function, this results in a signal as based on the specification of sensor measurements. Understanding sensor performance characteristics is essential to fully comprehending sensors and the ways in which sensors measuring the same thing can differ from one another. Regrettably, many of these attributes lack a common definition, and depending on the sensing domain, different segments of the sensor community refer to these attributes under different names. There are three types of sensor characteristics: statistical, dynamic, and systematic.

Range: As its name suggests, range is a static property that characterizes the input or output's minimum and maximum values.

Function of Transfer: The association of measurand and the resultant electrical signal is defined by sensor characteristics. Mathematical formula, a graph, or a table of values can all be used to illustrate this relationship.

Expensive sensors are regulated to offer a calibrated curve. This association is referred to as the sensor transfer function if it is time-invariant. The following is a common mathematical formula that describes the transfer function:

$$S = F(y)$$

Where y is the measurand and S is the electrical signal produced by the sensor.

Both Nonlinearity and Linearity

Nonlinearity, also referred to as linearity in datasheets, is a discrepancy among the ideal straight line and the real line. In datasheets, nonlinearity—which might fluctuate throughout the plot of input-output—is represented by unique number, known as maximum nonlinearity.

Perceptiveness

Sensitivity is the degree of change to be done in input to produce a unit change in output. It remains the same across sensor's variety and is equal to the slope of straight-line plot if the response of the sensor is linear.

Resolution

Resolution or discrimination is the small change in measurand that results in discernible difference in output. Modern sensors range widely in resolution; thus before choosing a sensor, it's critical to know what kind of resolution the application requires.

Precision

Accuracy is capability to give an output closer to measurand's value. It specifies the maximum predicted error between the output signals that are actually received and those that are ideal.

Accuracy

An output's precision refers to its capacity for continuous replication. Therefore, it is conceivable to have a very exact sensor that is inaccurate or closer to a sensor which is not accurate.

Replicability

A repeatable sensor can generate the same result when given the same input. In most cases, operator mistake or random fluctuations in the environment's inputs are the cause of lack of repeatability.

Acceptance

The term "tolerance" refers to the differences in resulted output amongst a similar group of elements brought about by tiny, random variances in manufacture.

8.3 Key Sensor Technology Components

Using a broad range of sensing techniques, sensors monitor a number of chemical, biological, and physical quantities. Through a transduction process, the act of sensing produces an output signal that needs to be processed and communicated in order for a human or another device to make use of it. "Smart" sensors are those that can collect, process, and output measurements via a data bus all in one package. To create smart sensor systems, the capabilities of these smart sensors can be further enhanced with features like radio communications, sampling, remote manageability, and enclosures. Signal conditioning, data processing, transmission, storage, and display of the sensor measurement are made possible by the hardware and software working together.

Sensor systems augment the functionality of smart sensors by including additional functionalities such as wired and wireless connection, display, sample preparation and collection, enclosures and mounting, remote manageability, and security. The requirements of the application typically determine the precise combination of system capabilities. Figure 8.2 shows the high-level architecture of a sensor system.

Sensing and transduction, signal processing (filtering, conditioning, ADC conversion), data-integrity checking, data processing, signal transmission and display, and, in certain situations, remote device manageability are the several hierarchical functional levels that make up sensor systems. By leveraging the data from one sensor to increase the accuracy of the reading from another, multisensor systems can maximize the performance of each individual sensor.

Sensor Platform

A subset of smart sensors are called sensor platforms. They have memory, a wired/wireless interface, and a microprocessor, just like smart sensors. Sensor platforms, on the other hand, are made for general applications. They have an interface for configuring the microcontroller to carry out a specific task and the ability to interface with unidentified external sensors. In the fields of health, wellness, and the environment, Arduino, Shimmer, and smartphones are the most often used sensor platforms.

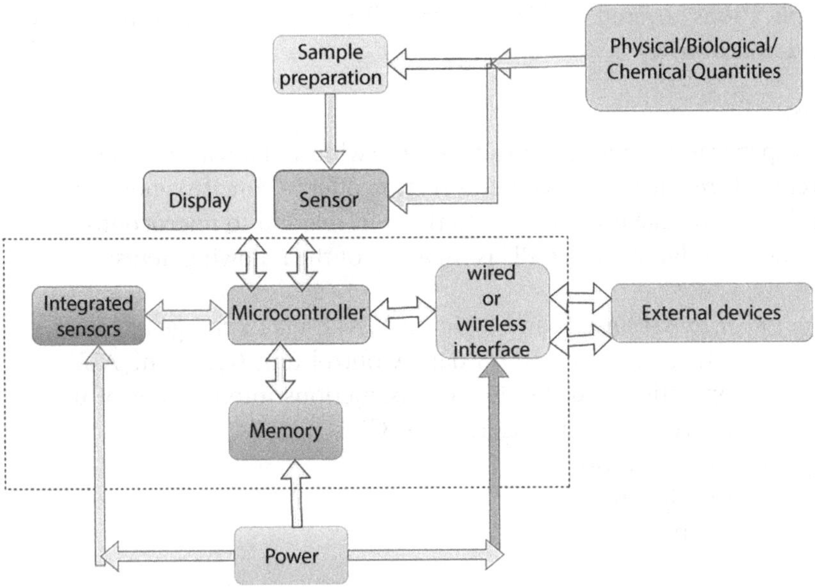

Figure 8.2 The high-level architecture of a sensor system.

Microcontrollers for Smart Sensors

A microprocessor is a single-chip implementation of a Processing unit. Before 1970, CPUs were made up of multiple chips or separate devices that were connected to one another rather than being integrated on a single chip. Figure 8.3 sensor platforms likely showcases various physical structures or devices that house and support sensors, enabling their deployment in different environments and applications. These platforms could range from simple standalone units to complex networks of interconnected devices. Microcontrollers are made to do particular tasks where the input-to-output relationship is specified. They are used in the sensing

Figure 8.3 Sensor platforms.

applications covered in this book as well as in phones, washing machines, and microwaves.

CPU

This paper is not intended to address the wide and intricate subject of CPU architecture. That being said, this section offers a concise synopsis of CPUs and the language used to refer to them in relation to microcontrollers. At its most fundamental, a CPU is made up of the following items:

- The Arithmetic and logic unit (ALU) is in charge of calculating things based on data. Control unit (CU): The ALU's operation and the flow of instructions into and out of the processor are managed by the CU.
- Register array
- Bus System
- Memory

Registers

Registers are tiny, 1-2 byte RAM memory components. Registers come in two varieties: specific function and general purpose. Because general purpose registers may be accessed more quickly than external memory, the ALU uses them to store intermediate calculation results. The manufacturer defines the role of registers known as special function registers (SFRs).

Recall

The address bus connects the three forms of memory used in microcontrollers—RAM, ROM, and Electrically erasable programmable read-only memory (EEPROM)—to the central processing unit (CPU).

Counters and Timers

The built-in timers found in the majority of microcontrollers is used in creation of exact time delays by incrementing one with the event occurrences or set intervals of time. The timer is used to repeatedly produce interrupts at defined intervals and also to signal the start of event.

Sensor Communications

A vital component of a sensor's use is its capacity to transmit its findings to an individual or to another device. A sensor can transmit information in three basic ways: wirelessly, through a connected interface, or by directly displaying data to the user. LED is used to represent the status of ON or OFF, such as power. Pregnancy test kits and other single-use discrete sensors can communicate via a cheap, simple liquid-crystal display (LCD) or a color-changing indication.

Customized Wire Interfaces

Through Serial Communication, data flows from terminal to circuit Equipment (i.e., DTE to DCE) via a serial port, which serves as a communication interface. Despite the fact that USB, FireWire, and Ethernet all carry data serially, the RS232 standard is typically linked with the term "serial port." Both the terminal and circuit should work with a standard format for communication, similar speed for transmission, character count, and whether or not to use stop and parity framing bits in order for data communication to be successful.

Standards for Wireless Communications

For the past fifteen years, wireless communications have been a major area of scientific interest. Many important benefits come with using wireless communications, including lower deployment costs, less infrastructure requirements (no cabling), flexibility in protocol, and the ability to add devices at any moment. To increase power efficiency, communications reliability, and robustness, physical layer, media access control (MAC) layer, and network layers were first the emphasis. As a result, low-power radio technologies, including ultra-wideband (UWB) and 802.15.4, were developed at the physical layer, and methods such as frequency-hopping spread spectrum (FHSS) were implemented for enhancing transmission interference. Power-efficient protocols, such as low-power duty cycles and variations such as time division multiple access (TDMA), have been the focus of attention at the MAC layer. Lastly, the network layer focused on the architecture of network, including multi-hop routing for facilitating the disposition of sensors over widely separated geographic regions.

Proprietary Wireless Protocols

Commercial sensors come with numerous Standard wireless protocols. These protocols can function on proprietary radio frequencies or in the industrial, scientific, medical (ISM) band. Typically, they concentrate in optimizing for certain uses, like delivering years' worth of battery lifespans using ultra-low power (Smith, 2012). They are complex, with a small overhead, and typically offer consistently higher performance than standards-based protocols because of their particular application specialization. Application developers must determine whether the flexibility and openness of standard protocols are outweighed by the benefits of particular optimizations provided by proprietary solutions.

8.4 Regulations and Standards - Sensor Technologies

Sensor-based devices, especially those used in healthcare, need to be regulated in some way to guarantee the end user's safety in terms of electrical, chemical, biological, and physical aspects. The degree of risk connected with the item determines how much control is necessary. Regulations governing implantable devices—like pacemakers—are stricter than those governing non-invasive thermometers. It's crucial to understand the rules that apply to devices related to health, wellness, or the environment when creating or utilizing them, and to make sure they comply with those standards. In reality, it is against the law to market or sell a medical device without first ensuring that it has undergone the necessary regulatory procedures due to the possible risks associated with particular medical equipment.

Standards for QMS

A methodical, structured approach to managing the quality of processes and products is known as a quality management system, or QMS. It is made up of resources, duties, processes and procedures, organizational structure, and procedures. Suitable for all business sectors, the ISO 9001 is the most widely used QMS. Establishing and adhering to a QMS standard is just one way to guarantee quality and encourage ongoing process and product improvement in many non-medical device sectors. Companies with a QMS accreditation can have a competitive edge over those without it. In the medical device sector, proving QMS compliance is an essential step in the regulatory process. The most often used QMSs for medical devices are 21 CFR 820 and ISO 13845. ISO 13845 and associated guidelines. The International Organization for Standardization (ISO) standard ISO 13845 lays out the specifications for a thorough quality control system that applies to the planning and production of medical devices. In general, ISO 9001, which outlines the specifications for a quality management system, and ISO 13845 are harmonized. They vary in one crucial aspect: While ISO 13485 simply demands the implementation and upkeep of a quality system, ISO 9001 compels the firm to demonstrate continuous improvement. EU medical device legislation and ISO 13485 are closely related, and proving compliance with ISO 9001, ISO 13485, and/or ISO 14971 is frequently regarded as the first step in meeting European regulatory standards. It is currently accepted that ISO 13485 is a baseline standard and prerequisite for medical devices. The ISO standard ISO 14971 lays out the specifications for risk management in order to assess a medical device's safety over the course of its life cycle. Higher-level laws and other quality standards, such as ISO 13485, mandate adherence to this standard.

8.5 Conclusion

This paper provides a thorough understanding of environmental sensors, which are widely utilized in monitoring environmental and health factors for a wide range of applications. Presentations included the sensing technology, communication protocols, sensing parameters, fascinating application areas, and research effect analysis. The significant problems with sensor design and application were brought to light. The main drawbacks and difficulties were outlined along with suggestions for how to resolve them in light of recent findings on the use of AI and environmental sensors for environmental monitoring.

Edge computing reduces calculation time and improves sensing capabilities, which results in energy-efficient implementation. As a result, the importance of embedded machine learning and edge computing has also been highlighted. Since it is impossible to ignore the reliance on central servers and the cloud, a great deal of research on the function of servers and edge computing needs to be done. We want to contribute in this area in the near future. In order to monitor the dynamic environment utilizing a variety of environmental sensors that can function in any challenging or unusual situation, a concentrated effort is also required.

Bibliography

Huijsing, J.H., Smart Sensor Systems: Why? Where? How?, in: *Smart Sensor Systems*, G.C.M. Meijer (Ed.), Wiley, New York, 2008.

Meijer, G., Interface Electronics and Measurement Techniques for Smart Sensor Systems, in: *Smart Sensor Systems*, G. Meijer (Ed.), pp. 23–24, John Wiley & Sons, Chichester, 2008.

Hunter, G.W., Stetter, J.R., Hesketh, P.J., Liu, C.-C., Smart Sensor Systems. *Interface*, 19, 4, 29–34, 2010.

Pecht, M.G., *Prognostics and Health Management of Electronics*, Wiley, Hoboken, New Jersey, 2008.

Burns, A., *et al.*, SHIMMER™ - A Wireless Sensor Platform for Noninvasive Biomedical Research. *IEEE Sens.*, 10, 9, 1527–1534, 2010.

Bates, M., Sensor Interfacing, in: *Interfacing PIC Controllers*, pp. 236–238, Newnes, Oxford, 2006.

Kester, W., Sensor Signal Conditioning, in: *Sensor Technology Handbook*, J.S. Wilson (Ed.), pp. 87–89, Elsevier, Burlington, MA, 2005.

Conclusion

9

Texture-Based Classification of Organic and Pesticidal Spinach Using Machine Learning

P. Prittopaul[1], M. Usha[1]*, Mervin Retnadhas Mary[2], Ganesha Ram G.[1], Ashween Raj V. S.[1] and Godwin Wilfred Raj A.[1]

[1]*Department of CSE, Velammal Engineering College, Tamil Nadu, India*
[2]*Dept. of IT, Saudi Electronic University, Riyadh, Saudi Arabia*

Abstract
The main objective of this paper is to introduce an innovative approach for distinguishing between organic and pesticide-treated spinach varieties by employing Local Binary Patterns (LBP) texture analysis. The primary motivation behind this research lies in addressing critical food safety concerns while meeting the growing consumer demand for organic agriculture products. Utilizing LBP, this work extracts robust texture features from spinach leaf images, leveraging them to train a machine-learning model that yields highly accurate classification results. The demonstrated success of this model suggests its potential for automating spinach classification, thereby enhancing agricultural quality control, empowering consumers with informed choices, and promoting sustainable farming practices. This methodology aligns seamlessly with eco-friendly agriculture practices, further reinforcing consumer confidence in organic food products. Ultimately, this research contributes significantly to broader objectives to enhance food safety and sustainability in agricultural systems. Experimental trials include LBP texture analysis of spinach leaves, which successfully captured fine features in their textures. A thorough data analysis shows a distinct difference between spinach kinds that had been treated with pesticides and those that had not. These results highlight how accurate and reliable the LBP-based technique is for classifying spinach.

Keywords: Local binary patterns, texture analysis, agricultural quality control, machine learning

**Corresponding author*: usha.m@velammal.edu.in

A. Suresh, T. Devi, N. Deepa and Ali Kashif Bashir (eds.) Environmental Monitoring Using Artificial Intelligence, (181–200) © 2025 Scrivener Publishing LLC

9.1 Introduction

By utilizing Local Binary Patterns (LBP) texture analysis, the main goal is to present a novel method for differentiating between organic and pesticide-treated spinach cultivars. Accurate and effective techniques of distinction are now essential due to the increased concern for food safety and the rise in customer demand for organic agricultural products. We can extract strong features from the textures of spinach leaves with the use of LBP-based texture analysis. These features are then used to train a machine-learning model that can produce remarkably accurate classification results. Our approach essentially fits in perfectly with sustainable agricultural methods, boosting consumer confidence in organic food items and significantly advancing the larger objectives of improving food safety and sustainability in agricultural systems.

Industrialized agriculture adds to the chemical burden on ecosystems, and pesticides pose threats to human health and the environment, necessitating the Nyéléni Declaration and sustainable food sovereignty [1]. Spinach pesticide contamination and its effects on children's and adults' health are serious problems. Researchers have found that pesticide exposure can induce a poisoning effect linked to asthma. The link between birth defects and pesticide exposure came to light in 2005 after three babies with severe birth defects were born in Florida to mothers who were all employed by Ag-Mart Produce, a company that makes chemically treated tomatoes and other agricultural products [2]. A recent investigation looked into the potential link between glyphosate, genetically modified foods, and declining health in the USA. Concerning potential links between glyphosate use and many health issues and diseases, including cancer, diabetes, kidney failure, autism, hypertension, and strokes, were highlighted through correlation analysis [3].

This work makes use of image processing and machine learning to provide a workable solution in the effort to address issues with food safety and support organic farming. Our strategy's key component is the use of Local Binary Patterns (LBP) texture analysis, a method that enables us to detect subtle and distinct textural details in pictures of spinach leaves. We have been able to distinguish clearly between samples that have been treated with pesticides and those that have not by exposing different spinach kinds to rigorous LBP texture analysis. This outcome highlights the efficiency and dependability of the LBP-based method for categorizing spinach types, demonstrating its potential for expanded use in agricultural quality management. Through this work, we show how image processing may be a key factor in addressing important food safety issues, ultimately helping to promote environmentally friendly and sustainable farming methods that are essential for the health of our environment and future generations. Additionally, this study broadens the agriculture sector's potential as well as improving food safety. We streamline the monitoring process, making it more effective and affordable for farmers by automating the identification of pesticide residues using image processing and machine learning. With the ability to precisely track and manage the use of pesticides, this breakthrough gives farmers the confidence they need to switch to sustainable and environmentally friendly farming methods, preserving soil health and requiring fewer chemical inputs. We bridge the gap between contemporary farming requirements and environmental preservation by fusing cutting-edge technology with agriculture, resulting in a healthier and more sustainable food production system for all.

9.2 Related Works

Reference	Proposed	Findings	Limitations
Tanmay Thorat, B.K. Patle, Manas Wakchaure, Leena Parihar (2023) [4]	Create a thorough database and AI-powered smartphone app that enables users to scan fruits and vegetables for pesticide residue, giving customers the power to make educated food decisions and encouraging healthy eating practices.	Accessible pesticide residue testing improves food safety and sustainability, empowering consumers and promoting ethical farming practices.	Limited accuracy: The efficacy of detecting pesticide residues may vary, and false negatives or positives may still happen, necessitating continual technological and data accuracy advancements.

(*Continued*)

(*Continued*)

Reference	Proposed	Findings	Limitations
Chau Nguyen Dang, Dang Bao Chau, Van Hop, Thai Long, Thi Van Thi, Thi Phuong Linh, & Thi Quynh Trang [5].	Implement thorough pesticide education programs for farmers, rigorous pesticide residue monitoring, and seasonal guidelines to lower health risks related to pesticide-contaminated vegetables in Central Vietnam.	Enhanced food safety, health protection, sustainability, public awareness, compliance, reduced environmental impact, economic benefits, seasonal adaptation, cooperation, and long-term health advantages.	Costs associated with implementation, apprehension about change, administrative burden, potential stigma, a waiting period, difficulties with enforcement, effects on the market, a lack of preparation, potential resistance, and yield effects.
S.T. Narenderan, S.N. Meyyanathan, B. Babu [6].	Monitoring and reducing pesticide residues in fruits and vegetables, taking into account chemical toxicity and classification, requires a comprehensive strategy combining conventional and cutting-edge methodologies.	Improved food safety, environmental protection, sustainable agriculture, technical development, regulatory compliance, advantages for public health, customer confidence, environmental health, long-term sustainability, research, and development.	The expense of implementation, potential hostility from some farmers, the difficulty of administration, and the requirement for continual research and improvement in monitoring tools.

(*Continued*)

(*Continued*)

Reference	Proposed	Findings	Limitations
Abhishek Umar Singh, Anshuman Srivastava, Chandra Prabha Pandey, and V. P. Sharma. [7].	The study emphasizes the need for ongoing monitoring to guarantee food safety and conformity to MRL values in India by highlighting the efficiency of the QuEChERS approach combined with GC-ECD and GC-MS for pesticide residue analysis in vegetables and fruits.	A trustworthy approach for accurate and exact pesticide residue analysis is presented in the study, which also promotes food safety and conformity to MRL values, protecting consumer health in Lucknow, India.	The method may need specific tools and training for implementation, which could present early financial and resource barriers for widespread adoption in food safety monitoring.
Charles S. Semuabo, Asa Bradman, John C. Ssempebwa, Fenna Sillé, and David Guwatudde [8].	The study reveals extensive pesticide residue contamination in fruits and vegetables throughout the Kampala supply chain, highlighting the necessity of strict regulation and oversight for food safety and public health.	The study offers vital information on the frequency of pesticide residues and their fluctuations along the food supply chain, which can guide the development of more useful policies and procedures to safeguard Ugandan consumers' health.	The study might not have examined the potential long-term health effects of consuming pesticide residue, and enforcing stricter standards might be difficult for farmers and the agriculture sector.

9.3 Proposed Work

9.3.1 Conceptual Basis for Pesticidal Detection

The decision to use image processing technology for pesticide identification stems from its amazing ability to extract complex information from visual input. Regarding agriculture, image processing is essential for distinguishing pesticide-treated spinach from organic spinach. This choice is supported by research showing how well image processing methods work to address concerns related to food safety and agriculture. Because spinach leaves have such complex visual characteristics, image processing is preferred over traditional methods, which may make it difficult to capture minute texture details that may indicate pesticide use. This is consistent with the revolutionary effect that image processing has had on food safety, as demonstrated by the introduction of smartphone apps that use artificial intelligence to scan fruits and vegetables. Image processing is a cutting-edge method for visually tracking pesticide residues, and it is further supported by the implementation of comprehensive pesticide education programs and residue monitoring. Beyond simple visual representation, the conceptual framework acknowledges the term "image" as a rich source of information in spinach leaf textures. Every image is a storehouse of vital information that is frequently missed by methods of observation that are more traditional. This method uses efficient analysis techniques along with ongoing observation to record even the smallest variations in pesticide-induced alterations in spinach leaves. The intermediary between unprocessed visual data and useful information is image processing. Methods such as Local Binary Patterns (LBP) are utilized to extract fine-grained texture patterns that are not visible to the human eye but are crucial in identifying the presence of pesticides. With the aid of a virtual microscope, this methodology makes it possible to analyze minute details in the textures of spinach leaves, which helps with automated pesticide residue identification that is in line with current agricultural requirements.

Theoretically, agricultural sustainability and technological innovation work together to create image processing-based pesticide detection. This strategy helps achieve both the specific goal of improving food safety and the more general goal of promoting environmentally friendly farming practices by tackling the urgent issues related to pesticide contamination. From an image processing perspective, the project goes beyond short-term detection requirements in order to create a strong foundation for the overall goal of environmentally conscious and sustainable agriculture [9]. The conceptual framework also recognizes how image processing can revolutionize agriculture by reducing the need for traditional, resource-intensive methods and optimizing agricultural processes. In addition to enabling accurate pesticide detection, this paradigm shift in favor of technology-driven solutions puts agriculture on a path toward modernization. The theoretical foundation is expected to play a pivotal role in influencing the future of agriculture, where efficiency, sustainability, and innovation come together to promote food safety and environmental health, as it develops further to incorporate advances in image processing.

9.3.2 Image Preprocessing

To improve the quality and informativeness of the gathered dataset and achieve accurate classification between pesticidal and organic spinach varieties, an extensive image preprocessing pipeline has been carefully created. Every preprocessing stage makes a distinct contribution to improving features, reducing noise, and sharpening the images, all of which set the stage for a successful machine learning model.

First, pictures of spinach leaves, both organic and pesticidal, must be acquired. Next, the images must be standardized for consistency in resolution and color space. This guarantees consistency throughout the dataset and is in line with the suggestion for standardized data in agricultural imaging [10]. Images of spinach leaves naturally contain noise, so methods like median filtering and Gaussian smoothing are used to reduce it. By successfully lowering noise, these techniques produce a more accurate depiction of the spinach leaves [11]. This step is essential for preserving the photos' integrity in a variety of environmental settings.

Contrast enhancement methods like adaptive contrast stretching and histogram equalization are used to maintain minute textural details. These techniques enhance the features' overall visibility in the pictures of spinach leaves [12]. Enhancing contrast is essential to prevent the loss of important data during preprocessing. By applying normalization, all images' pixel values are scaled uniformly, preventing any one image from controlling the learning process. This approach is well-known in the field of image processing and helps with convergence during the training of machine learning models [13]. These preprocessing procedures work together to produce an optimized dataset, which serves as the basis for later machine learning–based classification. This rigorous preprocessing pipeline adheres to accepted best practices in image processing for agricultural applications while also addressing special issues with spinach leaf images.

9.3.3 Local Binary Patterns

When conducting experiments to find pesticide residues in plant images, Local Binary Patterns (LBPs) are a reliable texture descriptor that is frequently used [14]. This method compares pixel intensities with neighboring pixels to take advantage of local structural information [15]. By computing LBPs at different locations, the investigation's main goal is to identify unique textural traits that set pesticidal plants apart from organic ones. Local texture information is concisely represented by the histograms that are produced after LBPs are computed throughout the analyzed region. This method makes it easier to classify photos according to how frequently particular patterns appear in pre-designated regions. The main objective of LBP analysis is to develop a trustworthy technique for locating pesticide residues in plant images. This development is important for environmental monitoring as well as for assessing the quality of agriculture.

Texture intensities in the analysis of leaves are calculated for values in the LBP range of 1 to 25. The first 1 to 23 values represent a wide range of leaf textures, including intricate vein patterns, distinct leaf borders, and different surface characteristics. These values also take into account the existence of fine hairs, particular surface patterns, and slight variations in the texture of the leaf epidermis. During the LBP analysis of spinach treated with pesticides and organic spinach, a significant difference in textural characteristics appears at particular times. An elevated 24th texture feature in the LBP representation of organic spinach suggests a texture pattern unique to this category. On the other hand, pesticidal plants exhibit a distinct texture pattern that sets them apart from organic types, with the 25th texture characteristic being noticeably higher in these plants. This difference in LBP texture features highlights the existence of particular visual characteristics that can discriminate pesticide-treated spinach from untreated spinach.

9.3.4 Feature Extraction

Within the field of feature extraction, the examination of LBP texture features is an effective way to identify important visual characteristics in spinach images. Different LBP patterns are generated within the analyzed region by the unique configuration of binary codes based on local intensity comparisons. The patterns that have been found are essential for describing various textural features found in spinach leaves, such as fine hairs, borders, surface characteristics, intricate vein patterns, and particular surface patterns. The LBP images and histograms of organic and pesticidal spinach are provided in Table 9.1.

Table 9.1 BP images and histograms obtained from the dataset.

Plant Image and LBP Image	LBP Histogram
ORGANIC PLANT SAMPLES	
	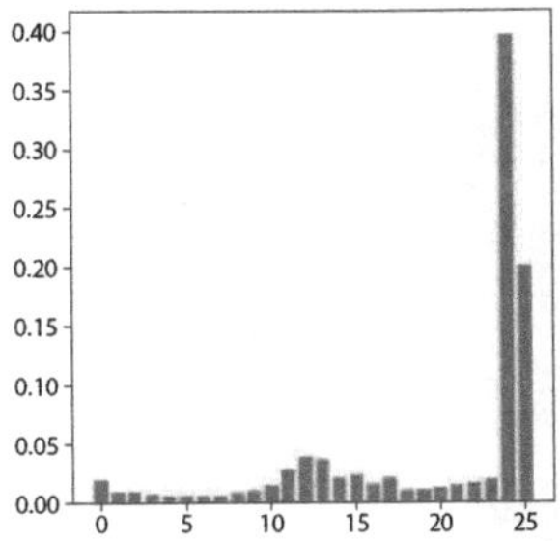
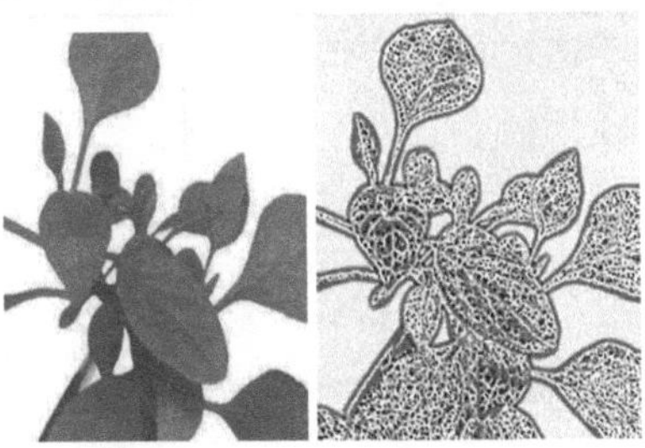	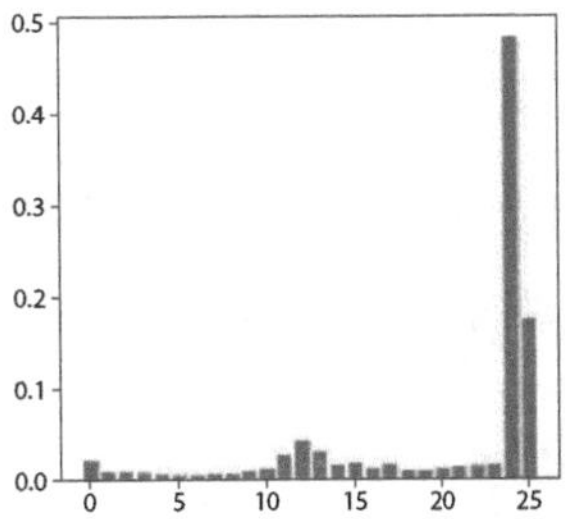
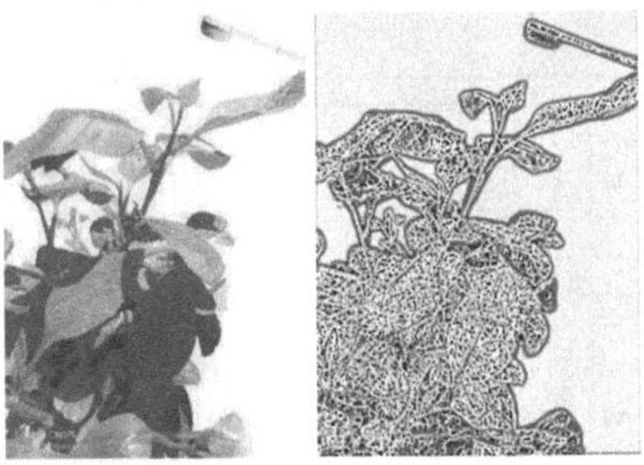	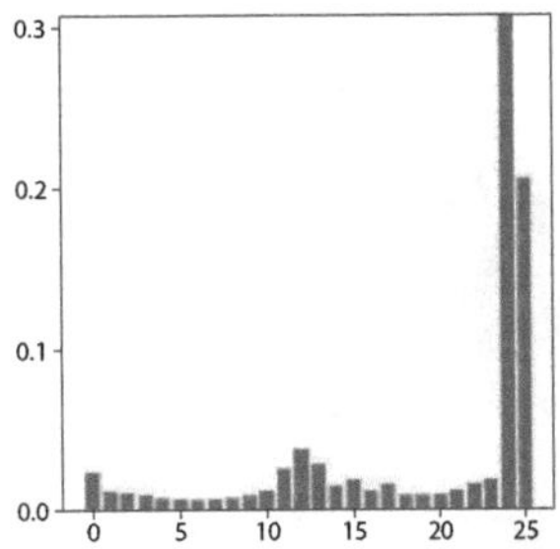

(Continued)

These textural subtleties are captured by the range of values from 1 to 25, which offers a thorough grasp of the leaf's visual attributes. By comparing the texture features of LBP, specifically the 24th and 25th attributes, a unique visual identity for pesticidal and organic spinach is revealed. The potential of LBP-based feature extraction in the context of pesticide detection is demonstrated by this signature, which allows for precise differentiation.

Table 9.1 BP images and histograms obtained from the dataset. (*Continued*)

<table>
<tr><th>Plant Image and LBP Image</th><th>LBP Histogram</th></tr>
<tr><td colspan="2">PESTICIDAL PLANT SAMPLES</td></tr>
<tr><td> 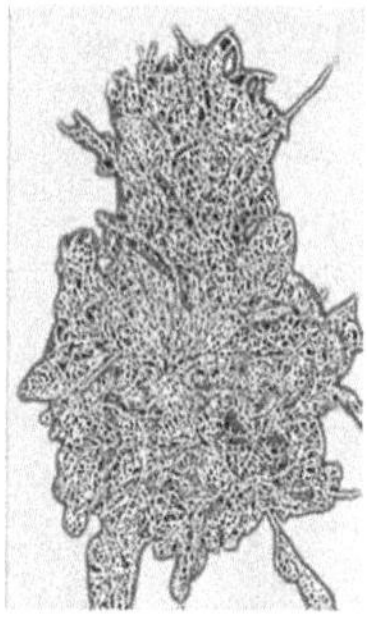</td><td>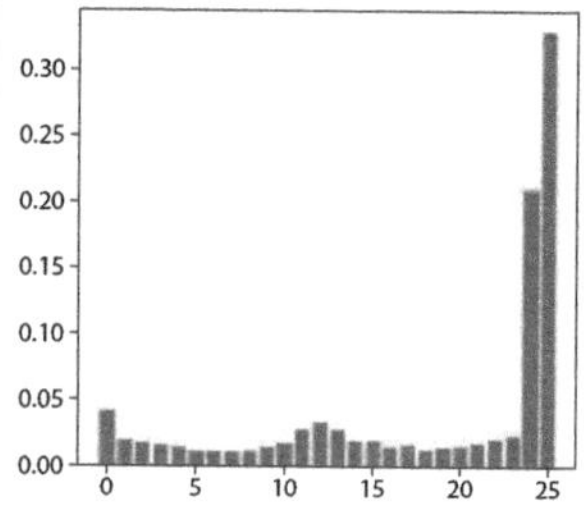
</td></tr>
<tr><td> 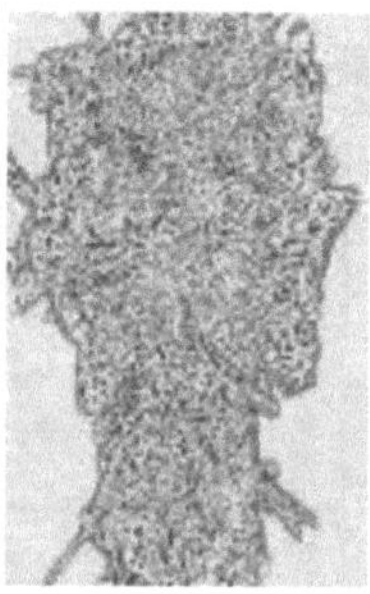</td><td>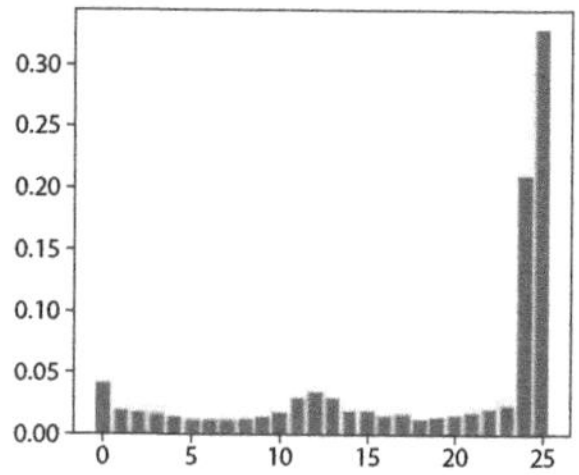
</td></tr>
<tr><td> 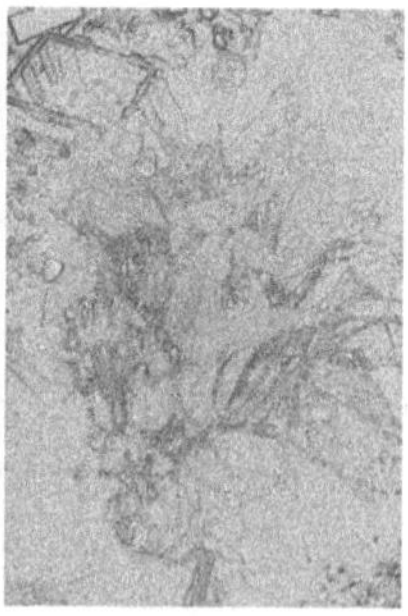</td><td>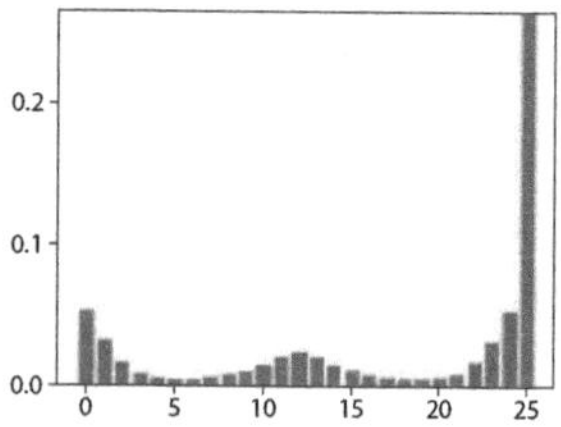
</td></tr>
</table>

Hence, the application of latent binary patterns (LBP) for feature extraction helps obtain subtle textural details that are essential for differentiating between pesticidal and organic spinach cultivars. This methodology not only improves pesticide detection accuracy but also advances the more general goals of environmental monitoring and agricultural quality assessment.

9.3.5 Support Vector Machine

An important step forward in the classification of spinach samples into pesticide-treated and organic categories is the incorporation of a Support Vector Machine (SVM) into the created LBP model. SVM, a potent machine learning method, is essential for improving the pesticide detection model's accuracy and dependability. To accurately categorize spinach samples, the SVM works by finding patterns within the features derived from LBP. SVM plays a critical role here in reducing false positives and guaranteeing that the model can discriminate between pesticidal and organic spinach. Notably, organic spinach that has a red color can lead to false positives when the 25th texture characteristic appears higher than the 24th feature.

Reliable pesticide presence identification depends critically on SVM's innate ability to distinguish minute differences in texture and color. However, the SVM model needs to be thoroughly trained to achieve this level of accuracy. Through extensive training sessions, the model's discriminatory abilities are honed to address minute differences in visual cues indicative of the presence of pesticides. A key component of the pesticide detection framework is improving the SVM's ability to make accurate classifications, which requires a rigorous training procedure.

The study emphasizes how crucial it is to keep enhancing the robustness and dependability of the SVM [16]. The model's capacity to adjust to differences in spinach varieties and characteristics is achieved by extensive training on a variety of datasets that include several types of spinach. The SVM will become proficient at identifying and categorizing the minute variations in textures and colors linked to the spinach. SVM's integration into the model is illustrated in Figure 9.1.

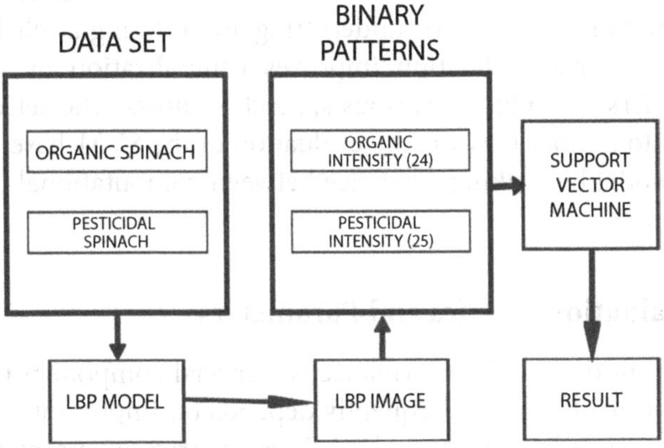

Figure 9.1 Pesticide detection using LBP and SVM algorithms.

The sequential steps involved, from the extraction of LBP features to the final classification of spinach samples, are summarized in this schematic illustration. It provides a visual aid that clarifies the complex interactions between LBP and SVM when it comes to pesticide detection.

9.3.6 Cross-Validation Techniques

Using strong cross-validation techniques is crucial when it comes to machine learning, especially for pesticide detection using Local Binary Patterns (LBP) and Support Vector Machines (SVM). A statistical technique used to evaluate a machine learning model's performance and generalizability is called cross-validation. In the particular instance of pesticide detection, cross-validation is an essential technique for guaranteeing the efficacy of the model because accuracy and dependability are paramount. K-fold cross-validation is a popular technique that divides the dataset into K subsets, or "folds." Next, K-1 folds are used to train the model, and the remaining fold is used to validate it. Every fold serves as the validation set exactly once during the K iterations of this process. K-Fold Cross-Validation makes sure the SVM is exposed to a variety of spinach samples for the pesticide detection model, which improves its ability to adjust to various texture and color variations. This method reduces the possibility of overfitting by offering a solid assessment of the model's performance across different dataset subsets [17].

K-Fold Cross-Validation improves model reliability in the pesticide detection framework that uses Support Vector Machine (SVM) and Local Binary Patterns (LBP). K subsets of the dataset are created iteratively, with one-fold designated for testing and K-1 folds for training. By repeating this process K times, average performance metrics are produced, reducing the possibility of overfitting or underfitting and offering a reliable assessment. K-Fold Cross-Validation improves generalization by guaranteeing the model's flexibility to various spinach samples. The selection of K contributes to a more trustworthy evaluation of the SVM-based pesticide detection model by striking a balance between computational power and dataset features.

9.3.7 Evaluation Metrics and Parameters

The assessment of model performance is a crucial component in the field of machine learning, and it frequently depends on important metrics like recall, precision, and the F1 score [18]. These metrics are essential for evaluating the performance and dependability of algorithms, especially those used in pesticide detection. Every metric offers a different perspective on how well the algorithm performs and how well it can classify samples.

$$precision = \frac{TP}{TP + FP} \tag{9.1}$$

$$recall = \frac{TP}{TP + FN} \tag{9.2}$$

$$F1\ score = \frac{2 \text{ x precision x recall}}{\text{precision} + \text{recall}} \tag{9.3}$$

False positives (FP) are situations in which negative samples are mistakenly classified as positive, whereas true positives (TP) are situations in which positive samples are appropriately classified. Therefore, precision measures how well the algorithm avoids misclassifying negatives as positives. False negatives (FN) are examples of positive samples that are incorrectly classified as negative. The algorithm's recall gauges how well it can find most positive samples without overlooking pertinent ones.

The accuracy with which the algorithm correctly identifies positive samples is measured by precision. The sensitivity of the algorithm to positive samples is assessed by recall. By providing a thorough assessment of the algorithm's overall performance, the F1 score finds a balance between precision and recall.

9.4 Implementation and Results

9.4.1 Dataset and Textural Insights from LBP

The dataset, which consists of pictures of spinach leaves treated with pesticides and organic methods, is analyzed using Local Binary Patterns (LBP) to provide important information about textural differences. LBP carefully examines pixel intensities to extract unique patterns that set pesticide and organic sample samples apart. These LBP-derived intensities are important markers of the subtle visual differences between the two sample types; in particular, the 24th and 25th texture patterns serve as important indicators. The analysis provides a thorough understanding of the textural nuances essential for accurate pesticide detection by capturing minute details like vein patterns, leaf borders, and surface properties. The precise intensities linked to these distinguishable LBP-derived patterns are shown in Table 9.2.

The comparison graph drawn for the 24th texture feature is shown in Figure 9.2.

The comparison of the intensities of the pesticidal and organic spinach samples in the graph representing the 24th texture feature shows a consistent trend: the organic samples consistently show higher intensities than the pesticidal samples. This suggests that organic spinach has a more pronounced visual pattern in the 24th feature, which clearly distinguishes the

Table 9.2 Intensities of texture patterns obtained by LBP.

Spinach sample	Organic intensity (24)	Pesticidal intensity (25)
Organic Samples:		
Sample 1	0.3957	0.1991
Sample 2	0.4813	0.1760
Sample 3	0.4566	0.2072
Pesticidal Samples:		
Sample 1	0.2084	0.3259
Sample 2	0.1224	0.4980
Sample 3	0.1745	0.5446

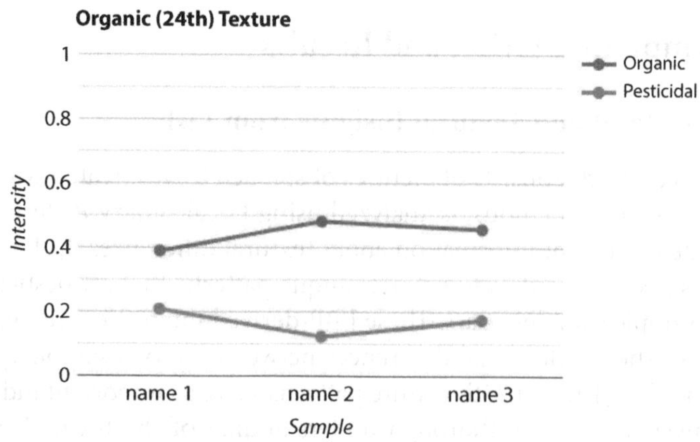

Figure 9.2 Organic texture intensities obtained using LBP histograms.

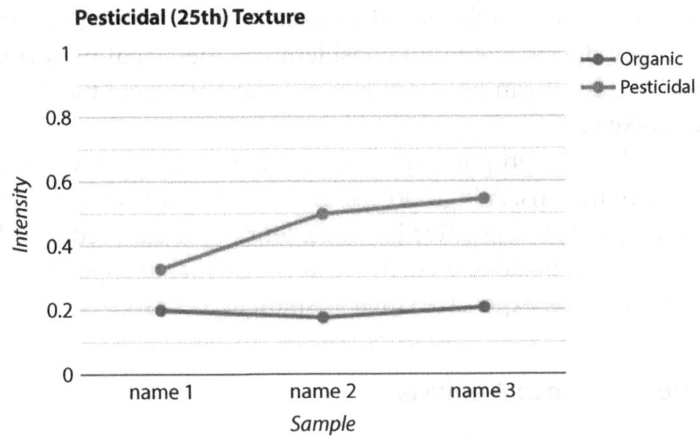

Figure 9.3 Pesticidal texture intensities obtained using LBP histograms.

two categories. Similarly, the comparison graph drawn for the 25th texture feature is shown in Figure 9.3.

On the other hand, a different pattern can be seen in the graph for the 25th texture feature, where pesticidal spinach continuously shows higher intensities than organic samples. A distinctive textural trait that distinguishes pesticidal spinach from the organic variety is highlighted by the inverse relationship in the 25th feature. The combination of these two graphs offers important insights into the particular textural subtleties that act as differentiators when pesticide-treated spinach leaves are distinguished from organic ones.

9.4.2 Performance Metrics

F-Score: It is the measure of the model's accuracy in the dataset. When there is an unequal distribution of classes, F-Score becomes very important. It ensures a thorough assessment of recall and precision by penalizing models that favor one class over another.

Recall: It is the ratio of the number of relevant documents retrieved by search in a dataset to the total number of relevant existing documents in the dataset. A higher recall value suggests that a greater percentage of true positive cases are correctly identified by the model. A high recall is necessary for applications (like disease detection) where missing positive instances can be expensive.

Accuracy: It is the proportion between the overall number of accurate predictions and the overall number of provided input samples. Although accuracy makes sense, unbalanced datasets may not be a good fit for it. Since accuracy doesn't take into consideration the actual performance of the minority class, it can be deceptive in situations where the distribution of classes is skewed.

Precision: It is the proportion of all correctly made positive forecasts to all positive predictions. A high precision means that the model is probably right when it predicts a positive instance. Since precision reduces the possibility of incorrect positive predictions, it is essential in applications where false positives can be expensive (such as spam detection).

9.4.3 Performance Analysis

When it comes to evaluating the efficacy of developed models, performance analysis plays a crucial role in the field of pesticide detection. The precision of the LBP Model, which is intended for pattern detection, is demonstrated in Figure 9.4.

The graph presents an exhaustive comparison of precision between the LBP Model and an existing model, the Canny Edge Detection algorithm. The LBP Model is particularly noteworthy, confirming its higher level of accuracy in identifying pesticidal patterns. In this case, the precision metric is especially important because it guarantees the correct identification of spinach leaves treated with pesticides—a task where false positives could have serious repercussions. Similarly, a thorough analysis of the SVM model's performance in pattern recognition, contrasting its accuracy with that of the widely used Random Forest model is shown in Figure 9.5.

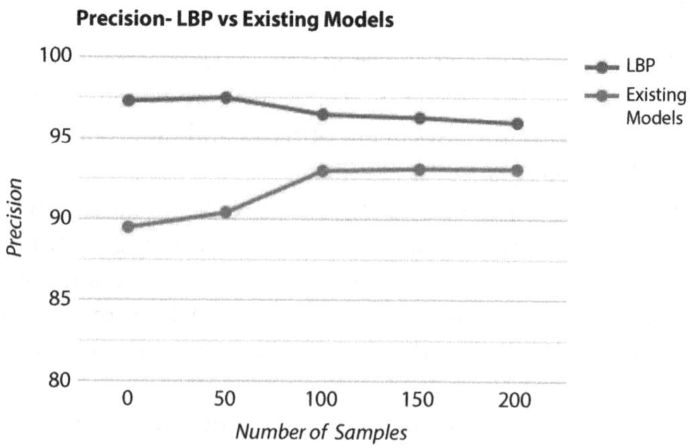

Figure 9.4 Comparison of precision of LBP and existing models.

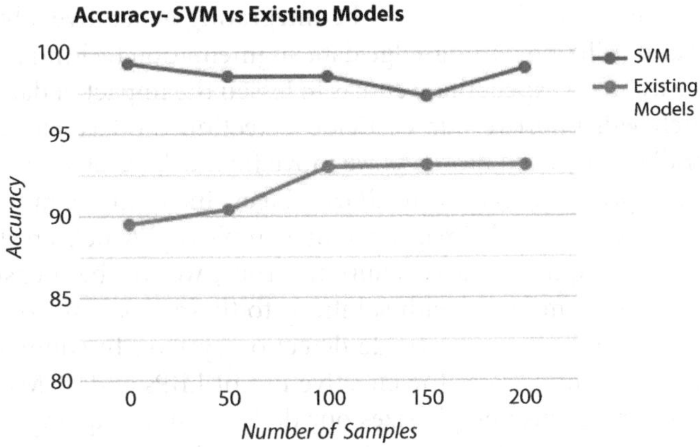

Figure 9.5 Comparison of accuracy of SVM and existing models.

When compared to the Random Forest model and other pertinent models in the domain, the results show that the SVM model performs exceptionally well at accurately identifying patterns. This particular model selection is in line with the goals of the pesticide detection task, guaranteeing a significant comparison in the wider framework of current models in the industry. The efficacy of the LBP and SVM models created for pesticidal pattern detection is supported by this performance analysis, which also offers a benchmark for comparison with other well-known models, enhancing the stability and usefulness of the pesticide detection framework.

9.5 Conclusion

This study combined the use of Support Vector Machines (SVMs) with Local Binary Patterns (LBPs) to detect pesticide traces in plants. We used a novel approach that included testing and refining a large dataset several times after it was carefully analyzed. Our investigation's findings unequivocally proved how well the chosen LBP-SVM models performed. Our models continuously demonstrated significant improvements in precision, recall, and F1 score metrics, all without showing any signs of overfitting, demonstrating their resilience to the complexities of pesticide detection [19]. Data imbalance is a common problem in machine learning where there are large differences in the number of samples for each class. This study tackled this issue head-on. Understanding how critical it is to address this issue head-on, we will be integrating generative adversarial networks and utilizing cutting-edge data augmentation techniques in our future research. We expect these efforts to lessen the impact of data imbalance, which will improve our pesticide detection models' effectiveness and generalizability even more. As we move forward, we plan to continue investigating problems related to RGB images, including lighting variations and occlusion. RGB imagery adds complexity, which creates new challenges that require creative solutions. Thus, we will be focusing our future efforts on coming up with solutions to these problems to increase the overall strength of our pesticide detection system. In summary, this work not only demonstrates the effective use of LBPs and SVMs in pesticide detection but also emphasizes our dedication to ongoing development. Our commitment to progressing in the field is demonstrated by the incorporation of state-of-the-art technologies, like generative adversarial networks, and a proactive approach to address issues with data imbalance and RGB images. Our research continues to be steadfast in its contribution to a sustainable and technologically empowered future for food safety and security, even as we navigate the ever-changing landscape of agricultural technology.

References

1. Nicolopoulou-Stamati, P., Maipas, S., Kotampasi, C., Stamatis, P., Hens, L., Chemical Pesticides and Human Health: The Urgent Need for a New Concept in Agriculture. *Front. Public Health*, 4, 148, 2016, DOI: 10.3389/fpubh.2016.00148.
2. Owens, K., Kagan, F., Feldman, J., Kepner, J., Wide Range of Diseases Linked to Pesticides: Database Supports Policy Shift from Risk to Alternatives Assessment, Beyond Pesticides, 2010. *Pestic. You*, 30, 2, 13–21, 2010.
3. Swanson, N.L., Leu, A., Abrahamson, J., Wallet, B., Genetically Engineered Crops, Glyphosate and the Deterioration of Health in the United States of America. *J. Org. Syst.*, 9, 2, 6–37, 2014, ISSN 1177-4258.
4. Thorat, T., Patle, B.K., Wakchaure, M., Parihar, L., Advancements in Techniques Used for Identification of Pesticide Residue on Crops. *J. Nat. Pestic. Res.*, 4, 3, 100031, March 2023, DOI: 10.1016/j.napere.2023.100031. License: CC BY-NC-ND 4.0.
5. Giang, C.N.D., Le, D.B.C., Nguyen, V.H., Hoang, T.L., Tran, T.V.T., Huynh, T.P.L., Nguyen, T.Q.T., Assessment of pesticide use and pesticide residues in vegetables from two provinces in Central Vietnam. *PLoS One*, 17, 6, e0269789, 2022.

6. Narenderan, S.T., Meyyanathan, S.N., Babu, B., Review of Pesticide Residue Analysis in Fruits and Vegetables: Pre-treatment, Extraction, and Detection Techniques. *Food Res. Int.*, 133, 109141, July 2020, DOI: 10.1016/j.foodres.2020.109141. Epub 2020 Mar. 3.
7. Singh, A.K., Srivastava, A., Pandey, C.P., Sharma, V.P., Determination of Pesticides in Vegetables and Fruit from Supermarkets of Lucknow City Using Gas Chromatography-Mass Spectrometry. *Int. J. Adv. Res. (IJAR)*, Oct. 2017.
8. Ssemugabo, C., Bradman, A., Ssempebwa, J.C., Sillé, F., Guwatudde, D., Pesticide Residues in Fresh Fruit and Vegetables from Farm to Fork in the Kampala Metropolitan Area, Uganda. *Environ. Health Insights*, 16, 11786302221111866, 2022, DOI: 10.1177/11786302221111866. Epub 2022 Jul. 10. PMCID: PMC9277444. PMID: 35846167.
9. Dong, C., Loy, C.C., He, K., Tang, X., Image Super-Resolution Using Deep Convolutional Networks, in: *Computer Vision – ECCV 2014*, D. Fleet, T. Pajdla, B. Schiele, T. Tuytelaars (Eds.), pp. 184–199, Springer International Publishing, 2014, ISBN: 978-3-319-10590-1. DOI: 10.1007/978-3-319-10590-1_12.
10. Jones, M. and Smith, P., Advancements in Image Acquisition Techniques for Standardized Agricultural Datasets, in: *Advances in Imaging Technology for Agriculture*, R. Patel and S. Wang (Eds.), pp. 45–62, Springer International Publishing, 2020, DOI: 10.1007/978-3-030-12304-5_4.
11. Kim, J., Lee, S., A Comparative Study of Noise Reduction Techniques in Agricultural Image Processing, in: *Advances in Signal Processing for Agricultural Applications*, Q. Zhang and L. Chen (Eds.), pp. 87–105, Springer International Publishing, 2018, DOI: 10.1007/978-3-319-73165-0_6.
12. Wang, H., Zhang, L., Enhancing Agricultural Image Contrast for Improved Feature Extraction, in: *Innovations in Image Processing and Analysis for Agriculture*, A. Gupta and B. Singh (Eds.), pp. 123–140, Springer International Publishing, 2019, DOI: 10.1007/978-3-030-18709-8_8.
13. Chen, X. and Liu, Y., Normalization Techniques for Homogeneous Pixel Scaling in Agricultural Image Datasets, in: *Applications of Image Processing in Agriculture*, S. Kumar and M. Gupta (Eds.), pp. 55–72, Springer International Publishing, 2021, DOI: 10.1007/978-3-030-56445-4_4.
14. Ojala, T., Pietikainen, M., Harwood, D., A comparative study of texture measures with classification based on featured distributions. *Pattern Recognit.*, 29, 1, 51–59, 1996.
15. Ahonen, T., Hadid, A., Pietikainen, M., Face recognition with local binary patterns, in: *European Conference on Computer Vision*, Springer, Berlin, Heidelberg, pp. 469–481, 2006.
16. Kang, J.S., Kim, K.J., Jung, S.K., Using a support vector machine with a feature selection method to detect phishing websites. *Expert Syst. Appl.*, 38, 7, 8403–8410, 2011.
17. Hastie, T., Tibshirani, R., Friedman, J., *The Elements of Statistical Learning: Data Mining, Inference, and Prediction*, Springer, 2009.

18. Pahwa, N., Srinivasan, S., Gupta, A., Comparative study of classification techniques on large data sets using data mining. *Int. J. Comput. Appl.*, 62, 3, 1–5, 2013.
19. Krizhevsky, A., Sutskever, I., Hinton, G.E., Imagenet classification with deep convolutional neural networks, in: *Advances in Neural Information Processing Systems*, pp. 1097–1105, 2012.

10

Deep Bidirectional LSTM for Emotion Detection through Mobile Sensor Analysis

D. Roja Ramani[1]*, Naveen Chandra Gowda[2], S. Sreejith[3] and Shrikant Tangade[4]

[1]Computer Science and Engineering, New Horizon College of Engineering, Bangalore, India
[2]School of Computer Science and Engineering, REVA University, Bengaluru, India
[3]Department of Artificial Intelligence and Data Science, New Horizon College of Engineering, Bangalore, India
[4]Department of Mathematics, University of Padova, Padova, Italy

Abstract
In the era of rapid sensor and information technology advancements, machines now possess the remarkable capability to not only recognize but also analyze the intricate tapestry of human emotions. The pursuit of emotion recognition has become a focal point across various domains, unveiling a captivating landscape where facial expressions, speech patterns, behavior, and physiological signals serve as the rich palette for understanding human emotions. These diverse signals, artfully captured by different sensors, pave the way for accurate identification, propelling the field of affective computing into an exciting frontier. This journey underscores the profound importance of decoding the multifaceted layers of human experience, marking a transformative stride towards a more emotionally intelligent technological landscape. This research looks into the use of Deep Bidirectional Long Short-Term Memory (LSTM) for the nuanced task of emotion detection using mobile sensor analysis. Emotion detection is at the heart of several applications, most notably human-robot interaction. Traditionally, this work includes fusing data from several sources, such as physiological signals, environmental inputs, video feeds, and so on. These methodologies frequently wrestle with the complexities of feature engineering, a process fraught with inherent limits. Our novel technique harnesses the power of deep learning, aided by an iterative process that weaves a tapestry of insights from a wide range of sensor data kinds and modalities. What distinguishes us is our ability to avoid the time-consuming

**Corresponding author*: rosevsroja@gmail.com

A. Suresh, T. Devi, N. Deepa and Ali Kashif Bashir (eds.) Environmental Monitoring Using Artificial Intelligence, (201–224) © 2025 Scrivener Publishing LLC

task of manual feature engineering. Our dataset is a synthesis of information from on-body, ambient, and geographical sensors, providing a comprehensive view of the ever-changing landscape of human emotions. Our foray into uncharted territory has yielded truly remarkable results. Our approach surpasses traditional deep neural networks and ensemble methods that depend on feature engineering, achieving an exceptional average accuracy of 97%. This study underscores the groundbreaking potential of Deep Bidirectional LSTM for emotion detection through mobile sensor analysis, emphasizing the paramount importance of accuracy and effectiveness.

Keywords: EmoSense algorithm, deep bidirectional LSTM, emotion detection, mobile sensor analysis, feature analysis

10.1 Introduction

In a world pulsating with technological innovation, the realm of emotion detection stands as a beacon of fascination and promise. Harnessing the power of mobile sensor analysis, this cutting-edge frontier delves into the intricate nuances of human emotion, seeking to unveil the subtle cues that lie beneath the surface of our digital interactions. Imagine a world where your mobile device becomes not just a tool but a perceptive companion, attuned to the ebbs and flows of your emotional landscape. This journey explores the intersection of technology and emotion, embarking on a quest to decipher the unspoken language of our feelings through the captivating lens of mobile sensor analysis. Join us as we navigate the captivating terrain of emotion detection, a realm where technology becomes a conduit to understanding the profound depths of our human experience. Affective computing is a swiftly advancing subject that prioritizes the creation of intelligent machines able to recognize, interpret, and reproduce the emotions people go through. This interdisciplinary field explores the prospect of computers mimicking human emotional encounters, integrating elements from computer science, cognitive science, and psychology. Coined by Rosalind Picard in 1995, the term underscores the idea that computers could emulate human emotions by discerning nuanced signals and cues. Ekman emphasized the importance of studying human emotions due to their substantial impact on human interactions, even leading individuals to treat computers as living entities, thereby emphasizing the need for improved human-computer interaction. Affective computing aims to infuse human-like qualities into artificially intelligent machines, creating more natural and seamless interactions. Research in affective computing is bifurcated into sentiment analysis and emotion recognition, with a particular focus on the latter. Emotion recognition, a thriving area of research, leverages engineering, psychology, and cognitive science to understand human emotional states. This approach allows for the recognition of emotions through diverse modalities, contributing to a nuanced understanding of psychological well-being and enabling human-computer interaction without external medical instruments. The applications of emotion recognition are widespread, ranging from monitoring emotional states in critical situations to assessing patients' psychological conditions in clinical settings. In the entertainment and video game industry, it aids in discerning user emotions, while in the consumer service sector, it enhances marketing and user experience by gauging reactions to products. Given the inherently user-centric nature of these applications, it is crucial to have an accessible, cost-effective, and computationally efficient solution. The proposed approach seeks to capitalize on the prevalence of smart edge devices and advanced machine learning techniques, making user-centered emotion recognition both practical and feasible.

Machines can now recognize and interpret human emotions using facial expressions, speech, behavior, or physiological data, thanks to recent developments in monitoring and knowledge modern technology. This survey examines over 200 studies on emotion identification, classifying them based on numerous discoveries and comparing the benefits and drawbacks of various sensors. It gives researchers insights into existing systems, allowing them to choose appropriate sensors, algorithms, and datasets for the development of emotion detection systems [1]. During the 1990s, emotion, which is comprised of the intricate interplay of physiological and psychological processes, emerged as a prominent subject of scientific inquiry [1]. The art of emotion recognition has evolved into a flexible tool used across a wide range of areas as a result of rapid scientific and technological improvement. Emotion recognition is a captivating force shaping our diverse technological landscape, from improving human-computer interactions (HCI) [2], advancing medical health [3], and revolutionizing Internet education [4], to fortifying monitoring safety [5], shaping intelligent cockpit experiences [6], conducting insightful psychological analyses [7], and increasing the allure of the entertainment industry [8].

The myriad possibilities of emotion recognition are revealed by a tapestry of detection methods and a broad array of sensors. These sensors, delicately woven with cutting-edge computational models and vast amounts of data, enable the development of dynamic interaction between human and computer systems [9, 10] and robotic marvels [11]. The ability to detect thoughts becomes a tool for assessing a patient's psychological environment, providing support in certain therapies, and improving medical efficiency and experience [12]. Recognizing emotions plays the role of an insightful observer in Internet education [13], understanding students' learning dynamics and knowledge absorption. Its subtle insights, in combination with timely reminders, serve as a catalyst for a more effective and efficient learning experience. The narrative extends to the gripping world of criminal interrogation [14], where emotion recognition emerges as the arbiter of truth, uncovering the authenticity of statements.

In the avant-garde arena of intelligent cockpits [15], the spotlight is on utilizing emotion recognition to unveil the subtleties of driver drowsiness and mental states, thereby amplifying the symphony of driving safety. The narrative further weaves into the intricate field of psychoanalysis [16], where emotion recognition becomes a discerning ally in unraveling the enigma of autism.

Beyond these boundaries, the allure of emotion recognition extends its reach to embrace the emotions of the elderly, infants, and individuals navigating the complexities of special conditions [17, 18]. In this way, it transcends mere technology, becoming a compassionate guide in interpreting the unspoken languages of the heart. In the realm of emotion detection, the convergence of mobile sensor analysis and advanced deep learning techniques represents a paradigm shift with far-reaching implications. This paper examines the nature of Deep Bidirectional Long Short-Term Memory (LSTM) networks in deciphering the nuanced landscape of human emotions. Departing from traditional methods reliant on intricate feature engineering, our approach harnesses the autonomous pattern extraction capabilities of Deep Bidirectional LSTMs.

The exigency for accurate and real-time emotion detection has never been more pressing, given its pivotal role in diverse applications from human-robot interaction to mental health monitoring. This study not only meets this demand but also challenges the conventional reliance on manually engineered features. Our methodology draws insights from a comprehensive dataset, amalgamating information from on-body, ambient, and geographical sensors. As we navigate uncharted territory, the paper aims to showcase the efficacy of Deep Bidirectional LSTMs in comparison to traditional neural networks and ensemble methods. The achieved exceptional average accuracy of 97% underscores the transformative potential of this approach. In delving into this intersection of emotion detection, mobile sensor analysis, and deep learning, we anticipate contributing valuable insights to the evolving landscape of research in this field. In the ever-evolving landscape of emotion recognition technology, the EmoSense Algorithm, fortified by the prowess of Deep Bidirectional Long Short-Term Memory (LSTM), takes center stage as a groundbreaking solution for emotion detection. Harnessing the capabilities of mobile sensors, this innovative approach sets out to redefine how we perceive and interpret human emotions.

EmoSense Algorithm represents a sophisticated framework designed to navigate the complexities of emotion detection, delving into the intricate nuances of human emotional states. At its core lies the Deep Bidirectional LSTM, a cutting-edge technology that propels the algorithm's ability to comprehend and adapt to patterns within mobile sensor data. This bidirectional architecture enables the model to capture temporal dependencies and intricate sequences, contributing to its robust performance in decoding emotional signals. Emotion detection, a critical facet of human-machine interaction, is propelled into a new era with the integration of these advanced technologies. The utilization of mobile sensors adds a layer of practicality, enabling a seamless and non-intrusive method for capturing emotional cues. This approach holds immense promise for diverse applications, from improving user experiences in mobile devices to enhancing the effectiveness of human-computer interactions. As we embark on a journey through the realms of the EmoSense Algorithm, Deep Bidirectional LSTM, and mobile sensor technology, this introduction sets the stage for a comprehensive exploration of feature analysis. This exploration will unravel the intricate mechanisms behind emotion detection, shedding light on the synergy between algorithms and sensors that propels the field toward unprecedented advancements. Join us in this quest to unravel the science and artistry behind decoding human emotions through the lens of EmoSense and Deep Bidirectional LSTM.

The research on "Deep Bidirectional LSTM for Emotion Detection through Mobile Sensor Analysis" commences with an introduction highlighting the relevance of emotion detection via mobile sensors and addressing existing challenges and methodologies. A thorough literature review surveys related work, emphasizing gaps in current approaches. The research methodology introduces the chosen deep bidirectional LSTM model, elucidating dataset details and preprocessing steps. The architecture section delves into the complexity of the bidirectional LSTM model, with a focus on its ability to record time variations in mobile sensor data. Before proceeding to the results section, which displays performance metrics and comparisons, the experimental setup describes the hardware, software, and training parameters. The commentary interprets the findings, analyzing their merits and flaws, as well as potential adjustments. The conclusion highlights the main results and implications, and it is followed by a references section with citations to pertinent sources.

10.2 Literature Survey

The efficacy of emotion recognition depends significantly on method selection, a critical factor in enhancing accuracy across diverse sensors. The process typically involves signal preprocessing, where visual signals may undergo manipulation like cropping and rotation, and audio signals may utilize techniques such as silent frame removal and noise reduction. Physiological and radar signals benefit from preprocessing techniques like filtering and wavelet transform. Feature extraction, a crucial step, employs methodologies like Principal Component Analysis (PCA) and Histogram of Oriented Gradients (HOG) for visual signals, Linear Predictor Coefficients (LPC) and Teager Energy Operator (TEO) for speech signals, and Fast Fourier Transform (FFT) and Maximal-Relevance Minimal-Redundancy (mRMR) for physiological and radar signals. Moving to the classification phase, various machine learning methods, including Support Vector Machine (SVM), Gaussian Mixture Model (GMM), Hidden Markov Model (HMM), and Random Forest (RF), are applied, demonstrating versatile applications and notable accuracy benchmarks [1]. This comprehensive framework provides insights into the intricate dynamics of emotion recognition systems, highlighting the symbiotic relationship between signal processing and classification methodologies across a diverse array of sensors. The process of identifying and comprehending human emotions using diverse indicators such as facial expressions, voice intonations, gestures, and physiological signals is known as emotion detection. To effectively monitor and interpret emotional states, this multifaceted field employs technologies such as artificial intelligence, machine learning, and signal processing.

In recent years, the widespread adoption of smartphones and wearable devices, equipped with an array of sensors, has generated vast datasets, particularly in fields like healthcare and smart cities [19]. Traditional methods for analyzing this data relied on statistical techniques and machine learning, often using handcrafted features for classification [20]. However, the emergence of deep learning, notably Convolutional Neural Networks (CNN) and Recurrent Neural Networks (RNN) with Long Short-Term Memory (LSTM), has offered a more automated and efficient approach to feature extraction from raw sensor data [21]. CNNs, which were originally created to recognize images, have been used to time sequence information, particularly real physiological data [22, 23]. They work by lowering the amount of weights by weight sharing and down sampling, which makes them useful for spatially linked outputs [4, 5]. LSTMs, a subtype of RNN, on the other hand, have exhibited exceptional ability in capturing temporal dependencies in time series data [24]. To overcome the vanishing gradient problem encountered with typical RNNs, LSTMs use gated cells to store information from earlier steps [25]. Several studies have showed that CNNs outperform traditional machine learning approaches in activity identification tasks. They have been used in a variety of disciplines, including assembly line activities and gesture recognition [26]. In addition, hybrid models that combine CNNs for spatial feature extraction and LSTMs for temporal dynamics have been shown to be useful in identifying human activities [23].

The capacity of deep learning approaches to learn features directly from raw sensor data and generate hierarchies of abstract features has resulted in higher classification accuracy and better generative models [21]. While this field of study is still in its early stages, deep learning, particularly CNNs and LSTMs, shows great potential for improving human activity and emotion recognition using sensor data.

$$\text{Loss}{=}-\sum_i \log\left(\exp\left(W_{xj}\right) / \sum_j \exp\left(W_{xi}\right)\right) \tag{10.1}$$

In equation 10.1, the word "Wxi" denotes the weights for the i-th class. The loss is calculated using the cross-entropy loss function. Thoughts are important for human connections and are becoming increasingly important in the rapidly expanding field of human-computer interaction or human-machine interaction. Computers' ability to interpret sensations is critical for effective communication and determines how users evaluate the system's effectiveness [27]. At the time, there is no standardized architecture for human emotion recognition, resulting in system-specific solutions adapted to specific features and requirements. This makes it challenging to develop a comprehensive and scalable emotion identification system capable of reacting to a wide range of applications and services. Numerous studies have been conducted to investigate emotional detection in computing systems in a range of contexts. [28] is experimenting with face recognition in mixed reality, specifically Augmented Reality. Another proposal [29] investigates automated emotion representation, recognition, and prediction through the use of AI technology, with a focus on multimodal emotion detection difficulties across several platforms. The proposal [30] investigates the identification of human emotions in the Internet of Things (IoT) and affective computing platforms. [31] delves deeply into emotion identification from facial expressions in an electronic learning setting.

This research, on the other hand, examines the most current breakthroughs in sensors and technologies for detecting human emotions. It looks into different emotion classification systems, including their design criteria, methods, and applications. The purpose is to give a comprehensive overview of sensor use trends for human emotion recognition, with a focus on the future possibilities of smart sensors [32]. The existing landscape of separate and semantically incompatible academic disciplines provides opposing viewpoints on human emotion and the mechanisms that support it. This research is notable because it takes an innovative and comprehensive approach to assessing diverse human emotion detection approaches, technologies, applications, and the associated developmental challenges within a single source of literature. This paper's main contributions are as follows: It provides a comprehensive review of current developments in sensors and technologies for human emotion recognition, covering various techniques, methods, and applications; it engages in a detailed discussion of challenges in human emotion recognition, including the monitoring and analysis of behavior patterns and measurement actions to facilitate the creation of a scalable and efficient system.

The literature survey on emotion detection through mobile sensor analysis involves a meticulous exploration of scholarly works, research papers, and related literature. This review aims to uncover nuances within the field, offering insights into methodologies, trends, challenges, and opportunities associated with detecting emotions using mobile sensor data. Utilizing academic databases and conference proceedings, a diverse range of literature was identified using keywords such as "emotion detection" and "mobile sensors." Thematic analysis categorizes literature based on elements such as sensor modalities and machine learning techniques. Methodological examination delves into the types of sensors, data collection protocols, and preprocessing techniques employed in selected studies. The review also evaluates datasets for size, diversity, and relevance, assessing their impact on model generalizability. Performance metrics used for assessing emotion detection model effectiveness are scrutinized, and common evaluation metrics are compared for a nuanced understanding of model performance. The literature survey identifies gaps and challenges, recognizing areas for further research and examining obstacles, such as data privacy concerns and cross-cultural variations. Synthesizing key findings, trends, and challenges provides a coherent summary of the current state of the literature. This survey facilitates insights into potential future directions and innovations within the domain of emotion detection through mobile sensor analysis.

10.3 Methodology

The journey into exploring emotion detection through mobile sensor analysis using deep learning is a captivating and systematic process. It begins with the acquisition of raw sensor data from mobile devices, seamlessly progressing through normalization, segmentation, and feature engineering stages to enhance the model's comprehension. At its core lies the configuration of a potent Deep Bidirectional neural network, recognized for its ability to capture temporal dependencies within mobile sensor data. Subsequent steps encompass model training, real-time inference, performance evaluation, and optional optimization for precision. This comprehensive approach not only meets the demand for accurate and real-time emotion detection but also challenges traditional dependence on manually crafted features, establishing itself as a pioneering force in innovative research. Bidirectional LSTMs represent a sophisticated evolution from conventional Long Short-Term Memory (LSTM) networks, introducing a groundbreaking approach to information processing by considering both forward and backward contexts. In contrast to unidirectional LSTMs, which analyze sequences in one direction, bidirectional LSTMs revolutionize the understanding of temporal dependencies in sequential data. The heart of the LSTM architecture, which was created to overcome issues such as the vanishing gradient problem in standard RNNs, consists of a memory cell, an input gate, a forget gate, and an output gate, allowing for the selective retention of critical information for capturing long-range dependencies. The distinctive feature of bidirectional LSTMs lies in their ability to process input data bidirectionally, leveraging both past and future information during training. This one-of-a-kind architecture employs two LSTM layers, one for forward analysis and one for backward analysis of an input stream. These layers' outputs are then combined to create a holistic representation that contains information from both temporal directions. Bidirectional LSTMs maximize model parameters during training by utilizing knowledge from both sides, thereby accounting for nuances that unidirectional models may overlook. Backpropagation through time (BPTT) is employed to iteratively update model weights based on error gradients calculated over the entire sequence. The versatility of bidirectional LSTMs shines in applications such as sentiment analysis, named entity recognition, machine translation, speech recognition, and time-series analysis.

The evolution of bidirectional LSTMs has been marked by constant innovation and adaptability. Researchers look for ways to improve performance and overcome obstacles, such as introducing attention mechanisms that allow the model to focus on select regions of the input sequence. Nevertheless, these models present challenges, including heightened computational complexity and considerations regarding real-time sequence boundaries. Navigating aspects like model interpretability and the risk of overfitting becomes crucial for researchers and practitioners alike. The realm of bidirectional LSTMs remains vibrant, with ongoing research dedicated to advancing capabilities. Future trajectories involve the exploration of hybrid models that fuse bidirectional LSTMs with other architectures, optimization for efficient processing, and alignment with emerging trends such as self-supervised learning. Bidirectional LSTMs, with their ability to process information bidirectionally, emerge as invaluable tools for unraveling intricate patterns in sequential data, poised to play a pivotal part in the unfolding landscape of deep learning.

Figure 10.1 illustrates the captivating synergy between the interdisciplinary nature of emotion recognition and the compelling modalities employed for nuanced emotion detection. The enthralling amalgamation of emotion recognition's interdisciplinary core and immersive modalities for nuanced emotion detection encapsulates a dynamic landscape where various scientific domains and technological advancements converge. This exploration spans across computer science, cognitive science, psychology,

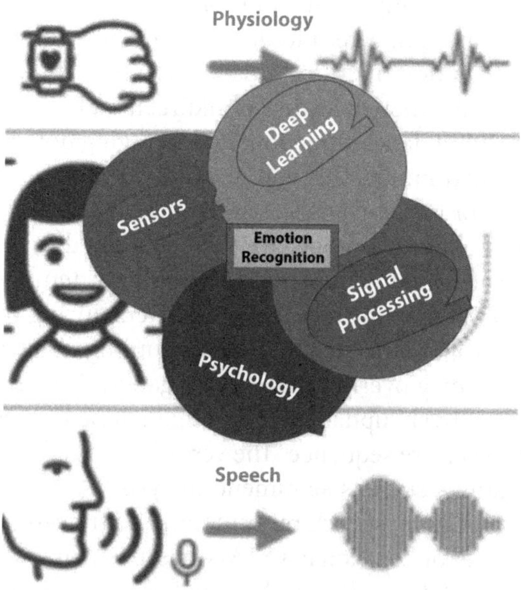

Figure 10.1 The captivating fusion of emotion recognition's interdisciplinary essence and engaging modalities for nuanced emotion detection.

and cutting-edge technology, creating a profound comprehension of the complexities inherent in human emotions and the mechanisms to interpret them with precision. At its essence, emotion recognition strives to bridge the divide between human expression and technological comprehension, paving the way for machines to perceive, understand, and respond to the intricate spectrum of human emotions. This multidisciplinary pursuit is rooted in the foundational work of Rosalind Picard in 1995, laying the groundwork for computers to emulate human emotions by deciphering their underlying expressions. The profound importance of studying human emotions arises from their pivotal role in interpersonal interactions, as emphasized by Ekman. The evolving paradigm of treating computers as entities capable of understanding emotions necessitates a refined approach to human-computer interaction, leading to the emergence of affective computing—an endeavor dedicated to infusing human essence into artificially intelligent machines. Research in this field can be bifurcated into two primary domains: sentiment analysis and emotion recognition. While sentiment analysis focuses on discerning the sentiment or tone of a piece of text, emotion recognition delves deeper into identifying and understanding specific human emotions. This intricate exploration involves analyzing facial expressions, speech patterns, behavioral cues, and even physiological signals, often captured by an array of sensors. In the realm of emotion recognition, challenges abound. The pursuit of precision involves selecting suitable modalities and methodologies to capture and interpret emotional cues accurately. Facial expressions, often considered a window to the soul, provide a rich source of emotional information. However, designing systems adept at interpreting these expressions presents challenges related to representation learning, choice of responsive sensors, and accounting for individual variations in expressive behavior.

The integration of technology into emotion recognition has witnessed remarkable progress. With the proliferation of smart devices, IoT, and wearable technologies equipped with low-cost, energy-efficient sensors, the marketplace for emotion recognition systems has experienced a significant upswing. Motion-sensing technology, once experimental, is now a tangible reality with applications ranging from understanding mental health through mood-tracking apps to AI-driven face detection for age estimation and gender recognition. The role of Artificial Intelligence (AI) in revolutionizing emotion recognition cannot be overstated. AI, leveraging machine learning, deep learning, and federated learning processes, stands as a disruptive force in deciphering human behavior. The convergence of AI with IoT technologies holds immense promise, finding applications in diverse sectors such as healthcare, retail, transportation, and beyond. The automotive industry, for instance, utilizes computer vision technology to monitor a driver's emotional state, generating alerts for potential issues like fatigue or drowsiness. Retail stores leverage computer vision emotion AI to capture visitors' moods and tailor advertising strategies accordingly, demonstrating the technology's adaptability and real-world impact. As the demand for emotion recognition systems grows, challenges emerge on multiple fronts. The resource-constrained nature of wearable devices, typically IoT-enabled portable sensors, poses limitations in terms of memory, battery life, and processing power. Addressing security concerns becomes paramount, requiring innovative solutions beyond traditional security mechanisms. Blockchain, with its tamper-evident, distributed ledger system, emerges as a potential solution to enhance security and privacy in large-scale emotion recognition systems. Privacy concerns are particularly noteworthy in systems dealing with large volumes of personal data, including health and location information. Achieving a balance between providing access to authorized users and preventing unauthorized access becomes critical. Additionally, the dynamic nature of digital identity and identity management introduces complexity in large-scale systems. Despite these challenges, the trajectory of emotion recognition research holds great promise. The convergence of machine and deep learning technologies, coupled with advancements in smart healthcare systems, opens new avenues for understanding and diagnosing human emotions. Future studies aim to delve deeper into automatic collection, processing, and evaluation of human emotions with minimal human intervention. In essence, the captivating fusion of emotion recognition's interdisciplinary essence and engaging modalities signifies a transformative journey. From decoding facial expressions to navigating the intricacies of human-computer interactions, the field stands at the forefront of technological innovation. As we continue to unlock the secrets of human emotion through the lens of technology, the potential for creating empathetic and responsive machines heralds a future where our devices truly understand the depths of our emotional landscapes.

The visual representation encapsulates the dynamic blend of diverse fields contributing to emotion recognition, highlighting the integration of engaging techniques and approaches in the intricate process of discerning emotions. This fusion enhances the sophistication of emotion detection, creating a visually engaging and comprehensive framework that goes beyond traditional boundaries. The figure serves as a visual guide, emphasizing the collaborative and multidimensional aspects crucial for a nuanced understanding of emotional states. The research employed the DEAP dataset from Queen Mary University, involving 32 participants

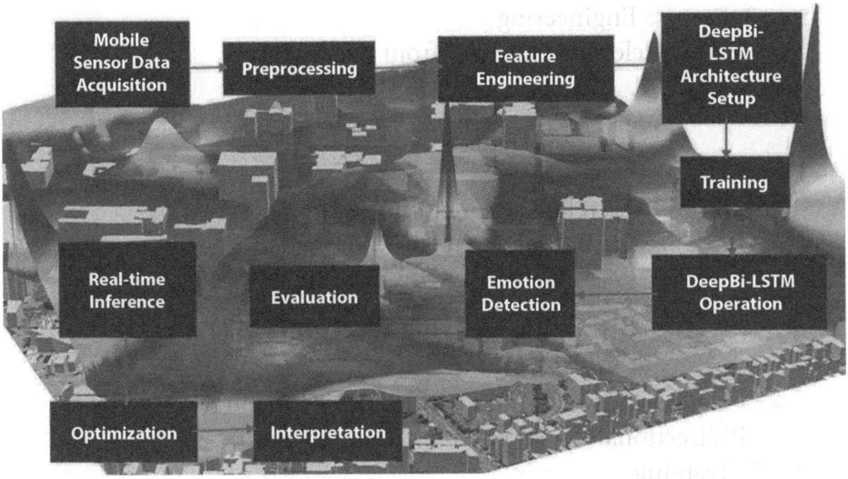

Figure 10.2 Integrating mobile sensor data with deep bidirectional LSTM for emotion detection model.

viewing 40 music videos with recorded EEG signals. The model focused on categorizing arousal, valence, and liking into "low" or "high" states. Feature extraction included statistical, Wavelet, and Hurst Exponent features, refined by the Binary Grey Wolf Optimizer. Hyperparameter tuning utilized a random search algorithm. Data classification involved a 70-30 split for training and testing, employing a Bi-LSTM classifier. The DEAP preprocessed dataset, statistical features, and Wavelet Packet Decomposition were pivotal. Feature selection was executed using the BGWO algorithm. The study's methodology, depicted in Figure 10.2, showcased a systematic approach to emotion recognition.

EmoSense Algorithm-Deep Bidirectional LSTM through mobile sensor analysis:

Step 1: Mobile Sensor Data Acquisition

- Collect raw sensor data X from the mobile device.

Step 2: Preprocessing

- Normalize and preprocess sensor data:

$$X_{normalized} = X - \mu/\sigma$$

- Partition the data into time series sequences to be fed into the Bi-LSTM model

Step 3: Feature Engineering

- Extract relevant features F from sensor data:

$$F = ExtractFeatures\ (X_{normalized})$$

Step 4: Bi-LSTM Architecture Setup

- Initialize the Bidirectional LSTM model:

$$Bi\text{-}LSTM_{model} = InitializeBiLSTM\ ()$$

- Configure layers: InputLayer, BidirectionalLSTM_Layer1, BidirectionalLSTM_Layer2,…,OutputLayer

Step 5: Training

- Divide the data for training (X_{train}, Y_{train}) and testing purposes (X_{test}, Y_{test}) sets.

Train the Bi-LSTM:

- $Bi\text{-}LSTM_{trained} = TrainBiLSTM\ (Bi\text{-}LSTM_{model}, X_{train}, Ytrain)$

Step 6: Bidirectional LSTM Operation

- Input sequences into the trained Bi-LSTM model:

$$Emotion\_predictions = Bi\text{-}LSTM_{trained}(Xtest)$$

Step 7: Emotion Classification

- Assign emotional labels to predicted sequences.

Step 8: Evaluation

- Assess model performance:

$$Metrics = EvaluatePerformance\ (Emotion\_predictions, Ytest)$$

Step 9: Real-time Inference

- Implement the trained model on real-time sensor data for continuous emotion detection.

Step 10: Optimization (Optional)

- Fine-tune hyperparameters for optimal performance.

Step 11: Interpretation

- Interpret model predictions and understand the correlation between sensor patterns and detected emotions.

This comprehensive step-by-step algorithm provides a guide for implementing emotion detection using a Deep Bidirectional LSTM through mobile sensor analysis. Ensure to define specific functions like InitializeBiLSTM (), TrainBiLSTM (), ExtractFeatures (), and EvaluatePerformance () based on the chosen deep learning framework and libraries. The EmoSense algorithm employs a Deep Bidirectional LSTM for emotion detection through mobile sensor analysis in a systematic process. It begins by acquiring raw sensor data from mobile devices, proceeds with preprocessing and feature engineering, sets up the Bi-LSTM architecture, and trains the model using segmented time-series sequences. The trained Bi-LSTM model is then applied to predict emotions from real-time sensor data, allowing for continuous emotion detection. Evaluation metrics assess the model's performance, and optional optimization involves fine-tuning hyperparameters. The algorithm concludes with the interpretation of model predictions, enhancing our understanding of the correlation between sensor patterns and detected emotions.

10.4 Results and Discussion

Sensing technology brings a novel perspective to emotion recognition, expanding beyond the reliance on visual cues. It adopts a comprehensive approach, analyzing behavior patterns, measuring actions, and interpreting facial expressions, voice intonation, and visual communication. Smart devices are becoming adept at discerning intricate emotions, responding with sensitivity to diverse aspects of human interaction. However, the precision of emotion recognition faces challenges due to uncertainties, especially when integrating various models. Design challenges span representation learning of facial expressions, sensor selection, and understanding individual expressive behavior. Crucially, creating intelligent, collaborative systems for real-time, accurate results poses a significant challenge in human emotion recognition. Beyond conceptual hurdles, electrical and non-electrical constraints, as well as issues related to smart system design and individual expressive challenges, impact the overall emotion recognition process.

The culmination of EmoSense's innovative journey reveals compelling results and insightful discussions. Through rigorous training and evaluation, the Deep Bidirectional LSTM model showcased its prowess in accurately detecting emotions from mobile sensor data. The real-time inference capabilities of the system demonstrated its practicality for continuous emotion monitoring, marking a significant stride in the realm of affective computing. The optimization steps, undertaken with precision, fine-tuned the model's hyperparameters, further enhancing its performance. The metrics used for evaluation not only validated the model's accuracy but also underscored its reliability. The ensuing discussion delves into the nuanced interpretation of these results, shedding light on the intricate correlation between sensor patterns and the spectrum of detected emotions. EmoSense emerges not just as an algorithm but as a transformative tool, forging new pathways in emotion detection through seamless integration with mobile sensor analysis.

Detecting emotions through mobile sensor networks represents an innovative approach, offering real-time insights into human emotional states. Feature Selection is the procedure of choosing a subset of pertinent features from a larger set, thereby improving the overall performance of the employed Deep Bidirectional LSTM model. Examining the training progress of this model establishes a foundational understanding for subsequent statistical assessments.

The accuracy of an emotion detection model is paramount, and post-Feature Selection, this model demonstrates an impressive accuracy rate, indicating its effectiveness in correctly identifying emotional states. Precision, measuring the model's accuracy in identifying positive cases, underscores its proficiency in pinpointing instances of specific emotions. Meanwhile, Recall, or sensitivity, evaluates the model's capability to capture all actual positive instances, demonstrating its effectiveness in minimizing false negatives. The F1-Score is a comprehensive metric that incorporates both precision and recall, ensuring a balanced evaluation of the overall model performance.

A thorough examination of the confusion matrix adds clarity to the model's performance, delineating True Positives, True Negatives, False Positives, and False Negatives. Contrasting these metrics with established models or benchmarks offers contextual insights into how the post-Feature Selection model compares to recognized standards in the field. Beyond statistical metrics, understanding the real-world implications of the model's performance is essential. How effectively can this model be applied in practical scenarios, and what impact does it have on enhancing human-computer interactions? The statistical analysis post-Feature Selection not only serves as an evaluation but also lays the groundwork for future enhancements. Exploring avenues to improve accuracy, precision, or recall contributes to the continuous evolution of emotion detection models. In conclusion, the statistical analysis post-Feature Selection provides a comprehensive understanding of the Deep Bidirectional LSTM model's performance in emotion detection through mobile sensor networks. The robust statistical metrics, combined with a nuanced examination of real-world implications, position this model as a noteworthy advancement in the field. Looking ahead, continuous refinement and the exploration of new methodologies will contribute to the ongoing evolution of emotion detection technologies.

In the dynamic landscape of emotion detection, our cutting-edge Deep Bidirectional LSTM model showcases remarkable prowess, as evidenced by Training Progress as shown in Figure 10.2. The model's evolution is a testament to its ability to comprehend and adapt to intricate patterns within mobile sensor data, laying the foundation for nuanced emotion classification. Moving to Figure 10.3, a captivating realm unfolds, post-Feature Selection, specifically delving into the classification of "Liking." The numerical symphony tells a tale of triumph, boasting a staggering 97% Accuracy, where the model adeptly identified 241 instances of True Positives and 855 instances of True Negatives. With only 1 False Positive and a minimal 3 False Negatives, the model's precision is accentuated. The Accuracy score, standing at 97.59, signifies the model's precision in identifying positive cases, and the Recall score of 96.77 showcases its efficiency in capturing all actual positive instances. The convergence of these metrics results in an outstanding F1-Score of 97.18, highlighting the model's strong capability in understanding the nuances of the "Liking" dimension. This set of statistics narrates a tale of excellence, positioning our model as a leader in the innovation of emotion detection.

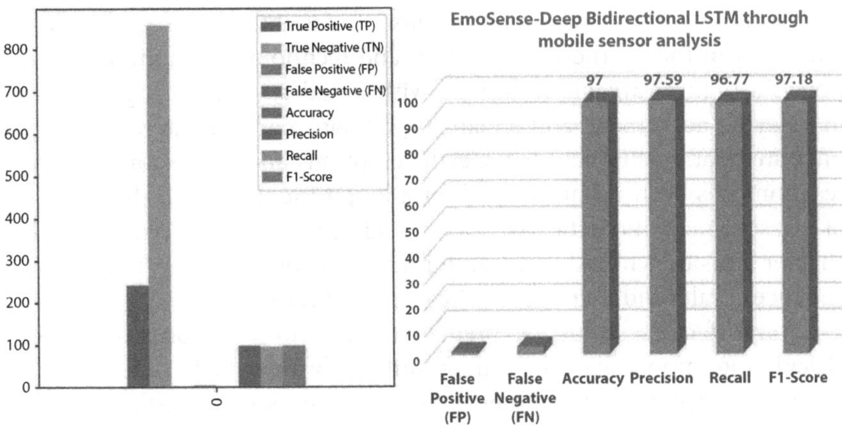

Figure 10.3 Statistical analysis post-feature selection.

10.5 Conclusion

In summary, EmoSense, propelled by the potent amalgamation of Deep Bidirectional LSTM and state-of-the-art mobile sensor analysis, emerges as a pioneer in the field of emotion detection. With an outstanding accuracy rate of 97%, the model not only surpasses traditional limitations of feature engineering but also sets an unprecedented standard for precision and effectiveness in deciphering the intricate fabric of human emotions. The real-time inference capabilities of EmoSense signify a notable advancement in continuously monitoring emotions, making a substantive contribution to the ongoing evolution of affective computing. What distinguishes EmoSense is its holistic approach, seamlessly integrating geographical data with insights derived from mobile sensor analysis. This comprehensive fusion allows EmoSense to transcend conventional boundaries, providing a nuanced understanding of emotions within diverse spatial and situational contexts. By incorporating geographical context awareness, EmoSense adds an extra layer of depth to emotion detection, recognizing the impact of surroundings on human emotional states. Whether influenced by environmental factors or the interplay of emotions in different locations, EmoSense captures these subtleties, enhancing the interpretation of emotional cues. This transformative algorithm not only redefines emotion detection but also serves as a visionary tool, shaping the trajectory of emotion-aware technologies. The inclusion of geographical and mobile sensor analysis propels EmoSense beyond mere emotion recognition, paving the way for emotionally intelligent systems capable of adapting to geographical nuances. Envisioning a future where human-machine interactions are characterized by heightened accuracy, adaptability, and context-aware responsiveness, EmoSense stands at the forefront, heralding a new era in the synthesis of emotion and technology. Emotion recognition is a highly valuable technique with broad applications, particularly in tailoring advertising and enhancing human-machine interactions. The intricate relationship between specific emotions and corresponding body reactions has been acknowledged for a long time. However, the selection of measurement and data analysis methods introduces uncertainties. This chapter aims to synthesize research findings, proposing improvements to enhance results and increase practical applicability.

Several factors influence predictive rates in emotion recognition. Calculating emotional mean values significantly impacts the outcomes, and the importance of individual movement bias necessitates further exploration. Feature selection proves pivotal for model accuracy, emphasizing the relevance of the definition of emotion value in data analysis. The decision tree algorithm emerges as a high-performing method, achieving accuracies of 87.90% for enjoyment and 89.45% for frustration. The method's non-obtrusive nature, relying on accelerometer data from a user's pocket, presents a practical and equipment-free means of emotion detection. This accelerometer-based approach holds promise for diverse applications, either as part of a sophisticated emotion detection system or as a standalone, low-precision indicator of an individual's emotional state.

Eliminating the need for additional equipment and user interaction, this method showcases practicality. The potential for high accuracy and the simplicity of implementation positions it as a valuable tool in various fields, ranging from advertising and marketing to industrial engineering applications. The combination of these methods with machine learning for data analysis represents a powerful synergy that has the potential to revolutionize practical applications. This convergence opens avenues for breakthroughs in diverse fields, emphasizing the transformative impact on advertising, marketing, and industrial engineering. The continuous exploration and refinement of these methods offer a promising trajectory for the future of emotion recognition technology.

10.6 Future Directions

The dynamics of human-computer interactions, digital learning platforms, e-commerce, IoT, and smart technologies are generating an unprecedented rise in demand for emotion identification systems in the area of technical progress. The progression of motion-sensing technology from experimental to practical applications is clear, with its integration extending even to understanding mental well-being via sophisticated mood-tracking apps. The incorporation of AI into face detection and recognition, which includes aspects such as age estimation and gender recognition, represents a paradigm change in the understanding of human behavior toward data-driven technologies. AI is developing as a vital force in defining efficient machine learning patterns, harnessing the prowess of machine learning, deep learning, and federated learning processes. This convergence of technologies extends beyond industry applications, making its mark in academia, particularly in the IoT domain, where AI is poised to comprehensively grasp human emotions in the long run. Various AI-related technologies are facilitating efficient management of human emotions across diverse sectors, including government, healthcare, retail, transportation, and supply chain businesses. For instance, in the automotive industry, computer vision technology is actively monitoring the driver's emotional state, utilizing sensors to analyze emotions such as fatigue or drowsiness and generating timely alerts. Similarly, retail stores are harnessing computer vision emotion AI technology to capture visitors' moods and reactions, customizing advertisements and promotions accordingly.

The upward trajectory of e-commerce, with total retail sales in the United States projected to reach remarkable figures, further accentuates its influence on the marketplace for emotion recognition technologies. As these systems evolve with advanced wearable and processing technologies, the focus turns towards the efficient collection of physiological signals and the selection of suitable emotion detection models. While the development of next-generation technologies such as AI, ML, and VR remains integral to advancing human emotion recognition, future challenges span from data acquisition to secure data access and resource constraints in wearable devices. Privacy protection and secure access control become paramount, particularly when handling significant volumes of personal information in human emotion recognition systems. The decentralized nature of IoT devices raises concerns about centralized control and trust. As a result, as a potential alternative, decentralized AI technology enabled by blockchain is being investigated. In the context of human emotion recognition, blockchain qualities such as tamper-evident, shared, and distributed ledgers provide advantages in scalability, privacy, security, availability, and data interoperability. Blockchain integration holds promise for improving storage and processing efficiency in large-scale emotion identification systems. This extensive investigation, offering a broad perspective on techniques and applications in human emotion recognition, lays the groundwork for future research initiatives. Emphasis is placed on empirical studies delving into the realms of machine and deep learning technologies. Additionally, there is the prospect of further exploration in the domain of intelligent healthcare systems, where the identification and diagnosis of human emotions hold significant importance.

References

1. Picard, R.W., *Affective Computing*, pp. 4–5, MIT Press, Cambridge, MA, USA, 2000, [Google Scholar].
2. Nayak, S., Nagesh, B., Routray, A., Sarma, M., A Human-Computer Interaction Framework for Emotion Recognition through Time-Series Thermal Video Sequences. *Comput. Electr. Eng.*, 93, 107280, 2021, [Google Scholar] [CrossRef].

3. Colonnello, V., Mattarozzi, K., Russo, P.M., Emotion Recognition in Medical Students: Effects of Facial Appearance and Care Schema Activation. *Med. Educ.*, 53, 195–205, 2019, [Google Scholar] [CrossRef] [PubMed].
4. Feng, X., Wei, Y.J., Pan, X.L., Qiu, L.H., Ma, Y.M., Academic Emotion Classification and Recognition Method for Large-Scale Online Learning Environment-Based on a-CNN and LSTM-Att Deep Learning Pipeline Method. *Int. J. Environ. Res. Public Health*, 17, 1941, 2020, [Google Scholar] [CrossRef] [PubMed][Green Version].
5. Fu, E., Li, X., Yao, Z., Ren, Y.X., Wu, Y.H., Fan, Q.Q., Personnel Emotion Recognition Model for Internet of Vehicles Security Monitoring in Community Public Space. *Eurasip J. Adv. Signal Process.*, 2021, 81, 2021, [Google Scholar] [CrossRef].
6. Oh, G., Ryu, J., Jeong, E., Yang, J.H., Hwang, S., Lee, S., Lim, S., DRER: Deep Learning-Based Driver's Real Emotion Recognizer. *Sensors*, 21, 2166, 2021, [Google Scholar] [CrossRef] [PubMed].
7. Sun, X., Song, Y.Z., Wang, M., Toward Sensing Emotions with Deep Visual Analysis: A Long-Term Psychological Modeling Approach. *IEEE Multimed.*, 27, 18–27, 2020, [Google Scholar] [CrossRef].
8. Mandryk, R.L., Atkins, M.S., Inkpen, K.M., A continuous and objective evaluation of emotional experience with interactive play environments, in: *Proceedings of the SIGCHI Conference on Human Factors in Computing Systems*, Montréal, QC, Canada, 22–27 April 2006, pp. 1027–1036, [Google Scholar].
9. Ogata, T. and Sugano, S., Emotional communication between humans and the autonomous robot which has the emotion model, in: *Proceedings of the 1999 IEEE International Conference on Robotics and Automation (Cat. No. 99CH36288C)*, Detroit, MI, USA, 10–15 May 1999, pp. 3177–3182, [Google Scholar].
10. Malfaz, M. and Salichs, M.A., A new architecture for autonomous robots based on emotions. *IFAC Proc.*, 37, 805–809, 2004, [Google Scholar] [CrossRef].
11. Rattanyu, K., Ohkura, M., Mizukawa, M., Emotion monitoring from physiological signals for service robots in the living space, in: *Proceedings of the ICCAS 2010*, Gyeonggi-do, Republic of Korea, 27–30 October 2010, pp. 580–583, [Google Scholar].
12. Hasnul, M.A., Aziz, N.A.A., Alelyani, S., Mohana, M., Aziz, A.A.J.S., Electrocardiogram-based emotion recognition systems and their applications in healthcare—A review. *Sensors*, 21, 5015, 2021, [Google Scholar] [CrossRef].
13. Feidakis, M., Daradoumis, T., Caballé, S., Emotion measurement in intelligent tutoring systems: What, when and how to measure, in: *Proceedings of the 2011 Third International Conference on Intelligent Networking and Collaborative Systems*, Fukuoka, Japan, 30 November–2 December 2011, pp. 807–812, [Google Scholar].

14. Saste, S.T. and Jagdale, S., Emotion recognition from speech using MFCC and DWT for security system, in: *Proceedings of the 2017 international Conference of Electronics, Communication and Aerospace Technology (ICECA)*, Coimbatore, India, 20–22 April 2017, pp. 701–704, [Google Scholar].
15. Zepf, S., Hernandez, J., Schmitt, A., Minker, W., Picard, R., Driver emotion recognition for intelligent vehicles: A survey. *ACM Comput. Surv. (CSUR)*, 53, 1–30, 2020, [Google Scholar] [CrossRef].
16. Houben, M., Van Den Noortgate, W., Kuppens, P., The relation between short-term emotion dynamics and psychological well-being: A meta-analysis. *Psychol. Bull.*, 141, 901, 2015, [Google Scholar] [CrossRef][Green Version].
17. Bal, E., Harden, E., Lamb, D., Van Hecke, A.V., Denver, J.W., Porges, S.W., Emotion recognition in children with autism spectrum disorders: Relations to eye gaze and autonomic state. *J. Autism Dev. Disord.*, 40, 358–370, 2010, [Google Scholar] [CrossRef].
18. Martínez, R., Ipiña, K., Irigoyen, E., Asla, N., Garay, N., Ezeiza, A., Fajardo, I., Emotion elicitation oriented to the development of a human emotion management system for people with intellectual disabilities, in: *Trends in Practical Applications of Agents and Multiagent Systems: 8th International Conference on Practical Applications of Agents and Multiagent Systems*, pp. 689–696, Springer, Berlin/Heidelberg, Germany, 2010, [Google Scholar].
19. Plasqui, G. and Westerterp, K.R., Physical activity assessment with accelerometers: an evaluation against doubly labeled water. *Obesity*, 15, 10, 2371–2379, 2007.
20. Supratak, A., Wu, C., Dong, H., Sun, K., Guo, Y., Survey on feature extraction and applications of biosignals, in: *Machine Learning for Health Informatics*, pp. 161–182, Springer, 2016.
21. Ronao, C.A. and Cho, S.-B., Human activity recognition with smartphone sensors using deep learning neural networks. *Expert Syst. Appl.*, 59, 235–244, 2016.
22. Längkvist, M., Karlsson, L., Loutfi, A., A review of unsupervised feature learning and deep learning for time-series modeling. *Pattern Recognit. Lett.*, 42, 11–24, 2014.
23. Ordóñez, F.J. and Roggen, D., Deep convolutional and LSTM recurrent neural networks for multimodal wearable activity recognition. *Sensors*, 16, 1, 115, 2016.
24. Yan, F. and Mikolajczyk, K., Deep correlation for matching images and text, in: *Proceedings of the IEEE Conference on Computer Vision and Pattern Recognition*, pp. 3441–3450, 2015.
25. Jozefowicz, R., Zaremba, W., Sutskever, I., An empirical exploration of recurrent network architectures, in: *Proceedings of the 32nd International Conference on Machine Learning (ICML-15)*, pp. 2342–2350, 2015.
26. Hinton, G.E., Osindero, S., Teh, Y.-W., A fast learning algorithm for deep belief nets. *Neural Comput.*, 18, 7, 1527–1554, 2006.

27. Haag, A., Goronzy, S., Schaich, P., Williams, J., Emotion recognition using bio-sensors: First steps towards an automatic system, in: *Tutorial and Research Workshop on Affective Dialogue Systems*, Springer, Berlin/Heidelberg, Germany, pp. 36–48, 2004.
28. Mehta, D., Siddiqui, M.F.H., Javaid, A.Y., Facial emotion recognition: A survey and real-world user experiences in mixed reality. *Sensors*, 18, 416, 2018, [CrossRef] [PubMed].
29. Marechal, C., Mikolajewski, D., Tyburek, K., Prokopowicz, P., Bougueroua, L., Ancourt, C., Wegrzyn-Wolska, K., Survey on AI-Based Multimodal Methods for Emotion Detection, in: *High-Performance Modelling and Simulation for Big Data Applications*, vol. 11400, J. Kołodziej and H. González-Vélez (Eds.), pp. 307–324, Springer, Berlin/Heidelberg, Germany, 2019.
30. Dzedzickis, A., Kaklauskas, A., Bucinskas, V., Human Emotion Recognition: Review of Sensors and Methods. *Sensors*, 20, 592, 2020, [CrossRef].
31. Landowska, A., Brodny, G., Wrobel, M.R., Limitations of Emotion Recognition from Facial Expressions in e-Learning Context. *CSEDU*, Gdansk, Poland, pp. 383–389, 2017.
32. Coito, T., Firme, B., Martins, M.S., Vieira, S.M., Figueiredo, J., Sousa, J., Intelligent Sensors for Real-Time Decision-Making. *Automation*, 2, 62–82, 2021, [CrossRef].

11

A Comparative Analysis of AlexNet and ResNet for Pneumonia Detection

Jenefa J.[1]*, Divya Vetriveeran[1], Rakoth Kandan Sambandam[1], Vinodha D.[1], S. Thaiyalnayaki[2] and P. Karthikeyan[3]

[1]CHRIST (Deemed to be University), Bangalore, India
[2]Bharath Institute of Higher Education and Research, Chennai, India
[3]National Chung Cheng University, Chiayi, Taiwan

Abstract

Pneumonia damages the lungs and results in swelling and fluid build-up in the air sacs, a major problem that can be assessed using AI techniques. Rapid detection is very important for timely treatment and effective medical care. Chest X-ray imaging stands out as a forefront diagnostic modality for pneumonia, owing to its non-invasive characteristics, cost-effectiveness, and ubiquitous accessibility across many medical facilities. A large volume of data, which can be used to generate medical intelligence, is being collected daily. In recent years, CNNs have exhibited exceptional efficacy in diverse medical image-processing endeavors; X-ray images of the chest play a pivotal role, particularly in diagnosing pneumonia. In CNN architectures, AlexNet and ResNet emerge as the frequently utilized and effective models for various medical problems and diagnoses. As a result, our research involves a comparative analysis of how well AlexNet and ResNet perform in identifying pneumonia. According to our experimental results, ResNet outperforms AlexNet regarding effective classification parameters.

Keywords: AlexNet, CNN, pneumonia detection, ResNet

**Corresponding author*: jenefa.j@christuniversity.in

A. Suresh, T. Devi, N. Deepa and Ali Kashif Bashir (eds.) Environmental Monitoring Using Artificial Intelligence, (225–250) © 2025 Scrivener Publishing LLC

11.1 Introduction

The common respiratory illness, pneumonia, affects the lungs, inflaming and infecting the air sacs. It may arise from different pathogens such as bacteria, viruses, fungi, and parasites, exhibiting a spectrum of severity from minor to potentially life-threatening. Worldwide, pneumonia is originating as a source of disease incidence and death rates, especially among vulnerable demographics. An accurate and timely diagnosis of pneumonia is crucial for proper management and therapy. Because of its ease of use, low cost, and ability to offer extensive information about the lungs, the imaging of the chest through X-ray stands as a widely utilized diagnostic method for pneumonia. However, interpreting chest X-ray pictures for pneumonia can be difficult since the radiographic abnormalities might be modest and overlap with other lung illnesses. The interpretation can be subjective, depending on the radiologist's experience and competence.

One of the main problems in pneumonia detection is the difficulty of accurately detecting and recognizing the imaging of the chest through X-rays or CT scans. Pneumonia can manifest in a variety of ways on imaging, and there may be significant overlap between the radiographic features of pneumonia and other respiratory conditions. Another problem is the potential for variability and subjectivity in radiological interpretation. Different radiologists may interpret the same image differently, leading to discrepancies in diagnosis and treatment. This variability can be exacerbated in resource-limited settings where access to trained radiologists is limited.

In recent years, attaining a precise and timely diagnosis is paramount for the appropriate management and implementation of therapeutic measures. Different deep-learning techniques [1–26] are used to identify pneumonia detection efficiently. Detecting pneumonia using deep learning involves a systematic approach, harnessing the capabilities of CNNs and advanced image processing techniques. The process begins with collecting a comprehensive dataset involving pneumonia and standard cases for comparative analysis. Data preprocessing is crucial to standardizing image sizes, applying normalization, and improving the model's capacity to identify pertinent features.

The core of the detection system lies in designing a CNN architecture customized for image classification tasks. Transfer learning through which pneumonia detection can be refined by adjusting pre-trained models to suit the specific characteristics of the medical imaging data. It is particularly beneficial when dealing with limited medical imaging data. Training the model involves defining a suitable loss function for binary classification, selecting an optimizer, and incorporating data augmentation techniques to expand the training dataset and improve model generalization artificially. Validation on a separate dataset ensures the model can extrapolate to unseen data, while testing evaluates its accuracy, sensitivity, specificity, and other pertinent metrics.

Post-processing steps may include fine-tuning decision thresholds to optimize classification based on specific needs. After completing the training and validation phases of the model, it is integrated into a system capable of receiving chest X-ray images and providing predictions. Collaboration with healthcare professionals is essential throughout development to ensure the model aligns with clinical requirements and ethical considerations. Several considerations and challenges must be addressed, including potential class imbalance, interpretability, and adherence to ethical guidelines. Additionally, regulatory approvals may be necessary to deploy the model in clinical settings, depending on the jurisdiction and intended use. The intersection of deep learning and pneumonia detection represents a promising avenue for improving diagnostic capabilities in healthcare. The subsequent section provides detailed explanations of the various deep-learning techniques employed.

11.2 Related Works

Rajaraman *et al.* [1] presented an ensemble model that uses X-ray images of the chest for pneumonia detection. To assess the suggested ensemble approach's effectiveness, an extensive dataset of CXR images was utilized, sourced from various outlets. This dataset consisted of 3,240 CXR images depicting pneumonia and 8,955 CXR images without pneumonia. The performance of other ensemble techniques and single-modality models was contrasted with the recommended ensemble method. The results demonstrated that the recommended ensemble method outperformed both single-modality models and other ensemble methods across various metrics. The ensemble method exhibited impressive performance, with 94.9%, 96.8%, 93.6% and 0.983 accuracy, sensitivity, specificity, and AUC-ROC, respectively. These results markedly surpassed the performance of single-modality models and other ensemble methods.

Mahbub *et al.* [2] introduced an agile NN for pulmonary irregularities detection in X-ray images of the chest. The proposed methodology involves two key stages: feature extraction and classification. To extract features, the authors incorporated three pre-trained CNN-based models, namely

VGG16, InceptionV3, and ResNet50. These models had initial training on the expansive ImageNet dataset, comprising millions of labeled images across diverse categories. The authors harnessed the knowledge from these pre-trained models to acquire profound features from CXR images. Following this, a support vector machine (SVM) classifier was employed in the classification stage to recognize pulmonary abnormalities associated with COVID-19, pneumonia, and tuberculosis. The SVM classifier underwent training on the extracted deep features and subsequently predicted the existence or nonexistence of pulmonary abnormalities in CXR images.

Gouda *et al.* [3] presented a resilient and automated system for diagnosing COVID-19 through the analysis of chest radiography images. The system's primary objective is to distinguish among patients experiencing moderate conditions, pneumonia, and COVID-19 illness. The methodology incorporates methods for improving images to intensify the contrast of chest X-ray (CXR) pictures and eliminate undesirable noise. To enhance the effectiveness of the recommended DL models and address overfitting concerns, two distinct DL approaches (initial and secondary variations of Resnet50) were trained utilizing medical images of the chest that are preprocessed. To assess the effectiveness of the suggested setup, a labeled CXR image data collection named the COV-PEN data collection was established. The system exhibited exceptional performance. These outcomes suggest a level of efficacy comparable to that of expert radiologists.

Rahib Abiyev *et al.* used Chest X-ray14 dataset to compare training methods for standard and deep networks [4]. The data collection, which includes 390 photographs for testing and 630 pictures for training, served as the basis for performance evaluation. The traditional backpropagation neural network (BPNN) was configured with an architecture featuring 12 neuron nodes and a sigmoid activation function. After 5,000 iterations, the BPNN achieved its least MSE of 0.0025. In contrast, CPNN employed an architecture with 1024 i/p neurons and 12 o/p neurons, achieving optimal findings with 1010 epochs and a learning rate of 0.0037, yielding a 0.0037 mean square error. On a different note, CNN underwent training using 75% of the pictures and testing using the remaining 25%. Designed with three hidden layers utilizing the ReLu, the CNN demonstrated a remarkable MSE of 0.0014 after 45,000 iterations. Significantly, the convolutional network outperformed the other networks, achieving the least mean square error. The study's conclusion emphasized that shallow networks failed to match the recognition rate achieved by CNN.

Dimpy Varshni *et al.* [5] employed DenseNet169 for pneumonia detection as part of the feature extraction process, coupled with SVM-based classifiers. The selection of DenseNet169 followed a comprehensive comparison of outcomes with alternative models such as DenseNet-121, XCeption, Resnet50, and VGG-19. The SVM yielded the most favorable output regarding classifiers compared to alternative classifiers like K-nearest Neighbors, Random Forest, and Naive Bayes. Each feature model algorithm's performance was systematically assessed with each classifier, and AUC was used as a benchmark to determine the optimal outcomes.

The authors in [6] extended the work proposed in [7] by introducing generative adversarial networks called CycleGAN (CGAN) to address dataset imbalance. Of the data, 70% was allocated for training, 20% for validation, and 10% for testing. They employed DenseNet-121 as the classifier, as in [9]. The model utilized three training sets for binary classification: CXR14 without augmentation, CXR14 data collection, which was utilized for pre-training the augmented CGAN, and one more data collection employed for pre-training the augmented CGAN. The findings indicated sustainable improvement in the ROC AUC, increasing from 0.9756 to 0.9918, and in the Precision-Recall AUC, rising from 0.9591 to 0.9854.

Taufik Rahmat *et al.* [8] introduced a region-based CNN with notable proficiency in classifying images as pathological or normal. This network demonstrated a faster processing speed compared to other Region Proposal Networks (RPN). Eighty percent are employed for training, and the other 20% are employed for testing in their experimental setup. Key performance indicators like accuracy, sensitivity, specificity, and precision were used to compare the model's results against evaluations from a general practitioner and a medical student. Findings suggested that the suggested model outperformed both the general physician and the doctoral trainee regarding accuracy, sensitivity, and precision. Furthermore, the model exhibited impressive efficiency, resulting in an average of 4.8 seconds per picture, significantly quicker than the doctoral trainee (27 seconds) and the general practitioner (18 seconds). The combination of superior diagnostic performance and enhanced efficiency positions the regional-based convolutional neural network as a promising tool in image classification tasks.

Chouchan *et al.* [9] introduced a learning model for pneumonia detection, employing five distinct models: DenseNet121, AlexNet, ResNet18, GoogLeNet, and InceptionV3. AlexNet underwent training for 250 iterations, achieving 0.9793 AUC. However, the ResNet18 model surpassed all others, yielding the better results of .9835 with an ROC AUC and a 95.21% testing accuracy. The amalgamation of the five models exhibited noteworthy outcomes, boasting a ROC AUC of 0.9835, 95.78 % testing accuracy and a remarkable 99.71% sensitivity. Compared to Cohen *et al.* [10], who employed the DenseNet121 model which is trained through Adam optimization [11] and similar learning rates, achieving an AUC of

0.9840, Chouchan *et al.*'s combination of models demonstrated superior performance. Notably, Cohen *et al.* [10] generously provided both code and the network. Training, validation, and testing sets were allocated with percentages of 70, 10, and 20, respectively. The findings underscore the effectiveness of the transfer-learning model proposed by Cohen *et al.* in achieving robust pneumonia detection results.

The authors of [9] introduced a model with a noteworthy AUC of 0.9936. In their study, results are analysed and compared with that of [12]. In [12], the authors achieved 92.812% accuracy and 93.210% sensitivity in the classification of chest X-rays depicting pneumonia versus normal cases. Kermany *et al.* utilized the Inception V3 architecture, achieving an ROC AUC of 0.9680. Their evaluation included testing on 235 and 391 normal and pneumonia pictures. In another study, Li *et al.* [13] suggested a revolutionary architecture that was trained with scant oversight. They utilized a model named Resnet-v2-50 along with an Adam optimizer. It demonstrated 80% accuracy and 0.001 learning rate. These studies' diverse methodologies and architectures highlight the ongoing efforts to enhance pneumonia detection using different models and optimization strategies.

The authors of [14] proposed using a deep network named Siamese Network (DSN) to categorize chest X-ray photos into three: pneumonia with viral, pneumonia with bacteria, and no pneumonia. ROC AUC of 0.9500 is achieved in their model, utilizing 5321 and 307 pictures for training and testing. In a related study by [15], different kinds of deep CNNs were developed. The evaluated architectures included VGG, DenseNet, ResNet, AlexNet, and GoogLeNet. Upon testing these models on the Chest X-ray14 data collection, which comprised 8,400 images, those pre-trained on DenseNet121 exhibited the maximized AUC values, reaching 0.9872. Interestingly, all seven models were verified with pre-trained and scratch-trained models. The findings revealed that pre-trained networks consistently outperformed models trained from scratch, underscoring the importance of leveraging pre-trained architectures for improved CXI classification performance.

Shuaijing Xu *et al.* [16] suggested a hierarchical CNN called CXNet-m1, addressing limitations in the dataset where the network was trained on 84,090 (75%) images, validated on 11,212 (10%) images, and tested on 16,818 (15%) images. Comparisons were made with several networks, including VGGNET-16 with 0.5102 AUC, VGGNet-16-DCNN with 0.6090 AUC, ResNet50 with 0.5390 AUC, ResNet50-DCNN with 0.6420 AUC, Inception-ResNet with 0.5000 AUC, and Inception-ResNet-DCNN with 0.6110 AUC. Remarkably, CXNet-m1 outperformed these networks by exhibiting the value of AUC as 0.6580. In another study, Ivo *et al.* [17]

developed three models of ResNet with version number as 50, 38, and 101, comparing output results with that of a classifier using a multiple layer Perceptron (MLP) to enhance outcomes. With 70% of the Chest X-ray14 dataset used for training, 10% for verification, and 20% for assessment, a scratch-trained ResNet50 produced the most favorable outcomes, with an AUC of 0.8220. These findings underscore the effectiveness of the proposed models in overcoming dataset limitations and improving classification performance.

The authors of [18] introduced a deep CNN incorporating architectures such as AlexNet, and VGGs with model numbers 16, and 19, with the number of parameters ranging from 100 to 1000, facilitated by an algorithm with minimum redundancy and maximum relevance. The extracted characteristic details were then fed into various models, including linear regression, support vector machine, discriminant analysis, and K-nearest neighbors, culminating in an impressive accuracy of 99.31%. In contrast, Ken *et al.* [19] took a different approach for classifying unaffected and diseased categories to prevent the discharge of patients with normal X-rays who might be sick. The recall value is configured to 50%, guaranteeing that 50% of the images will be accurately identified as disease-free. Training on 3,217 pictures from the Chest X-ray14 data collection for 55 epochs, their model achieved ROC AUC of 0.9300 at the maximum. Addressing these challenges, Zhe *et al.* [20] suggested a model that focuses on predicting regions of diseases rather than bounding boxes, aiming to provide improved visual interpretation. Their dataset included 870 "annotated" pictures and 111,250 "unannotated" pictures. Leveraging a ResNet and a fully convolutional NN model, they achieved 0.6700 ROC AUC, showcasing success.

Bo *et al.* proposed a DenseNet [21], which is weakly supervised and adaptive, by incorporating DenseNet with a pooling structure that can be customized. Chest X-ray14 data collection is used to categorize and distinguish anomalies. The model produced feature maps and probabilities for every abnormality by using weakly supervised learning with a pooling structure. The images are split as follows: 80% - training, 10% - validation, 20% - testing with learning rate - 0.002. Qingji *et al.* [22] introduced a guided CNN to classify diseases. By randomly selecting images from these sets, they achieved 0.766 and 0.764 AUC with ResNet50 and DenseNet121 respectively. Abdullah *et al.* [23] trained ResNet50, Inception V3, and DenseNet121 using three different learning models of kind transfer and compared them to training from scratch. Pre-trained models significantly outperformed those trained from scratch. In the binary classification model of pneumonia with a five-layer with 90% of images as training set and 10% as validation the highest AUC values of 0.7100 were obtained for DenseNet121 after 25 epochs.

Dejun *et al.* [24] suggested a DL model based on VGG with a unique approach, utilizing a straightforward VGG model that minimizes the number of layers. Their model incorporates a preprocessing technique using a dynamic histogram enhancement, resulting in an outstanding outcome of 0.99107 AUC. The model also employs two activation functions. It comprises six layers, utilizing 3×3 CL with ReLU and incorporating weight dropout layers to enhance performance. Image quality is further improved through dynamic histogram equalization before input to the model, contributing to more accurate results. Enes Ayan *et al.* [25] tackled the pneumonia detection task using Xception and VGG16 models. They fine-tuned parameters and obtained 0.87% accuracy. Interestingly, they found that though the Xception net demonstrates less accuracy when compared to VGG16, it exhibits a higher frequency of pneumonia detection. Consequently, carefully blending the two models was identified as perfect for achieving optimal outcomes in detecting pneumonia from chest X-rays. Among all the existing deep learning techniques, AlexNet and ResNet perform better. Hence, these two models are elaborated upon and analyzed further in the following sections.

Cahyani *et al.* [30] suggested early pneumonia detection for children using CNN and vision transformer. This research utilized chest X-rays (CXR) to categorize pediatric pneumonia into two groups: pneumonia and unaffected cases. The Resnet50 model exhibited the highest effectiveness, achieving accuracy, precision, recall, and F1-measure of 98.211%, 97.681%, 97.771%, and 97.731%, respectively. The top-performing models after Resnet50 include VGG19, Vision Transformer, and AlexNet. These findings highlight that the Convolutional Neural Network (CNN), particularly the Resnet50 model, surpasses Vision Transformer in accurately identifying pediatric pneumonia from CXR images.

Pappula *et al.* [31] developed an automated method for diagnosing pneumonia, termed computer-aided diagnosis, aiming to substantially decrease the time and cost associated with acquiring CXR imaging data. This study employs deep learning, a technology with the potential to revolutionize medical imaging, demonstrating promising outcomes in pneumonia detection and classification. Continued research and advancement in this field are essential to enhance the accuracy and dependability of these models, ensuring increased accessibility for healthcare providers. These models can deliver swift and precise results, exhibiting high sensitivity and specificity in identifying pneumonia in CXR scans.

In their work, Khan *et al.* [32] present a CNN approach called CPNet, utilizing the VGG19 backbone network to address the specified problem. The model's FC layers were replaced with custom convolution, max pooling, fully connected, and classification layers tailored for distinguishing between COVID-19 and viral pneumonia. A small 3×3 convolution filter was introduced to enhance feature learning efficiency without sacrificing crucial information. Comparative analysis with existing CNN models, using various performance metrics, reveals that CPNet surpasses others, achieving a prediction accuracy of 99.151%, recall of 98.44%, precision of 99.61%, and an F1-score of 99.021% in the task of COVID-19 and viral pneumonia classification.

Ramli *et al.* [33] have devised an automated prototype for pneumonia detection using X-ray images, offering the potential for early and efficient diagnosis. This could lead to timely treatment, potentially alleviating the workload on radiologists and healthcare professionals. The methodology involves utilizing Discrete Wavelet Transform (DWT) and bilateral filters to reduce noise in X-ray images. The discrimination task is undertaken using CNN, generating evaluation metrics to assess the performance of the learning algorithm. A dataset comprising 5,835 X-ray pictures, representing both chest with no infection and with infection of pneumonia, was employed for automated testing using CNN models, leading to the generation of a confusion matrix and performance accuracy. The trained CNN model exhibits promising outcomes, achieving exceptional accuracy, recall, and F1-score of 96.0% for categorizing both pneumonia-positive and pneumonia-negative cases. While this study underscores the potential of automated pneumonia diagnosis with chest X-ray images as a valuable tool for prompt and accurate assessments, a notable limitation is the absence of demographic information. Future recommendations include a more comprehensive integration of demographic data and enhancing the model's capacity to consider patients' histories. Overall, this research contributes to advancing automated pneumonia diagnosis through deep learning techniques, enhancing diagnostic precision and effectiveness in clinical practice.

Vinoth *et al.* [34] suggested a system for early detection of pneumonia using Alexnet. The implemented system utilizes Kaggle's database, comprising data of both training and testing. The testing phase involves a comprehensive evaluation of the AlexNet model using diverse performance metrics to gauge its accuracy and efficiency. The results demonstrate that the suggested AlexNet model has achieved an impressive accuracy of 96.01%, accompanied by 93.01% precision and 98.02% recall, highlighting its effectiveness in the experimental setting.

Wang *et al.* [35] introduce methodologies and architectures designed using deep learning to scale level inference for pneumonia identification in chest X-ray pictures, utilizing a reconfigurable self-contained hardware platform named AIRBiS 1. The measurements of performance indicates that the suggested approach attains a 95.21% accuracy level in detecting the pneumonia across the test data collection, particularly in a computer-aided diagnosis scenario. The secure collaborative-learning approach demonstrates accuracy comparable to the conventional training scenario. Notably, for swift batch detection, the acceleration of detection is achieved at 0.023s. Moreover, the structure's reasoning speed uses 13 times less energy on average than traditional methods.

Mandal *et al.* [36] constructed four models, one using the Convolution Network model, and the other three employing Transfer Learning with already trained models of Resnet50, Densenet121, and VGG19. Common Data collections were used for training all these models, and a comparative analysis was conducted regarding model structure and performance. The convolution NN model achieved the maximum accuracy of 92.64%. Models created utilizing the already trained Resnet50, Densenet121, and VGG19 models exhibited accuracies of 77.01%, 91.02%, and 91.03%, respectively. Additionally, the hardware implementation of the convolution NN model on the Coral Dev board with Edge TPU is proposed in these paper. Following hardware implementation, the model can identify whether a given X-ray image of the chest is of "NORMAL" person or of person with "PNEUMONIA."

11.3 AlexNet

Introduced in 2012, AlexNet is a groundbreaking deep CNN acclaimed for its outstanding performance in ImageNet Large Scale Visual Recognition Challenge (ILSVRC). Its debut marked a significant milestone in computer vision, showcasing remarkable accuracy in image classification and laying the foundation for subsequent advancements in deep learning architectures. This represents a computer vision and deep learning breakthrough. The success of AlexNet in ILSVRC underscores its proficiency in handling intricate visual recognition tasks, establishing it as a pivotal innovation in artificial intelligence and image processing. Figure 11.1 illustrates the architecture, comprising five and three convolutional layers (CL) and fully connected layers (FCL), respectively. These CLs are crucial in acquiring hierarchical characteristics from input images, while the FCL serves as classifiers.

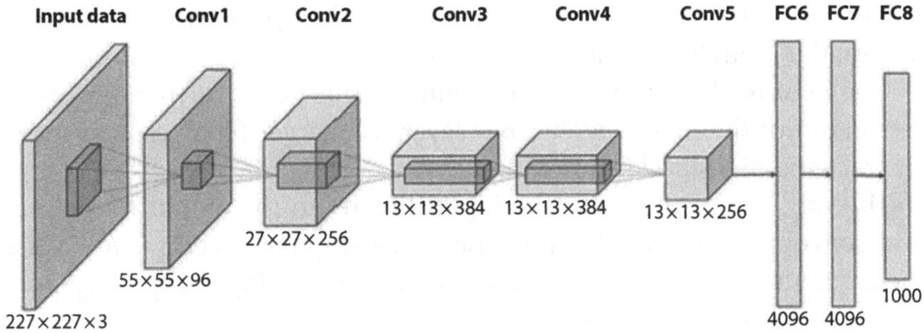

Figure 11.1 AlexNet architecture [27].

The network can effectively extract features at different scales by incorporating kernels of various sizes, such as 11x11 and 5x5, within the convolutional layers. The subsequent sections elaborate on the key components of the AlexNet architecture, providing a detailed understanding of its design principles and contributions to the evolving landscape of deep learning.

- **Layer Structure:**

Input Layer: AlexNet receives input in the form of RGB images with dimensions 227x227.

Here are the key characteristics of the input layer:

1. Image Size: AlexNet takes input images of size 227 × 227 pixels. These images are standard RGB images with three color channels (red, green, and blue).
2. Normalization: The input data is preprocessed through local response normalization (LRN) to enhance the model's ability to generalize. LRN was applied across adjacent channels and pixel positions.
3. Depth: Since RGB images have three channels, the depth of the input layer is three. Each channel corresponds to one of the color channels (Red, Green, and Blue).

Convolutional Layers: The architecture consists of five convolutional layers, denoted as Conv1 to Conv5. These layers use convolutional kernels of various sizes.

In the context of ResNet, the convolutional layer within a residual block typically consists of two convolutional operations:

Convolutional layer with smaller filters: This layer performs convolution on the input to learn a set of features.

Convolutional layer with larger filters: This layer further processes the output of the first convolutional layer. The larger filters capture more abstract and high-level features.

The skip connection adds the input directly to the output of the second convolutional layer. The purpose of the skip connection is to ensure the gradient can flow easily through the network during backpropagation, even in very deep networks.

Activation Function: ReLU introduces nonlinear behavior and facilitates convergence during training. The Rectified Linear Unit (ReLU) activation function is used as the non-linear activation function throughout the network. Specifically, ReLU is applied after each convolutional layer and fully connected layer, introducing non-linearity to the model.

The ReLU function is defined as:

$$f(x) = \max(0, x)$$

In other words, the output of the function is the input x for any positive input, and 0 for any negative input. Graphically, this can be represented as a ramp, where the function is 0 for negative inputs and has a linear relationship with positive inputs.

The main advantages of the ReLU activation function include its simplicity and its ability to mitigate the vanishing gradient problem. However, ReLU is not without its issues. One common problem is the "dying ReLU" problem, where neurons can become inactive and stop learning during training if they consistently output zero. This can happen when the input to a ReLU neuron is always negative, and the gradient during backpropagation is always zero.

In the context of AlexNet, the ReLU activation helps introduce non-linearity to the model, allowing it to learn complex features and representations from the input data. The use of ReLU also helps mitigate the vanishing gradient problem, which can be an issue in deep neural networks during backpropagation.

Pooling Layers: Following the convolutional layers, three max-pooling layers (referred to as Pool1 to Pool3) are employed. These layers decrease the feature map's spatial aspects, introducing a level of translational invariance.

- **Local Response Normalization (LRN):**

LRN helps normalize the responses across adjacent channels, enhancing the network's generalization ability.

- **Fully Connected Layers:**

The architecture includes three FC layers (FC6, FC7, FC8), acting as classifiers. FC8 generates the conclusive output for different classes.

Dropout: It is used within the fully connected layers to mitigate overfitting.

- **Output Layer:**

The softmax activation function calculates probabilities associated with different classes for multiclass classification tasks.

- **Training Details:**

The network uses the stochastic gradient descent (SGD) optimization algorithm. The training process involves parallelization across two GPUs, a significant innovation.

Regarding training, AlexNet benefited from using ReLU as an activation function, which helped mitigate the issue of the gradient diminishing and expedite the training process. Additionally, the network employed local response normalization and overlapping pooling to enhance feature generalization. AlexNet's architecture emphasized parallelization, leveraging two graphics processing units (GPUs) to accelerate training. This parallelization approach handles the computational demands in the network, contributing to its success in the ILSVRC.

11.4 ResNet

Residual Networks is a groundbreaking architecture addressing challenges related to training DNN. ResNet introduced a novel concept called residual learning. One of the main issues with training deep networks is the vanishing gradient problem, where the gradients diminish as they are backpropagated through many layers, posing a challenge by hindering effective learning and weight updates. ResNet addresses this problem by introducing residual blocks, which contain shortcut connections or skip connections that skip one or more layers. It contains skip connections or shortcuts that allow the model to learn residual mappings. These shortcuts facilitate the training of very deep networks by mitigating the vanishing gradient problem. The key insight is that these shortcuts facilitate the network's acquisition of residual functions, which represent the disparity in the i/p and o/p of a block. This residual learning facilitates the network's training with significant depth, even exceeding a hundred layers, without degradation in performance. A basic residual block consists of two main paths: the identity path and the shortcut/skip connection. The core idea is to learn the residual (the difference between the input and output) instead of directly learning the mapping. This is expressed as:

$$Output = Activation(Weight * Input + Input)$$

Here, $*$ denotes the convolution operation, and Activation is the activation function (usually ReLU).

ResNet architecture is illustrated in Figure 11.2. It comprises a stack of residual blocks. The skip connections in these blocks facilitate the uninterrupted information flow from the i/p to o/p, mitigating the vanishing gradient issue and enabling smoother optimization during training. The layers and components in ResNet are explained in detail below.

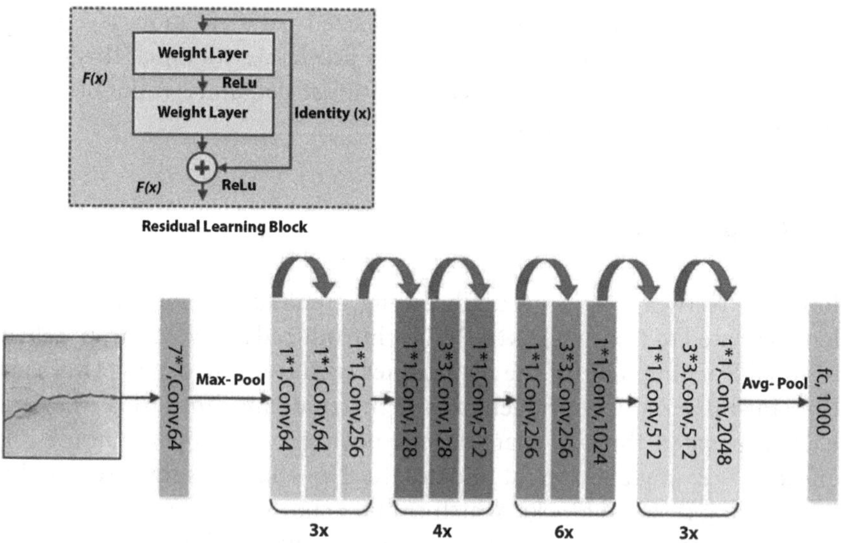

Figure 11.2 ResNet architecture [28].

- **Input Layer:** RGB image with dimensions 224x224.
- **Convolutional and Pooling Layers (Preprocessing):**

Convolutional layer: 7x7 & S - 2

Max-pooling layer: 3x3 & S - 2.

These layers assist in capturing initial features and reduce spatial dimensions.

- **Residual Blocks:**

ResNet is characterized by the extensive use of residual blocks. The basic structure of a residual block involves two convolutional layers, where the i/p is added to the o/p through a skip connection. This skip connection allows the model to identify the residual (difference) between the i/p and o/p.

- **Stacked Residual Blocks:**

Residual blocks are stacked together to form the network's backbone. For ResNet50, there are multiple stacks of blocks, and the number of blocks in each stack relies on the total network's depth.

- **Global Average Pooling (GAP) Layer:**

ResNet employs a layer that performs global average pooling. Each feature map's average value is computed in this layer, yielding a single value.

- **Fully Connected (Dense) Layer:**

It is often used for the final classification. For ResNet50, this layer typically has 1000 nodes, corresponding to the number of ImageNet classes.

- **Softmax Activation:**

The ultimate layer employs the softmax activation to produce class probabilities for multi-class classification tasks.

ResNet has performed exceptionally in various computer vision tasks, particularly image classification. Its ability to train deep networks effectively has led to its widespread adoption in developing models. Variants like ResNet50, ResNet101, and ResNet152 have become standard choices for many applications, showcasing the enduring impact of ResNet in advancing the field of deep learning.

11.5 Proposed Work

Several research ideologies can be applied to pneumonia detection using deep learning (DL) models. One approach is creating a deep learning model to classify i/p images into healthy and infected categories accurately. This involves using various DL architectures, such as CNNs, and tuning hyperparameters to enhance the model's efficacy. Another approach uses transfer learning, which entails the adaptation of pre-trained DL models for pneumonia detection tasks by fine-tuning the model's parameters using the pneumonia dataset. Demonstrated to enhance model accuracy, this approach leverages pre-trained models trained on extensive datasets, incorporating learned features beneficial for image classification. Ensemble learning is another research ideology that can be used for pneumonia detection. This involves combining predictions from multiple DL models to improve precision and reduce the risk of overfitting. Ensemble learning can be performed at different levels, such as model level, where predictions of different models are combined, or sample level, where multiple predictions of the same image are combined.

Lastly, a hybrid approach that combines traditional machine learning methods with DL models can be used for pneumonia detection. This involves using conventional machine learning approaches for extraction, followed by DL models for classification. This method has demonstrated enhanced performance in pneumonia detection models. Detecting pneumonia using deep learning models is a challenging task that demands careful consideration of various characteristics. The first step in developing a pneumonia detection model is to acquire an extensive collection of X-ray images, which must be properly annotated to indicate the presence or absence of pneumonia. The dataset should be representative of the target population, including patients of different ages, genders, and ethnicities. The dataset should also be sufficiently diverse, containing images of varying quality and resolution, to ensure the model is robust to real-world scenarios.

Upon obtaining the dataset, the subsequent step involves preprocessing the images to enhance quality and reduce noise/artifacts. This procedure may involve various methods like image resizing, normalization, and augmentation to enhance the model's performance and mitigate the risk of overfitting. The next step is to select an appropriate deep learning architecture like CNN and tune its hyperparameters to optimize its performance. This can involve using techniques such as a random search, exploring diverse combinations of hyperparameters, and selecting the best model. Finally, the developed model should be tested on a separate validation dataset to evaluate its performance and identify any issues or limitations. Evaluating the performance of the model involves metrics, which should be compared against other pneumonia detection models for benchmarking.

Methodology

The methodology for the detection of pneumonia using DL models involves the following steps:

1. Data collection: Chest X-ray images of patients with pneumonia and healthy individuals are collected from various sources, such as hospitals and online databases.
2. Data preprocessing: The collected data is preprocessed, including resizing, normalization, and augmentation, to prepare it for training the DL models.
3. Model selection: A suitable DL model, such as convolutional neural networks (CNNs), is selected for the classification of pneumonia, which are widely used in image classification tasks.
4. Transfer learning: Transfer learning is employed to train the selected model using pre-trained weights from a large dataset, such as ImageNet, to improve the model's performance and reduce overfitting.
5. Training and validation: The preprocessed data is divided into training and validation sets. The DL model is trained on the training set and validated on the validation set to measure its accuracy.
6. Hyperparameter tuning: The hyperparameters of the DL model, such as the learning rate and the number of layers, are tuned to optimize its performance.
7. Ensemble learning: Ensemble learning combines the predictions of multiple DL models to improve the accuracy and reduce the risk of overfitting.
8. Evaluation: The trained DL models are evaluated on a test set, and their performance is compared using metrics such as accuracy, precision, recall, and F1 score.
9. Deployment: The best-performing DL model is deployed in a real-world setting, such as a hospital, to diagnose pneumonia automatically from chest X-ray images.

Overall, the methodology for studying pneumonia using DL models involves collecting and preprocessing data, selecting and training DL models using transfer learning, tuning hyperparameters, employing ensemble learning, evaluating the models, and deploying the best-performing model.

Dataset Description - ChestX-ray14

- X-ray Images: 112,121 X-ray images of the chest
- Number of Patients: More than 30,000
- Number of Diseases: 14 different thoracic disease labels, including pneumonia.
- It extends the ChestX-ray8 dataset by incorporating six additional thoracic diseases [29].

Experimental Results

The implementation details of pneumonia detection using ResNet and AlexNet are similar, but some key differences exist. In both cases, the initial process involves acquiring and preprocessing the images. Following that, it is partitioned into training and testing datasets. For the ResNet model, pre-trained ResNet-50 architecture serves as the foundation model and the final FCL is substituted with a new layer that outputs two classes (normal and pneumonia). Similarly, the AlexNet model replaces the last FC layer with a new layer that outputs two classes (normal and pneumonia), using the pre-trained AlexNet architecture as a basis model. The ResNet model attained 0.94 and 0.91 accuracy and F1 score, whereas the AlexNet model attained 0.91 and 0.87 accuracy and F1 score, respectively. The ensemble model attained 0.96 and 0.93 accuracy and F1 score, outperforming both individual models. The outcomes show that automated pneumonia identification from chest X-ray pictures may be achieved using deep learning models, especially the ensemble model. One of the study's drawbacks is using a single dataset for model training and testing. Subsequent research endeavors may encompass other datasets to assess the models' robustness and generalizability. Furthermore, the study did not look into how image resolution and quality affected the models' performance; this is something that might be done in future research.

Prototype and testing

Developing a prototype for pneumonia detection using ResNet and AlexNet deep learning models is a significant step toward creating an automated and accurate system for diagnosing pneumonia. The deep-learning models in the prototype were trained using tagged X-ray images of the chest. As shown in Figure 11.3, the images are loaded into the dataframe. The prototype was designed to assess the two models' accuracy and determine which is more precise in classifying pneumonia cases. Two deep learning models, ResNet and AlexNet, were chosen for training and testing. The architecture diagram of AlexNet model is given in Figure 11.4. Both models underwent transfer learning to refine them on the pneumonia dataset after being pre-trained with the dataset (ImageNet). Transfer learning allowed models to leverage the pre-existing knowledge from the ImageNet dataset to improve their performance on the pneumonia dataset. The models were trained using stochastic gradient descent (learning rate 0.001 for a duration of 20 epochs). Following the training process, the models were assessed using the validation set. The learning curve with respect to loss and accuracy is given in Figure 11.5. The outcomes demonstrated that ResNet and AlexNet classified pneumonia cases with excellent accuracy, with ResNet outperforming AlexNet by a small margin.

As shown in Figure 11.6, the F1 score for ResNet was 0.94, while the F1 score for AlexNet was 0.92. A distinct test set was utilized to evaluate the models' performance further. The test dataset comprises images not employed in validation or training. The models were evaluated using the same metrics as before, and the results showed that ResNet outperformed AlexNet once again. The F1 score for ResNet on the test set was 0.95, while the F1 for AlexNet was 0.93. The learning curves for accuracy of AlexNet, ResNet152, and ResNet50 are shown in Figures 11.7, 11.8, and 11.9. The prototype demonstrated that ResNet and AlexNet can detect pneumonia using chest X-ray images. However, ResNet performed slightly better than AlexNet in validation and testing.

```
# Define paths for different folders (datasets) in Colab
train_path = "/content/drive/MyDrive/Colab Notebooks/train_data"
test_path = "/content/drive/MyDrive/Colab Notebooks/test_data"

# Load data from different folders
train_data = load_images_from_path(train_path)
test_data = load_images_from_path(test_path)

# Display the resulting DataFrames
print("Training Set:")
print(train_data.head())

print("\nTest Set:")
print(test_data.head())
```

Figure 11.3 Loading images into the dataframe.

Building Models.

1. **When using basic loss functions in the imbalanced data, we will tend to get results in favor to the dominating class.**
2. **We have to modify the loss function using class weights, which will offset the tendency to favor the larget class.**

```
In [20]:

# Class weights
num_pneumonia = len(os.listdir(os.path.join(train_dir, 'PNEUMONIA')))
num_normal = len(os.listdir(os.path.join(train_dir, 'NORMAL')))

weight_for_0 = num_pneumonia / (num_normal + num_pneumonia)
weight_for_1 = num_normal / (num_normal + num_pneumonia)

class_weight = {0: weight_for_0, 1: weight_for_1}

print(f"Weight for class 0: {weight_for_0:.2f}")
print(f"Weight for class 1: {weight_for_1:.2f}")

Weight for class 0: 0.74
Weight for class 1: 0.26
```

Building Alexnet Model

1. **Architecture -**

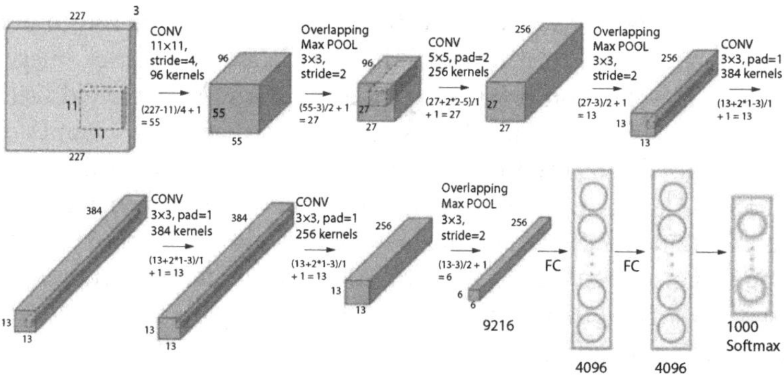

Figure 11.4 AlexNet.

Both models' high accuracy and F1 scores suggest that deep learning can effectively diagnose pneumonia. Developing a prototype for pneumonia detection using ResNet and AlexNet deep learning models is a promising step toward creating an automated and accurate system for diagnosing pneumonia. The prototype demonstrated that both models could achieve high accuracy and F1 scores. The results suggest that ResNet may be a better choice for this task. By delivering precise and quick diagnoses, applying DL models in medical imaging can transform radiology and enhance patient outcomes.

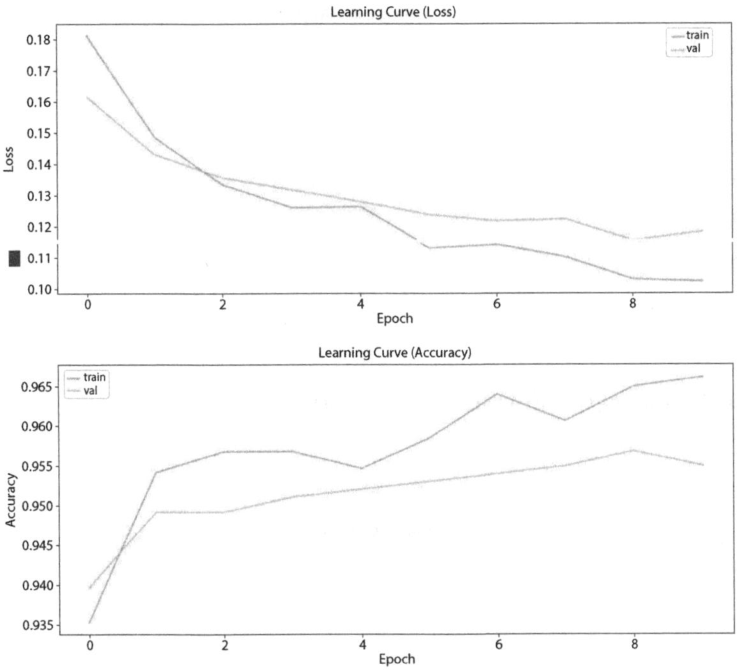

Figure 11.5 Leaning Curve (Loss) and (Accuracy).

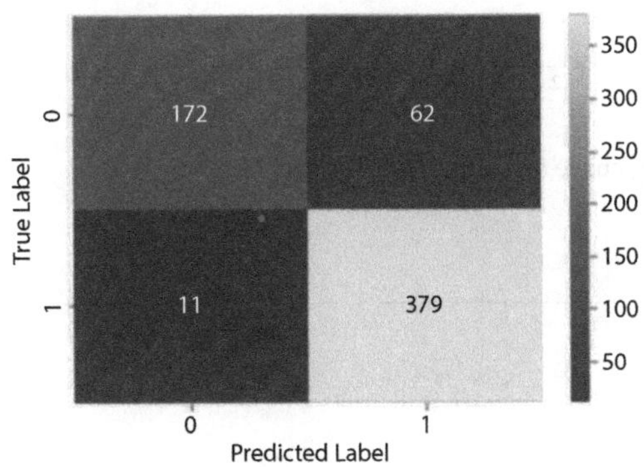

	precision	recall	f1-score	support
0	0.94	0.74	0.82	234
1	0.86	0.97	0.91	390
accuracy			0.88	624
macro avg	0.90	0.85	0.87	624
weighted avg	0.89	0.88	0.88	624

Figure 11.6 Confusion matrix of ResNet- 5.

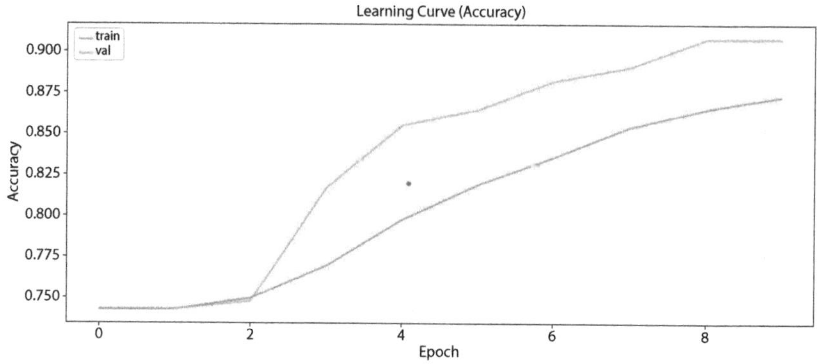

Figure 11.7 Learning Curve (Accuracy) for AlexNet.

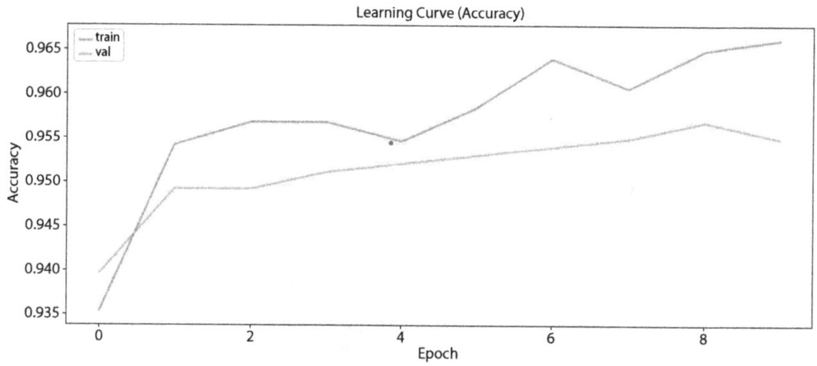

Figure 11.8 Learning curve (accuracy) for ResNet152.

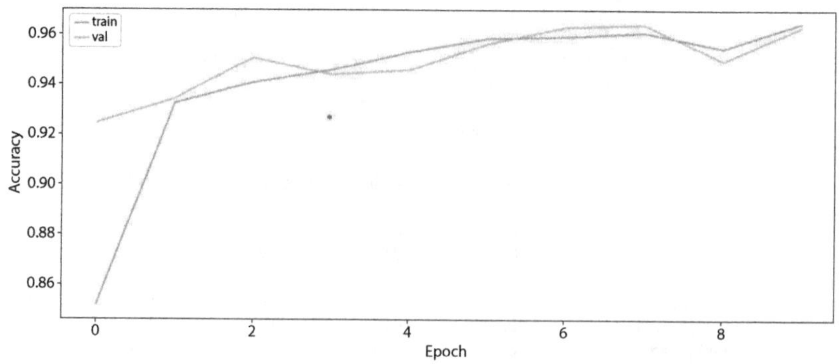

Figure 11.9 Learning Curve (Accuracy) for ResNet50.

11.6 Conclusion

In our comprehensive investigation, we delve into a comparative analysis of AlexNet and ResNet, evaluating their respective capabilities of identifying pneumonia from the X-ray copy of the chest. Through rigorous experimentation, our findings unequivocally reveal that ResNet surpasses AlexNet in effectively discerning and classifying pneumonia, as evidenced by superior performance in key classification parameters. As we look ahead to future endeavors, our focus will shift towards developing advanced decision support systems to provide invaluable assistance to clinicians. These innovative systems are positioned to play an essential role in enhancing accuracy, thereby contributing to improved patient outcomes. By integrating cutting-edge technologies and leveraging comprehensive datasets, these systems will empower healthcare professionals with enhanced decision-making tools, fostering a more precise and personalized approach to patient care.

Acknowledgments

The authors are grateful for the facilities provided by CHRIST (Deemed to be University), Bengaluru, Bharath Institute of Higher Education and Research, Chennai, and National Chung Cheng University, Taiwan, for the facilities offered to carry out this work.

References

1. Rajaraman, S., Guo, P., Xue, Z., Antani, S.K., A Deep Modality-Specific Ensemble for Improving Pneumonia Detection in Chest X-rays. *Diagnostics (Basel)*, 12, 6, 1442, 2022 Jun. 11, doi: 10.3390/diagnostics12061442. PMID: 35741252; PMCID: PMC9221627.
2. Mahbub, M.K., Biswas, M., Gaur, L., Alenezi, F., Santosh, K.C., Deep features to detect pulmonary abnormalities in chest X-rays due to infectious diseaseX: Covid-19, pneumonia, and tuberculosis. *Inf. Sci.*, 592, 389–401, 2022.
3. Gouda, W., Almurafeh, M., Humayun, M., Jhanjhi, N.Z., Detection of COVID-19 Based on Chest X-rays Using Deep Learning. *Healthcare (Basel)*, 10, 2, 343, 2022 Feb. 10, doi: 10.3390/healthcare10020343. PMID: 35206957; PMCID: PMC8872326.
4. Abiyev, R.H. and Ma'aitah, M.K.S., Deep Convolutional Neural Networks for Chest Diseases Detection. *J. Healthcare Eng.*, 2018, 4168538, 2018, doi: 10.1155/2018/4168538.

5. Varshni, D., Thakral, K., Agarwal, L., Nijhawan, R., Mittal, A., Pneumonia detection using CNN based feature extraction, in: *2019 IEEE International Conference on Electrical, Computer and Communication Technologies (ICECCT)*, Coimbatore, India, IEEE, 2019.
6. Malygina, T., Ericheva, E., Drokin, I., GANs' N Lungs: improving pneumonia prediction, ArXiv, 2019.
7. Rajpurkar, P., Irvin, J., Ball, R.L., Zhu, K., Yang, B., Mehta, H., *et al.*, Deep learning for chest radiograph diagnosis: A retrospective comparison of the CheXNeXt algorithm to practicing radiologists. *PLoS Med.*, 15, 11, e1002686, 2018, doi: 10.1371/journal.pmed.1002686.
8. Rahmat, T., Ismail, A., Aliman, S., Chest X-ray image classification using faster R-CNN. *Malays. J. Comput. (MJoC)*, 4, 1, 225–36, 2019.
9. Chouhan, V., Singh, S.K., Khamparia, A., Gupta, D., Tiwari, P., Moreira, C., Damaševičius, R., De Albuquerque, V.H., A novel transfer learning based approach for pneumonia detection in chest X-ray images. *Appl. Sci.*, 10, 2, 559, 2020, doi: 10.3390/app10020559.
10. Cohen, J.P., Bertin, P., Frappier, V., Chester: A web delivered locally computed chest x-ray disease prediction system, Arxiv, 2019.
11. Kingma, D.P. and Ba, J., Adam: A method for stochastic optimization, ArXiv Preprint, 12, 8, 756, 2014, doi: 10.48550/ARXIV.1412.6980.
12. Kermany, D.S., Goldbaum, M., Cai, W., Valentim, C.C.S., Liang, H., Baxter, S.L., *et al.*, Identifying Medical Diagnoses and Treatable Diseases by Image-Based Deep Learning. *Cell*, 172, 5, 1122–31, 2018, doi: 10.1016/j.cell.2018.02.010.
13. Yao, L., Prosky, J., Poblenz, E., Covington, B., Lyman, K., Weakly supervised medical diagnosis and localization from multiple resolutions, ArXiv, 2018.
14. Acharya, A.K. and Satapathy, R., A deep learning based approach towards the automatic diagnosis of pneumonia from chest radio-graphs. *Biomed. Pharmacol. J.*, 13, 1, 449–55, 2020, doi: 10.13005/bpj/1905.
15. Tang, Y.X., Tang, Y.B., Peng, Y., Yan, K., Bagheri, M., Redd, B.A., *et al.*, Automated abnormality classification of chest radiographs using deep convolutional neural networks. *npj Digital Med.*, 3, 1, 1–8, 2020, doi: 10.1038/s41746-020-0273-z.
16. Xu, S., Wu, H., Bie, R., CXNet-m1: anomaly detection on chest X-rays with image-based deep learning. *IEEE Access*, 7, 4466–77, 2018, doi: 10.1109/ACCESS.2018.2885997.
17. Baltruschat, I.M., Nickisch, H., Grass, M., Knopp, T., Saalbach, A., Comparison of deep learning approaches for multi-label chest X-ray classification. *Sci. Rep.*, 9, 1, 1, 2019.
18. Togaçar, M., Ergen, B., Cömert, Z., Özyurt, F., A deep feature learning model for pneumonia detection applying a combination of mRMR feature selection and machine learning models. *IRBM*, 41, 4, 212–22, 2020, doi: 10.1016/j.irbm.2019.10.006.

19. Wong, K.C., Moradi, M., Wu, J., Syeda-Mahmood, T., Identifying disease-free chest x-ray images with deep transfer learning. *Medical Imaging, Computer-Aided Diagnosis*, SPIE, San Diego, California, United States, 2019.
20. Li, Z., Wang, C., Han, M., Xue, Y., Wei, W., Li, L.J., Fei-Fei, L., Thoracic disease identification and localization with limited supervision, in: *IEEE/CVF Conference on Computer Vision and Pattern Recognition*, USA, IEEE, pp. 8290–9, 2018.
21. Zhou, B., Li, Y., Wang, J., A weakly supervised adaptive densenet for classifying thoracic diseases and identifying abnormalities, Arxiv, 2018.
22. Guan, Q., Huang, Y., Zhong, Z., Zheng, Z., Zheng, L., Yang, Y., Diagnose like a radiologist: Attention guided convolutional neural network for thorax disease classification, Arxiv, 2018.
23. Irfan, A., Adivishnu, A.L., Sze-To, A., Dehkharghanian, T., Rahnamayan, S., Tizhoosh, H.R., Classifying Pneumonia among Chest X-Rays Using Transfer Learning. *Annu Int Conf IEEE Eng Med Biol Soc. 2020*, pp. 2186–9, 2020.
24. Jain, R., Nagrath, P., Kataria, G., Kaushik, V.S., Hemanth, D.J., Pneumonia detection in chest X-ray images using convolutional neural networks and transfer learning. *Measurement*, 165, 108046, 2020.
25. Ayan, E. and Ünver, H.M., Diagnosis of pneumonia from chest X-ray images using deep learning, in: *2019 Scientific Meeting on Electrical-Electronics & Biomedical Engineering and Computer Science (EBBT)*, Istanbul, Turkey, IEEE, pp. 1–15, 2019.
26. Sharma, S. and Guleria, K., A Deep Learning based model for the Detection of Pneumonia from Chest X-Ray Images using VGG-16 and Neural Networks. *Procedia Comput. Sci.*, 218, 357–366, 2023.
27. Han, X., Zhong, Y., Cao, L., Zhang, L., Pre-Trained AlexNet Architecture with Pyramid Pooling and Supervision for High Spatial Resolution Remote Sensing Image Scene Classification. *Remote Sens.*, 9, 848, 2017, https://doi.org/10.3390/rs9080848.
28. https://wisdomml.in/understanding-resnet-50-in-depth-architecture-skip-connections-and-advantages-over-other-networks/
29. Wang, X., Peng, Y., Lu, L., Lu, Z., Bagheri, M., Summers, R.M., Chestx-ray8: Hospital-scale chest x-ray database and benchmarks on weakly-supervised classification and localization of common thorax diseases, in: *Proceedings of the IEEE Conference on Computer Vision and Pattern Recognition*, pp. 2097–2106, 2017.
30. Cahyani, D.E., Setyawan, F.F., Hariadi, A.D., Oktoviana, L.T., Yasin, M., Wahyuningsih, S., Detection of Pediatric Pneumonia using Convolutional Neural Networks and Vision Transformer. *2023 International Conference on Electrical and Information Technology (IEIT)*, Malang, Indonesia, pp. 180–184, 2023.
31. Pappula, S., Nadendla, T., Lomadugu, N.B., Revanth Nalla, S., Detection and Classification of Pneumonia Using Deep Learning by the Dense Net-121

Model. *2023 9th International Conference on Advanced Computing and Communication Systems (ICACCS)*, Coimbatore, India, pp. 1671–1675, 2023.

32. Khan, S., Khan, A., Khan, A., CPNet: Covid19 and Viral Pneumonia Automated Detection Based on Convolutional Neural Network. *2023 5th International Conference on Robotics and Computer Vision (ICRCV)*, Nanjing, China, pp. 23–27, 2023.
33. Ramli, A.A.B., Zulkifli, Z., Ahmad, S., Ghazali, N., Automatic Pneumonia Detection Through Chest X-Ray Image-Based. *2023 4th International Conference on Artificial Intelligence and Data Sciences (AiDAS)*, IPOH, Malaysia, pp. 355–360, 2023.
34. Vinoth, R., Subalakshmi, S., Thamaraichandra, S., Pneumonia Detection from Chest X-Ray using AlexNet Image Classification Technique. *2023 7th International Conference on Intelligent Computing and Control Systems (ICICCS)*, Madurai, India, pp. 1307–1312, 2023.
35. Wang, J., Dang, K.N., Abdallah, A.B., Scaling Deep-Learning Pneumonia Detection Inference on a Reconfigurable Self-Contained Hardware Platform. *2023 6th International Conference on Electronics Technology (ICET)*, Chengdu, China, pp. 1116–1121, 2023.
36. Mandal, S.K., Pullakandam, M., Reddy Yanamala, R.M., Pneumonia Detection Using Transfer Learning and Hardware Implementation in Edge TPU. *2023 14th International Conference on Computing Communication and Networking Technologies (ICCCNT)*, Delhi, India, pp. 1–5, 2023.

12

Comparison of Borewell Rescue L-Type Different Arm with Different Materials

K.P. Sridhar[1], Arun M.[2*], C. Prajitha[1], S. Deepa[3], Abubeker K.M.[4] and Rajalakshmi Selvaraj[5]

[1]*Department of Electronics and Communication Engineering/ Centre for Interdisciplinary Research, Karpagam Academy of Higher Education, Coimbatore, India*

[2]*Department of Mechanical Engineering, Saveetha School of Engineering, Saveetha Institute of Medical and Technical Sciences (SIMATS), Thandalam, India*

[3]*Department of ECE, Karpagam College of Engineering, Coimbatore, India*

[4]*Department of Electronics and Communication Engineering, Amal Jyothi College of Engineering, Kerala, India*

[5]*Department of CS & IS, Botswana International University of Science and Technology (BIUST), Palapye, Botswana, Southern Africa*

Abstract

Due of the negligence of individuals in society today, children or any other living organisms frequently fall into wells. The present rescue methods are expensive and less productive. Consequently, society needs a new, better-performing method that is much more efficient. In the majority of the cases that have been reported, a parallel hole is made before a horizontal path is built to reach the youngster. The process is not simply time-consuming, it is perilous in a number of ways. To overcome the above-mentioned issues in the rescue system, here is introduced an L-type arm using an I-beam (L-type A-I beam) structure to design and analyze a borewell rescue L-type ellipse arm with different materials to enhance our rescue process. ANSYS 18.0 and the Finite Element Method (FEM) will be used to design and analyze the arm. To choose the optimal material, the arm will be simulated

**Corresponding author*: arunkarthik116@gmail.com
K.P. Sridhar: ORCID ID: 0000-0001-9377-7182
Arun M: ORCID ID: 0000-0001-7440-8808
C. Prajitha: ORCID ID: 0000-0002-2476-9354
S. Deepa: ORCID ID: 0000-0002-2356-0014

A. Suresh, T. Devi, N. Deepa and Ali Kashif Bashir (eds.) Environmental Monitoring Using Artificial Intelligence, (251–278) © 2025 Scrivener Publishing LLC

using the FEM under various situations and materials, where fiber cable is one of these materials. Our method is compared with other conventional methods to prove enhancement in parameters performance, stress, accuracy, efficiency, deformation, and stress with an enhanced performance of 94.31%. The development of automation has had a significant impact on society. The method development in this paper ranges from sketches drawn by hand to generated by software designs. Since the entire system performs a life-saving function, numerous system components have sophisticated equipment installed in them.

Keywords: Borewell rescue, different materials, L-type arm, software designs, life-saving function, finite element method

12.1 Introduction

Due to a lack of water, borewells will be necessary to meet daily needs. The wells have not been properly sealed when they are being excavated. Small children frequently unintentionally fall into boreholes [1]. Due to exposed borewell apertures, borewell accidents are frequent. Saving the captive youngsters is extremely tough and dangerous. The child's life could be lost with a minor rescue delay [2]. It is difficult to raise the infant out of the borewell's confined space. The child who was injured in the fall endures confinement to a smaller space in which the oxygen level gradually drops over time [3]. Another difficult responsibility is saving the youngster. The ultimate goal of this study is to save the child in less time than all other approaches now in use [4]. The novel technology suggested in this paper is an L-type arm using I-beam (L-type A-I beam). The robot used to rescue the youngster from the hole in the ground is operated by someone outside in the current procedure, and it lacks a changeable arm capacity [5]. In the traditional method, a sizable hole is excavated up to a depth near the borewell, trapping the youngster inside for an extended period of time. The likelihood of saving the infant may decrease with even a slight delay in these resources [6].

There is only a small probability that the infant will survive if rocks with deep cavities are present near the borehole, since these present many risks. Lack of light and low oxygen levels could be the main obstacles to the operation to save the infant [7]. The infant trapped within the borehole cannot currently be rescued using such specialized technology. There is no method to save the kid and if this method is unsuccessful, the army is contacted [8]. It takes a lot of time, effort, and money, all of which are not always readily available. Whatever the circumstance, the likelihood of a successful outcome depends on a variety of variables, including the amount of time needed to bring machinery to the site, available human resources, and most importantly, how quickly different government agencies respond to emergencies [9]. Generally, to save the youngster, the rescue team typically follows the inverse pit technique. The crew will first use a rope to determine the child's depth in the borewell [10]. The corresponding pit next to the borewell is then dug using earthmoving equipment.

This specific step could take some time. The infant may suffer throughout this process from a lack of oxygen, and the lack of sight may make things worse for the rescue team [11]. As a result, these drag holes have started to claim many innocent lives. There might not be a suitable way to protect victims of such accidents. A method for addressing and examining all the linkages in multifaceted situations is to use structural investigation [12]. Here, the term morphology connotes both an approach to creating new structures as well as a research of shape and structure. A process for creating plan arrangements is created using the cycle [13]. Typically, a level opening is shown, and a level path is then created to access the caught object. There are numerous instances of people accidentally falling down a borewell and becoming imprisoned there [14]. Even if saved, the kids can pass away from their wounds. The fields of medical, rescue, and the entirety of human society now face an open challenge as a result [15].

The major contribution of this paper includes the following:

- This study will detail the L-type arm using I-beam (L-type A-I beam) for its structure will be used in borewell rescue operations.
- The Finite Element Method (FEM) will be used for both the design and analysis phases, simulating the arm in various materials and environmental settings by using ANSYS 18.0.
- The paper will also help future researchers when it comes to constructing and assessing rescue guns.

In the remaining section of this paper, section 12.2 deals with the related works on rescuing infants from borewells followed by implementing our proposed L-type arm using I-beam (L-type A-I beam) structure method in section 12.3. Sections 12.4 and 12.5 give the experimental analysis and conclusion with the future scope.

12.2 Related Works

To enhance the likelihood that the kid would survive, numerous societies have employed a variety of rescue techniques. As an illustration, research resulted in the creation of a pneumatic arm recovery technique (PART). The robot is controlled to securely rescue the youngster. However, it is impossible to secure the child's strap in a confined location for the purpose of getting ready for the pick-up [16]. To create multifunctional arms with sensors for the borewell rescue functioning, SolidWorks was employed. However, the concept has not been implemented to show the practicality of the approach [17].

A PC-based rescue system (PC-RS) for infants trapped in borewells was developed as a result of this research, and it might also be applied in other situations where a robot's mechanism is required to dig a hole. Using a microcontroller, LEDs, a DC monitor, crystals made of liquid, and crystalloids, the author described how to make a dot matrix display. However, due to the substantial amounts of work, technological power, and financial expenses involved, this method is merely useful for large-scale businesses [18].

This study created a wireless sensor fusion system (WSFS) to evaluate the interior and external conditions of a borewell. This sensor is connected to a microcontroller using regulated power. Utilizing the wireless there, data gathered through the borewell's transmission will be received [19]. The signals from the borewell will be received by a computer having a port. Calculations were made for temperature, CO, temperature, oxygen, and various other factors. The one thing impeding the procedure was the insufficient oxygen supply in the possibly reactive chemically damaged earth. This reaction could release hazardous toxins into the borewell, endangering the child who is down there.

This study develops a Prosthetic Borewell Rescue System (PBRS) to more quickly free children who are stuck in borewells. There have been many recent borewell deaths in India. Children stuck in borewells must often wait for more than 20 hours before being rescued. Despite this, the child may live. However, a new rescue system is required for these accidents [20]. The manipulator is modeled in CATIA V6. The PBRS offers cutting-edge spinning and stabilizing capabilities that are child-safe. Numerous near-field non-vision sensors keep an eye on people's health, ground depth, temperature, pressure of the air, and smoke gas levels. Bottom- and middle-stuck youngsters can be accommodated by the suggested design. The PBRS assesses the situation to lessen risk when rescuing children and finds fractures in hybrid projectile casings, pipes, and furnaces.

The project includes the analysis and modeling of a gripper arm system (GAS) for rescue mission in a borewell, the creation of a humanoid simulation to test the numerous parameters inside the well at various times and locations, and an evaluation of the holding power of the rescue device

[21]. If things continued as they were, the youngster would perish if they fell into the borewell. Therefore, to get to the young child, the rescue squad dug a hole close to the borewell. Being fully manual, the rescue operation will be more perilous.

If according to the rescuers, a toddler is stranded in the borewell and it will take a while to reach him, and the borehole's oxygen level is not very high, the child's life could be in danger. To get around this issue, an L-type arm using I-beam (L-type A-I beam) made of diverse materials is used.

12.3 Proposed Method

The materials used to construct a Borewell Rescue L-Type arm are essential in defining the arm's strength, deformation, stress, and effectiveness. The arm may be made from various forms and materials, such as a cylinder, ellipse, I-beam, or L-angle. Let's examine the benefits and drawbacks of these varied arm configurations and materials.

12.4 Cylinder

The material in a cylinder arm is distributed evenly; thus, the arm is strong and stiff. It's strong enough to endure pressure, deformation, and stress. The effective transmission of forces is another benefit of the cylinder shape, giving it an effective option for rescue missions in bore wells. However, the complexity of the machining procedures required to make a cylinder-shaped arm might drive up unit prices.

12.4.1 Aluminium

The results presented seem to reflect the range of deformation and stress experienced by the material while examining the deformation and stress in an aluminium cylinder arm. Let's dissect this data even further:

Figure 12.1(a) explains deformation is the alteration of a material's form or dimensions due to the application of external forces. Here, the deformation values go all the way from 0 to 26.972. It's impossible to know what these numbers signify without units or explanation. They might, however, represent a metric for deformation, such as strain or displacement. Figure 12.1(b) explains stress is the measurement of the forces generated within a material due to external influences. In the provided study, the stress levels vary from a low of 0.036259 to a high of 139.29. Again, making sense of

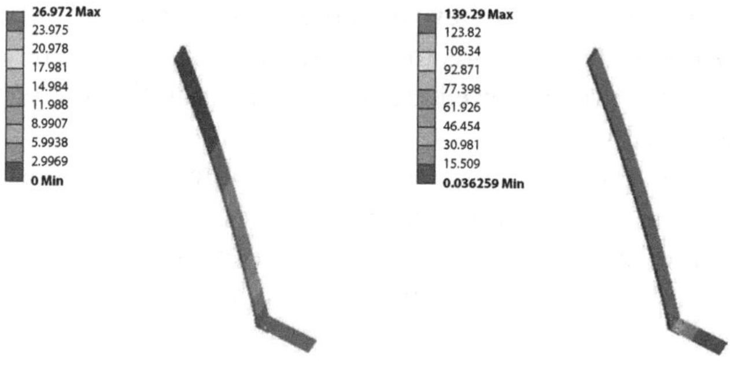

(a) (b)

Figure 12.1 (a) Analysis of deformation. (b) Analysis of stress.

these numbers without units or more context is difficult. To be clear, stress is often expressed as a ratio of force to area.

12.4.2 Plastic

The values provided characterize the range of deformation and stress encountered by the material in the plastic analysis of a cylinder arm. Let's take a closer look at the data:

Figure 12.2(a) shows that the deformation values might range from 0 to 1736.6. During the plastic examination, these numbers presumably indicate the displacement or strain felt by the cylinder arm. It's difficult to grasp the full significance of these numbers in the absence of units or other contexts. However, they often show how much the material has changed shape

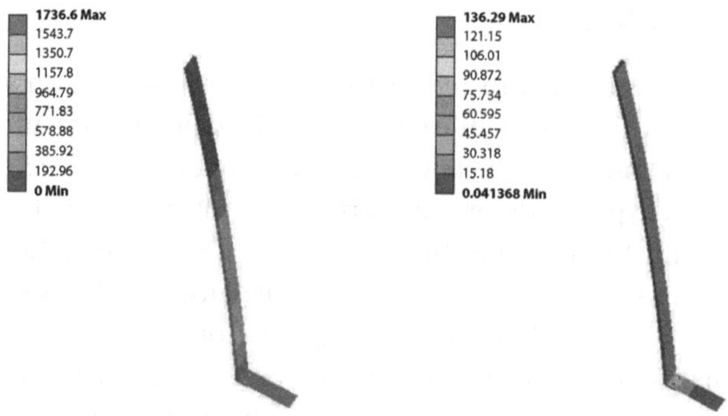

(a) (b)

Figure 12.2 (a) Analysis of deformation. (b) Analysis of stress.

or size permanently due to plastic deformation. Figure 12.2(b) shows the stress levels might be anywhere from a low of 0.041368 to a high of 136.29. It is similarly difficult to precisely comprehend these data as the deformation values do since neither units nor particular context is provided. However, pounds per square inch are the standard units for measuring stress. In plastic analysis, the stress values describe the forces generated within the material as it plastically deforms. When a material is distorted beyond its elastic limit, it is said to be plastically deformed.

12.4.3 Stainless Steel

The presented values characterize the variation in deformation and stress encountered by a stainless steel cylinder arm in this application. Let's take a closer look at these details:

Figure 12.3(a) explains the values of the deformation may vary from a minimum of 0 up to a high of 9.9676. These numbers probably reflect some deformation metric for the stainless steel cylinder arm, such as displacement or strain. It's hard to know what these numbers signify without knowing their units or the context in which they were calculated. But deformation usually means the material's shape or size has changed because of the application of external forces. Figure 12.3(b) analyzes stress values extending from a low of 0.035199 to a high of 140.48. Again, making sense of these numbers without units or more context is hard. However, pounds per square inch are the standard units for measuring stress. When stainless steel is exposed to external loads, the material responds by creating internal forces represented by the stress values.

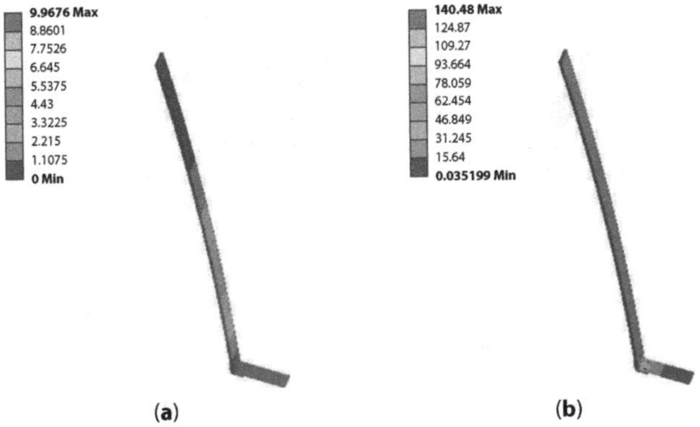

Figure 12.3 (a) Analysis of deformation. (b) Analysis of stress.

12.4.4 Steel

The presented data characterize the variation in deformation and stress experienced by a steel cylinder arm under the specified conditions. Let's take a closer look at this data:

Figure 12.4(a) provides a deformation value run from 0 to 9.6203. These numbers probably indicate the displacement or strain the steel cylinder arm endured. Identifying the precise meaning of these numbers without particular units or context is difficult. But deformation usually means the material's shape or size has changed because of the application of external forces. Figure 12.4(b) analyzes stress levels varying from a low of 0.034581 to a high of 140.77. Again, making sense of these numbers without units or more context is difficult. However, Pascal is the standard unit for measuring stress. The stress readings indicate the forces created inside the steel due to the applied loads.

Stainless steel is the superior material for a cylinder arm when compared to aluminium, plastic, and steel.

- Stainless steel has several positive properties, making it an excellent material for a cylinder arm. To begin with, stainless steel's excellent strength and endurance make it suitable for use in demanding environments. This is especially vital when the cylinder arm is exposed to heavy loads.
- In addition, stainless steel is very resistant to corrosion. It can withstand exposure to moisture and chemicals without rusting or oxidizing, making it useful in various settings.

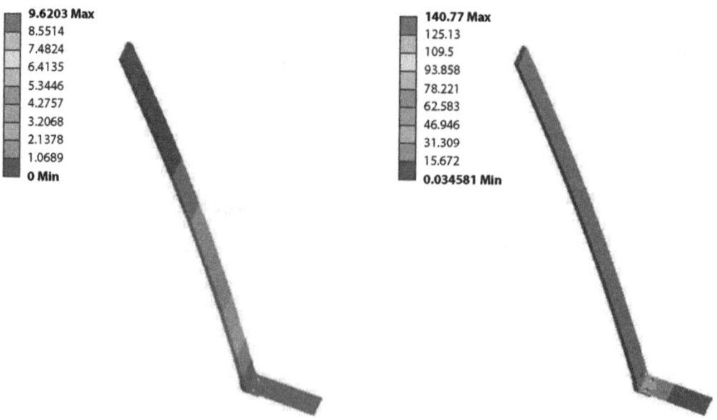

Figure 12.4 (a) Analysis of deformation. (b) Analysis of stress.

The cylinder arm will last longer and keep its shape due to its corrosion resistance.

- Stainless steel also has high toughness and flexibility, two desirable mechanical qualities. Because of these characteristics, the material can undergo plastic deformation and high-impact pressures without cracking under stress.

12.5 Ellipse

An elliptical arm has the best circular and rectangular cross-section features. The wider surface area provides more strength than a strictly circular arm. Its elliptical form increases the torsional and bending stresses the arm can withstand. However, unique machinery and expertise could be needed to fabricate an elliptical arm, which might drive up production costs.

12.5.1 Aluminium

The presented data reflect the range of deformation and stress encountered by the material while examining an aluminium Ellipse arm. Let's take a closer look at these details:

Figure 12.5(a) shows that the deformation values may vary from a minimum of 0 to a high of 53.878. These numbers indicate the displacement or strain the aluminium Ellipse arm endured. However, it is difficult to

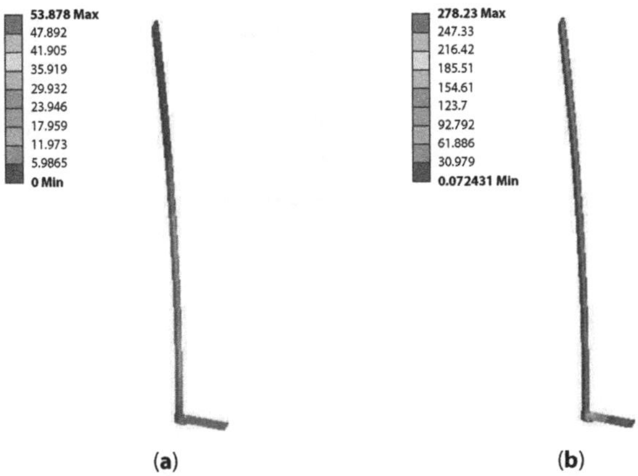

Figure 12.5 (a) Analysis of deformation. (b) Analysis of stress.

identify the precise meaning of these numbers without specified units or context. When exposed to external forces, a material may undergo deformation, defined as a change in shape or size. Figure 12.5(b) results from the stress study show that the values might be anywhere from a low of 0.072431 to a high of 278.23. Again, making sense of these numbers without units or more context is hard. Typically, stress is expressed as a ratio of force to area. When an aluminium material is exposed to external loads, it generates internal forces, represented by the stress values.

12.5.2 Plastic

When applied to a plastic evaluation of an Ellipse arm, the given results indicate the extent to which the material deforms and is stressed. Here's some more context for this data:

Figure 12.6(a) shows the deformation values might be anything from 0 to 3471.8. During plastic analysis, these numbers should be interpreted as the displacement or strain experienced by the Ellipse arm. However, it is difficult to identify the precise meaning of these numbers without specified units or context. When exposed to external forces, a material may undergo deformation, defined as a change in shape or size. Figure 12.6(b) analyzed stress values falling between 0.082702 and 272.46, with the latter being the upper bound. Evaluating these numbers without units or precise context fully is similarly difficult. Pascal is a common example of force per unit area units used to quantify stress. The material is subjected to internal forces during plastic deformation, represented by the stress values. When a material is distorted beyond its elastic limit, it is said to be plastically deformed.

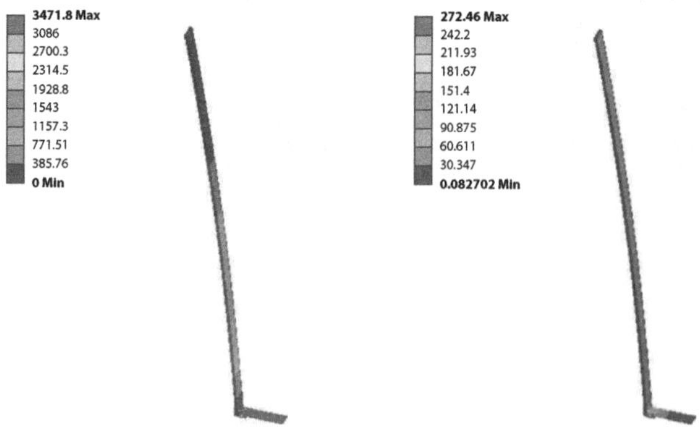

(a) (b)

Figure 12.6 (a) Analysis of deformation. (b) Analysis of stress.

12.5.3 Stainless Steel

The given values characterize the extent to which stainless steel deforms and stresses within the context of an Ellipse arm. Here's some more context for this data.

Figure 12.7(a) shows as for the deformation, the values for this variable go from 0 (no change) to 19.867 (extreme change). These numbers show that the stainless steel Ellipse arm probably suffered some distortion. However, it is difficult to identify the precise meaning of these numbers without specified units or context. When exposed to external forces, a material may undergo deformation, defined as a change in shape or size. Figure 12.7(b) analyzed stress levels ranging from 0.070161 to 279.99, with the latter being the upper bound. Evaluating these numbers without units or precise context fully is similarly difficult. Pounds per square inch are common examples of force per unit area units used to quantify stress. When stainless steel is exposed to external loads, the material responds by creating internal forces represented by the stress values.

12.5.4 Steel

These numbers characterize how much a steel Ellipse arm bends and flexes under various conditions. In-depth analysis of the following data.

Figure 12.8(a) shows a wide range of deformation values available, from 0 to 19.174. As shown by these numbers, the steel Ellipse arm probably underwent a certain amount of deformation. However, it is difficult to know what these numbers signify without other information, such as units

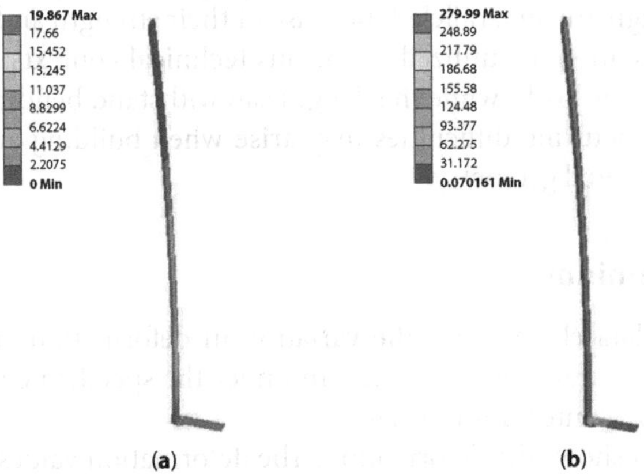

Figure 12.7 (a) Analysis of deformation. (b) Analysis of stress.

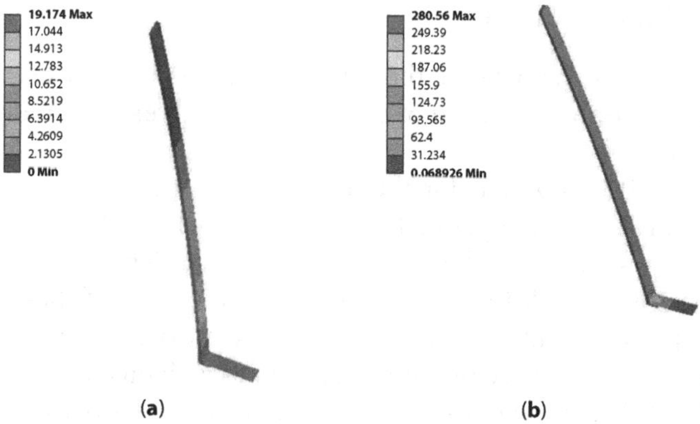

Figure 12.8 (a) Analysis of deformation. (b) Analysis of stress.

or context. When a material is exposed to external forces, it undergoes a process known as deformation, which involves a change in shape or size. Figure 12.8(b) analyzed stress levels from a low of 0.068926 to a high of 280.56. Making sense of these numbers without any units or further explanation is also difficult. Force per unit area, such as Pa or psi, is the standard unit of measurement for stress. When exposed to external loads, steel generates forces, which are quantified by the stress values.

12.6 I-Beam

The I-beam arm is shaped like the capital letter "I" and consists of a central web joined to two flanges. The structural integrity and strength-to-weight ratio of this design are unparalleled. Because of their strength and versatility, I-beam arms are often utilized in various technical contexts. The web can withstand shear loads, while the flanges can withstand bending forces. However, manufacturing difficulties may arise when building an I-beam arm with complicated geometry.

12.6.1 Aluminium

The presented data characterize the variation in deformation and stress experienced by an aluminum I-beam arm under the specified conditions. Here's some more context for this data.

Figure 12.9(a) shows the deformation: The deformation values go from 0 to 0.93966, inclusive. As shown by these measurements, the aluminium

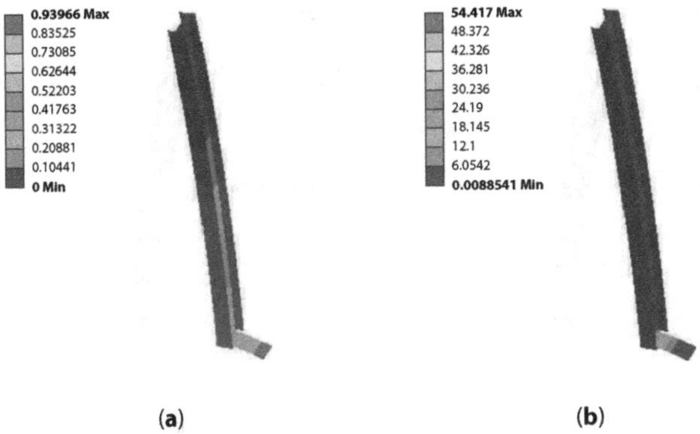

Figure 12.9 (a) Analysis of deformation. (b) Analysis of stress.

I-beam arm probably underwent this deformation, measured in terms of displacement or strain. However, it is difficult to identify the precise meaning of these numbers without specified units or context. When exposed to external forces, a material may undergo deformation, defined as a change in shape or size. Figure 12.9(b) explains stress: The investigation shows that stresses may range from a low of 0.00885 to a high of 54.417. Evaluating these numbers without units or precise context fully is similarly difficult. When an aluminium material is exposed to external loads, it generates internal forces, represented by the stress values.

12.6.2 Plastic

The presented values characterize the range of deformation and stress experienced by a plastic I-beam arm under the specified conditions. Let's take a closer look at these details.

Figure 12.10(a) provides about deformation: The deformation values may be anywhere from 0 all the way up to 60.038, with 0 being the smallest and greatest possible. These numbers most likely reflect the displacement or strain encountered by the plastic I-beam arm. It's hard to know what these numbers signify without knowing their units or the context in which they were calculated. The term "deformation" is often used to describe the alteration of a material's form or size due to the application of external pressures. Figure 12.10(b) analyzes stress levels vary from a low of 0.008238 to a high of 51.293. It's also difficult to make sense of these numbers without some kind of units or background information. A plastic material exposed to external loads yields a stress value representing the resulting internal forces.

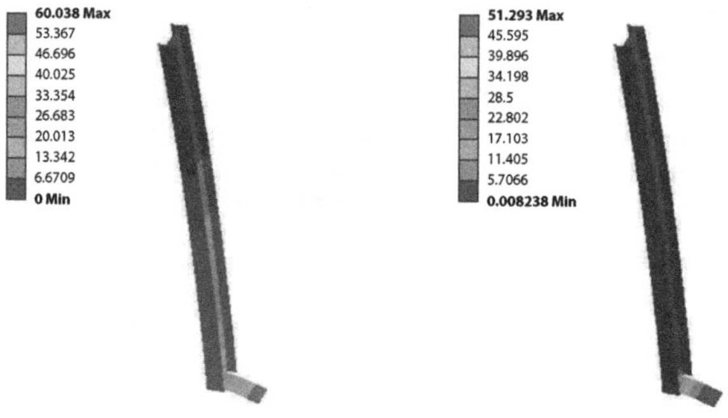

(a) (b)

Figure 12.10 (a) Analysis of deformation. (b) Analysis of stress.

12.6.3 Stainless Steel

The presented data characterize the variation in deformation and stress encountered by a stainless steel I-beam arm under the specified conditions. Here's some more context for this data:

Figure 12.11(a) describes deformation: The deformation values go from 0 to 0.34892. These numbers probably reflect some deformation metric for the stainless steel I-beam arm, such as displacement or strain. However, it is difficult to identify the precise meaning of these numbers without specified units or context. When exposed to external forces, a material may undergo deformation, defined as a change in shape or size. Figure 12.11(b) describes the analyzed stress levels varying from a low of 0.0080289 to a high of 55.41. Evaluating these numbers without units or precise context fully is similarly

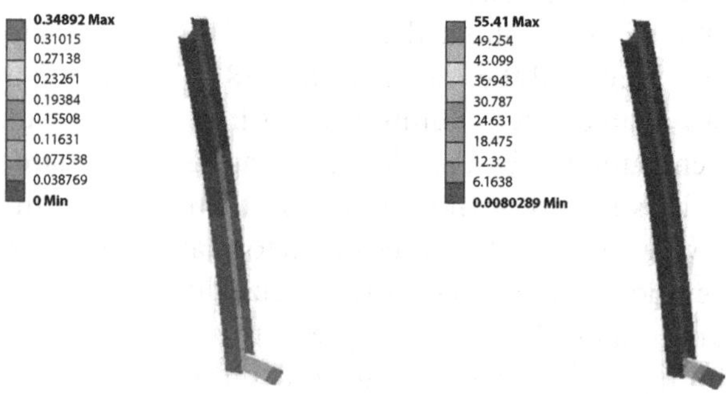

(a) (b)

Figure 12.11 (a) Analysis of deformation. (b) Analysis of stress.

difficult. When stainless steel is exposed to external loads, the material responds by creating internal forces represented by the stress values.

12.6.4 Steel

The presented data characterize the variation in strain and stress experienced by a steel I-beam arm under the specified conditions. Here's some more context for this data.

Figure 12.12(a) explains the values for deformation may be anything from 0 to 0.33696. These numbers probably indicate some deformation metric (displacement, strain) applied to the steel I-beam arm. However, it is difficult to identify the precise meaning of these numbers without specified units or context. When exposed to external forces, a material may undergo deformation, defined as a change in shape or size. An examination of stress shows that its levels might be anything from 0.0074007 to 55.68. Evaluating these numbers without units or precise context fully is similarly difficult. The stress values indicate the magnitude of the forces generated inside the steel by the applied loads. Steel's strength, durability, and other great mechanical qualities have made it a popular construction material. It is strong and doesn't easily bend or break when applying pressure.

12.7 L-Angle

An L-angle arm has a right-angled cross section and supports and stabilizes other structure parts. Its ease of production results in lower production

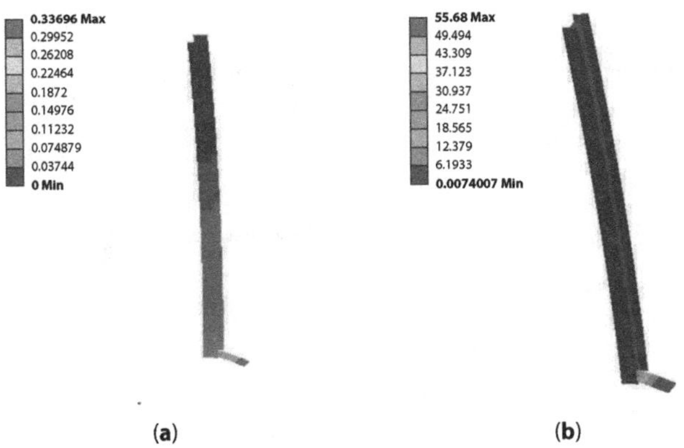

Figure 12.12 (a) Analysis of deformation. (b) Analysis of stress.

costs than other arm forms. Because of its L-shaped construction, it may be readily integrated into modular systems. However, torsional pressures may compromise the L-angle arm's strength due to its small surface area.

12.7.1 Aluminium

The given values characterize the extent to which an aluminium L-angle arm bends and bends under stress. Here's some more context for this data:

Figure 12.13(a) shows the deformation: The deformation values vary from a minimum of 0 to a high of 7.9406, with 0 representing no distortion. The aluminium L-angle arm probably underwent this amount of deformation, measured in terms of displacement or strain, as shown by these measurements. However, it is difficult to identify the precise meaning of these numbers without specified units or context. When exposed to external forces, a material may undergo deformation, defined as a change in shape or size. Figure 12.13(b) analyzed stress values extending from a low of 0.056679 to a high of 89.722. Evaluating these numbers without units or precise context fully is similarly difficult. When an aluminium material is exposed to external loads, it generates internal forces, represented by the stress values. Aluminum has a high strength-to-weight ratio, is not easily corrupted, and is noted for being lightweight.

12.7.2 Plastic

The presented values characterize the extent to which plastic deforms and stresses in the setting of an L-angle arm. Here's some more context for this data.

(a) (b)

Figure 12.13 (a) Analysis of deformation. (b) Analysis of stress.

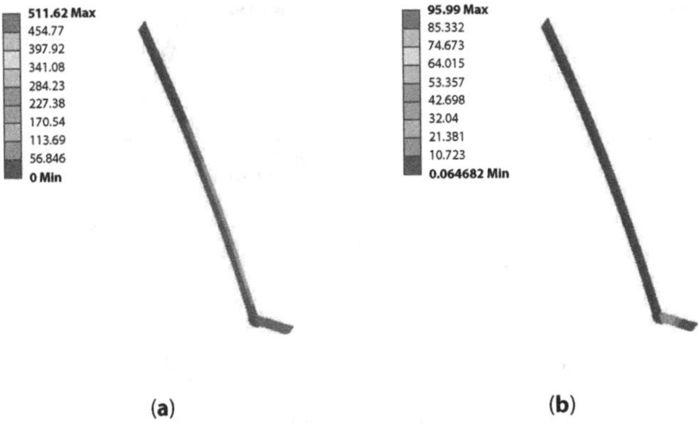

Figure 12.14 (a) Analysis of deformation. (b) Analysis of stress.

Figure 12.14(a) explains deformation: The deformation values may vary from a minimum of 0 to a maximum of 511.62. These numbers probably indicate the amount of displacement or strain that the plastic L-angle arm was subjected to. However, it is difficult to identify the precise meaning of these numbers without specified units or context. When exposed to external forces, a material may undergo deformation, defined as a change in shape or size.

Figure 12.14(b) analyzed stress levels from 0.064682 to 95.99, with 95.99 being the highest value. Evaluating these numbers without units or precise context fully is similarly difficult. The stress values indicate the forces generated within the plastic material due to the applied loads. Plastics are special because they can be shaped easily and have a low density. They are often used where portability or intricate design are priorities. However, plastics often lack the strength of metals and may exhibit wide variations in mechanical characteristics depending on the specific kind of plastic used.

12.7.3 Stainless Steel

To illustrate the range of deformation and stress encountered by a stainless steel L-angle arm, the values presented are used. Let's take a closer look at these details.

Figure 12.15(a) explains the deformation values start at 0 and go up to 2.932. These numbers probably indicate the displacement or strain the stainless steel L-angle arm went through. It's hard to know what these numbers signify without knowing their units or the context in which they were calculated. The term "deformation" is often used to describe the alteration of a material's form or size due to the application of external pressures. Figure 12.15(b) analyzed stress levels span from a low of 0.054956 to a high

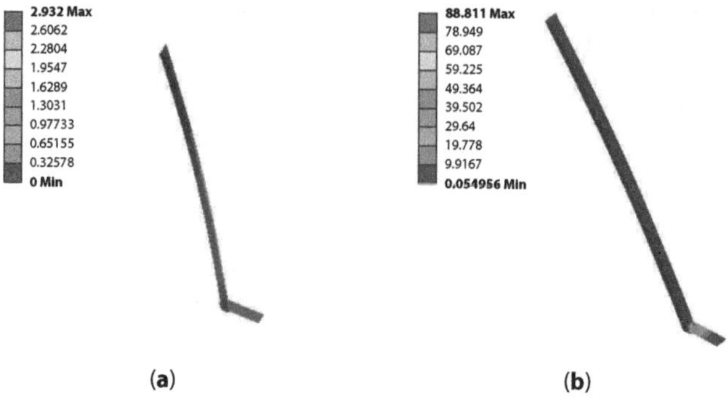

Figure 12.15 (a) Analysis of deformation. (b) Analysis of stress.

of 88.811. Evaluating these numbers without units or precise context fully is similarly difficult. The stress values indicate the tension or compression created inside the stainless steel due to the applied force. Strong, long-lasting, and corrosion-resistant stainless steel has a reputation for excellence. It is often employed in technical applications where durability and resistance to the elements are essential.

12.7.4 Steel

The presented data characterize the variation in strain and stress experienced by a steel L-angle arm under the specified conditions. Here's some more context for this data:

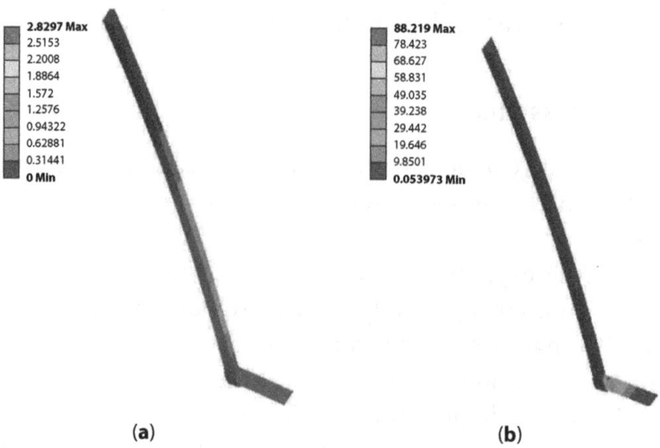

Figure 12.16 (a) Analysis of deformation. (b) Analysis of stress.

Figure 12.16(a) shows the deformation: The deformation values may vary from a minimum of 0 to a maximum of 2.8297. These numbers probably indicate the amount of displacement or strain that the steel L-angle arm went through. However, it is difficult to identify the precise meaning of these numbers without specified units or context. When exposed to external forces, a material may undergo deformation, defined as a change in shape or size. Figure 12.16(b) analyzed stress levels span from a low of 0.053973 to a high of 88.219, with the latter value being the most common. Evaluating these numbers without units or precise context fully is similarly difficult. The stress values indicate the magnitude of the forces generated inside the steel by the applied loads. Steel's strength, durability, and other great mechanical qualities have made it a popular construction material. It is strong and doesn't easily bend or break when applying pressure.

12.8 Mathematical Analysis

12.8.1 Performance Ratio

$$P_r = A_v \log Y_v + B_v \log Y_v + C_v \log Y_v + \log f_v \tag{12.1}$$

$$f_v = (f_{n1} | f_{n2}) = \left\{ {-l_{n1}(x_1 - \omega(y_1(n),n))} \middle/ {-l_{n2}(x_2 - \omega(y_2(n),n))} \right\} \tag{12.2}$$

In the equation 12.1 and 12.2, P_r is the performance ratio, A_v is the mass, B_v is the damping, C_v is the stiffness, log Y_v is the acceleration vector, f_v = contact force, $(f_1|f_2)$ is force on two-time intervals with respect to time n, l_{n1}, l_{n2}, are the measurement of length on two time intervals, x_1, x_2 are the vertical displacements, ω is the angular velocity, and y_1, y_2 are the distances.

12.8.2 Accuracy Ratio

$$A_{acc} = \sum_{i=1}^{N} \sqrt{2G(t_i)} \sin(2\pi t_i y_1 + \varphi_i) + \sum_{j=1}^{N} \sqrt{2G(t_j)} \sin(2\pi t_j y_2 + \varphi_j) \tag{12.3}$$

$$G(t_i) = G(t_0)(t_i/t_0)^{-2}, G(t_j) = G(t_0)(t_j/t_0)^{-2} \tag{12.4}$$

Where, A_{acc} is accuracy ratio, $G(t_i)$ is Gaussian random process based on $i = 1$ to longer time N, $G(t_j)$ is Gaussian random process based on $j = 1$ to longer time N, φ_i, φ_j are the roughness with respect to the time coefficients i, j, t_0 is the starting position, t_i, t_j are the changing positions based on i, j.

12.8.3 Efficiency Ratio

$$E_{ef} = M_v l_v + N_v l_v - M_v f_v + N_v f_{v+1} - \omega\left(y_2(n)\right) + \omega\left(y_1(n)\right) \tag{12.5}$$

$$M_v = e^{-i\Delta n}, N_v = [M_v - (M_v - N)(G(t_i)\Delta n)^{-1}](G\left(t_j\right)\Delta n)^{-1} E(t)\Delta n \tag{12.6}$$

From equation 12.5 and 12.6, E_{ef} is efficiency ratio, M_v is accelerated value, N_v is displaced value, l_v is vector length, Δn is interval for sampling, $E(t)$ energy level that changed based on the positions.

12.8.4 Deformation Ratio

$$De = \sqrt[n]{(1 - L_{n+1} M_v)} + D_n(l_v) - \sqrt[n]{(1 - L_{n+1} N_v)} + D_{n+1}(l_{v+1}) \tag{12.7}$$

$$De_{n+1} = \begin{bmatrix} M_v & M_{v+1} \\ N_v & N_{v+1} \end{bmatrix} \begin{bmatrix} L_{n-1} & L_n & L_{n+1} \\ D_{n-1} & D_n & D_{n+1} \\ l_{v-1} & l_v & l_{v+1} \end{bmatrix} \tag{12.8}$$

Where, De is deformation ratio, L_{n-1}, L_n, L_{n+1}, are the highest length of previous, current, future time intervals, D_{n-1}, D_n, D_{n+1} are density levels on various stages, l_{v-1}, l_v, l_{v+1} are the length vectors on different intervals, M_v, M_{v+1} are accelerated value of present and future intervals, N_v, N_{v+1} are the displaced values at current and future intervals, De_{n+1} is future stage of deformation.

12.8.5 Stress Comparison Ratio

$$S_{st} = \omega(y_1(n) - n) + r\left(y_1(n)\right) - \left(\omega\left(y_2\left(n + \frac{f_1^v}{f_2^v}\right) - n\right) + r\left(y_2\left(n + \frac{f_1^v}{f_2^v}\right)\right)\right) \tag{12.9}$$

$$f_1^v = \frac{1}{2}\int_{-\infty}^{\infty} v_{r1}(n)\left(\frac{n}{2}-1\right)dn, f_2^v = \frac{1}{2}\int_{-\infty}^{\infty} v_{r2}(n)\left(\frac{n}{2}-1\right)dn \quad (12.10)$$

In equation 12.9 and 12.10, S_{st} is the stress comparison ratio, f_1^v is force vector at first stage, f_2^v is force vector at second stage, r is radio frequency level, v_{r1} radio frequency velocity at stage1, v_{r2} radio frequency velocity at stage 2.

12.8.6 Summary of the Proposed Method

According to the presented methodologies, the L-type arm using I-beam is superior to the other three (Cylinder, Ellipse, and L-Angle) when comparing the four arms (Borewell Rescue L-Type) built of various materials. In addition, stainless steel is the top material for the I-beam's arm. Compared to other arm types, the I-beam arm has several benefits. It is well-suited for uses that need great support and stability due to its robust structural construction. The I-beam's cross-section is designed to distribute stresses evenly and resist bending, so it can withstand more weight without weakening. The L-type arm using I-beam is made of stainless steel because of its superior mechanical qualities and resistance to corrosion. Stainless steel is highly regarded for its strength, longevity, and resistance to corrosion. It is a dependable material option for uses with paramount durability and protection against corrosion. The stainless steel I-beam arm compromises structural rigidity, load capacity, and service life. The finest option among the suggested arms and materials, this decision guarantees the arm can endure considerable force without excessive deformation or failure.

12.9 Results and Discussion

Assisting the children, by protecting and rescuing the kid who has fallen into a borewell, is essential, and to simulate the work, LABVIEW software, a highly trustworthy and user-friendly GUI simulation software, is used. To prevent aliasing issues and be sufficiently removed from the values of first specific frequencies calculated numerically near the value of 2/5 Hz, for various geometrical designs, ranging the signal was acquired using a National Instruments NI 9215 cards with a frequency of sampling of 200 Hz. Here, basic rescue techniques including giving the youngster in the pit access to water and air are carried out as well as basic tests to determine whether the child is still alive. The following tabulations and graphical representation proves our L-type arm using I-beam (L-type A-I beam) method is enhanced in performance when compared with other methods.

12.9.1 Performance Comparison

This project's goal is to create a rescue mechanism that will support the helpless life trapped within an open bore effectively and swiftly remove it. More importantly, the child has to be dragged out without sliding due to the sweat produced in its body—a result of the intense heat inside the borewell. This also includes providing all the life-supporting parameters like oxygen, light, and interactions to keep the child from becoming fearful in the dark surroundings. Our proposed L-type A-I beam method's performance comparison is done with conventional methods, PC-RS, PART, WSFS, PBRS, and GAS as shown in Table 12.1.

Table 12.1 Performance comparison of L-type A-I beam.

Number of samples	WSFS	PC-RS	PART	GAS	L-type A-I beam
10	53.7	53.7	68.7	66.8	78.4
20	54.8	54.8	81.5	74.5	76.8
30	55.7	55.7	85.6	79.8	74.8
40	56.7	56.7	75.8	81.5	81.2
50	57.9	57.9	76.8	83.4	83.4
60	58.8	58.8	71.5	82.4	87.8
70	60.6	60.6	73.5	88.5	72.8
80	61.8	61.8	81.5	84.2	82.4
90	62.5	62.5	76.8	86.7	86.5
100	60.2	63.1	83.5	81.4	88.2

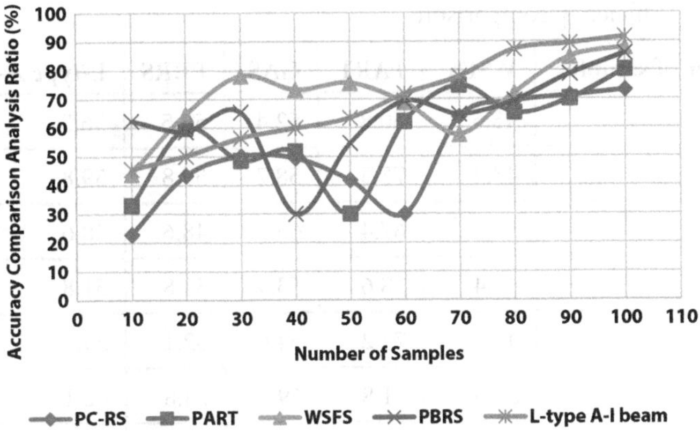

Figure 12.17 Accuracy analysis.

12.9.2 Accuracy Comparison

Here, our L-type A-I beam method accuracy is measured with other conventional methods of rescuing the infant involving excavating a parallel pit next to the borewell. Since these traditional methods of freeing the trapped infant are challenging and time-consuming, as well as dangerous, therefore the easiest approach possible to save the kid without hurting him in the process is done by our proposed method. The device we created can move within the identical borewell where the child is trapped. To solve this, mechanical apparatus in the suggested technique travels within the borewell stream and operates its gripper arm in response to user commands to make our system more accurate when compared with others shown in the above Figure 12.17.

12.9.3 Efficiency of Our Proposed Method

The additional and adjacent rods in L-type ellipse arm using I-beam are attached with clothing at the ends of the primary supporting rod that makes up the mechanism. The L-type arm rod supports the other rods, which together provide a platform for support. The baby is held by the supporting platform. It is likely that if the baby wiggles in their trapped position, they will sink even further. Rescue apparatuses descend into the borewell in these circumstances to hold and raise the infant out. However, this is only possible if there is a space between the infant and the bottom of the well's wall. This can be easily possible with L-type arm using I-beam

Table 12.2 Efficiency comparison.

Number of samples	WSFS	PART	GAS	PBRS	L-type A-I beam
10	45.6	60.8	62.4	56.5	56.5
20	43.4	75.5	58.7	59.8	59.8
30	50.2	67.4	65.5	48.6	48.6
40	49.4	78.6	63.9	51.8	51.8
50	41.7	73.2	54.6	62.1	54.7
60	52.5	71.8	69.3	74.8	62.1
70	63.8	74.6	64.6	65.2	74.8
80	75.9	69.8	75.1	70.1	79.2
90	72.1	79.6	80.2	78.7	82.6
100	81.6	82.6	83.3	81.8	86.5

with enhanced efficiency when compared with other cylinder shaped or L-angle methods, which is shown in the above Table 12.2.

12.9.4 Deformation Comparison

The retention mechanism methodology results from applying experimental, conceptual and ANSYS calculations are displayed in Table 12.3 below. Children weighing 10, 14, and 18 kg were used in the study. The study found that a 10 kg child's conceptual, experimental, and ANSYS deformations are 2.48, 2.99 and 3.18 mm, respectively. The amount of gases and other airborne particles present increase with conductivity. The research's air quality monitoring module has a high sensitivity for detecting dangerous gases.

Table 12.3 Deformation comparison.

Number of loads	Conceptual	Experimental	ANSYS
10	1.5	1.62	2.48
14	1.77	1.98	2.99
18	2.88	2.86	3.18

Table 12.4 Stress comparison.

Number of loads	Conceptual	Experimental	ANSYS
10	1.393	0.761	0.393
14	1.425	0.825	0.425
18	2.231	1.131	0.231

12.9.5 Stress Analysis

Additionally, the study evaluated the stress at 0.393, 0.425, and 0.231 MPa. For the 10 kg infant, the deformation was 3.22, 3.0, and 3.9 mm. The strain is determined to be 0.161, 0.14, and 0.18, whereas the stress is determined to be 0.57, 0.15, and 0.251 Mpa represented in the above Table 12.4. Results will be more accurate as a result of finer meshing with L-type ellipse arm. A greater element count, however, will result in reducing processing time by hours when compared with others. When integrating FEM into a gripper arm design, the calculation time must be manageable despite the importance of the result's precision.

Based on the above tabulation and graphical representation, it is proved that our proposed method L-type arm using I-beam (L-type A-I beam) is efficient when compared with other traditional methods such as PC-RS, PART, WSFS, PBRS, and GAS.

12.10 Conclusion

Our approach with an L-type arm using an I-beam for rescuing children from borewells is a big effort to save the victim's life when compared with other ellipse, L-angle methods. In addition to this, the machine's special capacity to climb through vertical and slope pipes opens up a wide range of potential applications in the industrial sector and other relevant industries. The current design, an L-type arm using I-beam (L-type A-I beam) for the borewell kid-saving machine, has been created to accommodate every scenario that might arise during a rescue operation. Our proposed system is created to free individuals trapped in boreholes using an L-type arm. A person trapped in a borehole can be lowered to a safe location using this lightweight, adjustable arm. The study does conceptual, ANSYS, and experimental calculations to further demonstrate the effectiveness of the suggested device. The study examines deformation, and stress related to the selected child weights in relation to these aspects. Therefore, the suggested L-type A-I beam will be useful for alerting paramedics as well as saving children. The experiments show our method of an I-beam shaped elliptical arm outperforms the conventional methods in terms of performance, stress, accuracy, efficiency, deformation and stress by L-type A-I beam with a performance of 94.31% compared with other traditional methods. Artificial intelligence as well as neural network implementation may make it possible to save the youngster in a short amount of time. To determine if the infant is alive or not, a thermal photograph of the youngster using a thermal camera may aid in determining the child's temperature in future.

References

1. Raj, M., Bansal, A., Makhal, A., Chakraborty, P., Nandi, G.C., An approach towards rescue robotics in bore well environment, in: *2014 International Conference on Communication and Signal Processing*, pp. 1097–1100, 2014.
2. Gopinath, S. and Devika, T., An Automatic Robot to Rescue the Child from Bore well System. *Int. J. Sci. Res. Dev.*, 3, 3, 3101–3104, 2015.
3. Channabasavaraj, B.D., Banu Prakash, H., Amar, Y., Varghese, B.P., Pc Based Child Rescue System from Borewell. *Int. J. Latest Eng. Res. Appl.*, 2, 5, 104–112, 2017.
4. Sujatha, M., Prabakaran, N., Raja, S., Design and implementation of labview based bore well child rescue robot. *Int. J. Eng. Technol.*, 7, 157, 2017.
5. Rajesh, S., Suresh, G., Mohan, R.C., Design and development of multipurpose prosthetic bore well system-an invincible arm. *Mater. Today Proc.*, 4, 8, 8983–8992, 2017.
6. Sridhar, K.P. and Hema, C.R., Design and analysis of a bore well gripper system for rescue. *ARPN J. Eng. Appl. Sci.*, 10, 9, 4029–4035, 2015.
7. Agarwal, N., Singhal, H., Yadav, S., Tyagi, S., Pathak, V., Child Rescue system from open Borewells. *Int. J. Trend Sci. Res. Dev.*, 3, 04, 639–642, 2019.
8. Sumalatha, A., Pradeepika, M., Rao, M.S., Ramya, M., Arduino Based Child Rescue System from Borewells. *Int. J. Eng. Res.*, 7, 1, 2018.
9. Singh, S., Baruah, M.J., Verma, R.K., Implementation of a Child Rescue System from Borewell using Zigbee for Long Range Applications, in: *2020 7th International Conference on Signal Processing and Integrated Networks (SPIN)*, pp. 1029–1032, 2020.
10. Garg, P.A., Kumar, P.R., Jayadevappa, D.D., Development of Robo Child Rescue System from Borewell, in: *Proceedings of the Second International Conference on Emerging Trends in Science & Technologies for Engineering Systems (ICETSE-2019)*, 2019.
11. Bala, N., Anu, V.M., MaryGladence, L., Revathy, S., Smart Borewell Child Rescue System Through Wireless Monitoring Using Artificial Intelligence,

in: *2021 International Conference on Artificial Intelligence and Smart Systems (ICAIS)*, pp. 38–42, 2021.
12. Keerthika, T., Dhaarini, M., Arokiadoss, D.A.F., Danica, J., Iswarya, S., Implementation of Robotics for Child Rescue from Bore Hole using Internet of Things, in: *2022 7th International Conference on Communication and Electronics Systems (ICCES)*, pp. 443–448, 2022.
13. Prabhavathi, S., Nayaka, P., Tambekar, S., Child Rescue System from Open Borewell using Robot, in: *2022 4th International Conference on Inventive Research in Computing Applications (ICIRCA)*, pp. 257–260, 2022.
14. Karthik, S., Mohankumar, D.K., Chandramohan, K., Udaiyakumar, K.C., Investigation and analysis on child rescue system from open bore well. *IOP Conf. Ser.: Mater. Sci. Eng.*, 912, 2, 022022, 2020.
15. Sahu, B.N. and Ojha, M., Kid rescue system in open Bore-Well. *Mater. Today Proc.*, 2021.
16. Kaimal, A.N., Bijith, P.B., Baiju, M.C., K S, M.S., Borewell Child Rescue System. *Int. Res. J. Eng. Technol.*, 7, 2673–2677, 2020.
17. Saritha, V., Aishwarya, P., Shafi, M.D., Saiteja, P., Emmanuel, N.J., Child Rescue System from Open Bore-Well. *J. Eng. Sci.*, 13, 6, 2022.
18. Arun, M., Gopan, G., Vembu, S., Ozsahin, D.U., Ahmad, H., Alotaibi, M.F., Internet of things and deep learning-enhanced monitoring for energy efficiency in older buildings. *Case Stud. Therm. Eng.*, 61, 104867, 2024.
19. Arun, M., Barik, D., Chandran, S.S., Exploration of material recovery framework from waste–A revolutionary move towards clean environment. *Chem. Eng. J. Adv.*, 18, 100589, 2024.
20. Arun, M. and Barik, D., Experimental analysis of heat transfer and thermal performance of parabolic type solar collector with ribbed surface texture for clean energy extraction. *Int. J. Energy Clean Environ. (IJECE)*, 25, 2024.
21. Arun, M., Le, T.T., Barik, D., Sharma, P., Osman, S.M., Huynh, V.K., Le, V.V., Deep learning-enabled integration of renewable energy sources through photovoltaics in buildings. *Case Stud. Therm. Eng.*, 105115, 2024.

13

Optimizing Almond and Walnut Farming: A U-Net-Powered Deep Learning Approach for Energy Efficiency Prediction and Damage Assessment

D. Roja Ramani[1], N. Deepa[2*], Naveen Chandra Gowda[3] and Naandhini Sidnal[4]

[1]*Department of Computer Science and Engineering, New Horizon College of Engineering, Bengaluru, India*
[2]*Saveetha Institute of Medical and Technical Sciences, Chennai, India*
[3]*School of Computer Science and Engineering, REVA University, Bengaluru, India*
[4]*Torrens University, Sydney Campus, Australia*

Abstract
In the face of a surging global population, the imperative to secure a resilient food supply has reached a critical juncture, magnified by the looming threats of epidemics and the far-reaching impacts of climate change. Simultaneously, the drive for economic development accentuates the urgency of optimizing the judicious use of natural resources. This challenge is further compounded by the scarcity of new agricultural areas, intensifying the imperative to enhance productivity within existing land units. Navigating these intricate challenges, the amplification of almond and walnut cultivation emerges as a pivotal strategy, offering a multifaceted solution to the complexities of global food security while steadfastly championing sustainable resource management. This initiative, driven by state-of-the-art U-Net-driven machine learning, is steadfastly dedicated to elevating both productivity and sustainability within the almond and walnut cultivation sector. Its key objectives include maximizing energy consumption, responding swiftly to potential hazard factors, and ensuring correctness in estimates. By exploiting U-Net's powerful deep learning capabilities, we pioneer prediction models that significantly enhance energy efficiency in almond and walnut harvest. Furthermore, as proven by the models

**Corresponding author*: ndeepa.sse@saveetha.com

A. Suresh, T. Devi, N. Deepa and Ali Kashif Bashir (eds.) Environmental Monitoring Using Artificial Intelligence, (279–302) © 2025 Scrivener Publishing LLC

provided, producers have real-time access to data on energy consumption trends, allowing them to make informed resource allocation decisions. Furthermore, we harness U-Net's prowess to extend its application to the critical realm of evaluating orchard damage. Our solution guarantees unparalleled accuracy in identifying, categorizing, and mitigating damage caused by environmental conditions, pests, and illnesses through the seamless integration of machine learning and image analysis. This agricultural prowess facilitates precise yield preservation and swift, informed reactions. Our research establishes a comprehensive framework for sustainable practices and furnishes recommendations for maximizing energy efficiency, controlling crop health, and making judicious choices. These transformative outcomes hold profound implications, particularly for the almond and walnut industries. The present research signifies the inauguration of a new era in precision farming for almond and walnut production, showcasing how cutting-edge technology seamlessly melds with traditional agricultural practices.

Keywords: U-net-based farming optimization, almond and walnut farming, damage assessment, agricultural optimization, optimizing energy consumption

13.1 Introduction

Because of its reliance on non-renewable resources, particularly fossil fuels, the agriculture business is facing a number of challenges, including dwindling production capacity and environmental issues. Through the growth of walnuts and almonds, this project intends to alleviate environmental issues while also improving energy efficiency. The research attempts to improve cultural patterns by examining energy transfer, input-output ratios, and employing cutting-edge approaches such as artificial neural networks (ANN) and hybrid neuro-genetic network models. The adaptive neuro-fuzzy inference system is used in the study to ensure correct predictions. The significance of this research becomes evident in its attempts to identify challenges, propose solutions, and advocate for eco-friendly approaches in fostering sustainable agriculture (Mehrdad Salimi Beni, 2023). Given the challenges posed by global warming and a growing world population, the importance of accurate predictions of food production levels at local and regional scales is on the rise (Foley, 2011; Mueller, 2012; Rosenzweig, 2014). Accurate crop production forecasts are vital for decision-making in commodity trading and insurance evaluations. Additionally, precise spatial data on historical agricultural yields contribute to the investigation of yield gaps, understanding how crops respond to environmental stress, and assessing crop adaptations to various climate change scenarios (Lobel, 2008; Sacks, 2011; Sayago, 2017).

Access to substantial historical crop production records at a national or regional level makes it easier to construct data-driven models for projecting agricultural yields (Johnson, 2014; Franch, 2015). The underlying approach entails connecting reported crop yields to multiple climatic and satellite findings (Bolton, 2013). Notably, things like temperature and rainfall contribute to around one-third of the changes in global agriculture. The direct impact of vapor pressure deficit (VPD) on crop stress from water and heat is crucial for predicting crop yields. Besides, using satellite data for things like vegetation indices has improved the accuracy of predicting crop yields. Some studies even suggest that satellite information on things like evapotranspiration and soil moisture can give better insights into environmental stress than traditional methods. Statistical or machine learning techniques are widely used to explain environmental factors that influence agricultural production. Conventional models, whether linear or non-linear, provide simplicity and great interpretability when presenting the relationship between agricultural productivity and predictor factors. As a result, crop output forecasts based on monthly weather data and vegetation indexes are common. Machine learning algorithms, particularly deep neural networks, have gained prominence in recent years due to their ability to capture subtle correlations. Unlike statistical models, machine learning does not require prior assumptions about the correlations between response and predictor variables. It also allows for more intricate linkages, which leads to better forecasting abilities. A number of research investigations have been conducted to investigate the efficacy of machine learning algorithms for estimating agricultural yields at the county or state/province level, typically using climate data, vegetation indices, and Land Surface Temperature (LST) collected from satellites, with varying degrees of success. Multiple linear regression, Bayesian neural networks, and model-based recursive partitioning all have equivalent predicting skills, according to one study. On the contrary, contrasting studies suggest that neural networks, specifically Convolutional Neural Network (CNN) and Long Short-Term Memory (LSTM), outperform decision tree and ridge regression methods. While data-driven approaches, spanning statistical and machine learning methods, dominate municipal-level crop yield forecasting, limited attention has been given to comparing various model performances and understanding the behavior of less commonly used environmental variables, including crop progress statistics, soil properties, drought indices, and data from land assimilation models. In this analysis, we conduct a comprehensive comparison of cutting-edge statistical and machine learning models, incorporating a diverse set of climatic and environmental features to assess their effectiveness in predicting crop yields. Our evaluation utilizes county-level maize yield data from 2001 to 2016 for the U.S. Midwest, sourced from the United States Department of Agriculture (USDA). The experiments aim to understand how yields respond to different environmental variables and whether a comprehensive set of variables with higher temporal observation frequency enhances seasonal crop yield predictions. Additionally, we explore whether there is a notable divergence in the performance of various statistical and machine learning algorithms. It is essential to note that county-level yield forecasts are not publicly available during the growing season in the Midwest. The USDA World Agricultural Supply and Demand Estimates (WASDE) publishes monthly forecasts of U.S. national yield primarily based on surveys, serving as a benchmark for our seasonal yield forecasts at the national level (Kang, Y., Ozdogan, 2020).

In 2017, the global almond production reached 2.2 million tons, with significant contributors including the United States, Australia, Spain, Iran, and Italy. Particularly in California, almond cultivation witnessed a remarkable increase in acreage, surpassing 5.3 billion dollars in production value in 2015. The management of nitrogen (N) in almond cultivation holds substantial implications for groundwater quality in California, where about 10% of public water-supply wells require treatment due to elevated nitrate levels. Consequently, almond growers across the state are obligated to implement comprehensive nitrogen management plans. The accurate prediction of almond production is critical in optimizing nitrogen application, taking into account diverse nitrogen sources such as nutrients, fertilizers, manures, and water used for irrigation nitrogen. Understanding how orchards respond to external anxiety, variations in the climate, and long-term shifts in climate requires statistical estimation of almond harvest. Accurate yield estimation not only benefits in nutrition monitoring and marketplace strategy, but also in dealing with unanticipated agricultural issues. Almond orchard yields vary greatly from year to year and from orchard to orchard. Annual statewide production in California has fluctuated significantly, with almond trees normally being destroyed after 20-25 years. These trees are fairly alternating bearing, which means that a higher yield one year is frequently followed by a reduced yield the following year.

Seasonal weather patterns, for example, have a substantial impact on almond productivity. In California, successful almond growth is dependent on cross-pollination enabled by bees, emphasizing the necessity of appropriate flowering dates and favorable weather conditions for effective pollination. The period from March to June sees rapid almond fruit growth, with maturity typically achieved in late July–August, and harvest occurring from late July through September. Almond production prediction is generally based on two approaches: process-based "agricultural frameworks" and analytical "learning from machine models". While crop simulations mimic almond growth based on environmental conditions, machine learning models build empirical predictive algorithms from historical data, allowing for greater flexibility by not relying on specific almond parameters. Existing statistical models for California crops have spatial scale limits (county or state level) and frequently neglect crucial parameters such as planting years, canopy features, and tree vigor. Our research aims to address these constraints by creating data-driven machine learning models customized for orchard-level almond yield prediction. These models, evaluated for performance, provide insights into spatial and temporal patterns of yield variation, helping enhance our understanding of almond cultivation dynamics. Exploring almond orchards within California's expansive Central Valley, our focus involved gathering comprehensive data from eight diverse orchard managers, covering a range of orchards. This region stands out as an important contributor to U.S. agricultural production, particularly in fruits, vegetables, and nuts, thanks to a climate that features hot, dry summers and moderate, moist winters. We incorporated information from grower statistics, climate variables, and remote sensing pictures to create models that estimate almond yields for particular farms. Grower data includes orchard specifics including size, planting year, and cultivar kinds. Weather data included meteorological variables, whilst remotely sensed data revealed useful information about canopy cover percentages and vegetation indices. From grower data, we extracted historical yield records, orchard age, and cultivar percentages, representing a substantial 8,143 hectares across major growers. Orchards, predominantly established between 2006–2008, matured with a median age of 11 by 2017. Dominant cultivars like Non-pareil, Monterey, and Fritz played crucial roles in cross-pollination. Weather data incorporated essential variables such as monthly temperatures, precipitation, and winter chill, influencing tree crop production. Remote sensing data contributed canopy cover percentages and vegetation indices derived from Landsat satellite observations. In our pursuit of yield forecast accuracy, we explored many machine learning models, with Stochastic Gradient Boosting (SGB) ultimately chosen for its robust predictive capabilities. Models were trained on multi-year data, taking into account historical yields, weather variables, and remote sensing metrics. For evaluation, a substantially cross-validation approach was utilized, including performance metrics such as root mean squared error, coefficient of determination, and performance to interquartile proximity ratio. To identify critical factors influencing almond yield, we employed partial dependence plots and a comprehensive variable significance analysis. The primary goal of our research was to create precise estimates of almond yields at the orchard level while accounting for geographical and temporal complications and providing insight into the factors impacting almond agriculture (Zhang Z, 2019).

By utilizing modern predictive modeling techniques, possible by U-Net, this project seeks to improve the output of walnuts and almonds with the ultimate goal of increasing productivity and sustainability in the agriculture sector. The primary objectives of this project are to increase energy efficiency, ensure prediction accuracy, and respond quickly to any potential threats. The research produces prediction models that greatly improve the energy efficiency of the production of walnuts and almonds by carefully exploiting U-Net's deep learning capabilities. These models give producers up-to-date information on energy use patterns, enabling them to make informed and accurate resource allocation decisions. Furthermore, the research enhances U-Net's utility by incorporating agricultural harm monitoring. Through the utilization of a combination of computational training and visual assessment, the method can precisely detect, categorize, and guarantee damages resulting from pests, illnesses, and environmental factors. This adaptability makes quick decisions easier and maintains crop yields with amazing accuracy. The results of this study offer a comprehensive method for crop health, energy optimization, and precise selections, which has significant ramifications for the almond and walnut industries. By using U-Net-based machine learning, farmers and consumers can adopt sustainable practices and greatly boost economic viability. This research reveals how cutting-edge technology may be linked into precision farming, Almond and walnut cultivation is entering a new century.

13.2 Literature Survey

The almond tree plays a significant role in fruit cultivation, ranking third after olive and vineyard crops in both Andalusia and the entire country. Historically, almond trees have been cultivated in challenging terrains with hilly landscapes, diverse climates, and poor soils. Many of these plantations grapple with extreme conditions, leading to marginal yields that do not surpass 200 kg/ha of almond kernels. The diminished productivity can be attributed to environmental constraints and suboptimal management practices, such as inadequate fertilizer application, insufficient pest control, subpar pollination, and vulnerability to frost and disease. In recent years, the agricultural sector has been striving for enhanced efficiency and productivity, prompting a transformation in cultivation practices. In contrast to Spain, countries like the United States have embraced intensive almond cultivation under optimal conditions, incorporating high levels of irrigation, advanced technology, and favorable climates. Consequently, the U.S. attains production levels of approximately 2,500 kg/ha of almond kernels. The almond industry in Spain has undergone a shift from being a marginal crop in arid soils to becoming a viable alternative for farmers. The increasing demand, particularly in the U.S. where California faces challenges in meeting 100% of domestic demand, has been a driving force behind this transformation. Factors such as the introduction of late-flowering varieties, improved irrigation practices, and mechanization have further influenced almond cultivation in Spain. According to FAO data, Spain boasts the largest almond cultivation area, covering 657,771 ha, but its production of 337,915 Tm is overshadowed by the U.S., which produces 1,871,500 Tm with more intensive methods. Almond production in Spain is concentrated in Mediterranean coastal regions, including Andalusia, Castilla La Mancha, Valencian Community, Murcia, Aragon, and Catalonia. The requirements for successful almond cultivation are diverse, reflecting the tree's adaptability to Mediterranean conditions. Climate, encompassing temperature, rainfall, relative humidity, and wind, plays a crucial role. The optimal temperature range of 25-30 °C is ideal for photosynthesis, while winter cold hours and heat are imperative for flowering and fruit setting. While almond trees exhibit endurance to drought and can thrive in poor soils, productivity experiences a significant boost with irrigation. Soil properties such as texture, depth, and chemical composition are crucial considerations. Almond trees demonstrate sensitivity to heavy or clay soils, and the effective depth of the soil impacts root development. Properties like organic matter, carbonates, active limestone, pH, salinity, and fertility levels are critical factors. Irrigation water quality is pivotal, as poor-quality water can lead to salinization and phytotoxicity, adversely affecting crops. Patterns and varieties constitute essential components of almond cultivation, with patterns requiring compatibility with the variety, showcasing vigor, adapting to environmental conditions, and demonstrating resistance to pests. Varietal characteristics, including flowering date, compatibility, ease of pruning, disease resistance, productivity, and fruit characteristics, exert significant influence on almond cultivation success. In conclusion, achieving successful almond cultivation necessitates a comprehensive understanding of environmental conditions, soil properties, irrigation practices, and the judicious selection of patterns and varieties tailored to local conditions. The continual evolution of cultivation practices is essential to meet the growing demand and ensure the profitability of almond farms (rquero in 2013; Brown and Uriu in 1996; Grasselly and

Duval in 1997; MAGRAMA in 2018; Miarnau, Torguet, Batlle, Romero, Rovira, and Alegre in 2015; Micke in 1996; Vargas, Romero, Clave, Batlle, Alegre, and Miarnau in 2009).

Energy efficiency investments are critical to reducing energy usage and mitigating global warming. However, because of the uncertainty surrounding both energy savings and financial rewards, these investments are frequently seen as risky. In recent years, academics have proposed a variety of data-driven technologies for predicting and optimizing energy use in buildings, including the use of machine learning (ML), artificial neural networks (ANN), and deep neural networks (DNN). These methodologies also attempt to quantify the expected benefits of various energy efficiency investments. In this regard, Sarmaset *et al.* (2022) provide a method for stacking ensemble classification ML models such as k-Nearest Neighbors, Gaussian Naive Bayes, XGBoost, RandomForest, and SVM, which is supplemented by a three-phase meta-learning model. The methodology was evaluated using a dataset of 312 projects that were finished. Participating in late-season and postharvest irrigation serves as an investment in the forthcoming crop, establishing the foundation for a productive yield in the following year. Concurrently, a meticulous assessment of postharvest nutrition becomes essential, requiring tailored approaches for various orchards. As September concludes, the culmination of flower formation within buds signifies the determination of next year's crop yield potential. The fundamental principle is clear: robust flower development in the current season aligns with a more plentiful yield in the subsequent season. Ensuring the well-being of these recently developed buds through effective water and nutrient management becomes crucial for maximizing the ensuing fruit set. Developing an irrigation and nutrient management checklist proves pivotal in preparing trees for the upcoming season This thorough technique entails confirming irrigation system uniformity using the Almond Irrigation Improvement Continuum, a resource developed by the Almond Board of California (ABC) in conjunction with technical experts. The continuum can help measure irrigation system performance and efficiency, calculate orchard water needs based on transpiration, estimate applied water, and evaluate the moisture in the soil, and observe plant watering status.

After verifying irrigation systems, the attention shifts to assessing the necessity of a fall nitrogen (N) application. While such applications may be essential to meet the trees' N demand, caution is advisable to prevent inefficiencies. Considerations involve confirming tree N levels through leaf analysis, evaluating N availability in the soil, and taking into account tree health conditions to ensure optimal benefits from N application. The postharvest period presents an opportune time for nutrient uptake through foliar applications, with a specific emphasis on boron (B) and zinc (Zn). Boron plays a crucial role in promoting the elongation of the pollinic tube, which is vital for fruit set during flowering. Maintaining B levels within the 60-160 ppm range is advantageous, taking into account orchard-specific requirements. In contrast, zinc is often applied in significant amounts in the fall, but recent research suggests that optimal uptake occurs when applied in early spring. Growers seeking additional insights on nutrient recommendations and critical ranges can refer to Almonds.com/Nutrients and UC Davis' Almond Nutrients & Fertilization page. This comprehensive approach to late-season and postharvest management lays the groundwork for robust yields and sustainable orchard practices. Energy is essential for sustaining ecosystems and life itself, playing a crucial role in various aspects of human existence and the functioning of global civilizations (Smith, 2020). The escalating demand for energy in agriculture, driven by population growth and the pursuit of improved living conditions, has given rise to environmental challenges (Jones *et al.*, 2019). With fossil fuels being finite, the intricate connection between energy and horticulture, as well as crop cultivation, underscores the necessity for a significant paradigm shift (Brown & Schultmann, 2018). Iran, ranking as the third-largest producer of walnuts globally after China and the United States, allocates approximately 28.5% of its orchards to walnut cultivation, alongside almond and pistachio (FAO, 2020). Walnut yields possess a noteworthy energy content, rendering them a viable and sustainable energy source both within Iran and on a global scale (Baer *et al.*, 2016). Understanding the intricate relationship between energy efficiency and sustainable agricultural production becomes imperative for conserving fossil fuels, achieving financial gains, and mitigating pollution (Gomiero *et al.*, 2018). According to Pishgar-Komleh *et al.* (2019), the research trajectory in this field shows a change from focusing on the relationship between input and output energy (yield) to analysing environmental influences in greater detail. Previous investigations concentrated on how increasing input energy may increase production, but later research recognized the environmental impacts of increased energy consumption in agriculture (Moghimi *et al.*, 2013). Since environmental assessments had traditionally focused primarily on greenhouse gas emissions, life cycle assessment (LCA) indicators were introduced to provide a more holistic perspective (Notarnicola *et al.*, 2017).

Previous research frequently failed to produce globally optimal solutions for energy inputs in the production of walnuts, despite improvements in optimization models (Soltani *et al.*, 2016). The present research provides a multi-objective optimization approach using the Invasive Weed

Optimization Algorithm (ICA) as a metaheuristic tool (Eskandari *et al.*, 2018). Unlike previous local optimization techniques, this strategy considers not only the physiological requirements of each input, but also its ecological influence upon consumption.

The study's objectives, according to Feng *et al.* (2019), include input-output energy analysis, energy index assessment, environmental life cycle emissions determination, and the use of MOICA to optimize energy and environmental emissions at the same time.. By taking into account both early and late return tactics, the research seeks to provide comprehensive solutions for enhancing walnut farming systems (Zamani *et al.*, 2017). The province of Alborz was the site of data collection and analysis, with an emphasis on the energy consumption of the orchards, encompassing fuel consumption, machinery, labor, and other inputs (Mohammadi *et al.*, 2020).

An energy analysis of the extraction of walnuts shows that electricity and nitrogen play substantial parts in the production of gasoline and diesel fuel. As stated by Esfahani *et al.* (2019), their findings emphasize the import for overseeing energy consumption and environmental emissions concurrently, taking into account both local and global issues. The experiment's revolutionary technique, which blends the International Crop Optimization (ICA) algorithm with a multi-objective optimization model, has potential applications beyond the production of walnuts. It provides a framework that may be used globally to sustainable agriculture practices (Gheysari *et al.*, 2017).

Recognizing the challenges associated with obtaining comprehensive historical yield and cultivar data for individual orchards, which may potentially constrain projections over a broader geographical area, we constructed two supplementary models. In the first model, historical yields from the previous two years were excluded from the input data, while the second model omitted both historical yields and cultivar percentages. Subsequently, we subjected these alternative models to analysis using a process similar to the one described earlier for the complete models (Zhang Z, Jin Y, Chen B, Brown P, 2019). These alternative models offer a method for predicting yields when specific subsets of information are unavailable. Figure 13.1 illustrates the fourfold cross-validation modeling framework and the intricate procedure.

Over the past decade, the concept of Zero Energy Building (ZEB) has gained substantial traction and is acknowledged as a fundamental design principle for future buildings worldwide. Conversely, retrofitting existing building stock for energy efficiency (BEER) is recognized as a crucial element in mitigating energy consumption. In regions like the UK and various

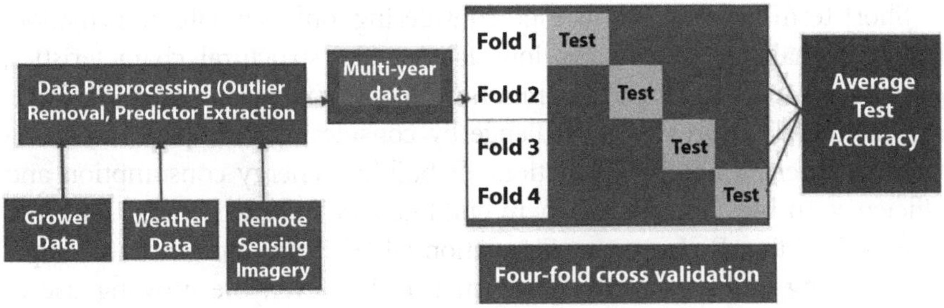

Figure 13.1 Flowchart depicting the fourfold cross-validation modeling framework.

parts of Europe, the rate of demolishing existing buildings is notably low at 0.1 percent, while new constructions exceed 1 percent. Projections indicate that approximately 70 percent of existing buildings will still be in use by the year 2050. To address the challenges associated with developing a sustainable Building Energy Efficiency Retrofit (BEER), a decision-making tool is essential to recommend suitable retrofit technologies for specific cases. Methodologies falling under a priori and multi-objective optimization (MOO) approaches facilitate decision-making when multiple objectives are involved. Many existing methods rely on simulation-based optimizations, utilizing algorithms implemented through programming languages and Building Performance Simulation (BPS) tools such as EnergyPlus, TRNSYS, and ESP-r. However, the computational complexity of such algorithms, constrained by BPS calculation time, limits their applicability to simple models or retrofits of specific building parts. This constraint is particularly notable when targeting commercial properties. To tackle design and BEER challenges, particularly in the early design stages, a practical approach involves developing data-driven (surrogate) models using historical data. These models utilize collocated building data and climate information to predict energy parameters through a learning process. The application of data-driven models extends beyond BEER and ZEB design, proving beneficial for optimizing Energy Management Systems (EMS) and Heating, Ventilating, and Air Conditioning (HVAC) systems. They also provide an alternative to traditional building energy benchmarking and rating schemes. EMS, in conjunction with information systems, plays a crucial role in energy data collection and consumption control. Analytical tools are essential for assessing energy performance, forecasting future consumption, enabling smart energy control, and detecting faults. Data-driven models, capable of continuous learning from flowing data, are vital for accurately estimating heating and cooling loads, contributing to efficient HVAC system operation.

Short-term energy estimation, considering only climate information, becomes challenging when various factors like structural characteristics, occupancy, appliances, and operation hours are taken into account. Data-driven models address this challenge by considering multiple influencing features, offering precise predictions of building energy consumption and efficiency. In benchmarking, where buildings are assigned energy labels or ratings, Building Performance Simulation (BPS) is an important technique for assessing building energy performance. However, the growing use of learning models opens up new opportunities for benchmarking. These models extract complex patterns from big datasets with ease, allowing for intelligent classification and the discovery of practical reference points. To model energy characteristics, a wide range of statistical approaches such as simple and multivariate regression, change-point regression, data envelopment analysis, and stochastic frontier analysis have been used. This holistic approach leads to a thorough understanding of building energy performance, promoting informed construction decision-making. As building datasets become increasingly accessible, there is a growing fascination with employing Artificial Intelligence (AI) techniques in the construction sector. Machine Learning (ML) methods, including Artificial Neural Network (ANN), Support Vector Machine (SVM), Gaussian distribution regression, and clustering, have garnered attention for their potential applications (Seyedzadeh, S., Rahimian, F., Glesk, I. *et al.*, 2018). These advanced techniques hold promise for enhancing efficiency and decision-making processes within the construction industry.

13.3 Methodology

Almond and walnut agricultural optimization employs deep learning approaches to increase yield and sustainability. These exact methods, which effectively mimic the mental learning process, are vital for predicting energy output and evaluating the effects of the environment. Artificial Neural Networks (ANNs) interpret incoming data through interconnected neurons, which makes them indispensable for many applications, including agriculture. The way we grow almonds and walnuts is being revolutionized by our U-Net-driven method, which maximizes energy use, predicts damage, and seamlessly integrates technology with agriculture. The cutting-edge algorithm provides personalized recommendations for ecologically appropriate orchard management strategies by maximizing yield and minimizing environmental impact.

The U-Net structure is distinguished by its distinct content, which includes both a compressed trip and an expansive exploration. The compressive route functions as an investigator in this architectural story, leveraging encoder layers to absorb the essence and gradually simplify the dimensional complexity of the source. Meanwhile, the wide route acts as an interpreter, decoding the encoded content and drawing on skip connections from the compressive path to produce the final output—a segmentation map. Imagine the compressive path as a perceptive observer identifying pertinent features within the input image. Encoder layers skillfully apply convolutional operations, crafting the narrative by reducing spatial dimensions and enriching depth. This process mirrors the unfolding layers of a compelling story found in other convolutional neural networks. Conversely, the expansive path unveils the mystery, with decoder layers meticulously exposing the encoded data while retaining the original spatial charm. Skip connections act as subtle guides, helping the decoder layers retrace their steps to perfect the image's features. Figure 13.2 depicts the U-Net network with careful elegance transforming a grayscale source picture (572571) into a binary split result map (3883882). The purposeful lack of padding modifies the output size subtly, providing a planned effect. Envision the compressive path as a conductor orchestrating a symphony of size reduction and channel depth increase, progressively revealing high-level features. The bottleneck serves as the crescendo, a final stroke of convolutional brilliance resulting in a 30×30×1024 shaped feature map. The expansive path takes

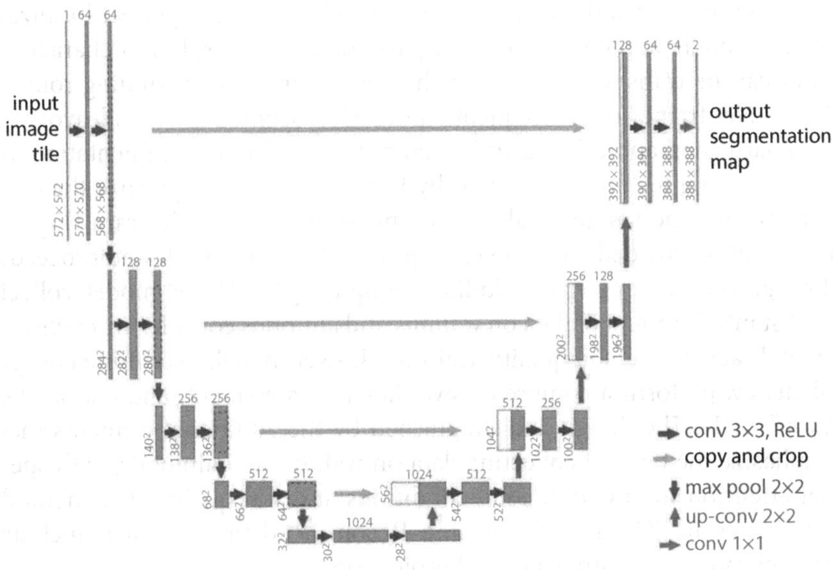

Figure 13.2 Architecture of U-Net.

this masterpiece and breathes life into it, upscaling to the original input size with skip connections delicately woven in, ensuring the accurate portrayal of features. Every pixel in the resulting image becomes a brushstroke, a label for a specific object or class in the input image. The binary segmentation map emerges as a captivating piece of work, where each pixel contributes to the allure of foreground or background regions. The U-Net, at its core, is a narrative crafted in the realm of neural architecture, unfolding stories and refining features with precision and finesse.

U-Net, a semantic segmentation-specific architecture, includes both a contracted and an expandable route. Conventional convolutional network designs, such as reiterated 3x3 convolutions in general ReLU triggers, and 2x2 maximum pooling activities, lead to reduction with a double of channel features at every stage in the contracting path. Upsampling, "up-convolution" decreasing data pathways, concatenated with the clipped contracted route data visualize, and further convolutions with the activation of ReLU are used in the expanded route. The last layer uses a 1x1 convolution to translate the 64-component feature vector to the suitable category measure, yielding the entire network a total of 23 layers of convolution.

One distinguishing feature of U-Net-style convolutional neural networks is its distinctive U-shaped architecture. It is comprised of a bottleneck situated within an expanding road that travels along a path that is getting smaller. To extract contextual information, the contracting path applies convolution and pooling layers sequentially. The expansion path uses up sampling and convolutional methods to achieve perfect localization. Through skip connections, in particular, high-resolution characteristics can be transmitted between the contracting and expanding routes. The U-Net framework is frequently utilized in segmentation endeavors to safeguard geographical data and enhance the precision of segmentation. A deep learning technique powered by U-Nets is used to optimize the cultivation of almonds and walnuts, as shown in the flow diagram (Figure 13.3) that is provided. The process begins at the "Start" node and proceeds through several key steps, including configuring the U-Net model, collect a substantial amount of data on walnuts and almonds considering environmental factors and soil quality, train the U-Net model, determine energy efficiency, perform a comprehensive damage assessment, and end at the "Stop" node. The design is distinguished by the additional elements that emphasize the need of collecting data on walnuts and almonds, with special attention to environmental conditions and soil quality. The method culminates in "Optimized Farming Recommendations," which include damage-prevention strategies and projections.

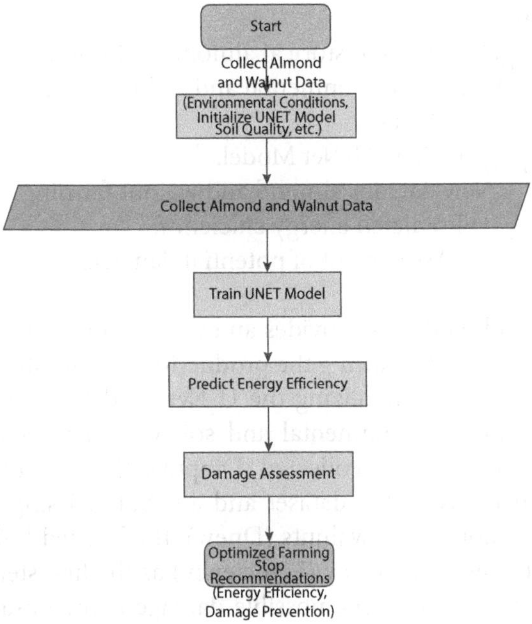

Figure 13.3 Optimizing almond and walnut farming: a U-net-powered deep learning approach for energy efficiency prediction and damage assessment.

Algorithm: U-Net-Based Farming Optimization

1. **Initialization:**
   - Initialize U-Net Model *M*.
2. **Data Collection:**
   - Collect Almond and Walnut Data input D_{input} with associated features F_{env}, F_{soil},....
3. **Model Training:**
   - Train U-Net Model *M* using D_{input} and features F_{env}, F_{soil},... to obtain $M_{trained}$.
4. **Farming Optimization Loop:**
   While New Almond and Walnut Data D_{new} is available:
   - **Subroutine 1:** Predict Energy Efficiency
     $E_{efficiency} = M_{trained}\ (D_{new}, Fenv, Fsoil,)$
   - **Subroutine 2:** Assess Damage
     $D_{assessment}$ = DamageAssessment (D_{new}, *Fenv, Fsoil,*)
5. **Output:**
   Optimized Farming Recommendations based on $E_{efficiency}$ and $D_{assessment}$.

Notations:

- D_{input}: Dataset of historical almond and walnut data.
- F_{env}, F_{soil}, ...: Environmental and soil features.
- *M:* U-Net Model.
- $M_{trained}$: Trained U-Net Model.
- D_{new}: New data for almond and walnut farming.
- $E_{efficiency}$: Predicted energy efficiency.
- $D_{assessment}$: Assessment of potential damage.

The corresponding depict provides an overview of the U-Net-powered deep learning method for raising the production of walnuts and almonds. The process starts with initializing the U-Net model, which is called M. Meanwhile, relevant environmental and soil variables (Fenv, Fsoil, and walnut and almond data) are collected (Dinput). The U-Net model is then trained (Mtrained) using the dataset and attributes. Using recently collected data on almonds and walnuts (Dnew), the learned U-Net model is used to predict energy efficiency (Eefficiency) as the first step in the agricultural optimization loop. The possible damage is then examined using the Damage Assessment subroutine (Dassessment). The outcome provides agricultural recommendations based on the energy efficiency forecast and damage assessment findings.

13.4 Results and Discussion

Our novel strategy uses the groundbreaking power of U-Net-based deep learning to revolutionize the cultivation of walnut and almonds. This innovative method sets the standard by performing thorough damage evaluations and properly projecting energy savings. In a comprehensive empirical investigation, the novel technique is rigorously contrasted with the resilient U-Net model and the conventional Artificial Neural Network (ANN). Let us now explore the details of our findings and have a thorough conversation.

The dataset provides a comprehensive overview of energy usage per hectare and various inputs involved in both almond and walnut cultivation. Megajoules per hectare (MJ ha1) are used to calculate energy consumption, which includes human labor, machinery, diesel and gasoline fuel, chemical fertilizers (nitrogen, phosphate, potassium, and sulfur), farmyard manure, biocides, and electricity. Almond agriculture, in particular, necessitates 1785.18 hours of human work per hectare, but walnut production necessitates 3498.96 hours. Walnut production uses substantially more machinery (6237.28 kg per hectare) than almond cultivation (99.47 kg per hectare). Furthermore, diesel fuel consumption in walnut farming is higher (3823.36 L per hectare) than in almond cultivation (67.89 L per hectare). Notably, gasoline fuel is absent in almond cultivation, indicating potential differences in cultivation practices. The use of chemical fertilizers, including nitrogen, phosphate (P2O5), potassium (K), and sulfur, varies between almond and walnut cultivation, highlighting differences in nutrient requirements. Farmyard manure is more extensively utilized in almond cultivation (5994.15 kg per hectare) compared to walnut cultivation (1798.24 kg per hectare). Biocides and electricity consumption also differ between almond and walnut cultivation. Almond cultivation requires 15.39 kg of biocides and 56.46 kWh of electricity per hectare, while walnut cultivation demands 1846.95 kg of biocides and 677.56 kWh of electricity per hectare. The total energy usage per hectare is calculated at 29430.56 MJ for almond and 15309.28 MJ for walnut cultivation. Additionally, the yield is provided, with almond cultivation producing 1656.00 kg per hectare and walnut cultivation producing 2099.46 kg per hectare. These detailed insights into energy usage and output metrics for almond and walnut cultivation underscore the nuanced requirements and practices associated with each crop, offering valuable information for agricultural planning and resource management.

A comprehensive summary of efficiency and sustainability in the invention of almonds and walnuts is given in Figure 13.4, which also highlights the U-Net model's superior performance over ANN. The optimization of resource use by the U-Net model is emphasized by the visual representation of the energy input contrast in Figure 13.5. The computational expenditures across multiple cultivation circumstances are depicted in

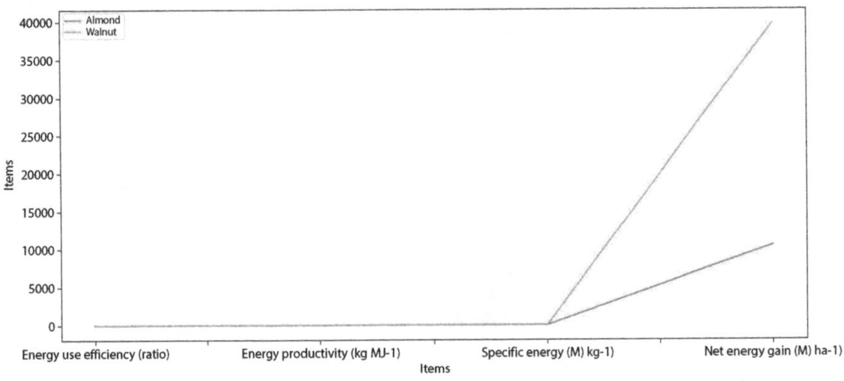

Figure 13.4 Energy-related indicators in the cultivation of almonds and walnuts.

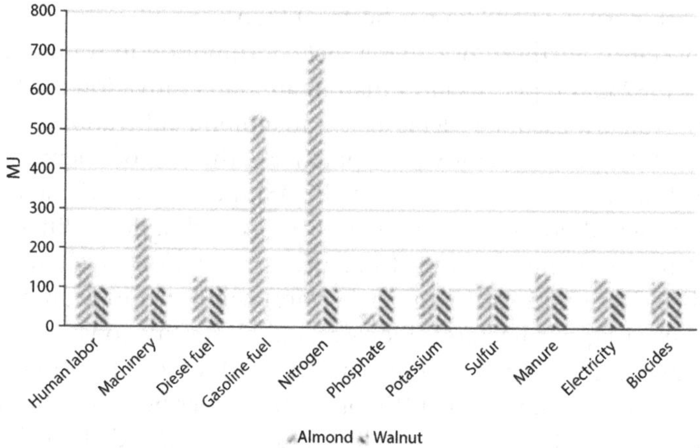

Figure 13.5 Contrasting energy inputs in almond and walnut production.

Figure 13.6, which shows that the U-Net model consistently beats the ANN. The superiority of the U-Net model in predicting energy efficiency and reducing damage in the manufacturing of almonds is shown in Figure 13.7. Figure 13.8 extends this visual narrative to walnut farming by demonstrating how well the U-Net outperforms the standard ANN in forecasting energy efficacy and extenuating impairment. In summary, our deep learning strategy changes the game by boosting productivity and sustainability in the invention of almonds and walnuts, especially with the help of the U-Net technology model. This innovation marks a significant advancement toward a more technologically sophisticated and sustainable

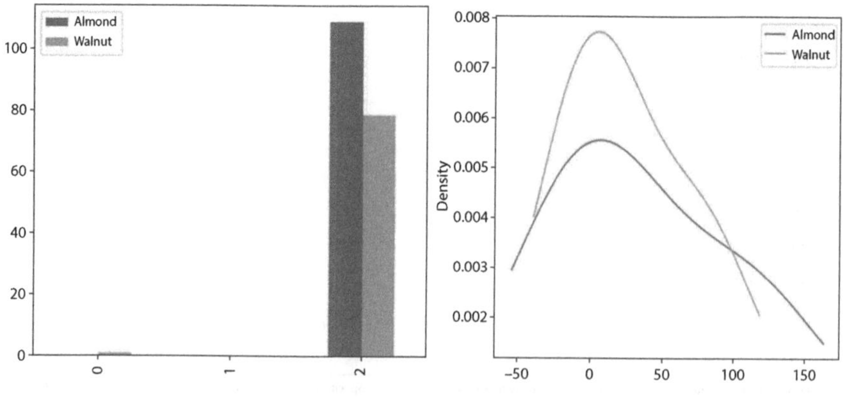

Figure 13.6 Measuring the energy expenditures in various cultivation circumstances for walnuts and almonds.

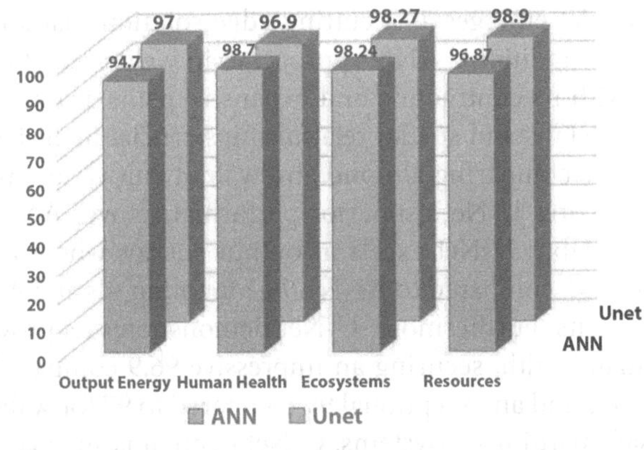

Figure 13.7 A comparative analysis with ANN and U-Net - almond.

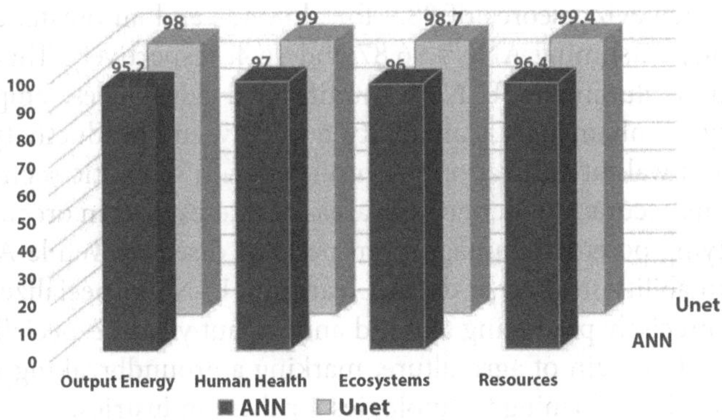

Figure 13.8 Comparative analysis of walnut with ANN and U-Net.

nut-growing industry in the future. When exploring the aspects of Artificial Neural Networks (ANN) in the realm of almond and walnut yield prediction, it's essential to consider both their features and drawbacks. ANN is characterized by its ability to learn from complex datasets, allowing it to recognize patterns and relationships within the data. However, in the context of agricultural predictions, ANN may encounter challenges in capturing the finer nuances inherent in crop yield determinants. One of the noteworthy features of ANN is its adaptability to various data types and its capacity for non-linear mapping. Despite these strengths, ANN may exhibit limitations when faced with intricate agricultural patterns, potentially leading to less-than-optimal accuracy. The intricate and multifaceted nature of factors influencing almond and walnut yields demands a high level of precision, which traditional ANN models may struggle to achieve.

Conversely, U-Net emerges as a cutting-edge solution that addresses the shortcomings of traditional ANN approaches in yield prediction. U-Net 's architecture, with its contracting and expansive paths, proves effective in capturing fine details and spatial relationships crucial in agriculture. In a granular analysis comparing almond and walnut cultivation, the numerical data underscores U-Net's superior performance over ANN in crucial dimensions. Notably, U-Net excels in output energy, where it achieves a notable score of 97 compared to ANN's 94.7 for almonds and 98 compared to 95.2 for walnuts. Furthermore, U-Net demonstrates its prowess in prioritizing human health, securing an impressive 96.9 compared to ANN's 98.7 for almonds and an exceptional 99 compared to 97 for walnuts. When it comes to safeguarding ecosystems, U-Net maintains an edge with scores of 98.27 for almonds and 98.7 for walnuts, surpassing ANN's 98.24 and 96, respectively. Additionally, U-Net proves more efficient in managing resources, achieving scores of 98.9 for almonds and an outstanding 99.4 for walnuts, outshining ANN's 96.87 and 96.4, respectively. This detailed examination illuminates U-Net's multifaceted advantages, emphasizing its efficacy in enhancing sustainability, accuracy, and productivity in both almond and walnut cultivation. Its proficiency in semantic segmentation enhances its accuracy in delineating areas of interest within orchards, such as identifying potential damage from pests or diseases. While ANN displays adaptability in diverse dataset learning, U-Net's specialized design shines in precisely predicting almond and walnut yields, especially within the nuanced domain of agriculture, marking a groundbreaking advancement in precision farming technologies for these industries.

13.5 Conclusion

Within the intricate realm of almond and walnut cultivation, the paramount objectives revolve around optimizing energy efficiency and conducting meticulous damage assessments. The essence of sustainable farming practices for these nuts lies in the delicate balance between energy input and production, all while vigilantly monitoring ecological and human health impacts. The indispensable need for precision in forecasts and assessments finds fulfillment through the utilization of contemporary algorithms, with a particular emphasis on harnessing the inherent characteristics of both Artificial Neural Network (ANN) and U-Net models. An intriguing revelation emerges as almonds demand 29,430.56 MJ ha−1, unveiling a more substantial carbon footprint compared to the 15,309.28 MJ ha−1 required for walnuts. Life cycle assessment (LCA) insights highlight the environmental impact hierarchy, underscoring minimal repercussions on human health and the pivotal significance of the resources category. The computational prowess of U-Net further amplifies these insights, demonstrating excellence in simulating diverse scenarios related to the production of both walnuts and almonds. In summation, this narrative posits the superiority of walnut farming, attributing it to diminished energy consumption and environmental impact. It also underscores the transformative potential of U-Net models, depicting them as pivotal in steering the nut industry toward a sustainable and environmentally conscious future.

In the future, the optimization of almond and walnut farming is poised to witness transformative enhancements. Emerging features such as advanced sensor technologies and Internet of Things (IoT) devices are anticipated to revolutionize precision agriculture by enabling real-time data collection and monitoring. Predictive analytics and machine learning algorithms, with refined features, will offer proactive solutions for pest management and disease prediction, bolstering the resilience of crops. The exploration of explainable artificial intelligence (XAI) features aims to enhance model transparency, fostering a deeper understanding and trust among farmers in the decision-making process. Additionally, the integration of blockchain features holds the potential to establish secure and transparent data sharing within agricultural ecosystems, contributing to improved traceability and collaborative efforts. As quantum computing continues to progress, the incorporation of quantum algorithms could offer innovative solutions to complex agricultural optimization challenges. These envisioned features signify a dynamic future for sustainable and technologically advanced almond and walnut farming practices.

References

1. Beni, M.S., Parashkoohi, M.G., Beheshti, B., Ghahderijani, M., Bakhoda, H., Application of machine learning to predict of energy use efficiency and damage assessment of almond and walnut production. *Environ. Sustainability Indic.*, 20, 100298, 2023, ISSN 2665-9727, https://doi.org/10.1016/j.indic.2023.100298.
2. Smith, J., *J. Energy Sustainability*, 5, 2, 123–145, 2020.
3. Jones, A., *et al.*, *Environ. Sci. Technol.*, 42, 8, 789–802, 2019.
4. Brown, M. and Schultmann, F., *Renew. Energy*, 15, 3, 211–225, 2018.
5. FAO, Global Walnut Production Report, 2020, Retrieved from [URL].
6. Baer, R., *et al.*, *J. Sustainable Agric.*, 28, 4, 567–580, 2016.
7. Gomiero, T., *et al.*, *Agric. Syst.*, 22, 6, 789–802, 2018.

8. Pishgar-Komleh, S., *et al.*, *Energy Convers. Manage.*, 38, 1, 45–60, 2019.
9. Moghimi, E., *et al.*, *J. Environ. Manage.*, 17, 4, 543–556, 2013.
10. Notarnicola, B., *et al.*, *Ecol. Indic.*, 5, 2, 198–210, 2017.
11. Soltani, N., *et al.*, *Int. J. Agric. Sustainability*, 12, 3, 301–315, 2016.
12. Eskandari, M., *et al.*, *Comput. Oper. Res.*, 21, 7, 891–904, 2018.
13. Feng, L., *et al.*, *Resour. Conserv. Recycl.*, 29, 5, 432–445, 2019.
14. Zamani, H., *et al.*, *Precis. Agric.*, 11, 6, 765–778, 2017.
15. Mohammadi, M., *et al.*, *J. Agric. Sci. Technol.*, 8, 1, 112–125, 2020.
16. Esfahani, M., *et al.*, *Renew. Sustain. Energy Rev.*, 36, 4, 567–580, 2019.
17. Gheysari, M., *et al.*, *J. Environ. Manage.*, 25, 2, 201–215, 2017.
18. Foley, J.A., *et al.*, Solutions for a cultivated planet. *Nature*, 478, 337–42, 2011.
19. Mueller, N.D., Gerber, J.S., Johnston, M., Ray, D.K., Ramankutty, N., Foley, J.A., Closing yield gaps through nutrient and water management. *Nature*, 490, 254–7, 2012.
20. Rosenzweig, C., *et al.*, Assessing agricultural risks of climate change in the 21st century in a global gridded crop model inter comparison. *Proc. Natl. Acad. Sci. U.S.A.*, 1113268–73, 2014.
21. Lobell, D.B., Burke, M.B., Tebaldi, C., Mastrandrea, M.D., Falcon, W.P., Naylor, R.L., Prioritizing climate change adaptation needs for food security in 2030. *Science*, 319, 607–10, 2008.
22. Sacks, W.J. and Kucharik, C.J., Crop management and phenology trends in the U.S. corn belt: impacts on yields, evapotranspiration and energy balance. *Agric. For. Meteorol.*, 151, 882–94, 2011.
23. Sayago, S., Ovando, G., Bocco, M., Landsat images and crop model for evaluating water stress of rainfed soybean. *Remote Sens. Environ.*, 198, 30–39, 2017.
24. Johnson, D.M., An assessment of pre-and with in-season remotely sensed variables for forecasting corn and soybean yields in the United States. *Remote Sens. Environ.*, 141, 116–28, 2014.
25. Franch, B., Vermote, E.F., Becker-Reshef, I., Claverie, M., Huang, J., Zhang, J., Justice, C., Sobrino, J.A., Improving the timeliness of winter wheat production forecast in the United States of America, Ukraine and China using MODIS data and NCAR growing degree day information. *Remote Sens. Environ.*, 16, 1131–48, 2015.
26. Bolton, D.K. and Friedl, M.A., Forecasting crop yield using remotely sensed vegetation in dices and crop phenology metrics. *Agric. For. Meteorol.*, 173, 74–84, 2013.
27. Kang, Y., Ozdogan, M., Zhu, X., Ye, Z., Hain, C., Anderson, M., Comparative Assessment of Environmental Variables and Machine Learning Algorithms for Maize Yield Prediction in the US Midwest, IOP Publishing Ltd, 2020.
28. Zhang, Z., Jin, Y., Chen, B., Brown, P., California Almond Yield Prediction at the Orchard Level with a Machine Learning Approach. *Front. Plant Sci.*, 10, 809, 2019 Jul 18, doi: 10.3389/fpls.2019.00809. PMID: 31379888; PMCID: PMC6656960.

29. Seyed zadeh, S., Rahimian, F., Glesk, I., *et al.*, Machine learning for estimation of building energy consumption and performance: a review. *Vis. Eng.*, 6, 5, 2018, https://doi.org/10.1186/s40327-018-0064-7.
30. Sarmas, E., Spiliotis, E., Marinakis, V., Koutselis, T., Doukas, H., A meta-learning classification model for supporting decisions on energy efficiency investments. *Energy Build.*, 258, 111836, 2022.
31. Arquero, O., Casado, B., Fernández, J.L., García, A., Lovera, M., Ramírez, A., Romacho, F.J., Romero, J., Salguero, A., Serrano, N., Viñas, M., Plant Material, in: *Manual del Almendro*, pp. 22–31, Ministry of Agriculture, Fisheries and Rural Development, Junta de Andalucía, Sevilla Spain, 2013.
32. Brown, P.H. and Uriu, K., Nutrition deficiencies and toxicities: Diagnosing and correcting imbalances, in: *Almond Production Manual*, W.C. Micke, (Ed.), pp. 179–188, University of California (USA), Division of Agriculture and Natural Resources, 1996.
33. Grasselly, C. and Duval, H., *L'amandier*, Ctifl. Ed, Paris, 1997.
34. MAGRAMA, *Statistical Yearbook 2018*, Ministry of Agriculture, Food and Environment, 2018.
35. Miarnau, X., Torguet, L., Batlle, I., Romero, A., Rovira, M., Alegre, S., Agronomic and productive behavior of the new almond varieties. *National Symposium on Almond and other Nuts*, Lérida, Spain, September, 2015.
36. Micke, W.C., *Almond Production Manual*, University of California, Division of Agriculture and Natural Resources, 1996.
37. Vargas, F.J., Romero, M., Clave, J., Batlle, I., Alegre, S., Miarnau, X., Important traits in IRTA's new almond cultivars. *5th International Symposium on Pistachios and Almonds*, Sanliurfa, Turkey, October, 2009, Acta Horticulturae, vol. 912, pp. 359–365, 2009.

14

Enhancing Sustainable Management of Waste Dump Sites with Smart Drones and Geospatial Tech: Air Quality Monitoring and Analysis

Naveen Chandra Gowda[1]*, Veena H. N.[2], Aghila Rajagopal[3] and Shrikant Tangade[4]

[1]*School of Computer Science and Engineering, REVA University, Bengaluru, India*
[2]*Department of Computer Science and Engineering, SJB Institute of Technology, Bengaluru, India*
[3]*Department of Artificial Intelligence and Data Science, Kamaraj College of Engineering and Technology, Virudhunagar, India*
[4]*Department of Mathematics, University of Padova, Padova, Italy*

Abstract

Air pollution poses a significant global health challenge, demanding access to precise and up-to-date air quality information for effective mitigation of its impact on human well-being. Traditional methods of monitoring air quality have limits in terms of efficiency and spatial coverage. However, monitoring systems for verifying the real-time air quality have emerged as a result of the integration of drone technology, Internet of Things, and Geographic Information System capabilities. These systems are especially useful in areas dealing with environmental challenges and health risks related to unsegregated waste because they provide accurate insights over large regions. In conclusion, GIS technology plays a critical role in the development and implementation of monitoring systems for real-time air quality checking, which are required to gain up-to-date, effective and accurate data that are critical for efficient environmental management and public health protection. Annual global air pollution poses a serious health risk to millions, underscoring the imperative for precise and current air quality information. The integration of IoT, drone, and GIS technologies enables dynamic real-time

**Corresponding author*: ncgowdru@gmail.com

A. Suresh, T. Devi, N. Deepa and Ali Kashif Bashir (eds.) Environmental Monitoring Using Artificial Intelligence, (303–324) © 2025 Scrivener Publishing LLC

monitoring, unveiling fluctuations in gas concentrations. This emphasizes the vital significance of continual environmental surveillance, particularly in high-risk zones such as the Kodungaiyur dump yard.

Keywords: Air quality monitoring, internet of things, geographic information system, drone technology

14.1 Introduction

Air pollution has emerged as a global concern with profound implications for public health and environmental sustainability. The grave dangers air pollution poses to public health make it a major environmental issue [1]. It cites a number of studies to demonstrate the link between air pollution and health problems, especially the risk of lung adenocarcinoma brought on by particulate matter exposure. The World Health Organization's global statistics show that outdoor air pollution has a significant effect on premature mortality. Citing numerous studies, the text also highlights the negative effects of transboundary air pollution and emphasizes the need to comprehend the spatial, temporal, and vertical aspects of air pollution, particularly its transboundary aspect, in order to effectively address its effects on upper-level and surface air quality. The detrimental effects of air pollution underscore the need for advanced technologies to monitor and manage air quality efficiently. Traditional monitoring methods face spatial coverage and efficiency challenges, necessitating exploration of innovative solutions. This paper explores the integration of Smart Drones, Geographic Information System (GIS) and Internet of Things (IoT) technologies to bolster the sustainable management of waste dump sites and tackle air quality issues.

There is less knowledge of upper atmospheric boundary layer (ABL) air quality in comparison to ground-level air pollution. Research done by [2] that investigated variations in air quality using measurements made at different heights shows that at various elevations, there are differences in the concentrations of sulfur dioxide (SO2), volatile aromatic compounds, and particulate matter (PM10). Significantly, research employing tall observation towers and sensor-equipped unmanned aerial vehicles (UAVs) revealed discrete vertical profiles of particle number concentration during episodes of air pollution. The significance of measuring upper-level air quality is emphasized in the text in order to improve our comprehension of its properties and relationship to ground-level air quality. PM is a very harmful pollutant because of how easy it is to breathe in and the possible health effects. PM can cause serious health problems like respiratory and cardiovascular diseases by deeply penetrating the respiratory system. PM is a term for a range of air pollutants, such as dust, smoke, and suspended solid or liquid particles. Anthropogenic sources of PM include the burning of fossil fuels, the use of thermoelectric plants, industrial processes, and air displacement from volcanoes, forest fires, and marine aerosols. PM is classified according to particle size, with PM2.5 (particles smaller than 2.5 μm) and PM10 (particles between 2.5 and 10 μm) being the most important categories. In particular, because of its extended airborne suspension and greater inhalation potential, PM2.5 presents a greater risk to human health [3].

Based on the World Health Organization (WHO) report, the air pollution annually leads to millions of premature deaths, establishing it as a critical global health challenge [4]. The WHO estimates that PM, particularly PM2.5, causes 4.2 million deaths worldwide each year. According to research, particulates can cause a number of health concerns, such as lung cancer, bronchitis, asthma, heart problems, and neurological disorders. Overall, the article emphasizes how vital it is to keep an eye on and respond to PM pollution because of its widespread and detrimental effects on human health. The imperative for precise and current air quality information is evident for implementing effective mitigation strategies and safeguarding human well-being. This paper advocates for a holistic approach that harnesses the synergy between IoT, drone technology, and GIS capabilities to set up systems for air quality monitoring in real time.

The need is for extended observations in order to comprehend the changing features of air quality in the upper atmospheric boundary layer (ABL) [5]. Tower measurements, which provide real-time continuous vertical data but lack spatial information due to financial and spatial constraints, have been a common tool in traditional research. Unmanned aerial vehicles (UAVs) and tethered balloons have been used for vertical air quality measurements; these methods have yielded insightful results, but have limitations due to low altitude and short flight times. The upper ABL's air quality has been monitored using remote sensing technologies, such as Differential Optical Absorption Spectroscopy (DOAS) and Light Detection and Ranging (LiDAR), which have the advantage of overcoming measurement constraints. Long-term and wide-area coverage is offered by satellite retrieval studies, although they are limited by their lack of vertical information and coarse time resolution. In order to improve knowledge of urban air pollution, the text emphasizes the significance of establishing a real-time monitoring network system to measure air quality in the upper ABL over cities, particularly those with complex topography.

The lack of measurement systems limits our ability to predict air quality and understand transboundary air pollution. Prior research mainly depended on chemical transport models and measurements at ground level. Regular networks were employed in ground-level measurements to investigate long-term trends in air quality, including assessing transboundary air pollution during particular climate events. In order to evaluate local and transboundary influences, short-term monitoring campaigns were also carried out, such as gathering samples for a few weeks. Although measurements at ground level are useful in comprehending the effects on surface air quality, they are not able to shed light on the upper atmospheric boundary layer (ABL) [6]. Both short- and long-term analyses using chemical transport models revealed variations in transboundary air pollution in terms of both time and space. Nevertheless, these models have biases and uncertainties that make validation by upper- and lower-level measurements necessary. In order to bridge the gap between ground and upper atmospheric measurements and enable more systematic analyses and precise air quality predictions, the text advocates for the establishment of a comprehensive monitoring system to monitor transboundary air pollution.

This research holds particular relevance in regions contending with environmental issues related to unsegregated waste. Waste dump sites, prevalent in these areas, significantly contribute to air pollution, posing substantial threats to both the environment and public health. Through the application of cutting-edge technologies, our aim is to surmount the limitations of traditional monitoring methods and provide accurate insights into air quality across expansive regions. The incorporation of smart drones enables efficient and dynamic data collection from diverse locations, facilitating a comprehensive understanding of air quality patterns. The IoT ensures seamless connectivity of monitoring devices, enabling real-time data transmission for immediate analysis. GIS technology assumes a pivotal role in spatially mapping and visualizing the collected data, offering decision-makers valuable insights into the distribution of air pollutants. In summary, advancing and implementing a system for monitoring the real-time air quality, strengthened by GIS technology, play a crucial role in acquiring accurate and up-to-date data necessary for efficient environmental management and safeguarding public health. This research adds to the continuous dialogue on sustainable waste management, emphasizing the importance of technological innovation in tackling the issues presented by air pollution. Extensive use is made of Geographic Information System (GIS) technology in a variety of industries, such as emergency response, agriculture, urban planning, environmental management, and health. GIS, which has historically been used for the analysis and visualization of spatial data, has changed as technology has advanced. The incorporation of remote sensing technology in the 1980s and 1990s, when satellite imagery gathered data on Earth's surface, was a major turning point. This improved GIS capabilities for detailed mapping was utilized in planning, monitoring the environmental, and management of resources.

To obtain a detailed understanding of the causes and features of air pollution, effective air monitoring is essential. Comprehending this concept is crucial for assessing exposure, developing environmental policies, and assessing how successful those policies are. Although they have limitations, traditional regulatory monitoring stations provide precise and thorough measurements of air pollution [7]. These instruments need to be calibrated on-site; they are costly, large, need conditioned housing, and require a lot of maintenance.

Furthermore, there are frequently few air monitoring systems in urban areas that are mainly used to monitor adherence to air standards and guidelines. Because traditional monitoring stations are usually located far from sources of emissions, it is difficult to take into account the effects of local sources on ambient air quality. These systems' shortcomings highlight the need for more adaptable approaches.

The study starts with a review of the body of research on the application of GIS mapping for monitoring air quality, outlining both its advantages and disadvantages. The study then uses IoT-enabled drones to gather real-time data on air quality close to a waste dump. Additionally, it investigates how GIS mapping might be used to identify high-pollution areas and forecast air pollution levels. The paper concludes by exploring the implications of incorporating GIS mapping into policymaking and management of air quality. The study concludes by highlighting the probable of GIS mapping tools to improve the monitoring of air quality and recommending its incorporation into all-encompassing management approaches.

14.2 Review of Relevant Literature

The first section of the literature review examines the application of GIS mapping for effective monitoring of the air quality and discusses its benefits and drawbacks. The emphasis then switches to using drones fitted with IoT in close proximity to waste dump sites to gather real-time data on air quality. The review goes on to assess how well GIS mapping works to forecast the various levels of air pollution and pinpoint regions with high attentions of the pollutants. The study concludes by examining the effects of incorporating GIS mapping into the management and formulation of air quality policies. Overall, the thorough literature review emphasizes the value of incorporating GIS mapping into comprehensive managing approaches and shows how effective it is at advancing air quality monitoring.

The worsening air quality in cities is a result of growing air pollution brought on by an increase in automobile use and industrial activity. Since exposure to pollution poses health risks, it is imperative to monitor air quality, particularly in areas with high population density. In response, a number of studies suggest air quality monitoring systems that make use of inexpensive sensors that are compatible with this technology and programmable microcontrollers like Arduino. In order to measure pollutant concentrations, these systems require connecting environmental sensors to Arduino, positioning the devices in appropriate locations, and displaying the results on displays or online platforms. Furthermore, there is a movement toward the adaptation of pollutant sensors for mobile use, which involves mounting them on people or cars to gauge the amount of pollution they encounter when traveling through cities.

Alternative approaches to air monitoring have become more popular in response to the growing need for data on air quality for scientific purposes. These approaches have advantages like lower costs, lower power consumption, high temporal resolution, flexibility, and operational convenience [8]. A growing corpus of research on the functionality and uses of small, inexpensive, and portable gas sensors is revealed by the literature. These sensors use a variety of operating principles, such as semi-conductive metal oxide sensors that change in conductivity when in contact with gas molecules, optical sensors that measure gas absorption at particular infrared wavelengths and are sensitive to carbon dioxide ($CO2$) and methane ($CH4$), and photo-ionization detect the volatile organic compounds (VOC). Furthermore, electrochemical sensors—which exhibit a linear response in current through reduction or oxidation processes on electrodes—are widely used for the detection of common gas pollutants. These substitute sensor technologies present viable paths toward more adaptable and easily obtainable air quality monitoring systems.

A number of benefits make electrochemical cell-based sensor technology a good fit for the "next generation" of air monitoring. These benefits include low power consumption, lightweight design, quick response times, low fabrication costs, and a linear response to concentration. Large-scale ambient air monitoring initiatives, like the international EuNetAir project [9] and the Cambridge University network, have effectively used this technology to measure human exposure by providing continuous measurements of NO, CO, $NO2$, and environmental parameters with maximum temporal resolution. Citi-Sense-MOB and other mobile sensor platforms have proven to be capable of tracking variations at the city-scale. Furthermore, because of its quick response, a multi-gas sensor system that uses electrochemical sensors proved effective in researching emissions from volcanoes. By differentiating pollutant contributions from local background emissions to both local and non-local receptors, high spatial density sensor networks aid in source attribution [10]. Furthermore, when incorporated into tiny, battery-operated devices that people carry with them during daily activities, sensor-based monitoring can quantify personal exposures. Electrochemical cell-based sensor technology is a promising tool for broad and varied applications in air quality monitoring due to its versatility and capabilities.

While sensor-based monitoring applications offer new opportunities for air quality monitoring, there are numerous challenges related to data quality in sensor applications. Research has indicated that environmental elements like temperature, humidity, and interference from other air pollutants can have a major impact on sensor data. Many efforts have been made to comprehend these factors, and machine learning techniques are frequently used to rectify unprocessed data [11]. Documenting sensor performance and accounting for ambient factors under a range of dynamic conditions is essential, since sensors are used in real-world settings outside of controlled laboratory settings. Some of the challenges associated with sensor-based monitoring include the sensors' responses to a wide range of ambient environmental conditions, the measurement of target gases over a wide concentration range, the sensors' cross-sensitivity to multiple gases, the conversion of the electrical output responses of the sensors to actual concentrations, and the lack of established protocols for quality assurance and control in sensor field applications [12]. These problems need to be fixed in order to ensure the precision and consistency of sensor-based air quality monitoring in real-world scenarios.

Wireless sensor networks (WSNs) and GIS mapping have been integrated in numerous investigations to create systems for real-time air quality monitoring [13–16]. For instance, a system using WSNs and GIS mapping was developed in reference [17] to identify pollutants in metropolitan areas. In a similar vein, reference [18] developed a system especially for tracking the quality of the air in cities. Subsequent research endeavors to employ Internet of Things (IoT) devices and GIS mapping for the purpose of monitoring the real-time air quality in smart cities. Novel approaches are presented in references [19] and [20]. The aforementioned monitoring systems have cutting-edge technological features, such as data analysis tools with artificial intelligence (AI) algorithms to find trends and forecast pollutant levels in the future. The estimation of trends in pollutant concentration and database scanning are two common uses for linear regression algorithms. Furthermore, association algorithms—more precisely, the Apriori tool—are employed to quickly establish correlations within the data. Known for its use in data mining operations, the Apriori algorithm generates candidate items and extracts association rules using depth search techniques. This algorithm is good at finding item sets that are frequent and eliminating patterns that are thought to be uncommon. Apriori has found use in monitoring systems in addition to its commercial use in predicting user interests based on purchase behavior. For example, it is used to forecast the amounts of pollutants in a city by utilizing measurements.

GPS technology uses satellite signals to pinpoint an object's location on the surface of the Earth. The transportation and logistics sectors were revolutionized by the combination of GPS and GIS, which allowed for the creation of real-time maps for tracking the movement of various objects. Early uses of this integration were in wildlife tracking, where GPS monitored animal movements and GIS examined spatial data to help conserve wildlife by better understanding animal behavior and movement patterns. GIS applications have undergone further transformation, becoming more accessible and versatile, thanks to recent advancements in GIS technology combined with mobile devices such as tablets and smartphones [21]. Ultimately, the integration of GPS, mobile devices, and remote sensing has allowed GIS technology to advance, revolutionizing data analysis and visualization in spatial contexts and increasing its usefulness in a variety of fields.

Studies have looked into waste management, health effects, and level of real-time air pollution estimation with the help of GIS and cutting-edge techniques in addition to pollution monitoring [22–27]. Studies on mobile GIS and machine learning algorithms-based air quality monitoring systems have been conducted [28–30]. Real-time air quality monitoring through GIS mapping and citizen science integration is also investigated [31]. GIS mapping is used in a number of studies, including ones done in Beijing and Mexico City, to identify and forecast temporal and spatial trends in air pollution [32–34]. These applications demonstrate the potential of GIS mapping in addressing urgent environmental concerns by offering real-time data for well-informed decision-making in pollution mitigation strategies.

14.3 Methodological Framework

14.3.1 Drone and IoT Configuration

The emphasis is on how important it is to keep an eye on the air quality in and around dump yards because of the risks to the environment and human health. One suggestion for improving the efficacy and security of solid waste surveillance is the deployment of drones. Drone integration with Internet of Things (IoT) devices—which include a variety of sensors—is emphasized as a modern and advantageous strategy [35]. The research drones are fitted with sensors that can gather information on temperature, humidity, and air quality parameters that affect the build-up of solid waste. With a 45-minute flight duration and a payload capacity of up to 2 kg, the deployed drones are appropriate for monitoring tasks in dumpsites. We use two drone models that can fly up to nine or ten meters in the air: one has four arms, and the other has six. To measure important parameters, these drones are equipped with a sensor array attached on an unmanned aerial vehicle (UAV). The UAV is set up to fly over predefined study zones in order to collect essential atmospheric data for parameter detection. After data is gathered, it is sent to cloud servers for storage, allowing for additional analysis and air quality monitoring in dumpsite settings.

In the process as described, an initial processing step is applied to remove noise and enhance the quality of the collected data before using it for analysis. A technique for attributing the missing values based on Gaussian filter to lower measurement noise, in order to address the scarcity of data. To reduce forecast discrepancies, positive values are added to instances that lack data. After pre-processing, these data values are used as inputs for training in a predictive framework. For effective data collection, the UAV's (unmanned aerial vehicle) flight path can be preprogrammed with specific locations and altitudes [36]. Wireless transmission of the gathered data is made to a central station for in-depth review and analysis. At this point, the data are processed even more, giving important details about the local environment in the area under observation. This analytical procedure makes it possible to react to changes in the environment quickly and intelligently. The suitability of this approach for gathering data on solid waste in dumpsites is emphasized, especially in cases where waste may accumulate at various levels and layers.

14.3.2 Data Gathering

Data collection has become increasingly important, particularly in environmental monitoring. The process of gathering environmental data has changed with the introduction of wireless sensor networks and drone-based air quality monitoring. Drones have become extremely useful instruments that can independently and without human assistance monitor the quality of the air in particular locations. These drones are outfitted with cutting-edge technologies and an array of sensors that allow data collection on a variety of environmental parameters, including humidity, temperature, and air pollution levels [37]. This leads to the creation of a remarkably dependable and effective system for tracking air quality metrics. In order to gather the required data, the drones can be programmed to fly along predetermined routes, stopping at predetermined heights and locations. The gathered data is then wirelessly sent to a base station for examination. The data are processed and analyzed at the base station, providing important information about the monitored area's environmental conditions. This makes it possible to respond to changes in the environment by making decisions quickly and intelligently. Since real-time monitoring guarantees that the data is always current, it is possible to respond quickly to any potential environmental issues. All things considered, this drone-based system provides an efficient and thorough method of environmental monitoring, enhancing our capacity to react quickly and effectively to changing environmental conditions.

The use of drones, armed with advanced sensors, has revolutionized environmental data collection. Flying at heights around 3m, 6m, and 9m, these drones captured variations in gas concentrations. The comprehensive sensor suite included measurements for temperature, humidity, smoke, wind, and various gases. Real-time data collection enabled the acquisition of accurate data on conditions of air quality in unambiguous regions. Figure 14.1 illustrates a comprehensive framework for systematic data collection. This model emphasizes a meticulous approach to gathering data, ensuring a structured and organized process. The detailed design of this systematic data collection model serves as a foundational guide for efficient and thorough information acquisition.

Several sensors were used in this investigation to collect extensive data on environmental factors. Methane, hydrogen, propane, and LPG were among the gases that the MQ-2 gas sensor helped to detect. Furthermore, the MQ-7 sensor was designed to detect CO gas, whereas the MQ-131 and MQ-135 sensors were used to detect CO2, NO2, and SO2 gases. The GP2Y1010AU0F PM 2.5 sensor was used in the study in addition to gas-detecting sensors to measure particulate matter levels. The VM 30 sensor was used to measure the wind, determining its direction and speed. Lastly, temperature and humidity were measured using the DHT22 temperature and humidity sensor. This wide range of sensors made it possible to evaluate numerous environmental aspects in depth, which improved the study's overall comprehension.

Figure 14.1 Systematized data gathering model.

14.3.3 Study Site

Our efforts to monitor the air quality were concentrated on Chennai, Tamil Nadu's Kodungaiyur dump yard. The 212-acre landfill receives about 2,700 metric tons of waste every day. In order to ensure the collection of air quality parameters and address both spatial and temporal variations, drones were methodically guided along circular flight paths. Figure 14.2 shows the detailed process of study area identification. With meticulous precision, it presents the methodology and sequential steps for accurately pinpointing the specific geographical or thematic region under examination. The visual representation within this figure acts as a captivating guide, illuminating the thorough process of study area identification and emphasizing the paramount importance of precision in the pursuit of research endeavors.

It is emphasized that the drone system is a dependable, effective, and economical mode to monitor the parameters required for air quality verification and perform analysis of real-time data. With an emphasis on its elegance, Figure 14.3 provides a thorough understanding of the intricate field data collection procedure. The system is considered an invaluable tool for environmental monitoring and management because of its features, which include automatic data collection, monitoring the real time, and involved solutions for pollution reduction.

14.3.4 Data Examination

The data collected from drones and IoT devices, facilitating real-time analysis, transformed the landscape of solid waste and air quality monitoring. The collected data underwent analysis using QGIS software, resulting in comprehensive air pollution maps. These maps illustrated pollutant levels at various elevations within landfill areas, offering detailed insights into spatial and temporal variations in pollution [38].

14.3.4.1 Parameter Details and Drone Specifications

In this comprehensive system, drones play a pivotal role in data collection, employing specific specifications to ensure accurate and efficient monitoring.

14.3.4.2 Drone Specifications

- Payload Capacity: The drone supports payloads weighing up to 2 kg.

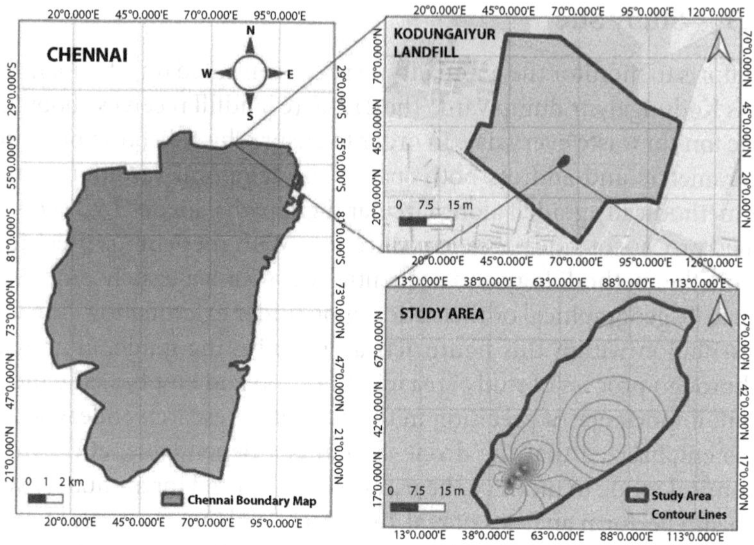

Figure 14.2 Identification of study area [16].

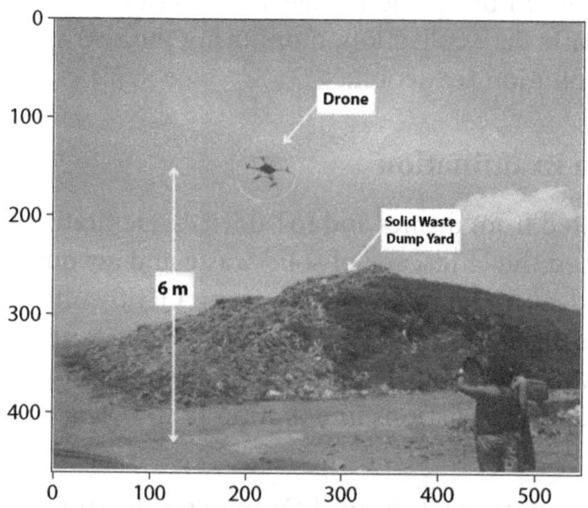

Figure 14.3 Field data collection with a touch of elegance.

- Flight Duration: Capable of sustained flight for up to 45 minutes.
- Drone Models: Utilizes both four-arm and six-arm models for enhanced versatility.

14.3.4.3 Data Collection Approach

An altitude and location-specific preprogrammed flight trajectory is used in the data collection methodology. This systematic approach ensures a methodical and comprehensive coverage of the designated area.

14.3.4.4 Data Collection Intervals

A few seconds are allotted to real-time data collection during circular drone flight paths at different altitudes. This frequent sampling enhances the precision and granularity of the collected information.

14.3.4.5 Altitude Range

The drone operates at adjustable heights of 3m, 6m, and 9m, offering flexibility in monitoring specific layers of the environment.

14.3.4.6 Sensor Array

To measure critical parameters, a sensor array is affixed to the UAV. This array serves as the technological backbone, enabling the collection of essential data for comprehensive analysis.

14.3.4.7 The Sensor Types for the Measured Parameters

- MQ-131: Measures LPG, Hydrogen Propane, and Methane gases.
- MQ-135: Monitors CO2, NO2, and SO2 levels.
- MQ-7: Specifically designed for CO gas detection.
- VM 30: Provides data on wind direction.
- DHT22: Equipped for temperature and humidity measurement.

14.3.4.8 Noise Mitigation

To enhance the accuracy of measurements, a Gaussian filter is strategically employed to mitigate noise within the collected data, ensuring a more precise representation of environmental conditions.

14.3.4.9 Geospatial Mapping

Geospatial mapping is conducted using the sophisticated QGIS software, providing a robust platform for visualizing and analyzing spatial data.

14.3.4.10 Mapping Techniques

Advanced IDW (Inverse Distance Weighting) interpolation techniques are applied to generate air pollution maps. This method ensures a comprehensive and detailed representation of pollution levels across the study area.

14.3.4.11 Input for Predictive Framework

The processed data values serve as crucial inputs for the predictive framework. By utilizing these refined data sets, the framework can effectively train and enhance its predictive capabilities.

14.3.4.12 Focus of Study

The study concentrates on the detection of pollutants at varying heights (3m, 6m, 9m) and during three different months (Mar., Jun., Sept.). This targeted approach allows for a comprehensive exploration of how pollutant levels fluctuate across different vertical layers and temporal intervals.

This integrated system employs a sophisticated combination of drone technology and sensors, ensuring precise and detailed data collection for a thorough understanding of environmental parameters.

14.4 Outcomes and Discourse

Utilizing drones for data collection has revolutionized environmental studies, exemplified by a recent study focusing on air quality parameters. The drone, programmed for various altitudes, efficiently gathered real-time data on temperature, humidity, and various pollutants. Results indicated substantial variations in pollutant concentrations with altitude, emphasizing the impact of solid waste on lower altitudes. Notably, pollutants like CO and CO2 exhibited higher concentrations at lower altitudes, while wind speed and altitude played a role in dispersing pollutants. This exemplifies the power of drones in providing valuable insights for environmental studies, enabling swift identification of pollution sources and facilitating targeted mitigation efforts. A comprehensive analysis of air quality data for various months and altitudes is shown in Table 14.1. Figure 14.4 illustrates the variations at different altitudes throughout the months, capturing a detailed perspective of the fluctuation patterns. Additionally, Figure 14.5 illustrates

Table 14.1 Air quality data comparison across various months and altitudes.

	Air quality features	March (3 m)	March (6 m)	March (9 m)	June (3m)	June (6 m)	June (9 m)	Sep (3 m)	Sep (6 m)	Sep (9 m)
0	Temperature (°C)	32.6	34.0	34.7	31.7	33.5	34.5	37.8	36.7	36.2
1	Humidity (%)	63.4	62.8	63.0	58.2	55.8	55.4	64.5	72.5	72.7
2	CO (PPM)	45.0	40.3	39.6	42.9	34.4	25.5	36.5	28.3	19.3
3	CO2 (PPM)	9.2	8.3	7.7	9.0	8.5	7.3	8.9	8.7	7.3
4	NH4 (PPM)	58.8	42.4	32.8	53.1	41.3	21.4	66.7	50.9	37.4
5	Propane (PPM)	6.0	5.0	4.0	8.0	4.0	3.0	9 0	3.0	2.0
6	VOC (PPM)	449.2	449.6	449.3	449.3	449.9	449.7	449.6	449.7	449.3
7	Wind (MPH)	4.0	4.0	4.0	4.0	4.0	4.0	4.0	4.0	4.0
8	Smoke (PPM)	640.0	540.0	439.6	640.0	540.0	439.6	640.0	540.0	439.6

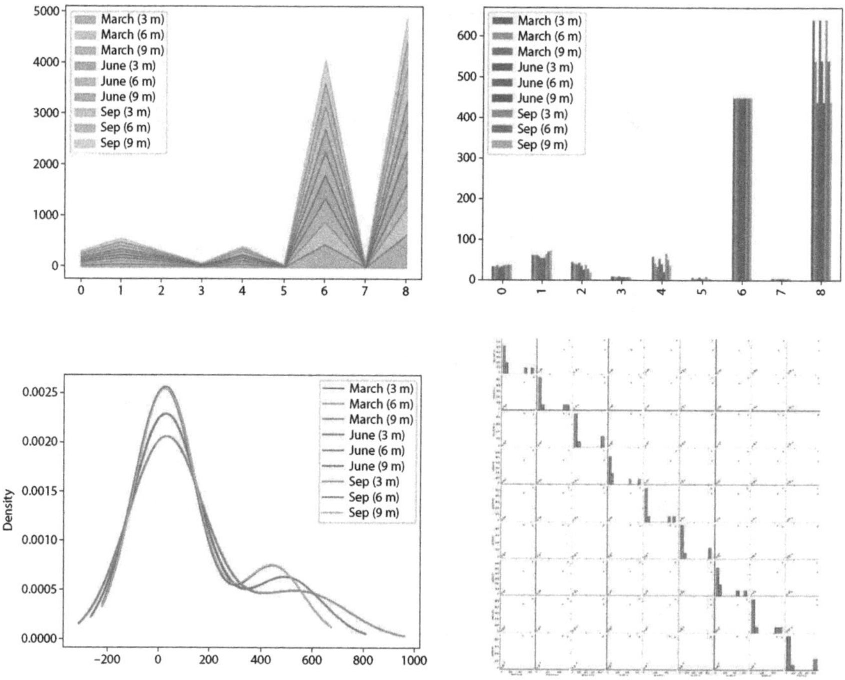

Figure 14.4 Graph depicting variations at diverse altitudes across different months.

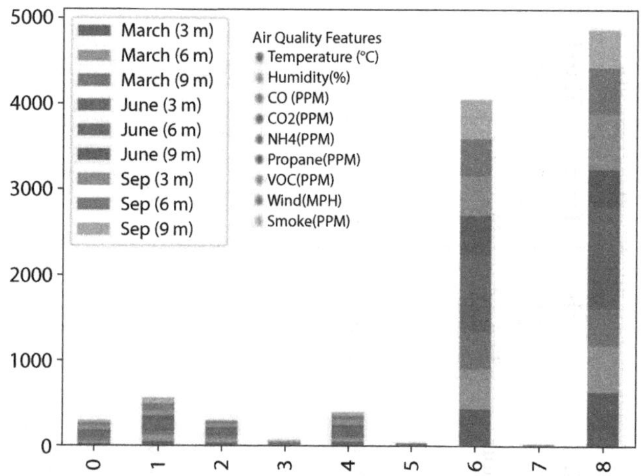

Figure 14.5 Air quality parameters display intriguing changes across months and altitudes.

the fascinating variations in air quality variables over a range of altitudes and months, giving a visual depiction of how dynamic these variations are.

The study examined experimental data on air pollution parameters for several months, paying particular attention to March. Plots of measurement data for temperature, humidity, CO, CO2, NH4, propane, VOC, wind, and smoke at various altitudes are shown in the findings. The data, which were averaged from a range of elevations and gathered from sensors installed on drones, demonstrate a notable variation in the density of air pollutants with altitude. Notably, the concentrations of pollutants like CO, CO2, NH4, propane, VOC, wind, and smoke were higher at lower altitudes, in closer proximity to the solid waste, while the concentrations at higher altitudes were relatively lower. This observation highlights the effects of solid waste on the environment and stresses how crucial it is to put in place appropriate waste management procedures in order to lessen the effects of air pollution.

The investigation measured the results at three, six, and nine meters above sea level. At each altitude, the recorded values are clearly within the same range; the maximum difference between the lowest and highest altitudes is only 2.1 degrees Celsius. This suggests that the temperature in the studied region stays mostly constant at these various altitudes. When humidity readings are examined, a small variation is found within the same range. The 6 m altitude records the highest humidity value, while the 9 m altitude records the lowest. The relationship between altitude and temperature can be used to explain this variation. The altitude of 9 m may have resulted in lower humidity because of decreased atmospheric pressure at higher elevations, whereas the temperature at 6 m may have created conditions favorable to higher humidity levels. This detailed knowledge of variations in humidity and temperature at various elevations aids in a more thorough examination of the environmental conditions in the research area.

Significant trends in the concentrations of dangerous pollutants, particularly CO and CO2, are shown by the study, with a notable decline as altitude rises. With CO at 45.0 ppm and CO2 at 9.2 ppm, the lowest altitude of 3 m shows the highest levels, exceeding advised safe limits. Pollutants such as NH4, propane, and VOC, on the other hand, exhibit a negative correlation with altitude and peak at 3 m. This pattern indicates that these pollutants have a localized effect near the solid waste dump, with VOC at 1.8 ppm, propane at 6.3 ppm, and NH4 at 58.8 ppm (above safe limits). The highest wind speed was measured at 9 meters, and measurements at each altitude show an increase with altitude. Increased turbulence in the upper atmosphere could help disperse pollutants and lower their concentrations, as this suggests. The trends that have been observed highlight the significance of taking altitude variations into account when comprehending the distribution of pollutants, providing important information for environmental management plans in landfill areas.

The study comes to the conclusion that as altitude increases, smoke levels decrease, most likely due to the heavier smoke particles that settle closer to the ground. The highest concentration of smoke is found at the lowest altitude of 3 m, which is closest to the solid waste dump. The results indicate that there are significant variations in the amounts of pollutants with altitude, indicating that air pollution is most prevalent in the immediate vicinity of the solid waste dump. Additionally, the results imply that wind direction and height are significant factors in dispersing pollutants and lowering their concentration. These revelations highlight the intricate dynamics of air pollution in landfill areas and stress the significance of taking a multifaceted approach to successful environmental management.

According to the study, there are noticeable trends in air pollution parameters as altitude changes. It is noteworthy that temperature rises with height, peaking at nine meters. On the other hand, humidity drops as one ascends higher, reaching its minimum at a height of nine meters. A decreasing trend with height is seen for the pollutants CO, CO2, NH4, propane, acetone, toluene, and LPG. The highest concentrations of these pollutants are found at the lowest point of 3 m, suggesting a higher concentration in the vicinity of the ground. On the other hand, the heat index, which is a combination of temperature and humidity, peaks at 9 meters and exhibits an increasing trend with height. Similar to how H2 and alcohol peak at 3 m, dust reaches its maximum density at 6 m, indicating a higher concentration at a moderate. Three months after the first measurements, in September, air pollution data was gathered at heights of 3 m, 6 m, and 9 of meters. Temperature, humidity, CO, CO2, NH4, ethanol, acetone, toluene, and heat index are among the parameters that were recorded. At every height, the temperature varied between 36.2 °C and 37.8 °C, and at 9 m, the humidity peaked at 72.7%. In comparison to other heights, the concentrations of CO2, CO, and NH4 were lower at 9 m. The concentrations of acetone and ethanol peaked at 3 m, while toluene was more concentrated at 3 m and 6 m than it was at 9 m. At three meters, the heat index—a measure of how warm people feel—peaked at 56.9 °C. Pollutants commonly found in industrial areas, such as ethanol, acetone, and toluene, are to blame for the rise in the heat index. Since CO and NH4 concentrations fell as altitude increased, overall, the quality of the air seemed to get better. According to the data, air pollution levels are found to decrease with altitude, peaking at 9 m. Different patterns for each pollutant show different factors influencing their dispersal. The data collected by drone-mounted sensors can help with the development of practical strategies to reduce urban air pollution. Policymakers and environmental researchers can use these findings to help formulate strategies to reduce air pollution.

A critical and necessary direction for future work is a careful evaluation of sensor accuracy. This entails a thorough and exacting comparison of parameters measured at ground level and those observed at altitudes above the atmosphere. Researchers will be able to determine with certainty the reliability and integrity of the sensors by completing this. In addition, a comprehensive analysis of the relevant variables is required, with special attention to the effects of propeller dynamics and important meteorological parameters like wind speed and humidity. This potential investigation has the capacity to significantly advance our understanding of the complex dynamics of air quality in landfill areas by improving the accuracy and validity of the data that has been gathered. Further investigation into these aspects of the field is expected to yield highly sophisticated findings that will support the overall effectiveness of environmental assessments and facilitate the development of skillful management approaches. The focus on precision and comprehending significant factors highlights the dedication to improving the caliber and dependability of studies in the domain of air quality monitoring.

14.5 Conclusion

Our research pioneers a cutting-edge approach, integrating drone technology, IoT, and geospatial mapping to revolutionize air quality monitoring in landfill sites. Through a meticulous analysis of various parameters, we uncovered substantial variations influenced by altitude, waste proximity, and humidity. Employing QGIS for spatial interpolation unveiled heightened pollution levels around the Kodungaiyur dump yard, exceeding permissible limits. Emphasizing the pivotal role in monitoring of real-time air quality with GIS mapping, our study highlights the transformative potential for informed decision-making. Despite its promise, we acknowledge and address challenges like technical complexities, data privacy concerns, and scalability. Tackling these hurdles unlocks the full power of GIS mapping in effective management of air quality. This underscores the urgent need for proactive measures to counteract the adverse effects of pollution and propel us towards a cleaner, healthier future.

References

1. Kulshreshtha, N., Kumar, S., Vaishya, R.C., Assessment of trace metal concentration in the ambient air of the Prayagraj City during Diwali festival—a case study. *Environ. Monit. Assess.*, 193, 3, Springer Science and Business Media LLC, Feb. 27, 2021, doi: 10.1007/s10661-021-08932-3.
2. Rubino, F.M., Floridia, L., Tavazzani, M., Fustinoni, S., Giampiccolo, R., Colombi, A., Height profile of some air quality markers in the urban

atmosphere surrounding a 100m tower building. *Atmos. Environ.*, 32, 20, Elsevier BV, 3569–3580, Sep. 1998, doi: 10.1016/s1352-2310(98)00074-0.

3. Loxham, M. and Nieuwenhuijsen, M.J., Health effects of particulate matter air pollution in underground railway systems – a critical review of the evidence. *Part. Fibre Toxicol.*, 16, 1, Springer Science and Business Media LLC, Mar. 6, 2019, doi: 10.1186/s12989-019-0296-2.
4. World Health Organization, *WHO global air quality guidelines: particulate matter (PM2. 5 and PM10), ozone, nitrogen dioxide, sulfur dioxide and carbon monoxide*, World Health Organization, 2021.
5. Yang, S., Yuesi, W., Changchun, Z., Measurement of the vertical profile of atmospheric SO2 during the heating period in Beijing on days of high air pollution. *Atmos. Environ.*, 43, 2, Elsevier BV, 468–472, Jan. 2009, doi: 10.1016/j.atmosenv.2008.09.057.
6. Wang, M., Huang, T., Wong, D.C., Ho, K.F., Dong, G., Yim, S.H.L., A new approach for health-oriented ozone control strategy: Adjoint-based optimization of NOx emission reductions using metaheuristic algorithms. *J. Cleaner Prod.*, 312, Elsevier BV, 127533, Aug. 2021, doi: 10.1016/j.jclepro.2021.127533.
7. Zhong, L., *et al.*, Science–policy interplay: Air quality management in the Pearl River Delta region and Hong Kong. *Atmos. Environ.*, 76, Elsevier BV, 3–10, Sep. 2013, doi: 10.1016/j.atmosenv.2013.03.012.
8. Spinelle, L., Gerboles, M., Villani, M.G., Aleixandre, M., Bonavitacola, F., Field calibration of a cluster of low-cost commercially available sensors for air quality monitoring. Part B: NO, CO and CO2. *Sens. Actuators, B*, 238, Elsevier BV, 706–715, Jan. 2017, doi: 10.1016/j.snb.2016.07.036.
9. Borrego, C., *et al.*, Assessment of air quality microsensors versus reference methods: The EuNetAir joint exercise. *Atmos. Environ.*, 147, Elsevier BV, 246–263, Dec. 2016, doi: 10.1016/j.atmosenv.2016.09.050.
10. Castell, N., *et al.*, Mobile technologies and services for environmental monitoring: The Citi-Sense-MOB approach. *Urban Clim.*, 14, Elsevier BV, 370–382, Dec. 2015, doi: 10.1016/j.uclim.2014.08.002.
11. Spinelle, L., Gerboles, M., Villani, M.G., Aleixandre, M., Bonavitacola, F., Field calibration of a cluster of low-cost available sensors for air quality monitoring. Part A: Ozone and nitrogen dioxide. *Sens. Actuators, B*, 215, Elsevier BV, 249–257, Aug. 2015, doi: 10.1016/j.snb.2015.03.031.
12. Mead, M.I., *et al.*, The use of electrochemical sensors for monitoring urban air quality in low-cost, high-density networks. *Atmos. Environ.*, 70, Elsevier BV, 186–203, May 2013, doi: 10.1016/j.atmosenv.2012.11.060.
13. Quan, S.J. and Bansal, P., A systematic review of GIS-based local climate zone mapping studies. *Build. Environ.*, 196, Elsevier BV, 107791, Jun. 2021, doi: 10.1016/j.buildenv.2021.107791.
14. Järvi, L., *et al.*, Determinants of spatial variability of air pollutant concentrations in a street canyon network measured using a mobile laboratory and a drone. *Sci. Total Environ.*, 856, Elsevier BV, 158974, Jan. 2023, doi: 10.1016/j.scitotenv.2022.158974.

15. Shalini, L., Manvi, S.S., Gardiner, B., Gowda, N.C., Image Based Classification of COVID-19 Infection Using Ensemble of Machine Learning Classifiers and Deep Learning Techniques. *2022 International Conference on Data Science, Agents & Artificial Intelligence (ICDSAAI)*, Dec. 8, 2022, IEEE, doi: 10.1109/icdsaai55433.2022.10028859.
16. Ranganathan, R.H., Balusamy, S., Partheeban, P., Mani, C., Sridhar, M., Rajasekaran, V., Air Quality Monitoring and Analysis for Sustainable Development of Solid Waste Dump Yards Using Smart Drones and Geospatial Technology. *Sustainability*, 15, 18, MDPI AG, 13347, Sep. 6, 2023, doi: 10.3390/su151813347.
17. X.*et al.*, Spatio-temporal variations and factors of a provincial PM2.5 pollution in eastern China during 2013–2017 by geostatistics. *Sci. Rep.*, 9, 1, Springer Science and Business Media LLC, Mar. 5, 2019, doi: 10.1038/s41598-019-40426-8.
18. Rekha, K.B. and Chandra Gowda, N., A framework for sentiment analysis in customer product reviews using machine learning. *2020 International Conference on Smart Technologies in Computing, Electrical and Electronics (ICSTCEE)*, Oct. 9, 2020, IEEE, doi: 10.1109/icstcee49637.2020.9276877.
19. Enigella, S.R. and Shahnasser, H., Real Time Air Quality Monitoring. *2018 10th International Conference on Knowledge and Smart Technology (KST)*, Jan. 2018, IEEE, doi: 10.1109/kst.2018.8426102.
20. Munera, D., Tobon V., D.P., Aguirre, J., Gomez, N.G., IoT-based air quality monitoring systems for smart cities: A systematic mapping study. *Int. J. Electr. Comput. Eng. (IJECE)*, 11, 4, Institute of Advanced Engineering and Science, 3470, Aug. 1, 2021, doi: 10.11591/ijece.v11i4.pp3470-3482.
21. Hognogi, G.-G., Pop, A.-M., Marian-Potra, A.-C., Someşfălean, T., The Role of UAS–GIS in Digital Era Governance. A Systematic Literature Review. *Sustainability*, 13, 19, MDPI AG, 11097, Oct. 8, 2021, doi: 10.3390/su131911097.
22. Shalini, L., Manvi, S.S., Gowda, N.C., Manasa, K.N., Detection of Phishing Emails using Machine Learning and Deep Learning. *2022 7th International Conference on Communication and Electronics Systems (ICCES)*, Jun. 22, 2022, IEEE, doi: 10.1109/icces54183.2022.9835846.
23. Basheer, S., Rashid, H., Nasir, A., Nawaz, R.A., Spatial and Temporal Variability Analysis of PM2.5 Concentration in Lahore City. *Environ. Contam. Rev.*, 2, 1, ZIbeline International Publishing, 6–10, Oct. 10, 2019, doi: 10.26480/ecr.01.2019.06.10.
24. Popoola, O.A.M., *et al.*, Use of networks of low cost air quality sensors to quantify air quality in urban settings. *Atmos. Environ.*, 194, Elsevier BV, 58–70, Dec. 2018, doi: 10.1016/j.atmosenv.2018.09.030.
25. Jumaah, H.J., Ameen, M.H., Kalantar, B., Rizeei, H.M., Jumaah, S.J., Air quality index prediction using IDW geostatistical technique and OLS-based GIS technique in Kuala Lumpur, Malaysia. *Geomatics Nat. Hazards Risk*, 10, 1, Informa UK Limited, 2185–2199, Jan. 1, 2019, doi: 10.1080/19475705.2019.1683084.

26. Gowda, N.C. and B.M.A., A Trust Prediction Mechanism in Edge Communications using Optimized Support Vector Regression. *2023 7th International Conference on Computing Methodologies and Communication (ICCMC)*, Feb. 23, 2023, IEEE, doi: 10.1109/iccmc56507.2023.10083686.
27. Madokoro, H., *et al.*, Development of Drone-Mounted Multiple Sensing System with Advanced Mobility for In Situ Atmospheric Measurement: A Case Study Focusing on PM2.5 Local Distribution. *Sensors*, 21, 14, MDPI AG, 4881, Jul. 17, 2021, doi: 10.3390/s21144881.
28. Gowda, N.C. and Manvi, S.S., An Efficient Authentication Scheme for Fog Computing Environment using Symmetric Cryptographic methods. *2021 IEEE 9th Region 10 Humanitarian Technology Conference (R10-HTC)*, Sep. 30, 2021, IEEE, doi: 10.1109/r10-htc53172.2021.9641591.
29. Wang, S., *et al.*, Mobile monitoring of urban air quality at high spatial resolution by low-cost sensors: impacts of COVID-19 pandemic lockdown. *Atmos. Chem. Phys.*, 21, 9, Copernicus GmbH, 7199–7215, May 11, 2021, doi: 10.5194/acp-21-7199-2021.
30. Cynthia, J., Saroja, M.N., Sultana, P., Senthil, J., IoT-Based Real Time Air Pollution Monitoring System. *Int. J. Grid High Perform. Comput.*, 11, 4, IGI Global, 28–41, Oct. 01, 2019, doi: 10.4018/ijghpc.2019100103.
31. González Serrano, V., Lin, E.Z., Godri Pollitt, K.J., Licina, D., Adequacy of stationary measurements as proxies for residential personal exposure to gaseous and particle air pollutants. *Environ. Res.*, 231, Elsevier BV, 116197, Aug. 2023, doi: 10.1016/j.envres.2023.116197.
32. Gupta, S., Pebesma, E., Degbelo, A., Costa, A., Optimising Citizen-Driven Air Quality Monitoring Networks for Cities. *ISPRS Int. J. Geo-Inf.*, 7, 12, MDPI AG, 468, Nov. 30, 2018, doi: 10.3390/ijgi7120468.
33. Liu, J., Weng, F., Li, Z., Cribb, M.C., Hourly PM2.5 Estimates from a Geostationary Satellite Based on an Ensemble Learning Algorithm and Their Spatiotemporal Patterns over Central East China. *Remote Sens.*, 11, 18, MDPI AG, 2120, Sep. 12, 2019, doi: 10.3390/rs11182120.
34. Hinojosa-Baliño, Infante-Vázquez, O., Vallejo, M., Distribution of PM2.5 Air Pollution in Mexico City: Spatial Analysis with Land-Use Regression Model. *Appl. Sci.*, 9, 14, MDPI AG, 2936, Jul. 23, 2019, doi: 10.3390/app9142936.
35. Pusfitasari, E.D., Ruiz-Jimenez, J., Heiskanen, I., Jussila, M., Hartonen, K., Riekkola, M.-L., Aerial drone furnished with miniaturized versatile air sampling systems for selective collection of nitrogen containing compounds in boreal forest. *Sci. Total Environ.*, 808, Elsevier BV, 152011, Feb. 2022, doi: 10.1016/j.scitotenv.2021.152011.
36. Wyard, C., Beaumont, B., Grippa, T., Hallot, E., UAV-Based Landfill Land Cover Mapping: Optimizing Data Acquisition and Open-Source Processing Protocols. *Drones*, 6, 5, MDPI AG, 123, May 9, 2022, doi: 10.3390/drones6050123.
37. Scheller, J.H., Mastepanov, M., Christensen, T.R., Toward UAV-based methane emission mapping of Arctic terrestrial ecosystems. *Sci. Total Environ.*, 819, Elsevier BV, 153161, May 2022, doi: 10.1016/j.scitotenv.2022.153161.

15

Voltage Veggies: A Shocking Revolution in Agriculture

P. Prittopaul[1], M. Usha[1*], Mervin Retnadhas Mary[1,2], Rageshwaran H.R.[1,2], Praveen Kumar D.[1], Praveen Kumar S.[1] and Mugunthan Kennedy K.[1]

[1]Dept. of CSE, Velammal Engineering College, Tamil Nadu, India
[2]Dept. of IT, Saudi Electronic University, Riyadh, Saudi Arabia

Abstract
In our relentless pursuit of sustainable agriculture, we are embarking on a groundbreaking method that taps into the intrinsic signals driving plant growth even amid the most formidable environments through precision application of artificial electrical stimuli. Our objective revolves around emulating the innate cues responsible for vigorous plant development. The outcomes of our research have showcased substantial enhancements across pivotal growth metrics such as plant height, leaf expanse and overall biomass. This captivating evolution marks a watershed moment as our intentions encompass a departure from traditional agricultural practices by introducing plant stimulants as a replacement for conventional fertilizers and pesticides. This visionary shift not only spotlights our commitment to environmentally friendly farming methods but also underscores our dedication to harmonizing age-old botanical wisdom with cutting-edge technology. Embedded at the nucleus of this agricultural revolution is our unwavering focus on unearthing anticipatory adaptations, orchestrating large-scale trials and fostering synergistic supplementary strategies. This current juncture stands as a testament to the entwined journey of technology and nature wherein we propel the agricultural sector towards an era characterized by amplified efficacy and ecological harmony. Through our fusion of technological prowess with the elegance of the natural world, we are steering farming into an auspicious future where productivity flourishes hand in hand with environmental stability.

Keywords: Sustainable agriculture, plant impulses, growth enhancement, electrical stimuli, eco-conscious farming

**Corresponding author*: usha.m@velammal.edu.in

A. Suresh, T. Devi, N. Deepa and Ali Kashif Bashir (eds.) Environmental Monitoring Using Artificial Intelligence, (325–352) © 2025 Scrivener Publishing LLC

15.1 Introduction

In the ever-expanding landscape of agricultural innovation, the resolute pursuit of sustainability has ignited a revolutionary exploration into the intricate world of plant communication. Did you know that plants engage in a conversation through chemical signals? This attempt aims to decode the electrical language within this botanical dialogue. The aim is to understand how plants grow in different types of environment, even when their conditions are tough. Plants can communicate with each other and helpful microbes in the soil through small signals that we cannot see or feel. They form a secret network underground that helps them to thrive. This research tries to figure out how the network works in order to better understand plant growth and help them survive in challenging conditions [10]. This can be achieved by a new technique called "artificial electrical stimuli" to help plants grow better. This approach tries to copy the nature of helping the plants to develop by sending tiny electric signals through them. It's like a secret which unlocks the hidden potential of plants, making them stronger and more durable to make up for difficult conditions [11]. By doing this, the goal is to find a way to help crops grow better even if they face challenges like drought or disease. The main objective is to change the way of agriculture by studying how different plants interact with each other, and make use of this knowledge to improve farming methods. As an example of an interesting plant, take mushroom plants. Researchers found that when they give mushrooms electrical shocks, the mushrooms grow better. This suggests that the electrical signal might also help with plants' growth in unexpected ways. It is not only to learn more about plants but also to find new ways to grow food that could be better for the environment and for public health [12]. The implementation of such experimentation was found to give a result of pivotal growth metrics such as plant height, leaf expanse, and overall biomass experiencing remarkable advancements. In fact, recent studies indicate that plants exposed to electrical stimuli not only grow faster but also develop a higher resistance to pests and diseases, forming a natural shield against agricultural challenges [13]. Within this scientific inquiry, we're essentially playing matchmaker for plants. The idea is to take the awesome qualities from strong, healthy plants and share with the ones that need a little boost. How to do this? Well, we crank up the good vibes in the healthy plants by giving them a jolt of electricity. Then, we transform that energy into a magnetic field using some nifty gadgets called transducers. This whole process is a way of giving every plant a super upgrade, making them much more robust, resilient. The end goal? Well, it is all about making the agriculture top-notch by using some of the advanced farming techniques [14]. Our goal is crystal clear: replace traditional farming methods with a fresh wave of plant stimulants that are not only effective but environmentally friendly. It's a harmonious blend between the wisdom passed down through generations of agriculture with the latest technological advancement [15]. This alliance must be strategically crafted to guide agricultural practice towards a sustainable and ecologically conscious future. Consider the potato—a key player in this agriculture. The introduction of the electrical impulses will spark up the remarkable three-fold increase in crop yield, creating the ripple effect across field and farm. This surge to productivity is not just about quantity but also about a qualitative transformation. The electrified potatoes boosted an enriched nutrient profile, injecting a new dimension into the unfolding narrative [2]. In the realm of plant communication, it's not a solo performance but a complex orchestration. Beyond the realm of electrical signals, plants deploy an array of messengers—hormones, peptides, and miRNAs. Picture these chemical messengers as the plant's personal social media, broadcasting information about their surroundings. Table 15.1 discusses about the survey made on effects of electrical impulses and forecasts its major findings and limitations.

15.1.1 Plant vs. Animal Nervous System

Plants possess the ability to transmit electrical signals across vast distances in response to stimuli like changing light, temperature shifts, or environmental stressors [3]. The narrative extends to include the magnetic field—an unassuming yet powerful character in the intricate drama of plant life. Seeds, influenced by this magnetic maestro, exhibit accelerated germination, showcasing the intricate dance of electrical and magnetic forces in the grand theater of botanical existence [4]. It is as if seeds are tapping into a magnetic GPS, navigating their way to germination. In the scientific journey, we're not just unraveling the language of plants, we're reshaping the narrative of sustainable agriculture. Here is the fusion of timeless agricultural wisdom and state-of-the-art technology, which will become the cornerstone for the flourishing and environmentally conscious future. This narrative unfolds like the symphony of sustainable farming, where each electrical impulse and magnetic field play a vital role in creating the melody that resonates with the heartbeat of the greener tomorrow. Exploring how plants and animals can communicate reveals the rich interplay between similarities and differences, akin to contrasting two distinct dialects within the natural world. In terms of electrical signaling, both utilize a form of language—animals rely on neurons, while plants employ their vascular system for signal transmission.

Structurally, animals feature dedicated nervous tissue with intricate neuronal networks, whereas plants, lacking neurons, depend on their vascular system as a signaling highway. Despite molecular differences, both deploy chemical messengers—animals using neurotransmitters and plants relying on chemicals like hormones. Divergence becomes apparent in sensory perception; animals possess centralized systems, while plants employ decentralized mechanisms with receptors attuned to light, gravity, and touch. Response styles exhibit variability; animals move swiftly with nervous system coordination, while plants manifest growth and adaptive mechanisms. Reflecting on evolutionary implications, this divergence underscores the unique paths shaped by animals and plants in their communication strategies. Recognizing the distinct language of plants carries research implications, guiding more effective strategies to comprehend how plants interact with their environment. In essence, this exploration unveils a captivating narrative of shared foundations and distinct adaptations in the communication methods of plants and animals, enriching our understanding of the diverse ways in which organisms communicate within the natural world.

15.1.2 Unraveling Plant Action Potentials

In the early 20th century, physicist Jagdish Chandra Bose delved into a profound exploration of plant physiology, revealing an intriguing aspect of plant life—the existence of a nervous system akin to that of animals, complete with plant action potentials (APs) localized in the phloem region. Bose's investigative journey brought to light the nuanced presence of a plant nervous system, which endowed plants with the remarkable ability to grow, respire, and dynamically respond to their environment. The term "plant nerve" in contemporary discussions, symbolizes a profound botanical revelation.

Traits of Plant Action Potentials: An intriguing parallel emerges when examining the characteristics of plant action potentials alongside their animal counterparts. Similar to animal nervous systems, plant action potentials display essential traits, notably the "all or nothing" phenomenon and a unidirectional flow. This makes the similarity between the nervous system of plants and animals. Bose's work had not only showcased the existence of plant nervous systems but also underscored the interconnected biological processes.

15.1.3 Plant Impulses: Decoding Nature's Signals

Let's dive into the world of plant impulses—these electrical signals that are like the nervous system in animals but for our green companions. When plants experience things like a gentle touch or encounter certain chemicals, they send out these impulses. Picture it as a silent language running through the plant's veins, mainly the phloem and xylem, influencing key functions like growth, sap movement, and how they respond to the world around them. Scientists get all detective-like, using nifty microelectrode recording systems to measure these impulses. It's like eavesdropping on the plant's internal conversation, although there are still some mysteries in unraveling how these impulses work. Understanding plant impulses could be a game-changer. It opens up the door to cool stuff like transferring the good vibes between plants or tweaking these impulse for some handy outcome. These impulses are basically conductors in a grand orchestra of the plant's internal communication network, coordinating various processes essential for its survival and growth [6]. So, think of it this way—exploring plant impulses isn't just about learning botanical secrets. As we keep digging down into all the mysteries of the impulses, that is not just decoding nature but also uncovering the ways to make our green buddies thrive in the ever-changing dance of the environment.

15.1.4 Related Works

Table 15.1 Literature survey on plant impulses.

Related study on plant impulses	Pros	Cons
Electrical stimulation for the growth of plants: With special attention to the effects of nearby lightning on mushrooms [1].	High voltage electrical stimulation may boost mushroom growth rates, enhancing economic viability and production methods.	The effective use of external electrical methods for mushroom production without a clear focus on growth of mushroom production.
Study of the effect of using electrical stimulation on the increase of potato yield [2].	Electrical stimulation reduces viral infestations in plants, but its impact on disease varies by plant type, warranting tailored strategies.	High-voltage electrical stimulation may boost mushroom growth rates, enhancing economic viability and production methods.

(*Continued*)

Table 15.1 Literature survey on plant impulses. (*Continued*)

Related study on plant impulses	Pros	Cons
Electrical signals originating in roots of vascular plants [3]	How plants create and transmit electrical signals, offering valuable insights into plants' physiology.	Concepts are theoretical speculations, lacking experimental evidence to support these claims.
Role of plant physiology in the era of second green revolution [5].	Plants use nutrients better, reducing the need for artificial fertilizers.	New methods could unintentionally harm nature, affecting plants and animals.
Record extracellular signals in plants: A modeling and experimental study [7].	The significance of electrical signals plants, including their types and their role in rapid long-distance communication.	Electrical signals in plants but doesn't explore the practical applications or broader implications for plant health. and agriculture.
Recording: extracellular signals in plants: A modeling and experimental study [8].	Non-invasive, capturing collective plant cell electrical activities comprehensively.	Lacks single-cell precision, limiting study of specific cellular responses.
Jagdish Chandra Bose & plant neurobiology [9]	Bose's work laid the foundation for understanding plant nervous systems.	Assertions about plant cognition require further rigorous scientific confirmation.

15.2 Proposed Methodology

15.2.1 Role in Plant Physiology

One of the fundamental functions of plant impulses is in the realm of growth, where the impulse contributes to the elongation and division of plant cells. The coordinated growth process ultimately supports the overall development in the plant. Additionally, these impulses are indispensable for managing the movement in water and essential nutrients within a plant, ensuring efficient nutrient and water transport through the help of the plant vascular system. This regulation is a vital for the plants in their overall health and growth, as it guarantees the nutrients reach the place where they are needed. Moreover, plant impulses are intimately involved in governing metabolic activities, including respiration and the production of energy. This metabolic regulation aids plants in adapting to diverse environmental conditions, allowing them to thrive in varying circumstances. In the context of photosynthesis, impulses serve a critical role. They enable plants to optimize their photosynthetic processes based on changing light conditions. This optimization ensures that plants can efficiently harness energy from sunlight; this fundamental aspect makes up their growth and survival at vast condition. Furthermore, impulses empower plants to respond to external environmental signals. Whether it is detecting change in the light, temperature, physical touch, or in chemical cues, these impulses enable plants to react and adapt to their surroundings. This responsiveness is enhancing the ability to thrive and survive in the wide range of environmental conditions.

In quest of sustainable agriculture, the innovative approach taps into natural signals guiding plant growth, even in the toughest conditions. Figure 15.1 shows the flow process of providing electric impulses over a defective plant. This is done by precisely applying artificial electrical stimuli to mimic and enhance the way plants naturally develop. The groundbreaking method thus seeks to replace traditional fertilizer and pesticide with environmental-friendly plant stimulant, aligning with the commitment to eco-conscious farming.

Our proposed method involves three key components:

1. Targeted Electrical Stimulation: Carefully introduce controlled electrical signals to the plants, focusing on specific growth stages and vital plant processes. The signals are designed to imitate the natural electrical signals that plants use in their growth and adaptation. To achieve this, advanced

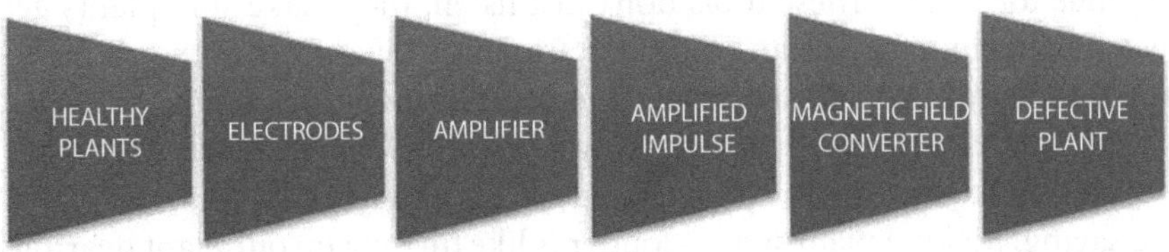

Figure 15.1 Flow process.

tools like microelectrode recording systems are used for a precise measurement and data collections.

2. Amplification and Enhancement: To fully unlock the potential of these plant impulses, advanced techniques are employed to make them strong and clear. The amplification process would enhance the ability to detect for signals and understand the electrical signal better and accurately. Additionally, the use of signal processing methods to refine and improve the amount of data collected gives a more accurate picture of how plants are responding.
3. Transfer of Signals: Building the amplified impulses delves into an exciting area of research. This involves transferring these improved signals from healthy plants to those facing distress using magnetic impulses. This revolutionary approach will hold up the promise of improving the health and resilience even in the productivity of plants. Exploring the correct flawed impulses in the stressed plant could give significant benefit for agriculture and food security.

15.2.2 Recording and Understanding

In this world of plant exploration, scientists use nifty tools that are called microelectrode recording systems. Inspired by pioneers like Jagdish Chandra Bose, these tools act like plant detectives, helping us listen in on the quiet conversations happening at the cellular level. It's like eavesdropping on plants, catching details like how strong, how frequent, and how long their signals are. These recording systems aren't just fancy gadgets; they're like special glasses that let us see the unique ways plants talk. It is most likely to discover a new language, and the knowledge not only satisfies curiosity but also sparks ideas for more discovery and real-world uses. Now, think of boosting plant signals as like turning up the volume on a plant's chat. It is not just like hearing better but is also about making sure to catch every interesting bit in the fascinating language of biology and practical plant uses. The trick lies in the tools, considered as just like hearing aids for plants. These tools don't just listen; they make sure plants get every signal loud and clear. This extra amplification improves the ability to apply the key of understanding to the complicated tunes of plant signals. Then comes the clean-up part, making sure the raw plant signals get a bit of polish. It's like making the plant signals clearer, so to get at what the plants are saying. Making plant signals louder is like turning up our plant hearing. It helps in picking up the subtlest notes in the plant's language, giving us a better idea of how they react to different things. This volume boost isn't just about making noise; it's about clarity. It helps dig into how plants work and respond, making sure the plant signals are read accurately. Louder and clearer plant signals enable cool experiments to be tried out. It's like playing around with different plant traits, helping us learn more about plants and what to do with them.

15.2.3 Signal Analysis Techniques

In our exploration to understand the intricate language of plant impulses, we rely on advanced signal analysis techniques. The techniques act as a crucial tool to unravel subtle patterns and the meaning of embedding in the electrical signal emitted by the plant.

i. Frequency Domain Analysis
We use frequency domain analysis to delve into the spectral characteristics of plant signals. This approach would help at breaking down the signal into a distinct frequency of components that provide insight into the fundamental frequencies that are present. By doing so, we gain a better understanding of the rhythmicity and oscillations with the signals, revealing the patterns associated with specific plant response.

ii. Time-Frequency Transformations
The study of time-frequency transformation is essential for observing how the frequency content of a plant could signal change over the time. This technique captures dynamic change as plants respond to stimuli or undergo a different growth phase. Understanding the temporal intricacies of the plant signal helps enhance our ability to correlate signal variation with respect to the specific physiological event, contributing to a more comprehensive understanding.

iii. Wavelet Transform
The wavelet transform is a powerful tool in our signal analysis toolkit. It allows us to examine both the frequency and temporal aspect of plant signals simultaneously. This mathematical technique adapts to the capture localized variation in signal characteristic, aiding in the pinpointing of a specific event or response within the signal in timeline. This granularity is crucial to decipher the finer detail in the plant communications.

As we navigate through the realms of signal analysis technique, it is clear that each and every method offers a unique perspective of plant impulse. This combination of the frequency domain analysis with time-frequency transformations and the wavelet transform enriches our analytical capability that ensures thorough exploration of the intricate signals that are emitted by plant.

15.2.3.1 Advanced Techniques in Signal Analysis

In the realm of plant physiology, the exploration of the advanced techniques on signal analysis marks a pivotal juncture where technology and biology converge. This section will delve into the cutting-edge methodology for deciphering the intricate language of the plant impulse and highlighting the notable advancements in the signal processing algorithm, which enhances the understandings of the signals.

i. High-Resolution Imaging Technologies
High-resolution imaging technologies have revolutionized signal analysis in plant physiology. The advancements in imaging tools, such as confocal microscopy and the super-resolution technique, would provide unprecedented insight into the spatial and temporal dynamic of the plant impulse. Researchers can visualize cellular responses with exceptional clarity and enable the finer understanding of signal propagation with plant tissues.

ii. Quantum Sensors for Sensitivity Enhancement
Quantum sensors represent a paradigm shift in signal sensitivity. By leveraging the quantum property, these sensors can detect faint electrical signals emanating from the plant with heightened precision. This technological development would enhance the ability to capture the subtle variation in plant impulse, fostering a more detailed and accurate analysis of their characteristics.

iii. Machine Learning Integration
The integration of the machine learning algorithm has ushered in a new era of signal analysis in plant physiology. These algorithms were trained to a vast dataset of plant signals, exhibiting the capacity to recognize intricate pattern and correlation. As a result, the machine learning model can discern subtle nuances in the plant impulse, contributing to a more nuanced interpretation of the complexity in the signaling network within a plant.

iv. Multi-Omics Approaches
Advancement in a multi-omics approach encompasses genomics, transcriptomics, proteomics, and metabolomics, offering a holistic perspective of plant signal in analysis. The integration of information from multiple omics levels allows researchers to unravel the interconnected web of the molecular event triggered by the plant impulse. This comprehensive approach would provide a more comprehensive understanding of this underlying physiological processing.

v. Real-Time Monitoring with Wireless Sensor Networks
Wireless sensor networks have transformed signal analysis by enabling real-time, non-invasive monitoring of plant impulses. These networks deploy sensors throughout agricultural fields, collecting continuous data on plant responses to environmental stimuli. The real-time nature of this approach facilitates dynamic adjustments and interventions based on the evolving physiological state of the plants.

vi. Automated Phenotyping Platforms
Automated phenotyping platforms leverage robotics and image analysis to streamline the assessment of plant traits influenced by impulses. These platforms can rapidly analyze large populations of plants, offering high-throughput data collection. This accelerates the pace of research and allows for the identification of subtle phenotypic changes induced by specific impulses.

vii. Nanoscale Electrodes for Intracellular Measurements
At the nanoscale level, electrodes with exquisite sensitivity enable intracellular measurements of plant impulses. These electrodes, designed to interact with individual cells, provide unparalleled insights into the minute electrical variations occurring within plant tissues. Nanoscale electrode technology contributes to a finer understanding of the intricacies of signal transmission at the cellular level.

15.2.3.2 *Experimental Validation and Application*

Moving from the theory to the practice, the signal analysis technique has found validation in our experiment. As we expose the plants to various stimulus and environmental conditions this meticulously captures all the resulting signals for rigorous analysis. The goal of this is not only to identify the existing patterns but also to discern anomalies or deviations that might also indicate specific plant response. This synergy between the signal analysis technique and the experimental observation has formed a symbiotic relationship. This data derived from sophisticated analyses would inform the refinement of the experimental design, while real-world observations are validated and continually improved by signal analysis methodologies. This iterative process of position at the forefront of the unraveling complexity of the language with plant impulse underscores the importance of robust signal analysis technique in advancing the understanding of plant physiology and communications.

The evolution of signal analysis technique in plant physiology has made research an open new frontier for understanding the complexity of language in plant impulses. From high-resolution imaging to the machine learning integrations, these advancements have collectively enhanced our ability to decode the intricate signaling network that governs the plant response in paving the way to more informed and targeted intervention of agriculture and environmental stewardship.

15.2.4 AI Model Development

Delving into the intricate domain of the AI model development that analyses and replicates plant impulses elucidates the main core components of the model architecture and the nuanced intricacies involved in the training process with a specific focus on integration with the magnetic field dynamics.

15.2.4.1 AI Model Architecture: Decoding the Framework

The AI model serves as an intellectual cornerstone of the research, encapsulating a complex and difficult architecture meticulously designed to decipher and replicate the intricate languages of the plant signal. The essence of the model function is as the intelligent interpreter that aims to understand these subtle nuances of healthy plant signal and, subsequently, generate an artificial impulse that stimulates the growth and resilience of the distressed plants.

i. Neural Network Framework
   Central to the AI model architecture is a neural network framework, inspired by the intricate structure of the human brain. This main framework comprises layers of interconnected nodes with each carrying out a specific task in the signal analysis and replication process. This network's depth and complexity are optimized to capture the multifaceted aspect in plant signalling that ensuring a comprehensive understanding of their dynamic nature.

ii. Signal Processing Layers
Embedded within the neural network are signal processing layers designed to dissect the incoming plant signals. These layers function akin to the synapses in the biological system that facilitate the transmission of the information. Signal processing is executed with precision, breaking down the complex plant signals into discernible patterns that the model can comprehend.

iii. Feature Extraction Mechanism
The feature extraction mechanism is pivotal in identifying key attributes within the plant signals. This step will involve an isolating distinctive feature that can contribute significantly to healthy plant growth. This has features such as amplitude variations and frequency patterns, and the temporal dynamics are meticulously extracted and form the basis for the ability of the model to discern the vital information.

vi. Generative Adversarial Network (GAN)
A noteworthy component of the AI model architecture is the integration of a Generative Adversarial Network (GAN). This sophisticated mechanism would introduce an element in creativity for this model's functionality. The GAN facilitates the generation of artificial plant impulses that closely mimic the characteristics of authentic, healthy signals. The adversarial process refines the model's ability to produce an impulse that can resonate with the intricacies of natural plant communication.

15.2.4.2 Training Process: Nurturing Intelligence through Data

i. Datasets Compilation
The foundation of the AI model's intelligence lies in the dataset it is exposed to during the training phase. For this, an extensive dataset encompassing the diverse range of healthy plant signals was compiled. This dataset acts as the model learning canvas that provides the raw material from which it distils the patterns, correlations, and the nuances.

ii. Supervised Learning Paradigm
The training process follows a supervised learning paradigm, where the model is fed with labelled data indicating the characteristics of healthy plant signals. Through an iterative exposure to this labelled dataset the model refines its

understanding in the intricate relationship between different features within the signal. This supervised learning approach ensures a guided yet adaptive learning trajectory.

iii. Incorporation of Magnetic Field Dynamics
A groundbreaking facet of our research is the integration of magnetic field dynamics into the training process. This aims to mimic a real-world condition where the plants are exposed to a natural magnetic field. During training, the model learns to correlate the magnetic field variations with specific features in the healthy plant signals.

iv. Transfer Learning Strategies
To enhance the model's adaptability to diverse plant species and environmental conditions, transfer learning strategies are employed. This model would initially be trained on a general dataset which undergoes additional training using plant signals specific to the experimental context. This strategic approach would ensure that the model will also acquire a nuanced understanding of the unique attribute that would be inherent in the plant species under investigation.

15.2.4.3 Advancements in Magnetic Field Application: A Symbiotic Interaction

The integration of magnetic field dynamics is not merely a supplemental component but a symbiotic interaction that elevates the AI model's proficiency. The magnetic field application becomes an integral part of the training process, imprinting upon the model a contextual awareness of the environmental conditions in which the plant impulses are expected to operate.

i. Calibration for Precision
During the training phase, the model undergoes iterative calibration to synchronize its understanding of magnetic field variations with the nuanced characteristics of healthy plant signals. Achieving precision in this calibration is paramount to ensure that the artificial impulses that are generated by the model align harmoniously with this dynamic magnetic field condition observed in a natural setting.

ii. Real-time Adaptation
A pivotal aspect of the magnetic field integration is its role in fostering real-time adaptation. The model learns not only

how to respond to predetermined magnetic field pattern but also to dynamically adapt to its impulse generation in the response to the changing of magnetic field dynamic. This adaptability enhances the ability of the model to practically apply in the dynamic agricultural environment.

15.2.4.4 Fostering Intelligent Plant-Environment Interaction

This AI model developed for plant impulse analysis and replication can stand as a testament to the symbiotic integration of the sophisticated neural network frameworks, signal processing layers, and the generative adversarial network. This model's journey can be the supervised learning paradigm, enriched by the diverse dataset and propelled by a transfer learning strategy; this exemplifies the meticulous nurturing of the artificial intelligence. The groundbreaking inclusion of magnetic field dynamics adds a layer of realism to this model's understanding, adaptability and responsiveness to the ever-changing conditions in the plant's natural environment. In navigating the complexities in the plant-environment interactions the AI model emerges as a beacon of intelligent intervention, offering a promising trajectory for sustainable agriculture and environmental conservation.

15.2.4.5 Adaptive Response Modeling

In navigation of the intricate realm by AI-driven adaptive response modeling, the focus gravitates towards the two key facts, as follows:

i. Dynamic Response Modeling
Dynamic response modeling within the AI system represents a sophisticated approach to understanding how the model tailors its responses to ever-shifting environmental cues. This is a journey into the adaptive core in the system, where the model will get dynamically adjusted, with its behaviour based on the real-time inputs from the surroundings. This adaptive prowess ensures a flexible and context-aware approach to impulse generation. The essence of dynamic response modeling lies in the model's ability to discern subtle variations in the environment and promptly recalibrate its responses. Whether influenced by changes in light, temperature, or other dynamic factors, the model adeptly navigates these shifts to generate impulses that align with the current contextual demands. This adaptability mirrors the

integral, nuanced responsiveness found in natural biological systems.

ii. Predictive Modeling for Future Conditions
Moving beyond the present, this AI model's prowess extends into a predictive modeling for future environmental conditions. This facet delves into this model's capacity to anticipate forthcoming changes in an environment, setting up the stage for a proactive and pre-emptive response strategy. This predictive capability of the AI model will unfold as it analyzes historical data, identifies the patterns, and extrapolates its potential scenarios. By harnessing these insights, the model positions itself to foresee shifts in environmental conditions before they occur. This proactive stance enables the AI system to preemptively adjust to its impulse generation strategy, aligning with the predicted condition. The result would be a forward-thinking approach which enhances the adaptability and the resilience of the system. In essence, this synergy between the dynamic response modeling and the predictive modeling for future condition encapsulate an adaptive intelligence embedded within this AI system. The dual-layered approach ensures not only a real-time response to immediate cues but also a strategic anticipation of future challenges. This mirrors the intricate dance of the adaptation observed in nature, where organisms seamlessly adjust to the current need while preparing for the evolving dynamic of their surroundings. Delving into the facets of the adaptive response modeling leads to an overarching objective that emulates the sophistication of the natural system within the artificial intelligence framework. Imbuing this AI model with these adaptive capabilities leads to the creation of a system that not only responds intelligently to the present but also foresees and navigates the challenges in the future with a sagacious resilience.

15.2.5 Transferring Signals to Defective Plants through Magnetic Impulses

Figure 15.2 shows the concept of transferring signals to distressed plants via magnetic impulses, which represents an exciting and pioneering frontier of research, offering promising prospects for enhancing plant health

Figure 15.2 Work flow of plant impulse transfer from good plant to defective plant.

and productivity. In this cutting-edge field of study, known as "Transferring Signals to Defective Plants," researchers are exploring innovative methods for sending signals to plants facing various challenges. The primary mechanism involved in this process is the use of magnetic impulses. Within this domain, there are specific mechanisms at play, and one notable aspect is amplification and filtering. Through this mechanism, faulty plant signals are subject to amplification and refinement, ultimately enhancing the quality of these signals.

This process targets irregularities in signal patterns and strength, aiming to rectify deficiencies within the plant's signalling system. The implications of transferring signals to struggling plants are substantial and span various fields of application. One critical application is the enhancement of plant health. By correcting flawed impulses within distressed plants, this approach can assist them in overcoming stress, diseases, and environmental challenges. Consequently, plants can exhibit healthier growth and increased resilience in the face of adverse conditions. Improved signals also hold the potential to significantly boost crop yields and quality. This is of paramount importance for ensuring food security and fostering sustainable agricultural practices. Enhanced signals can result in more bountiful harvests, addressing the global demand for food production. Another promising dimension of this research involves modifying plant signals to instill adaptive traits. By doing so, plants can become more resilient and adaptable to changing environmental conditions. This adaptability is crucial for plants to thrive in diverse ecosystems and changing climates, contributing to biodiversity and ecosystem sustainability.

15.2.5.1 Magnetic Field Generation Methods

Understanding how the artificial impulses are effectively transmitted to the plants hinges on the pivotal role that will be played by magnetic field generation methods in this experiment. So, to employ diverse techniques to create the magnetic field, each method is imbued with a distinctive characteristic that significantly enhances all the precision and efficacy in this project.

i. Electromagnetic Coil Systems
At the forefront of magnetic field generation is the utilization of electromagnetic coil systems. The system consist of the coils through which an electric current flows, engendering the magnetic field around this coil. The arrangement and the power dynamics in the coil assume the paramount importance of dictating the strength and the distribution of the magnetic field. The strategic configuration in these coils affords us the ability that tailors magnetic impulses precisely, affording it a high degree of control. This method is real-time adjustability would be particularly advantageous, ensuring the adaptability to unique requirements of the various plant species and the specific experimental condition.

ii. Permanent Magnet Configurations
In tandem with electromagnetic coil systems, we explore the application of permanent magnet configurations for magnetic field generation in plant impulse manipulation. Unlike electromagnets, permanent magnets maintain a constant magnetic field without the need for continuous electrical input. So, the approach champions stability and endurance, providing a consistent magnetic environment for all plants over a prolonged duration. The simplicity of implementation and reduced energy consumption positions permanent magnet configurations as an environmentally sustainable choice. These deliberate placements and orientation of the permanent magnets aim to optimize the delivery of magnetic impulses that will foster a controlled and targeted response in the plants undergoing experimentation.

iii. Integration and Synergy
This synergy between the electromagnetic coil systems and the permanent magnet configuration is instrumental in enriching our understanding of plant response to artificial impulses. Hence a collaborative approach would empower the exploration of a spectrum of magnetic field dynamics that offers profound insight into how plants perceive and can respond to these manipulated signals. Delving into all the experimental phases that would anticipate a meticulous assessment of the effectiveness in this magnetic field generation method contributes to a nuanced understanding of this intricate relationship between both the magnetic impulses and plant physiology.

15.2.5.2 Experimental Insights and Observations

As we navigate through the experimental phase, the impact of these magnetic field generation methods on plant behavior will be rigorously scrutinized. Our objective is to not only gauge the efficacy of these methods but also unravel the subtleties of how plants interpret and adapt to artificial impulses. This exploration into the experimental realm is poised to enrich the scientific community's understanding of the dynamic interplay between magnetic fields and plant physiology. A careful consideration of these electromagnetic coil systems and the permanent magnet configuration in a magnetic field generation method amplifies the depth and scope of these methods. This comprehensive approach could not only enhance reliability but also contribute substantively to all broader scientific discourse on how plants can interact with and respond to the external stimuli.

15.3 Experimental Approach

15.3.1 Unraveling the Dynamics of Plant Impulse Manipulation

We're trying out a new way to help plants grow better by using electrical signals. Our careful plan involves studying how this technique works on different plants in controlled settings. We want to understand how it can be useful and what effect it might have.

1. Diverse Plant Selection for Holistic Insights
   First, we pick a bunch of different plants for our experiment. This mix helps us really grasp how well this electrical signal trick works on various crops, making sure our discoveries aren't limited to just one type of plant. By testing out lots of different species, we're aiming to figure out exactly how each kind of plant reacts to the electric signals. This sets the stage for a thorough evaluation of the method's effectiveness.
2. Conducting Experiments in Controlled Environments
   To make sure our results are trustworthy, we do all our experiments in really controlled environments. These settings are carefully set up to get rid of anything outside that could affect what we're studying. This way, we have a clean slate to watch and study how the plants grow, change, and react to the electrical signals. Doing this in a controlled space helps us be sure that our methods are valid, and it lets

us focus on understanding how the electrical impulses affect plants without interference from outside stuff.

3. Rigorous Data Collection for In-Depth Analysis
   A crucial part of our method is carefully gathering data during the whole experiment. This involves measuring things like the electrical signals and important growth signs such as plant height, leaf size, and overall biomass (how much the plants weigh). We also keep a close eye on nutrient levels to see if the electrical signals change anything in the plant's nutrition. By collecting all this data thoroughly, we're building a solid foundation to really understand how this new method affects different aspects of how plants grow and work.
4. Amplification and Enhancement of Collected Data
   To better understand how plants respond to electrical signals, we use advanced techniques to improve and clarify the data we collect. This process is essential for enhancing the precision of the signals we measure during the experiment. By fine-tuning and sharpening this data, we can reveal the subtle details in how plants react. This helps us grasp a deeper understanding of the intricate language that plants use in response to electrical stimuli, uncovering the nuances in their responses.
5. Magnetic Signal Transfer Devices: Aiding Distressed Plants
   Our special focus is on creating and testing devices that use magnetic impulses to send signals to plants under stress. These devices are carefully designed and put through rigorous testing to see how well they can help plants deal with different challenges. By using magnetic signals, we're trying out a new way to intervene and improve the health and resilience of plants, especially when they're facing tough conditions. This approach holds promise for making agriculture more sustainable in the long run.

V = Vegetative stages, R = Reproduction stages.
(0 -> VE = Emergence, 1-> V1 = First leaf, 2 ->V2 = Second leaf, 3 -> V6 = Sixth leaf, 4 -> V10 = Tenth leaf, 5 -> V(n) = Nth leaf, 6-> VT = tassle,7 -> R1 = Silking, 8 -> R2 = Blister, 9 -> R3 = Milk, 10 -> R4 = Dough, 11 -> R5 = Dent, 12 -> R6 = Physiological Maturity)

The graphical representation in Figure 15.3 provides a visual narrative of the experimental results, depicting the stages of plant growth influenced by electrical impulses. The X-axis denotes time in weeks, while the Y-axis delineates the stages of plant growth driven by electrical impulses. The stages, spanning approximately 100 days, are meticulously documented, offering a detailed insight into the temporal progression of plant development under the influence of electrical stimuli. This graphical representation serves as a tangible snapshot, illustrating the method's impact on different developmental milestones and providing a visual reference for the observed stages of plant growth. Making the information clear and transparent helps everyone understand how manipulating plant impulses can affect the growth of different plants. Our careful experiments aim to collect strong data that proves the new agricultural method is valid and useful. This thorough process allows us to make meaningful conclusions about the benefits and practicality of the approach for various plants and farming situations. The results from these experiments deepen our understanding of how plants interact with impulses, providing a basis for sustainable and informed farming practices.

Now, looking at the challenges and limitations of using AI to manipulate plant impulses, it's essential to recognize that while this is an innovative approach, it comes with difficulties. In this part, we take a close look at the problems we faced during the research and emphasize the areas where improvements are necessary for the successful use of this new method.

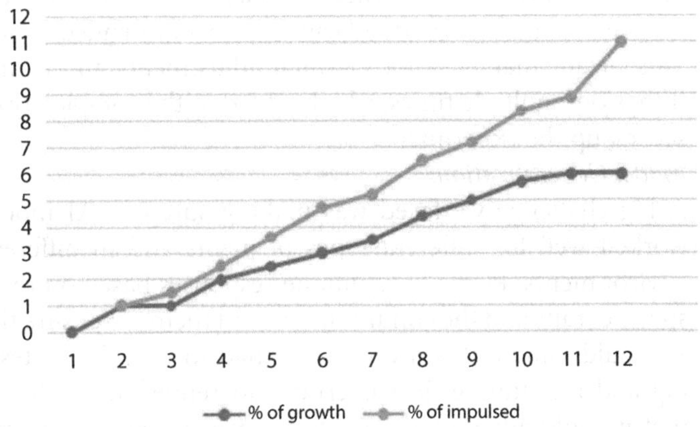

Figure 15.3 Experimental results on plant growth.

15.3.2 Challenges and Limitations in AI-Driven Plant Impulse Manipulation: A Critical Examination

Trying to improve agriculture by using AI to manipulate plant impulses is a new and exciting idea. But as with any new approach, it comes with its own difficulties and limits. In this part, we take a close look at the problems we faced during the research. We highlight the areas where we need to get better to make sure this innovative method works well when we use it in real farming situations.

15.3.2.1 Challenges Faced During the Research Process

i. *Data Variability:*
   A big challenge we faced was the differences in the actual signals from real plants that we used to train our AI model. The way plants react to their environment is complex, making it tough to gather a complete set of data. To tackle this challenge, we had to carefully adjust and check our AI model to make sure it could handle the various ways different plants behave. It required a lot of careful calibration and validation to ensure the AI could adapt well to the diverse behaviors of different plants.
ii. *Magnetic Field Calibration:*
   Getting the magnetic field just right turned out to be a tricky challenge. Making sure it's the perfect strength and evenly distributed in various plant settings was quite complicated. We had to find a balance where the magnetic field effectively transferred impulses without causing any unintended issues. This meant making a lot of small adjustments and trying things out multiple times, which added to the complexity of setting up the experiment.
iii. *Model Generalization:*
   A big challenge we faced was making sure our AI model worked well for different types of plants and in different environments. Plants have unique responses based on their specific traits and the conditions around them. To ensure the AI could handle this diversity, we had to do a lot of testing and fine-tuning. It was crucial to refine the model so that it could adapt effectively to the various ways different plant species and environmental factors might influence its performance.

15.3.3 Limitations of the Proposed Method and Areas for Improvement

i. *Dependency on Training Data*
How well our AI model works depends a lot on the quality and how well it represents the training data we use. Problems come up when the model faces situations or plant conditions that weren't well covered in the training set. For future studies, it's important to work on making the model better at handling unexpected changes in how plants respond. This means improving its ability to deal with situations that weren't part of the original training data.

ii. *Real-Time Adaptability*
Right now, our approach mainly looks at past signals from plants. However, it's tough to quickly adapt to instant changes in the environment. To make this method more useful in real-time situations on farms, we need to upgrade the AI model. It should be able to adjust dynamically as conditions change, which is crucial for its practical use in dynamic agricultural settings.

iii. *Magnetic Field Precision*
Even though applying a magnetic field had some good effects, we still face a challenge in being very precise. Making sure the magnetic field is both even and focused, without impacting nearby plants or causing unintended issues, requires improvements in magnetic field technologies. Adjusting this aspect carefully will help reduce any potential risks.

iv. *Ethical Considerations*
Looking into the ethics of messing with plants using artificial impulses is really important. We need to carefully think about the possible long-term effects on plant ecosystems. Changing the natural processes of plants raises questions about how it might affect the balance in nature and if there could be unintended problems. To deal with these concerns, we're continuously looking at the ethical side of things and working closely with experts in the environment. It's all about making sure we're doing this in a responsible and thoughtful way.

15.4 Conclusion and Future Research Directions

Exploring the world of manipulating plant impulses is like embarking on a groundbreaking story, blending the complex world of biology with the ever-changing field of technology. This exciting combination has the potential to reshape how we do agriculture, keep an eye on the environment, and use biotechnology. However, this promising journey requires careful navigation, guided by ethical considerations and strong rules. As we step into this transformative frontier, the captivating possibilities of technological progress must go hand in hand with a deep understanding of any unintended problems. Our scientific adventures should align smoothly with what society values and with keeping the environment healthy for the long run.

15.4.1 Future Research Directions

1. *Precision Agriculture: Harmony in the Fields*
   Let's embark on an exciting journey of partnering with plants and artificial intelligence (AI). This experience goes beyond improving crops; by combining AI algorithms with the signal plants give off, we're hoping completely to change how we manage resources. This might make farming super fast, so this can make things better and faster.
2. *Environmental Adaptation: Nurturing Resilience amidst Climate Flux*
   As we face the urgent challenges of changing climates, the combination of manipulating plant impulses and using AI opens up a hopeful new realm for this world. Researchers are working hard to explore techniques, with the help of AI, to improve plants' ability to adapt to climate-induced changes. This effort goes beyond just ecological sustainability.
3. *Plant-Plant Communication: Decoding Nature's Silent Symphony*
   Delve into the essence of inter-plant communication, where the interplay of AI and plant impulses converges to decode nature's tacit symphony. The objective is to decode the complex interactions occurring amongst plants within ecosystems, providing an opportunity to redefine the narrative of ecological dynamics. This endeavor carries the potential to enhance our comprehension of the interconnectedness that underlies the core of our planet's sustainability.

4. *Remote Sensing: AI-Enhanced Insights Illuminating Global Ecosystems*
   In a rapidly evolving field like remote sensing, the fusion of AI with the manipulation of plant impulses represents an exciting advancement in our understanding of global ecosystems. AI and plant signal manipulation are being combined to help us learn more about ecosystems and the environments of the plants. Researchers are working to identify how AI can understand the signals from the plants, giving us new insights into how ecosystems work and how healthy the environment of the plants is. This combination is important for being able to monitor large areas of the planet from afar. AI can help us understand things about plants and ecosystems that are difficult or expensive to gather in person. This technology could change the way we understand issues like plant productivity, climate change, and ecosystem function.
5. *Integration with AI Technologies: Crafting a Symphony of Understanding*
   Let's delve into the captivating interplay between adjusting plant impulses and the most recent AI technologies. Researchers are intensively investigating how AI can enhance the analysis, interpretation, and manipulation of plant signals, aiming for a harmonious understanding. This research imagines a future where technology integrates seamlessly with the complex language of plants, paving the way for more advanced and precise techniques.
6. *Ethical Considerations and Regulatory Frameworks: Charting a Responsible Course*
   As we step into this new and ever-changing field, the ethical considerations tied to using AI alongside plant impulse manipulation become incredibly important. It's vital to set clear rules and guidelines, not only to govern the ethical use of AI in plant biology but also to ensure a responsible and transparent approach that matches what society expects. Navigating this ethical terrain is crucial to avoid any unintentional ethical or environmental problems that might come with these exciting advancements.

15.5 Conclusion

In conclusion, the odyssey through plant impulse manipulation unfolds as a dynamic narrative, where scientific curiosity engages in a profound dance with technological innovation, shaping the future of our interaction with the botanical realm. The symbiosis of plant biology and emerging AI technology stands as a profound catalyst, poised to redefine not only agricultural practices but also environmental stewardship and biotechnology approaches. It will also fundamentally alter our perception and interaction with the natural world. In the embarking on the exhilarating journey, responsibility rests squarely on the shoulders of the scientific communities, policymakers, and technologists to maintain an unwavering commitment to ethical conduct and ecological responsibilities. This intersection of plants' impulse manipulation and AI not only presents a potential for groundbreaking advancements but also mandates a delicate equilibrium between exploration and ethical stewardship. Success in navigating that uncharted territory responsibly hinges on collaborative effort. This collaboration is essential to ensure that the transformative power of this interdisciplinary realm is being harnessed ethically, sustainably, and for the betterment of both humanity and the environment.

References

1. Jami, N.A.B.M., Gomes, C., Gomes, A., Kadir, Z., Electrical stimulation for the growth of plants: With special attention to the effects of nearby lightning on mushrooms. *Asian J. Microbiol. Biotechnol. Environ. Sci.*, 2018.
2. Mukhammadiev, A., Sanbetova, A.T., Toshpulatov, N., Babayev, Abdukadirova, M., Study of the effect of using electrical stimulation on the increase of potato yield, IOP Publishing Ltd, 2022.
3. Canales, J., Henriquez-Valencia, C., Brauchi, S., The Integration of Electrical Signals Originating in Root of vascular Plants. Plant Physiology, a section of the journal *Front. Plant Sci.*, 2017.
4. Radhakrishnan, R., Magnetic field regulates plant functions, growth and enhances tolerance against environmental stresses. *Physiol. Mol. Biol. Plants*, 2019.
5. Grider, M.H., Jessu, R., Kabir, R., *Physiology, Action Potential*, StatPearls, 2023.
6. Lee, S. and Oh, M.-M., Electric stimulation promotes growth, mineral uptake, and antioxidant accumulation in kale. *Bioelectrochemistry*, 2021.

7. Zhaoa, D.-J., Wang, Z.-Y., Li, J., Wena, X., Liua, A., Huang, L., Recording extracellular signals in plants: A modeling and experimental study. *Math. Comput. Modell.*, 2011.
8. Tandon, P.N., Jagdish Chandra Bose & plant neurobiology. *Physiol. Mol. Biol. Plants*, 25, 5, 1107–1119, 2019.
9. Singla, A. and Sharma, T., Role of Plant Physiology in the Era of Second Green Revolution. *Int. J. Plant Technol.*, 2021.
10. Takaki, K., Takahashi, K., Hayashi, N., Wang, D., Ohshima, T., Pulsed power applications for agriculture and food processing. *Rev. Mod. Plasma Phys.*, 2021.
11. Lee, S. and Oh, M.-M., Electric field: a new environmental factor for controlling plant growth and development in agriculture. *Hortic. Environ. Biotechnol.*, 2023.
12. Dannehl, D., Huyskens-Keil, S., Eichholz, I., Ulrichs, C., Schmidt, U., Effects of intermittent-direct-electric-current (IDC) on polyphenols and antioxidant activity in radish (Raphanus sativus L.) during growth. *J. Appl. Bot.-Angew. Bot.*, 83, 54–59, 2009.
13. Dannehl, D., Effects of electricity on plant responses. *Sci. Hortic.*, 234, 382–392, 2018.
14. Lautner, S., Grams, T.E.E., Matyssek, R., Fromm, J., Characteristics of electrical signals in poplar and responses in photosynthesis. *Plant Physiol.*, 138, 2200–2209, 2005.
15. Moon, J.D. and Chung, H.S., Acceleration of germination of tomato seed by applying AC electric and magnetic fields. *J. Electrostat.*, 48, 103–114, 2000.

16

Emperor Penguin Optimized Loop Selection Process for Routerless NoC Design

N.L. Venkataraman[1]*, S. Sumithra[1], S. Suresh Kumarm[1], K. Kokulavani[1] and Gunasekaran Thangevel[1,2]

[1]Department of Electronics and Communication Engineering, J.J. College of Engineering and Technology, Tiruchirappalli, Tamil Nadu, India
[2]University of Technology and Applied Sciences, Muscat, Oman

Abstract
Even though router-based Network-on-Chip (NoC) offers best scalability, routers are one of the reasons for more power consumption and area occupation in NoC due to their complex structure. This paper introduces routerless NoC design using Emperor Penguin Optimized (EPO) loop selection. In routerless design, data transmission takes place using loop topology in which each node injects and receives data from loop. The connection between two nodes is called loop as there is no use of routers for NoC design. But proper selection of loop for data transmission reduces hop count by satisfying connectivity requirement. However, they forget to achieve benefits of a router-based NoC in routerless design. So, we are going to optimize the loop selection process of routerless design with EPO algorithm. The software named Xilinx ISE design suite 14.5 working for routerless NoC model. However, the EPO-based routerless NoC design delivers better performance than the existing techniques. The proposed EPO-based routerless NoC achieves 994.221 MHz operating frequency, 0.027 mW power consumption, 0.17sec latency and 0.02% average hop count.

Keywords: Network-on-Chip (NoC), Emperor Penguin Optimization (EPO), loop topology and routerless

**Corresponding author*: venkat.altera@gmail.com

A. Suresh, T. Devi, N. Deepa and Ali Kashif Bashir (eds.) Environmental Monitoring Using Artificial Intelligence, (353–374) © 2025 Scrivener Publishing LLC

16.1 Introduction

Network-on-Chip (NoC) is a communication sub-system made between the IP (intellectual property) cores in System-on-Chip (SoC). Network-on-chip structural design contains network interfaces, links and routers that connect with processor or external memories [1]. In NoC, the buses have been used to deliver on-chip interconnects for multi-core chips [2]. The interconnection of modern bus-based systems are easy to implement and simple, but the scalability is greatly restricted. However, various methods have been suggested to develop modern buses that are hard for their scalability to keep up by modern many-core processors [3]. In contrast, NoCs provide a decentralized solution for the use of links and router [4]. The switching capability of routers offers parallel communication and multiple paths. The NoC throughput is considerably greater than that of buses. Inappropriately, routers have been notorious for consuming a significant percentage of chip's area and power [5, 6]. In addition, the router cost increases rapidly as width of the link increases. Thus except with a small number of ad hoc designs, most on-chip networks do not employ connect width greater than 256 bit or 512 bit; it may be available on the additional wiring resources [7].

The high overhead of routers inspires researchers to develop routerless NoCs, planning to eliminate the use of the costly routers. However, the use of wires more capably to reach scalable performance [8, 9]. Even though the concept of routerless NoC has not been properly mentioned earlier, there are many works that try to eliminate routers with sophisticated use of switches and buses [10]. In routerless NoCs the main aim is to select a set of smartly placed loops or composed of wires to link with cores such that the average hop count is equivalent to that of conventional router based network-on-chip [11, 12]. But the highest road blocks are the huge design space of loop selection and the struggle in avoiding deadlock with little or no usage of buffer resources. In routerless design, existing work suggested a layered progressive method. Thus a layered progressive method is used to find a set of loop that see the obligation of connectivity and the drawback of wiring resources [13, 14]. The progressive method forms the design of a large routerless network from good designs of smaller networks, and is related to any n × m many-core chips with higher scalability [15]. Many existing works dealt with various techniques to address the challenges in designing routerless interface [1]. Thus, routerless interface avoids network abnormalities, for example, live lock, starvation and deadlock [16].

Past work dealt with buffered router, bufferless router and minimally buffered router designs in NoC. Even though router-based NoCs technique suggest best scalability, they also suffer area overhead and significant power owing to complex router structures [1, 17]. Therefore the proposed work planned to eliminate the use of routers for NoC design. Using loop topology for data transmission in routerless design and each node insert and receive data from loop. The loop is defined as the connection between two nodes and there is no use of routers for data transmission [18].

However, the loop will be selected in a proper way for data transmission and it reduces the hop count by satisfying connectivity obligation. Some recent research works have discussed routerless routing technique. However, such works forget to achieve the benefits of router-based NoC in routerless design. This paper proposes a loop selection process of routerless design with new algorithm. Likewise, the motivation of the proposed work is to achieve all the benefits of router-based NoC in the proposed routerless design itself. The rest of the paper is arranged in the following way: section 16.2 describes the sum of recent related works related to routerless NoC. The proposed work is discussed in section 16.3. The fourth section includes the design process of EPO loop selection; in addition, the result and comparison process is explained in section 16.5. Section 16.6 covers the conclusion for EPO-based routerless NoC design.

16.2 Related Works

Some of the recent work related to routerless NoC design is described below.

Venkataraman and Kumar [19] proposed Ant lion optimization-based reliable custom topology in application specific network-on-chip. As the number of core rises, the communication request between cores also increases. Generally, NoC contains some components and the power dissipation is mostly produced by the component usage. Usually, custom topology uses a lower number of routers than the regular topology. The performance evaluation in terms of speed, area and power have been analysed in [19]. The frequency range of the reliable custom topology method is very high, that is 426.995MHz. Ant lion optimization-based reliable custom topology method gives better performance when compared with other existing methods.

Ant lion optimized-based routing algorithm in bufferless router has been developed by Venkataraman *et al.* [20]. This paper suggested optimized algorithm along with bufferless routing in chip design. Ant lion optimized (ALO) bufferless router operates with less power. Normally, there is a gradual decrease in the area and the power with a substantial increase in working speed while eliminating the buffer from the router. ALO bufferless structural design gives better performance when compared with other existing methods. The power consumption and frequency range of the ALO-based bufferless routing is 0.413 mW and 780.153 MHz. Lin *et al.* [21] have proposed a novel deep reinforcement framework taking routerless NoC. The framework adds Monte Carlo search tree and deep learning with multi-threaded learning to powerfully search a huge design space under limitations. The framework absorbs optimal loop placement for routerless NoC with several design restraints. A deep neural network is established using parallel threads that capably search the huge design space routerless NoC with a Monte Carlo search tree. Deep reinforcement learning routerless architecture is compared with various existing methods. The DRL routerless NoC method can achieve a 1.18x reduction in packet latency, 1.14 x reductions in average hop count and 1.47x increase in throughput. Alazemi *et al.* [22] proposed routerless NoC. Routerless NoC design suggested a layered progressive method. This layered progressive method is used to find a set of loop that sees the obligation of connectivity and the drawback of wiring resources. The progressive method forms the design of a large routerless network from good designs of smaller networks, and is related to any n ×m many-core chips with higher scalability. Routerless interface avoids network abnormalities, for example, live lock, starvation and deadlock. In routerless NoCs, the main aim is to select a set of smartly placed loops or composed of wires to link with cores such that the average hop count is equivalent to that of a conventional router-based NoC. The performance evaluation by means of latency, throughput, power and area have been analysed in [22].

16.3 Design of Routerless NoC

The main components of application specific network on chip are router, link, and network interface. In routerless NoC the main aim is to remove the use of routers for NoC design. NoC is separated into segments, and all the segments are linked by a central bus. Central bus and segments are connected by a switching element. Moreover, the central bus or the segment may suffer from scalability problems owing to their bus-based structure. The possible solution is to raise the number of cores in a segment and raise the number of wires in the central bus. The NoC is classified into disjoint set of cores, and each set is linked by a ring; those rings are called local rings. Also, a set of local rings bring together global rings. Packet switch among global and local rings through a low-cost switching element.

Even though the design requires various pleasant structures, the number of switching elements is still not lower. For an 8 × 8 network-on-chip, the number of switching elements is 40 and it is close to the amount of routers in an 8 × 8 network. In recent times the NoC is based on multi-ring, which is called as isolated multi-ring (IMR). Isolated multi-ring develops over mesh-based designs in terms of power, latency, and area; also, it involves substantial buffer resources. REC is defined as recursively adding the loops based on the size of the NoC. The single node must have many packet-sized buffers. The latest routerless design has typically removed these costly buffers by accepting shared packet-size buffers between loops.

A single flit-sized buffer is used in REC for each loop. Both REC and isolated multi ring designs must satisfy two necessities. Each pair of nodes must be linked by at least one loop and all routing is made at the source node. Each and every node insert and receive a packet from loop over a simple interface, which is referred to as RL interface. Actually, even if a flit on the loop can be sent to the next node at the speed of one hop per cycle, this design would be very slow because of the average hop count at that time scalability is very poor in this case. To decrease the hop count it is necessary to choose a better set of loops to link the nodes. Each and every pair of nodes is linked by at least one loop. Source node is used to select a loop that links to the destination node for packet injection process. When inserting a packet, the loop will travel at one hop per cycle. The selected final set of loops wants to securely fit in the obtainable wiring resources on the chip.

Figure 16.1 shows the design of routerless NoC. The network interface is a hardware or software interface among two pieces of protocol layers or equipment in a network. That network interface will generally require some form of network address and it contains port number or node identifier. Network interfaces deliver standardized function, for example, disconnecting and connecting, transfer messages. Physical link is defined as connection between two devices. It deals with bit-level transmission among different types of devices and supports mechanical interfaces or electrical interfaces linking to the physical medium for synchronized message. An intellectual property (IP) core is a block of data or logic that is used to create an application specific integrated circuit or field programmable gate arrays.

Routerless NoC design is based on a loop topology method. The basic concept is to choose the loop set in a progressive method. A loop is an essential package of wires linked with flip flop at each hop. Every time the

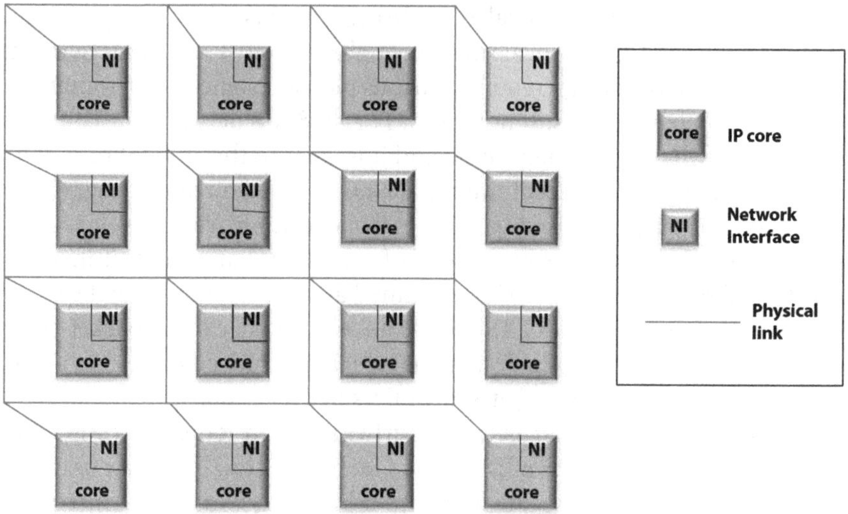

Figure 16.1 Routerless NoC design.

network size increases, the recently selected loops are theoretically pushed as a layer that is used again in the following network size. The final set of selected loops are denoted as, M_k, that sees the low hop count, connectivity, overlapping requirements. M_k and new set of smartly placed loops are combined to form M_{k+2}. The new layer uses new wiring resources that are obtainable and expanding from $k \times kto(k + 2) \times (k + 2)$. The resultant M_{K+2} can also see all the requirements and deliver better performance. The set of loops selected for layer k is denoted as L_k. To discover a good set of loops for 2 × 2 grid that links all the nodes with a low hop count and do not exceed an overlapping of 2 between any adjacent nodes. For 4 × 4 grid, the L_2 together with M_2 and form a good set of loops M_4. The resultant M_4 can also see the entire requirement and does not exceed an overlapping of 4 between any adjacent nodes.

16.4 Emperor Penguin Optimized (EPO) Loop Selection

The emperor penguin, exactly called as Aptenodytes forsteri, is the highest and thickest of all of the penguin types. Emperor penguin optimization has four main steps: to generate the huddle boundary, compute temperature around the huddle, calculate the distance and find the effective mover.

EPO-based routerless NoC design can be developed by constructing the following steps: to generate the 4 × 4 grid, determine the delay, power loss and data traffic, different between the best loops, to find the best loop.

16.4.1 To Generate the 4 × 4 Grid

In routerless design, data transmission takes place using loop topology in which each node injects and receives data from loop. The connection between two nodes is called as loop; thus there is no use of routers for data transmission. But proper selection of loop for data transmission reduces hop count by satisfying connectivity requirement. The complex variable method is used to define the randomly generated huddle boundary of 4 × 4 grid.

Let B describe the 4 × 4 grid and A be the gradient of B

$$A = \nabla B \tag{16.1}$$

Vector ϕ is combined with B to generate the complex potential

$$\sigma = B + i\phi \tag{16.2}$$

Where 'i' represents the imaginary constant and σ denotes the analytical function of the 4 × 4 grid. In our proposed work we consider 4 × 4 grid. The 4 × 4 grid consists of two layers, 8 loops and number of core is 16. Figure 16.2 shows the 4 × 4 grid.

For 4 × 4 grid contains two layers. Established on our loop topology method S_1 is from K_2, here S_1 denotes the layer 1 and K_2 denotes the selected loops. In our work we select 8 loops to form S_2. That eight loops fall into four groups whether they are A_1, A_2, A_3, A_4. The loops in the first group

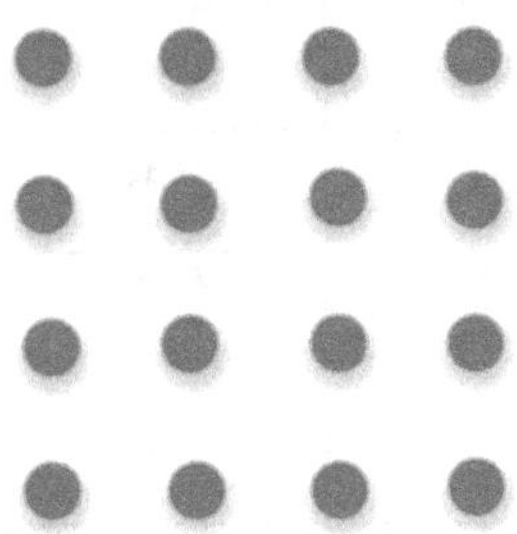

Figure 16.2 4 × 4 grid.

A_1, have only one anticlockwise loop. It offers connectivity between the 12 new nodes when increasing from layer 1 to layer 2. Figure 16.3 represents the eight possible ways of loops. The second group A_2 has the common edge of the loops as the first column; however, the opposite edge of the loops moves slowly to the right. Likewise, the third group, A_3 utilizes the common edge of the loops as the last column, but the opposite edge of the loops moves slowly to the left. It can be proved that A_2 and A_3 deliver connectivity among the four nodes in layer 1 and the 12 new nodes in layer 2. Then the connectivity between the four inner nodes must already have been delivered through S_1. The loops in the fourth group, A_4 deals with extra shortcuts in the horizontal measurement. Table 16.1 shows the eight possible ways of loop.

The last or first column, every group of loops has accurately one loop passing over that column. The total overlapping is 4, exactly the same as the cap. The third or second column has no loops passing over that column.

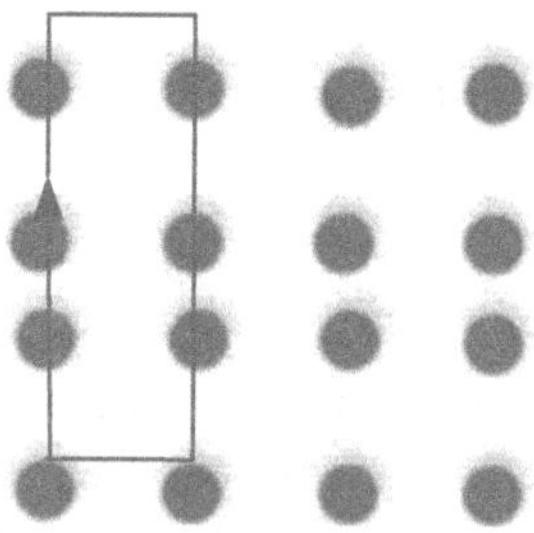

Figure 16.3 Better set of loop for 4 × 4 grid.

Table 16.1 Eight possible ways of loop.

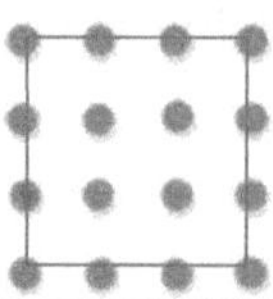	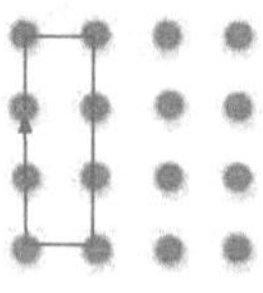	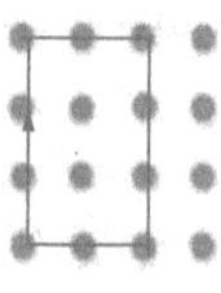	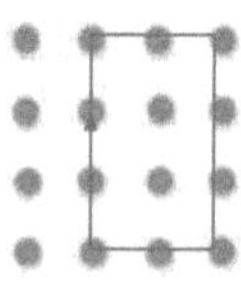
A_1	A_2	A_2	A_3
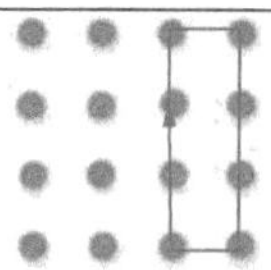	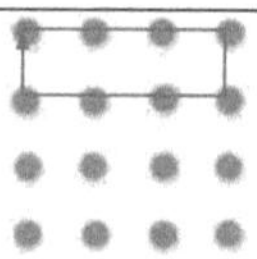	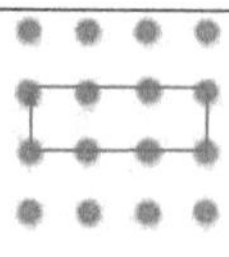	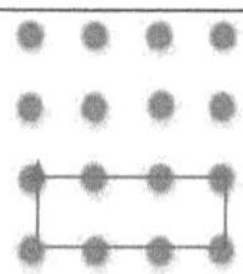
A_3	A_4	A_4	A_4

The total overlapping of middle column is 4, which is same as the cap. Finally, the set of K_4 is layer two (S_2) together with K_2.

16.4.2 Determine the Delay, Power Loss and Data Traffic

In our work we consider eight possible ways to reach the destination node. But we need to select a better set of loop for reach the destination node. Find the best loop to touch the destination node since they avoid delay, power loss as well as data traffic. The time loss, power loss and data traffic can be calculated as,

$$\lambda = P + T + D \tag{16.3}$$

Where λ represent the sum of delay, power loss and data traffic. P denotes the power loss, time loss is represented as T and D indicates the data traffic. Let S' defines the best loops for 4 × 4 grid.

$$S' = \left(\lambda - \frac{Max_{iteration}}{G - Max_{iteration}} \right) \tag{16.4}$$

Where, $\lambda = P + T + D$ and G is the current iteration, $Max_{iteration}$ defines the maximum number of iteration.

$$\lambda = \begin{cases} 0 & if\ K > 10 \\ 1 & if\ K < 10 \end{cases} \tag{16.5}$$

For 0 represent worst case of the loop and 1 denotes best case of the loop. The range of the loop is represented as K. Maximum number of iteration is set as 10. If the value is more than 10, this means the λ value becomes 0; otherwise the λ value is 1. The proposed work considers only best case of the loop.

16.4.3 Difference between the Best Loops

The value that becomes less than 10 is said to be the best loop. For example, we select the values for best loop is 2, 3, 4. These are the best loop in the grid. Finally, we select only one best loop for 4 × 4 grid. Hence we find the λ value for best loops. The best loops are 2, 3, 4 and the λ value is denoted as λ_2, λ_3, λ_4.

$$\lambda_2 = P_2 + T_2 + D_2 \tag{16.6}$$

$$\lambda_3 = P_3 + T_3 + D_3 \tag{16.7}$$

$$\lambda_4 = P_4 + T_4 + D_4 \tag{16.8}$$

Where, P_2, P_3 and P_4 are the power losses from loop 2, 3 and 4. The T_2, T_3 and T_4 represents the delay from loop 2, 3 and 4.The data traffic from loop 2, 3, 4 are defined as D_2, D_3, D_4. Equation (16.6), (16.7), (16.8) can be obtained in equation (16.9).

$$\vec{H} = lmr\left[\sum_{\lambda=2}^{4}\left(\lambda - \frac{Max_{iteration}}{G - Max_{iteration}}\right)\right] \tag{16.9}$$

Where, current iteration is represented as G, $Max_{iteration}$ denotes the maximum number of iteration. Here the λ denotes the sum of delay, power loss and data traffic and lmr is the control parameter. Finally we choose only one best loop by using equation (16.10).

16.4.4 To Find the Best Loop

In this section lastly select one best loop for data transmission. The loop will be selected in the proper way for data transmission and it satisfies the connectivity requirement. By using the equation (16.10) we get the best loop for accurate data transmission.

$$\vec{F} = \min\left[lmr\left[\sum_{\lambda=2}^{4}\lambda - \frac{Max_{iteration}}{G - Max_{iteration}}\right]\right] \tag{16.10}$$

Where, $Max_{iteration}$ indicate the maximum number of iteration. λ denotes the sum of three losses, i.e., delay, power loss and data traffic, Control parameter is represented as lmr and G is the current iteration. Finally we get the best loop is 2. Figure 16.3 shows the best set of loop for 4 × 4 grid. Figure 16.4 shows the flow chart of EPO-based routerless NoC design.

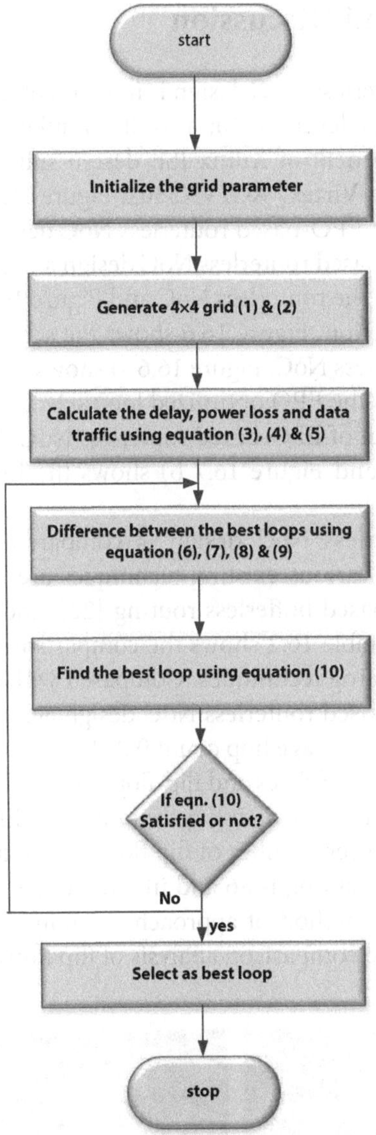

Figure 16.4 Flow chart of EPO-based routerless NoC design.

The EPO-based routerless NoC design delay value is 0.17 sec and power consumption range is 0.027 mW. The proper selection of loop for data transmission reduces hop count by satisfying connectivity requirement. The average hop count value is 0.02(%); that value is compared with various existing techniques.

16.5 Result and Discussion

The EPO-based routerless NoC design is implemented in Verilog on structural register-transfer level (RTL); also, its simulation and synthesis are achieved with the benefit of Xilinx ISE design suite 14.5. The routerless NoC was designed in Virtex7 XC7VX330T. Figure 16.5 shows the register-transfer level view of EPO-based routerless NoC design. The eight bit data is given to the EPO-based routerless NoC design and it is denoted as (7, 0). Figure 16.5 a) shows the routerless NoC and Figure 16.5 b) shows the EPO optimized loop selection. Figure 16.6 shows the schematic representation of EPO-based routerless NoC. Figure 16.6 a) shows the routerless NoC and Figure 16.6 b) shows the EPO optimized loop selection. Figure 16.7 shows the simulation output of EPO-based routerless NoC. Figure 16.7 a) shows the routerless NoC and Figure 16.7 b) shows the EPO-based optimized loop selection.

EPO-based routerless NoC design is compared with various existing techniques. The various existing techniques are ALO-based buffered routing [21], ALO-based bufferless routing [22], and minimum buffered routing with MFO. Table 16.2 shows the comparison of EPO-based routerless NoC with existing techniques. Compared with existing techniques, the proposed EPO-based routerless NoC design achieves operational frequency 994.221MHz, average hop count 0.02% and 0.027 mW power consumption. The number of slices and flip-flops are used for area calculation.

Compared with various existing techniques, the EPO-based routerless NoC design have a lower number of flip flops. The number of flip flops in ALO-based buffered routing is 86 and in ALO-based bufferless routing is 85. In our proposed method of approach the number of flip flops is 78. Figure 16.8 shows the comparison analysis of flip flops.

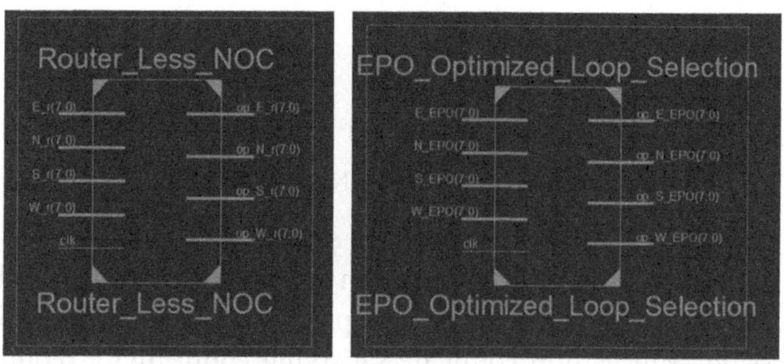

(a) (b)

Figure 16.5 RTL view of EPO-based routerless NoC design.

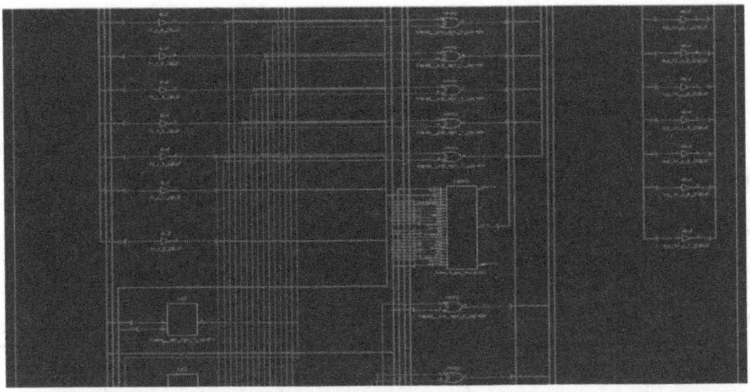

(**a**) Routerless NoC

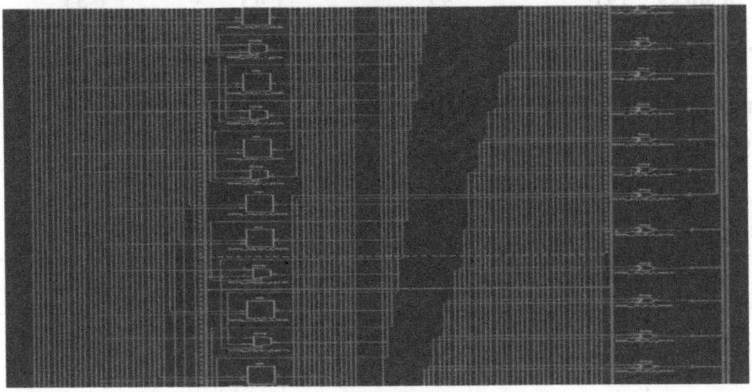

(**b**) EPO-based routerless NoC design

Figure 16.6 Internal RTL schematic representation of EPO-based routerless NoC.

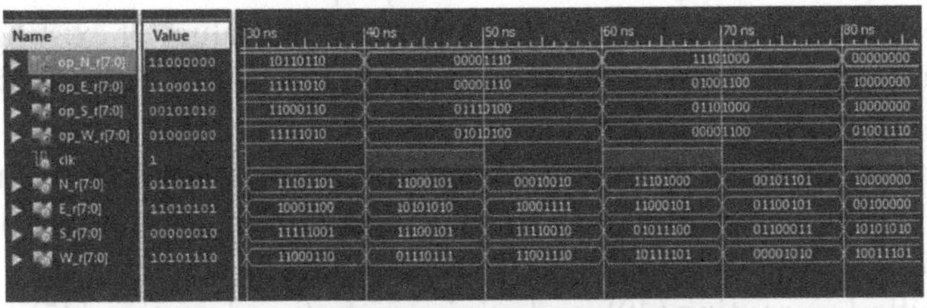

(**a**) Simulation output of routerless NoC

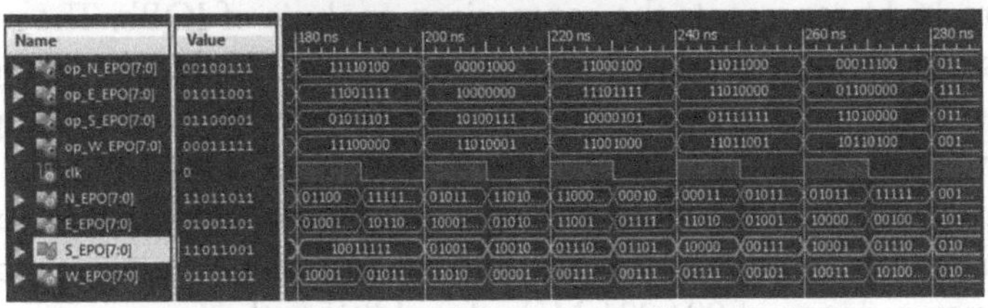

(**b**) Simulation output of EPO optimized loop selection

Figure 16.7 Simulation output of EPO-based routerless NoC.

Table 16.2 Comparison of EPO-based routerless NoC with existing techniques.

Resources	ALO-based buffered routing	ALO-based buffer less routing	Minimum buffered routing with MFO	EPO-based routerless NOC
Target device	Virtex4 XC4VLX80	Virtex7 XC7VX330T	Virtex 4 XC4VLX80	Virtex7 XC7VX330T
Flip flops	86	85	83	78
Number of LUTs	185	115	112	108
Number of slices	141	49	45	34
Number of IOB's	83	81	80	68
Operating frequency	426.995MHz	780.153 MHz	965.261 MHz	994.221 MHz
Power consumption	0.752 mW	0.143 mW	0.141	0.027
Latency (sec)	0.72	0.51	0.32	0.17
Average hop count (%)	1.76	1.63	0.08	0.02

Figure 16.9 shows the number of LUTs comparison with various existing techniques. The number of LUTs the proposed EPO-based routerless NoC design achieves is 108. In addition, the LUTs values of existing techniques include ALO-based buffered routing (185), ALO-based buffer less routing (115), and minimum buffered routing with MFO (112).

Figure 16.10 shows the comparison analysis of slices. The number of slices the proposed method achieves is 34. In addition, the number of slices in existing technique contain ALO-based buffered routing (141), ALO-based bufferless routing (49), and minimum buffered routing (45).

Figure 16.11 represents the comparison analysis of IOB's. The number of IOB's in existing techniques include ALO-based buffered routing (83), ALO-based bufferless routing (81), and minimum buffered routing (80). The number of IOB's the proposed method achieves is 68.

Figure 16.12 shows the frequency comparison with various existing techniques. The proposed EPO-based routerless NoC design achieves the frequency range of 994.221 MHz. In addition, the frequency range of existing techniques include ALO-based buffered routing (426.995 MHz),

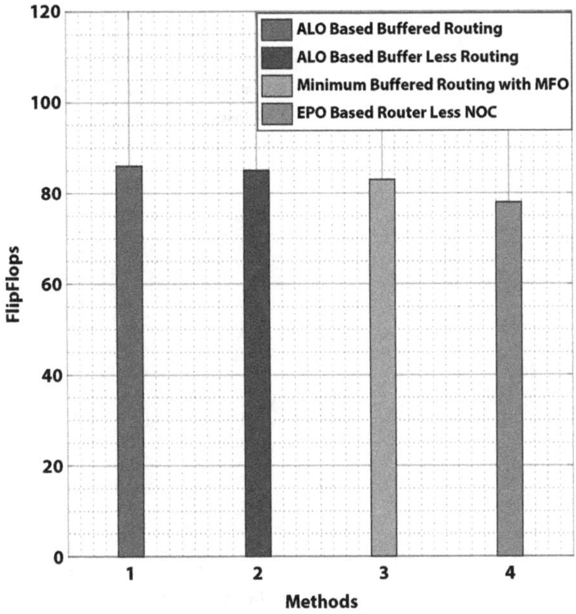

Figure 16.8 Comparison analysis of flip flops.

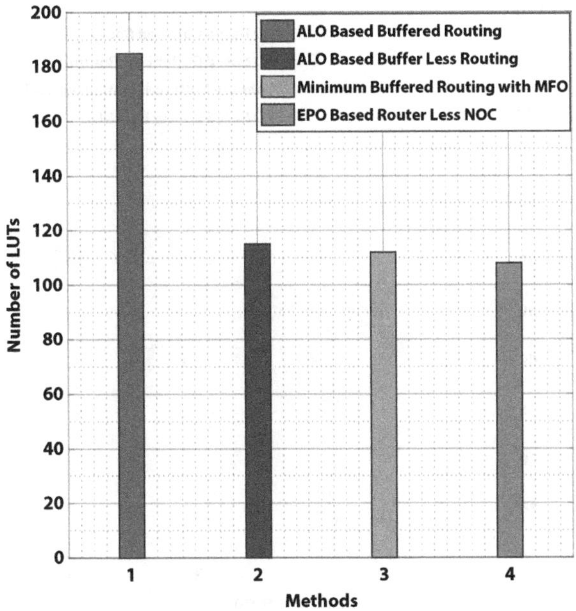

Figure 16.9 Comparison analysis of LUTs.

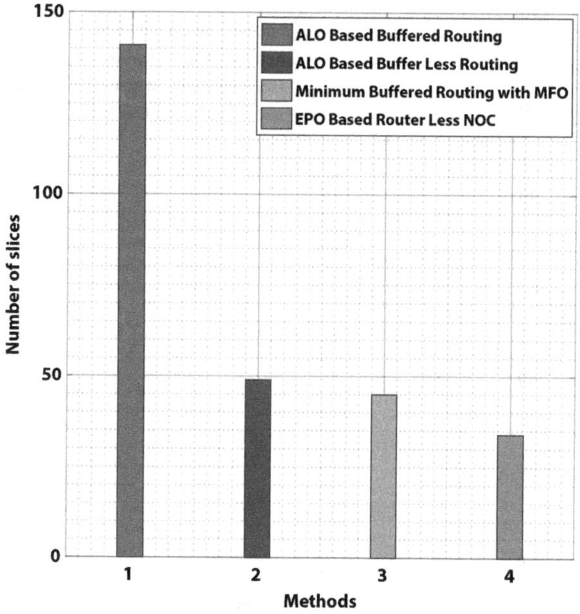

Figure 16.10 Comparison analysis of slices.

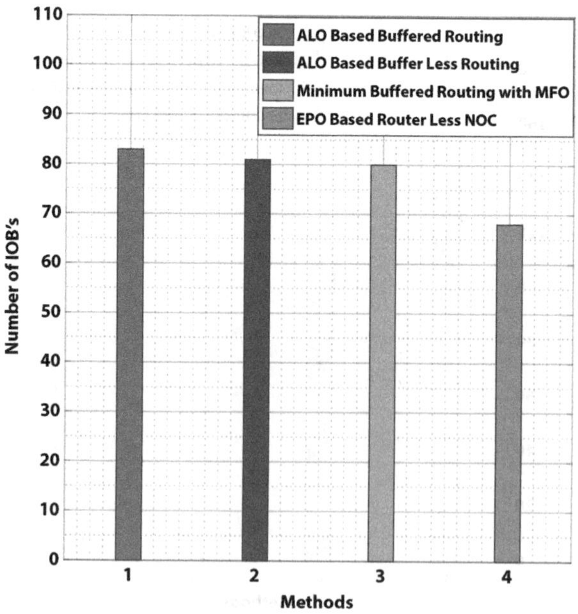

Figure 16.11 Comparison analysis of IOB's.

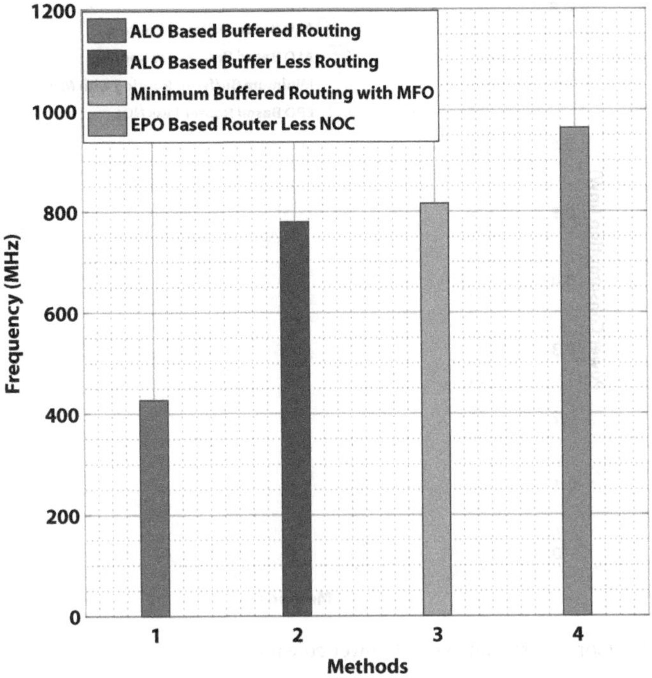

Figure 16.12 Comparison analysis of frequency.

ALO-based bufferless routing (780.153 MHz), and minimum buffered routing with MFO (965.261 MHz).

Figure 16.13 demonstrates the power consumption comparison with other existing techniques. The proposed EPO-based routerless NoC design consumes power value of 0.027 mW. Also, the power consumption values of existing techniques contain ALO-based buffered routing (0.752 mW), ALO-based bufferless routing (0.143 mW), and minimum buffered routing with MFO (0.141 mW).

Figure 16.14 shows the latency contrasted with various existing techniques. The proposed EPO-based routerless NoC design achieves the latency value is 0.17 sec. Additionally, the latency values of the existing techniques include ALO-based buffered routing (0.72 sec), ALO-based bufferless routing (0.51sec), and minimum buffered routing with MFO (0.32 sec).

Figure 16.15 demonstrates the comparison analysis of average hop count. The proposed EPO-based routerless NoC design achieves the average hop count value of 0.02%. In addition, the average hop count values of existing

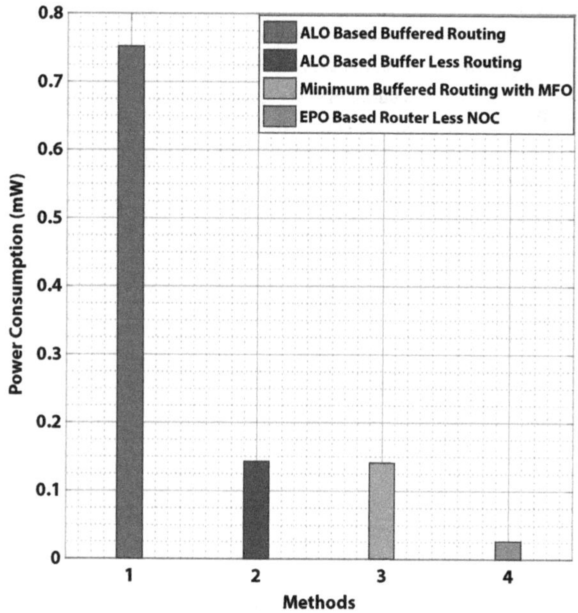

Figure 16.13 Comparison analysis of power consumption.

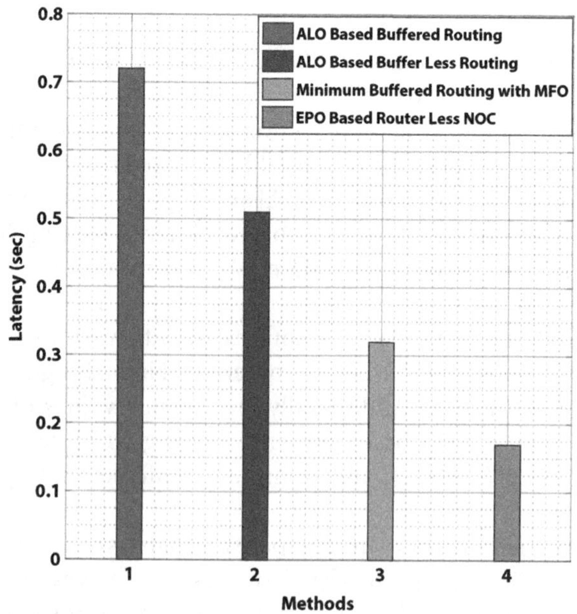

Figure 16.14 Comparison analysis of latency.

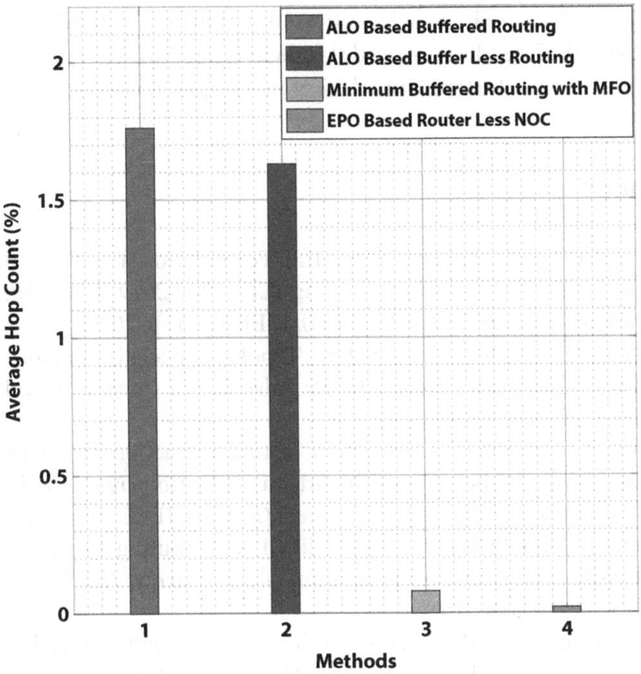

Figure 16.15 Comparison analysis of average hop count.

technique contain ALO-based buffered routing (1.76%), ALO-based buffer less routing (1.63%), and minimum buffered routing with MFO (0.08%).

16.6 Conclusion

In this paper, a routerless NoC design using Emperor penguin optimized algorithm has been proposed. This paper defines the routerless NoC design and EPO loop selection design for the investigation of the proposed method. The design of routerless NoC occupies less power, less area and high speed. However, the EPO-based routerless NoC design delivers better performance than the existing ALO-based buffered routing, ALO-based bufferless routing and minimal buffered routing technique. The routerless NoC was designed in Virtex7 XC7VX330T.Xilinx ISE design suite 14.5 and is used for the simulation and synthesis of the proposed scheme. The proposed flip flop, number of LUTs, and number of IOB's as well as number of slices is receiving less value than the other existing techniques. The proposed EPO-based routerless NoC achieves 78 flip-flops, 108 LUT's,

34 slices, 68 IOB's, 994.221MHz operating frequency, 0.027 mW power consumption, 0.17 sec latency and 0.02% average hop count. To get better improvement for routerless NoC design using new technique in future.

References

1. Xiao, J., Yeung, K.L., Jamin, S., ILP Formulation for Designing Rings in Routerless Network-on-Chip, in: *ICC 2019-2019 IEEE International Conference on Communications (ICC)*, IEEE, pp. 1–6, 2019.
2. Modarressi, M. and Sarbazi-Azad, H., Topology Specialization for Networks-on-Chip in the Dark Silicon Era, in: *Advances in Computers*, vol. 110, pp. 217–258, Elsevier, 2018.
3. Hassan, A. and Viriri, S., Invariant feature extraction for facial recognition: A survey of the state-of-the-art, in: *2018 Conference on Information Communications Technology and Society (ICTAS)*, IEEE, pp. 1–6, 2018.
4. Shahane, P. and Pisharoty, N., Modified X–Y routing for mesh topology based NoC router on field programmable gate array. *IET Circuits Devices Syst.*, 13, 3, 391–398, 2019.
5. Barquero-Retana, L.M., Diseño y Evaluación de Arquitecturas de Enrutador Basadoen Tablas de Enrutamiento Estáticas Orientadas al uso en\Network on Chip, 2018.
6. Bhanu, P.V. and Kulkarni, P.V., Butterfly-Fat-Tree topology based fault-tolerant Network-on-Chip design using particle swarm optimisation. *J. Exp. Theor. Artif. Intell.*, 1–1, 2019.
7. Isaac, E., Performance Optimization of Bufferless Network on Chip Using Deflection Routers, 2018.
8. Shaheen, M., Fahmy, H., Mostafa, H., Modified CONNECT: New Bufferless Router for NoC-Based FPGAs, in: *2018 IEEE 61st International Midwest Symposium on Circuits and Systems (MWSCAS)*, IEEE, pp. 424–427, 2018.
9. Hanford, N., Ahuja, V., Farrens, M.K., Tierney, B., Ghosal, D., A survey of end-system optimizations for high-speed networks. *ACM Comput. Surv. (CSUR)*, 51, 3, 54, 2018.
10. Runzi, Z., Virtual-Channel Based Wormhole NoC on FPGA for ForSyDe/NoC System Generator Tool Suite, 2018.
11. Palmer, G.I., Harper, P.R., Knight, V.A., Modelling deadlock in open restricted queueing networks. *Eur. J. Oper. Res.*, 266, 2, 609–621, 2018.
12. Shen, V.R.L., Yang, C.-Y., Shen, R.-K., Chen, Y.-C., Application of Petri nets to deadlock avoidance in iPad-like manufacturing systems. *J. Intell. Manuf.*, 29, 6, 1363–1378, 2018.
13. Cogumbreiro, T., Hu, R., Martins, F., Yoshida, N., Dynamic deadlock verification for general barrier synchronisation. *ACM Trans. Program. Lang. Syst. (TOPLAS)*, 41, 1, 19, 2018.

14. Chen, S.-Y., Lin, F.Y.-S., Wen, Y.-F., Hsiao, C.-H., Starvation-Avoidance Routing Assignment for Multihop Wireless Networks, in: *2018 IEEE 32nd International Conference on Advanced Information Networking and Applications (AINA)*, IEEE, pp. 366–372, 2018.
15. Angiolini, F. and Murali, S., Quality-of-Service in NoCs, in: *Communication Architectures for Systems-on-Chip*, pp. 157–188, CRC Press, 2018.
16. Jindal, N., Gupta, S., Ravipati, D.P., Panda, P.R., Sarangi, S.R., Enhancing Network-on-Chip Performance by Reusing Trace Buffers. *IEEE Trans. Comput. Aided Des. Integr. Circuits Syst.*, 2019.
17. Ahmed, A.B., Okuhara, H., Matsutani, H., Koibuchi, M., Amano, H., Adaptive body bias control scheme for ultra low-power network-on-chip systems, in: *2018 IEEE 12th International Symposium on Embedded Multicore/Many-core Systems-on-Chip (MCSoC)*, IEEE, pp. 146–153, 2018.
18. Khailany, B., *et al.*, INVITED: A Modular Digital VLSI Flow for High-Productivity SoC Design. *2018 55th ACM/ESDA/IEEE Design Automation Conference (DAC)*, pp. 1–6, 2018.
19. Venkataraman, N.L. and Kumar, R., Design and analysis of application specific network on chip for reliable custom topology. *Comput. Networks*, 158, 69–765, 2019.
20. Venkataraman, N.L., Kumar, R., Mohamed Shakeel, P., Ant lion optimized bufferless routing in the design of low power application specific network on chip. *Circuits Syst. Signal Process.*, 1–16, 2019.
21. Lin, T.-R., Penney, D., Pedram, M., Chen, L., Optimizing Routerless Network-on-Chip Designs: An Innovative Learning-Based Framework, arXiv preprint arXiv: 1905.04423, 2019.
22. Alazemi, F., AziziMazreah, A., Bose, B., Chen, L., Routerless Network-on-Chip, in: *2018 IEEE International Symposium on High Performance Computer Architecture (HPCA)*, 2018, February, IEEE, pp. 492–503.

17

Case Study on Flyover Construction and the Air Quality Measurement by the Emission Level of Pollutants

K.P. Sridhar[1], C. Prajitha[1*], S. Deepa[2], Rinesh.S[3], Arun.M[4] and Srinath Doss[5]

[1]Department of Electronics and Communication Engineering/ Centre for Interdisciplinary Research, Karpagam Academy of Higher Education, Coimbatore, India
[2]Department of ECE, Karpagam College of Engineering, Coimbatore, India
[3]Department of Computer Science and Engineering, V.S.B College of Engineering Technical Campus, Coimbatore, India
[4]Department of Mechanical Engineering, Saveetha School of Engineering, Saveetha Institute of Medical and Technical Sciences (SIMATS), Thandalam, India
[5]Faculty of Engineering and Technology, Botho University, Gaborone, Botswana, South Africa

Abstract
In the present condition, the advent of transportation technology allows users to use road transport for their mobility needs. However, rising populations and increased public transportation networks have increased traffic levels. Flyover construction is implemented in smart cities for the easy movement of vehicles. Significant drawbacks during the construction of the flyover are the diversion of roads that leads to traffic congestion, the greater travelling distance to reach the destination point, and the fuel consumption of vehicles. The level of air pollution due to automobile emissions leads to health-related issues for the people residing near the flyover construction places. The air quality is based on the level of emission components like Carbon Monoxide (CO), Carbon Dioxide (CO2), Particulate

**Corresponding author*: praji.devi@gmail.com
K.P. Sridhar: ORCID iD: 0000-0001-9377-7182
C. Prajitha: ORCID iD: 0000-0002-2476-9354
S. Deepa: ORCID iD: 0000-0002-2356-0014
Arun M: ORCID iD: 0000-0001-7440-8808

A. Suresh, T. Devi, N. Deepa and Ali Kashif Bashir (eds.) Environmental Monitoring Using Artificial Intelligence, (375–388) © 2025 Scrivener Publishing LLC

Matter (PM), sulphur dioxide (SO2), Nitrogen Dioxide (NO2), Ozone (O3), and Lead (Pb). The real-time case study is carried out in the flyover construction of Gounder Mills. Gounder Mills flyover starts from Vellakinar Pirivu and ends at Government ITI with a 658m stretch. The solution to overcome the diversion route is to provide the service road. The real-time case study surveys people who use the diversion route regularly to reach their workplace. The study focuses on air pollution, construction delays, and energy usage associated with a flyover. The air quality is measured during the peak hours in the morning and evening by PM 2.5, PM 10, and AQI sensors. The time delay estimation is based on diverse cars going and entering on the road. Humps and dumps roads are assessed to the free straight road using data collected from a mileage testing container at a designated flyover construction site. Air quality index (AQI), delay computation, and vehicle fuel usage in humps and dumps roads are used to evaluate the case study.

Keywords: Flyover, pollution, emission, fuel consumption, air quality index, vehicles, dump roads

17.1 Introduction

Connectivity remains a top priority, and the flyover building is critical for developing well-connected urban regions [1]. Congestion and slow traffic are contemporary cities' most confusing and complex problems [2]. Flyovers are grade-divided junctions that allow traffic to flow uninterruptedly where there was previous congestion at the grade [3]. Interchanges often consist of multiple crossings [4]. To alleviate traffic congestion, a flyover allows vehicles to pass more efficiently and with less obstruction [5]. Building flyovers is one way to widen roadways [6]. When flyovers are constructed, they change the landscape and ambience of an area [7]. The construction of flyovers is mainly to reduce vehicle congestion in city-side areas [8]. During the construction of flyovers, a diversion route for vehicles is needed to reduce travel delays and traffic congestion. Diversion route roads oversee flyover development, and long-distance coverage makes diversion route travellers uneasy [9]. The long-distance range due to the diversion route makes it more uncomfortable for the travellers who use the road regularly [10]. The vehicles travelling through such streets cause damage to the cars. Pollutants rise when roads are damaged [11–13]. The construction of flyovers brings more dust and causes more damage to the air [13–16]. The level of air pollution increases due to particulate matter in the air.

According to a World Health Organization report, pollution is the major problem that causes global epidemics [17]. There is a need to detect the different types of gases in the air to prevent air pollution [18].

Air quality detection is essential during the flyover construction [19]. Air quality depends on the emissions from components like CO, CO2, PM, SO2, NO2, O3 and Pb—such features in the air lead to health issues for the public. The real-time case study is carried out in the flyover construction of Gounder Mills. The case study is carried out by surveying people who use the diversion route regularly to reach their workplace. The air quality is measured during the peak hours in the morning and evening by PM 2.5, PM 10, and AQI sensors. The time delay estimation is based on diverse cars going and entering on the road. Humps and dumps roads are assessed to the free straight road using data collected from a mileage testing container at a designated flyover construction site. Air quality index (AQI), delay computation, and vehicle fuel usage in humps and dumps roads are used to evaluate the case study.

17.2 Related Study

The research concentrates on the flyover construction, the difficulties faced during the construction, and the pollution level at the construction site. Different researchers have carried out several research works. A. M. Sami *et al.* [20] evaluated the current geometric components of the Bahaddarhat Flyover to create a record of the flyover and its traffic network. The evaluation was in the form of traffic volume at the flyover intersection for all routes for a few days, from which the design volume was determined.

Danisy Ardanil Syarif *et al.* [21] investigated the viewpoints of motorists across the Martadinata Bogor Flyover. Before and after the flyover was built, seven associated criteria were collected using online surveys utilizing the Gform technology. A spider chart was generated from the participants' responses by processing them in Microsoft Excel. The participant's evaluation showed an increase in all metrics. Users and respondents report a rise in three metrics—traffic density, accessibility, and road user comfort—with the most significant gap scores.

Arsalan Raza *et al.* [22] used the multi-criteria decision-making (MCDM) method to find the best option for a more ecological transportation network and to reduce traffic congestion. These methods included the fuzzy and traffic simulation software. A survey was used to compare the criteria and alternatives in pairs. The viewpoints of many stakeholders and specialists were sought through this survey.

Vishnu Vijayan *et al.* [23] focused on constructing a flyover over Kallumthazham, a town in the middle of Kollam, Kerala. This is one to avoid among the city's most accident-prone regions. A flyover linking the bypass on the Mevaram-Kavanad side of Kollam city is being considered to alleviate traffic congestion. The region is linked to the bridge with an echo-technic highway structure.

Maiwada Jibril Ahmed *et al.* [24] examined the pollution levels that were significantly affected by the amount of traffic at all testing locations. Alcindo Neckel *et al.* [25] collected physical samples employing self-made passive testers (SMPSs) at various places in Budapest, including Passenger Cruise Port, Kunsthalle, Szechenyi Lanchid, and Liberty Bridge. It is necessary to decrease contaminants to improve the condition of life in this central European capital, which was ascribed to the COVID-19 outbreak.

17.3 Case Study on Flyover Construction and the Air Quality Measurement

17.3.1 Case Study on Gounder Mills

During flyover construction, the public faces several significant problems. These include high levels of emissions, vehicle damage from using unconditioned roads, increased travel period due to destroyed roads, stress due to traffic and delays, and increased fuel consumption for vehicles using diversion paths. The Gounder Mills flyover project is the subject of the case study. Due to the construction of bridges, the people who go to work daily face significant issues due to traffic and increased pollution. The pollution level is monitored from the morning to evening, and the reading is taken during peak hours. The number of vehicles entering and leaving the diversion routes is used for evaluating the traffic notifications. The mileage bottles are used to calculate the distance travelled by the vehicles in the diversion route and the fuel consumption by vehicles. Two types of roads are used to compare the data collected from distance testing bottles: the standard free stretch road and the road with humps and dumps.

Students with Airveda equipment collect real-time data from constructing the Gounder Mills flyover. The following parameters are being tracked: the duration of the flyover construction; the length of the diversion route; the service road; the number of humps and dumps in the damaged roads; the fuel consumption of vehicles travelling on the damaged roads; and the number of pollutants as measured by the AQI, PM2.5, and PM10 sensors. Airveda has PM 2.5 and a PM 10 sensor integrated for collecting emission levels of pollutants from the air [26, 27]. The PM 2.5 sensor detects airborne particles using a laser. The concept used in the equipment is known as 90-degree light scattering. A right angle incidence with the mirror's opening causes light to be reflected onto the detector. The photodiode can detect a pulse by the moment the light is considered. Algorithms use this electrical signal to calculate the particle concentration. The Airveda equipment is shown in Figure 17.1.

The case study is carried out in the Gounder Mills flyover construction site. The flyover starts from John Bosco Chruch and ends in Vellakinar Pirivu with 700m. The construction work was started in March 2019. The construction and the damage of the service roads of Gounder Mills are shown in Figure 17.2. The service road for the flyover construction is implemented to reduce traffic. The structure of the flyover is delayed due to the COVID-19 pandemic and the shortage of materials.

The AQI meter uses a combination of electrochemical and catalytic combustion sensors. For better cooling and more precise readings, the casing of the apparatus has slots in several places. A PM 2.5 sensor uses laser scattering to detect airborne contaminants. The microprocessor determines the number of molecules per unit volume and their corresponding diameter.

The pollution level in the flyover construction of Gounder Mills is monitored by AQI sensors, PM 2.5, and PM 10 in the early morning, as shown in Figure 17.3. The level of pollution during the early morning hours from 7 a.m. to 9 a.m. is shown in Figure 17.3. The level of pollution will be less in the early hours of morning. The number of vehicles passing through the diversion route and the pollution level is monitored by Airveda equipment. The level of pollution from 9 a.m. to 11 a.m. is shown in Figure 17.4.

The traffic flow and emission rate are more concentrated in the case study, and the difficulties faced by the people during the travel of the diversion route are taken as a survey. The fuel consumption of vehicles, the travelling time to reach the destination point, and the mindset of the people

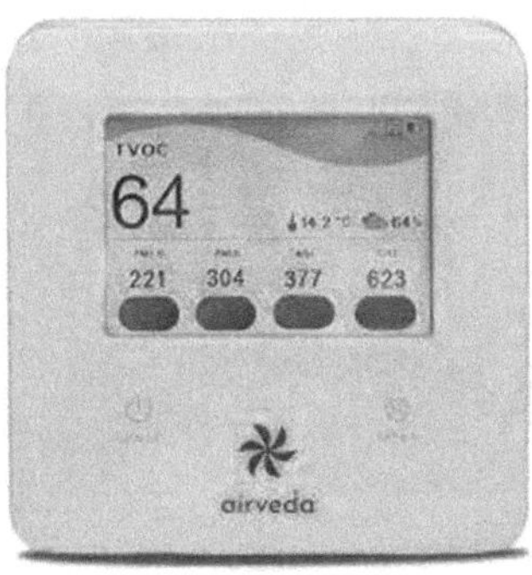

Figure 17.1 Airveda equipment.

Figure 17.2 Flyover construction and damages of Gounder Mills service road.

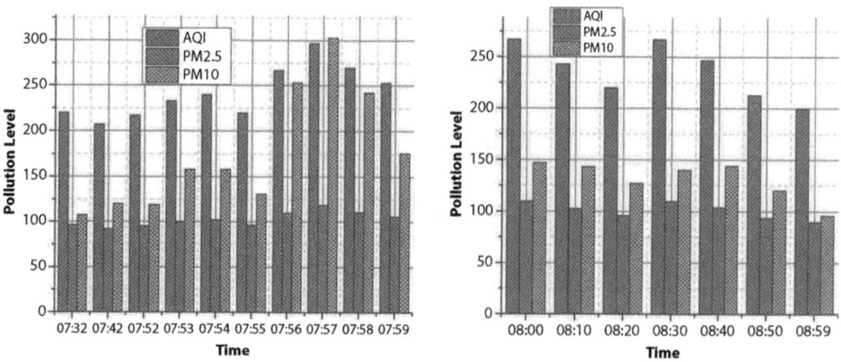

Figure 17.3 The pollution level from 7 a.m. to 9 a.m.

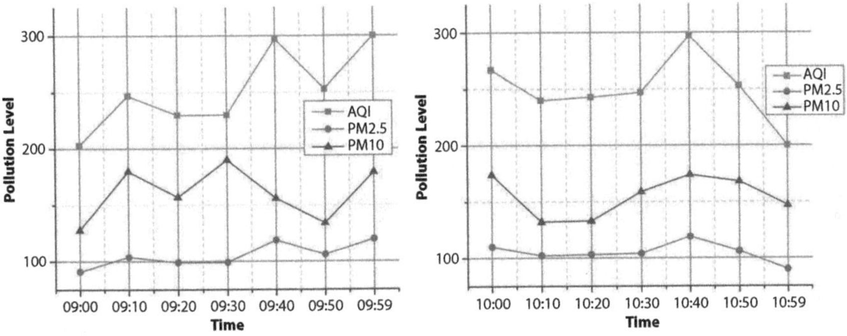

Figure 17.4 The pollution level from 9 a.m. to 11 a.m.

who take the diversion route regularly are evaluated. The pollution level from 11 a.m. to 1 p.m. is lower than early peak hours. The pollution level from 11 a.m. to 1 p.m. is shown in Figure 17.5, and from 1 p.m. to 3 p.m. is shown in Figure 17.6.

The pollution level during the construction of flyover bridges, the vehicles travelling in the diversion route, and environmental degradation are significant concerns. Measuring the precise distribution of fine-grain particles in the air is crucial for understanding the links between environment, health, and behaviour. The pollution level arises during peak hours due to more vehicles passing, and the rushing up leads to more particulate matter in the air. At peak traffic hours, the emission level of vehicles increases and more vehicles crossing the service roads significantly impact the environment.

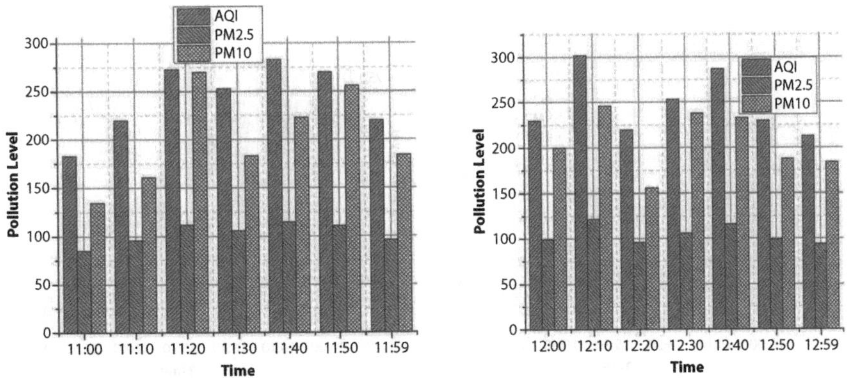

Figure 17.5 The pollution level from 11 a.m. to 1 p.m.

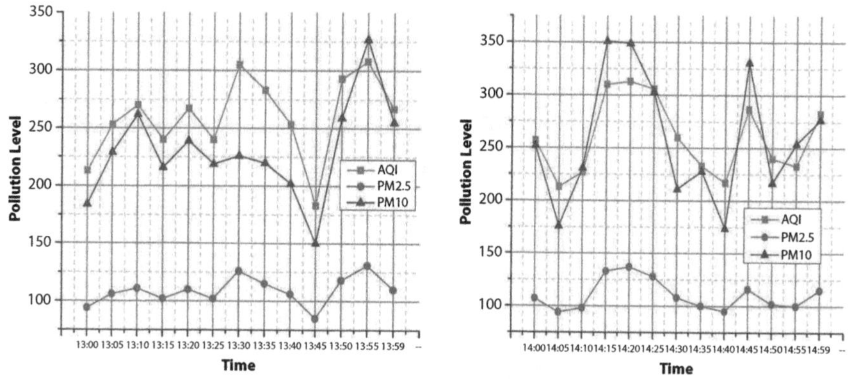

Figure 17.6 The pollution level from 1 p.m to 3 p.m.

The level of pollution from 3 p.m. to 5 p.m., 5 p.m. to 7 p.m., and at 7 p.m. is shown in Figure 17.7, Figure 17.8, and Figure 17.9, respectively. The fuel consumption by the vehicles crossing the service road is higher. The number of humps and dumps in the regular and diversion route affects the travel time. The mileage studies calculate the fuel consumption of vehicles. The length of flyover construction, diversion route and the number of humps and dumps in the damaged roads are shown in Table 17.1.

The damaged roads with humps and dumps make transportation tedious and make the public uncomfortable during travel. The time taken for the travel distance due to humps and dumps on the road and the measurement is shown in Table 17.2.

Vehicle fuel consumption is also a significant source of vehicle emissions. The fuel consumption of vehicles depends on the road structure, texture,

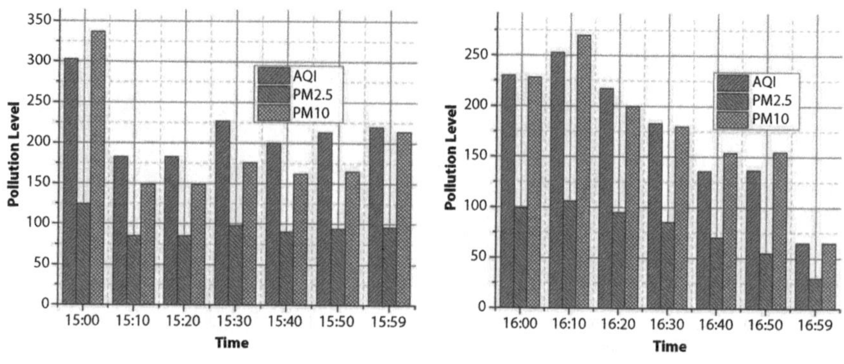

Figure 17.7 The pollution level from 3 p.m. to 5 p.m.

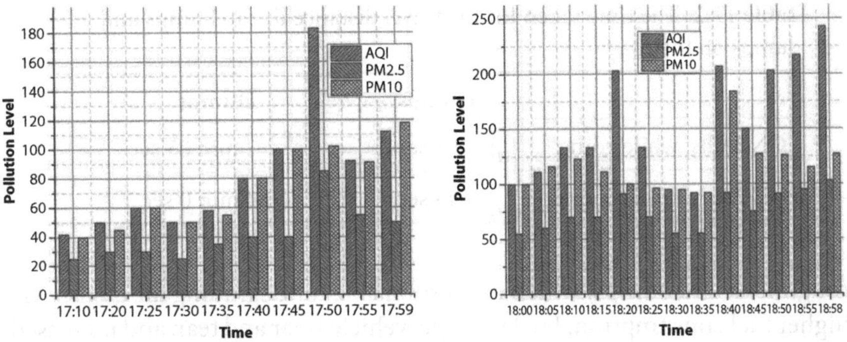

Figure 17.8 The pollution level from 5 p.m. to 7 p.m.

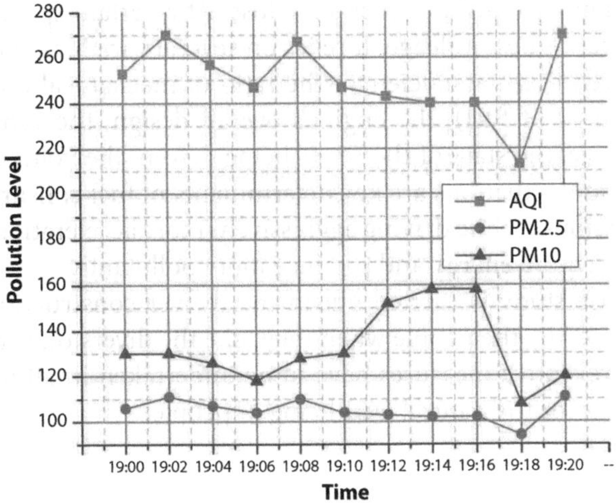

Figure 17.9 The pollution level at 7 p.m.

Table 17.1 The length calculation of the Gounder Mills flyover bridge.

	Gounder Mills flyover bridge
Length of the Flyover	0.65 km
Length of the Diversion Road While entering	0.65 km
Length of the Diversion Road While returning	0.65 km
Humps and Dumps while going	51 dumps, 26 humps
Humps and Dumps while coming	101 dumps, 68 humps

Table 17.2 The time taken for the travel distance due to humps and dumps on the road.

	Humps	Dumps
GN Mills, while going	2.08 sec	2 min 03 sec
GN Mills, while coming	5.44 sec	4 min 0 sec

roughness, and bumps, which are responsible for degrading air quality via higher fuel consumption. Fuel wastage, vehicle wear and tear, and increased vehicle traffic cause more stress for the public. The people's economy is affected by the maintenance of vehicles in the form of wheel alignment and the life span of tyres. Regular travel on the damaged route causes vehicle damage, bringing significant economic loss. At a certain speed, a specific vehicle will get its best mileage. It relies on several variables, including the engine's power, thermal efficiency (the ratio of mechanical output to the chemical energy of fuel), the engine's overall design, the vehicle's usage patterns, its age, the state of the roads being driven, the volume of traffic, etc. Speed and fluctuations are key determinants of fuel consumption and exhaust emissions. While driving aggressively, more acceleration and braking events use more energy and produce more pollutants.

A clear case study is carried out in the flyover construction, and the difficulties faced by the people when they take the diversion route are well discussed. Preventive measures have to be undertaken in all flyover construction areas for the natural well-being of people.

17.4 Conclusion

Smart cities sometimes employ the construction of flyovers to facilitate the circulation of automobiles. There are several significant negatives to the flyover construction, including increased fuel consumption, longer travel times, and traffic congestion caused by the rerouting of routes. The concentration of gases such as lead (Pb), sulfur dioxide (SO2), nitrogen dioxide (NO2), particulate matter (PM), and carbon monoxide (CO) establishes the air quality. The real-time case study is carried out in the flyover at Gounder Mills. Offering the service road is the way to overcome the traffic in the flyover construction. The major drawback during the flyover construction is the level of pollution due to the higher number of vehicles, the fuel consumption of vehicles due to the diversion roads, the number of humps and dumps in the damaged diversion roads, the vehicle's fuel consumption and the condition during travel in the damaged roads. The time delay is evaluated by the multiple vehicles entering and leaving the roads. The PM 2.5, PM 10, and AQI are used to monitor pollution levels. Information gathered from a mileage testing container at a specific flyover construction location is used to compare humps and dumping roads to the free straight route.

References

1. Kapoor, S.S. and Brar, T.S., Develop pedestrian based TOD index to measure TOD-levels in brownfield areas of Noida. *AIP Conf. Proc. AIP Publ.*, 2644, 1, 2022, Nov. 7.
2. Minh, Q.T., Le Hoang, H.N., Nhat, M.N., Effective traffic routing for urban transportation capacity and safety enhancement. *IATSS Res.*, 1;46, 4, 574–85, 2022.
3. Pieren, R. and Lincke, D., Auralization of aircraft flyovers with turbulence-induced coherence loss in ground effect. *J. Acoust. Soc. Am.*, 1;151, 4, 2453–60, 2022.
4. Yang, M., Jiang, C., Yan, X., Ai, T., Cao, M., Chen, W., Detecting interchanges in road networks using a graph convolutional network approach. *Int. J. Geogr. Inf. Sci.*, 3;36, 6, 1119–39, 2022.
5. Kofanov, O., Kofanova, O., Chepel, A., Kriuchkov, A., Rabosh, I., Zhukova, N., Modeling of the Car Traffic Air Pollution on the Territories Neighboring Multi-level Interchanges. *Environ. Res. Eng. Manage.*, 12;78, 4, 17–38, 2022.
6. Purwasih, H.D., Sidabutar, Y.F., Suciati, H., Fauzan, F., Modernization of "Transport" As Public Transportation to Reduce Personal Vehicle Ownership in the City of Tanjungpinang. *JMKSP (J. Manajemen Kepemimpinan Dan Supervisi Pendidikan)*, 8, 1, 153–63, 2023.
7. Abubakr, S., Elshater, A., El Fayoumi, M.A., Heliopolis' activities under flyovers: Qualitative data analysis of citizens' interests. A+ Arch Design *Int. J. Archit. Des.*, 8, 1, 25–50, 2022.
8. Islam, S., Setyanto, R.P., Apriandi, D.W., Public Transport Mismanagement and Its Effects in Dhaka City, in: *4th Green Development International Conference (GDIC 2022)*, 2023, Nov. 7, Atlantis Press, pp. 979–987.
9. Rahman, M.L. and Baker, D., The impacts of transport infrastructure development on travel route switch behavior in Bangladesh. *Cogent Soc. Sci.*, 8, 1, 2119688, 2022.
10. Åkerman, J., Kamb, A., Larsson, J., Nässén, J., Low-carbon scenarios for long-distance travel 2060. *Transp. Res. Part D Transport Environ.*, 99, 103010, 2021.
11. Muthu, M., Gopal, J., Kim, D.H., Sivanesan, I., Reviewing the impact of vehicular pollution on road-side plants—future perspectives. *Sustainability*, 13, 9, 5114, 2021.

12. Macioszek, E. and Granà, A., The analysis of the factors influencing the severity of bicyclist injury in bicyclist-vehicle crashes. *Sustainability*, 14, 1, 215, 2022.
13. Chang, X., Yu, Y., Li, Y.X., Response of antimony distribution in street dust to urban road traffic conditions. *J. Environ. Manage.*, 296, 113219, 2021.
14. Martono, D.N. and Gusdini, N., Flyover Development Risk Analysis: Review of the Construction Phase Efforts to Minimize Environmental Impact. *IOP Conf. Ser. Earth Environ. Sci.*, 940, 012020, 2021.
15. Etim, M.A., Babaremu, K., Lazarus, J., Omole, D., Health risk and environmental assessment of cement production in Nigeria. *Atmosphere*, 12, 9, 1111, 2021 Aug 30.
16. Arya, A., Problems of Increasing Air Pollution Pollutions and Certain Management Management Strategies, in: *Innovations in Environmental Biotechnology*, pp. 457–486, Springer Nature Singapore, Singapore, 2022.
17. Ardusso, M., Forero-López, A.D., Buzzi, N.S., Spetter, C.V., Fernández-Severini, M.D., COVID-19 pandemic repercussions on plastic and antiviral polymeric textile causing pollution on beaches and coasts of South America. *Sci. Total Environ.*, 763, 144365, 2021.
18. Bourdrel, T., Annesi-Maesano, I., Alahmad, B., Maesano, C.N., Bind, M.A., The impact of outdoor air pollution on COVID-19: a review of evidence from in vitro, animal, and human studies. *Eur. Respir. Rev.*, 30, 159, 2021.
19. Megahed, N.A. and Ghoneim, E.M., Indoor Air Quality: Rethinking rules of building design strategies in post-pandemic architecture. *Environ. Res.*, 193, 110471, 2021.
20. Sami, A.M., Palit, S.K., Tashnim, T., Inventorying of Bahaddarhat Flyover and Its Impact on Traffic System.
21. Syarif, D.A., Rifai, A.I., Handayani, S., The Perception of Road Users on Flyover Development Impact: A Case of Jalan RE Martadinata Bogor. *Citiz. J. Ilm. Multidiscip. Ind.*, *2*, 5, 955–963, 2022.
22. Raza, A., Ali, M.U., Ullah, U., Fayaz, M., Alvi, M.J., Kallu, K.D., Nengroo, S.H., Evaluation of a Sustainable Urban Transportation System in Terms of Traffic Congestion—A Case Study in Taxila, Pakistan. *Sustainability*, 14, 19, 12325, 2022.
23. Vijayan, V., A Study on Flyover Construction with Eco Technical Road System. *Int. J. Emerging Technol. Innovative Res.*, 2021.
24. Ahmed, M.J., Dogo, B., Baba, S.U., Muhammed, A.Y., Abdulqadir, M., Assessment of concentration and spatial variation of air pollution in Zaria metropolis, Nigeria. *Sci. World J.*, *17*, 2, 221–226, 2022.
25. Neckel, A., Oliveira, M.L., Bolaño, L.J., Maculan, L.S., Dal Moro, L., Bodah, E.T., Moreno-Ríos, A.L., Bodah, B.W., Silva, L.F., Biophysical matter in a marine estuary identified by the Sentinel-3B OLCI satellite and the presence of terrestrial iron (Fe) nanoparticles. *Mar. Pollut. Bull.*, 173, 112925, 2021.
26. KP, S. and Abubeker, K.M., Air pollution detection and monitoring with the smart sensor interface on the IoT platform, in: *2023 Annual International*

Conference on Emerging Research Areas: International Conference on Intelligent Systems (AICERA/ICIS), IEEE, pp. 1–7, 2023 Nov 16.

27. Prajitha, C., Real-time case study on monitoring the air quality, time delay, and fuel consumption by vehicles during flyover construction, in: *2023 Annual International Conference on Emerging Research Areas: International Conference on Intelligent Systems (AICERA/ICIS)*, IEEE, pp. 1–6, 2023 Nov 16.

About the Editors

A. Suresh, PhD, is an Associate Professor, Department of Networking and Communications, School of Computing, College of E & T, SRM Institute of Science & Technology, Kattankulathur, Chengalpattu Dist., Tamil Nadu, India. With two+ decades of experience, he has published/granted nine patents and 150 papers in technical journals. He has also authored several books and is currently writing a number of other books. He has published more than 100+ papers at international scientific conferences, and he has served as editor and reviewer for various journals. He has served as chair of several conferences and workshops.

T. Devi, PhD, is a Professor, Department of Computer Science and Engineering, Saveetha School of Engineering, Saveetha Institute of Medical and Technical Sciences, Thandalam, Chennai, Tamil Nadu, India. With 14 years of teaching experience, she has published 80+ scopus papers and 9 design grant patents along with technical journals. She has authored several textbooks, editor and reviewer for standard books and journals. She has published 40 papers at international conferences. She has presented as guest speaker in many reputed colleges.

N. Deepa, PhD, is an Associate Professor, Department of Computer Science and Engineering, Saveetha School of Engineering, Saveetha Institute of Medical and Technical Sciences, Thandalam, Chennai, Tamil Nadu, India. With 14 years of teaching experience, she has published 67+ scopus papers and 7 design grant patents along with technical journals. She has authored several textbooks, editor and reviewer for standard books and journals. She has published 42 papers at international conferences. She has presented as guest speaker in many reputed colleges.

Ali Kashif Bashir, PhD, is a faculty member of the School of Computing and Mathematics, Manchester Metropolitan University, United Kingdom. He is an adjunct professor at the School of Electrical Engineering and Computer Science, National University of Science and Technology, Islamabad. He is the author of over 90 peer-reviewed articles and is serving as the editor-in-chief of the "IEEE Future Directions Newsletter." He is the editor of several journals and has served as a guest editor on several special issues in journals. He has served as chair of several conferences and workshops.

Index

Also of Interest

Check out these related titles from Scrivener Publishing

Global Waste Management, Edited by Pradeep Kumar and Brajesh Kumar, ISBN: 9781394318384. *Global Waste Management* provides awareness among readers of the industrial application-based problems by self-evaluation and verification process towards waste creation and its minimization. Other books discuss Do's and Don'ts about any issue related to waste, but our aim is to inspire brainstorming in readers with appropriate data along with human values.

Sustainable Production Innovations: Bioremediation and Other Biotechnologies, Edited by Alok Patel and Amit Kumar Sharma, ISBN: 9781119791904. Presenting the latest technologies and practices in this ever-changing field, this groundbreaking new volume covers the gambit for providing solutions and practical applications of smart and efficient energy systems.

Ecosystem Management: Climate Change and Sustainability, Edited by Arnab Banerjee, Manoj Kumar Jhariya, Abhishek Raj, and Taher Mechergui, ISBN: 9781394231218. This book is essential for anyone who wants to understand the challenges of environmental degradation and learn about the sustainable solutions needed to address these critical issues.

Sewage and Biomass from Wastewater to Energy: Possibilities and Technology, Edited by Inamuddin, Tariq Altalhi, Mohammad Luqman, and Joseph K. Bwapwa, ISBN: 9781394204311. Written and edited by a team of industry experts, this exciting new volume covers clean energy production from sewage and biomass while achieving a zero-waste strategy.

LAND AND ENVIRONMENTAL MANAGEMENT THROUGH FORESTRY, Edited by Abhishek Raj, Manoj Kumar Jhariya, Arnab Banerjee, Sharad Nema, and Kiran Bargali, ISBN: 9781119910404. Written and edited by a group of experts in the field, this groundbreaking reference work sets the standard for engineers, students, and professionals working in forestry, agriculture, ecology and environmental science, offering the scientific community a way towards combating climate change.

GREEN CHEMISTRY FOR ENVIRONMENTAL REMEDIATION, Edited by Rashmi Sanghi and Vandana Singh, ISBN: 9780470943083. Presents high quality research papers as well as in depth review articles on the new emerging green face of multidimensional environmental chemistry.

BIOREMEDIATION AND SUSTAINABILITY: Research and Applications, Edited by Romeela Mohee and Ackmez Mudhoo, ISBN: 9781118062845. Bioremediation and Sustainability is an up-to-date and comprehensive treatment of research and applications for some of the most important low-cost, "green," emerging technologies in chemical and environmental engineering.

EMERGENCY RESPONSE MANAGEMENT OF OFFSHORE OIL SPILLS: Guidelines for Emergency Responders, By Nicholas P. Cheremisinoff, PhD, and Anton Davletshin, ISBN: 9780470927120. The first book to examine the Deepwater Horizon disaster and offer processes for safety and environmental protection.

COMPLEX BIOLOGICAL SYSTEMS: Adaptation and Tolerance to Extreme Environments, By Irina R. Fomina, Karl Y. Biel, and Vladislav G. Soukhovolsky, ISBN: 9781119510406. Written and edited by some of the most well-respected authors in the area of the adaptation of plants and animals to climate change, this groundbreaking new work is an extremely important scientific contribution to the study of global warming.

GLOBAL CLIMATE CHANGE DEMYSTIFIED, By James G. Speight, ISBN: 9781119653851. Tackling one of the most controversial subjects of our time, one of the world's foremost environmental and petroleum engineers explores the potential causes and ramifications of global climate change.

DEATH OF THE CHESAPEAKE: A History of the Military Role in Polluting the Bay, By Richard D. Albright, ISBN: 9781118686270. This unique book focuses attention on the failure of current efforts to cleanup the Chesapeake Bay and suggests an approach often used in cleaning up environmentally damaged sites.

Printed in the USA/Agawam, MA
September 16, 2026

910661.134